Logic and Pragmatism

Logic and Pragmatism

Selected Essays by
Giovanni Vailati

Translated by
Claudia Arrighi

Edited by
Claudia Arrighi
Paola Cantù
Mauro De Zan
&
Patrick Suppes

CSLI
PUBLICATIONS
Center for the Study of
Language and Information
STANFORD, CALIFORNIA

Copyright © 2009
CSLI Publications
Center for the Study of Language and Information
Leland Stanford Junior University
Printed in the United States
13 12 11 10 09   1 2 3 4 5

Library of Congress Cataloging-in-Publication Data

Logic and pragmatism : selected essays / by Giovanni Vailati /
edited by Claudia Arrighi ... [et al.].

p.   cm. – (CSLI lecture notes ; no. 198)

Includes bibliographical references and index.
ISBN-13: 978-1-57586-591-1 (cloth : alk. paper)
ISBN-10:   1-57586-591-2 (cloth : alk. paper)
ISBN-13: 978-1-57586-590-4 (pbk. : alk. paper)
ISBN-10:   1-57586-590-4 (pbk. : alk. paper)
1. Pragmatism. 2. Logic.
I. Arrighi, Claudia. II. Title. III. Series.

B3652.V332E5 2009
195 –dc22   2009029827
CIP

∞ The acid-free paper used in this book meets the minimum requirements
of the American National Standard for Information Sciences—Permanence
of Paper for Printed Library Materials, ANSI Z39.48-1984.

CSLI was founded in 1983 by researchers from Stanford University, SRI
International, and Xerox PARC to further the research and development of
integrated theories of language, information, and computation. CSLI headquarters
and CSLI Publications are located on the campus of Stanford University.

CSLI Publications reports new developments in the study of language,
information, and computation. Please visit our web site at
http://cslipublications.stanford.edu/
for comments on this and other titles, as well as for changes
and corrections by the authors, editors, and publisher.

Contents

Preface

This book is the result of a joint cooperation of several scholars that are interested in Vailati's works for different reasons, but who have in common the belief in the opportunity of making a wide selection of his texts available for the first time in the English language, thus enabling a revival of Vailati's studies.

Vailati's work became known quite early, given that his complete writings were published soon after his death in 1911.[1] However, in the first half of the 20th century, neoidealism in Italy came into a strong hegemonic position; this philosophical movement rejected the dialogue between science and philosophy and refused to consider pragmatism as a philosophical movement, and Vailati's figure, who had always pleaded against the polarization into 'two cultures', was soon forgotten. It was not until the fall of Fascism and the end of the Second World War that Vailati's writings came to be appreciated again in Italy. A list of references on Vailati that is included in the Selected Bibliography at the end of this volume shows an interest in several aspects of his work, ranging from economics to philosophy of knowledge, from logic to ethics and philosophy of religion, from history of science to psychology.

In 1959 Vailati's rich correspondence, his manuscript annotations and his library were acquired by the Department of Philosophy of the University of Milan. This allowed for the publication of a new, extended edition of Vailati's writings by Mario Quaranta in 1987,[2] and the edition in 1971 by Giovanni Lanaro of Vailati's correspondence including letters to Pareto, Mach, Welby, Fogazzaro, Vacca, Brentano, Papini, Prezzolini, and from Enriques, Croce, Calderoni, Amato Pojero, and Salvemini.[3] Although Lanaro's edition already contains a vast selec-

---

[1] M. Calderoni, U. Ricci, Giovanni Vacca (eds.) *Scritti di G. Vailati, 1863-1909.* Leipzig-Firenze: Barth, 1911.

[2] M. Quaranta (ed.) *Scritti. Giovanni Vailati*, Bologna: Forni, 1987

[3] G. Lanaro (ed.), *Giovanni Vailati. Epistolario, 1891-1909.* Torino: Einaudi,

tion of Vailati's letters, further correspondence with Amato Pojero, Croce, and Brentano has been published at a later date,[4] and some unpublished correspondence with Russell, Pikler, Wohlwill, Duhem, and Schiaparelli has been recently edited on the Yearbook of the *Vailati Study Center*[5] in Crema—Vailati's hometown,— a center which promotes researches on Vailati and the publication of materials from the Archive.

This year, being the centenary of Vailati's death, a revival of interest in his works has taken place, especially in Italy, where two International Conferences (Milan, October 7–8; Bologna October 11–13) will analyze several aspects of Vailati's philosophy and epistemology. A great deal still remains to be said and this volume, which arose from a conjoint project of Mauro De Zan, the director of *Vailati's Center* in Crema, and Patrick Suppes, Lucie Stern Professor of Philosophy Emeritus in Stanford, is intended not only as a means to celebrate the centenary of Vailati's death, but also as a tool for future research.

The reasons for the choice of the essays contained in this volume are only partly evident from the title. On the one hand the chosen writings serve to illustrate Vailati's original form of pragmatism, which does not date only from Vailati's collaboration with the Italian Pragmatist group formed by Papini and Prezzolini around the journal *Leonardo*, but is also connected to Vailati's participation to the Italian school of Mathematical Logic. Paola Cantù and Mauro De Zan show in their presentation of Vailati's life and works the relevance of his interest for the logical problem of definition but also for the historical study of scientific ideas, and of his critical analysis of the conceptions of Hume, Berkeley, Brentano and of Positivist scientists. Vailati's contribution to pragmatism, as shown in the essay by Maria Caamano and Patrick Suppes, includes the development of a criterion to establish empirical meaningfulness based on predictive elements, and in particular on conditional expectations, underlining the important role of deliberate actions as the grounds for objectivity—both in language and science.

On the other hand the chosen writings will also show Vailati's interest for science and the humanities, and his early criticism of the

---

1971.

[4]See A. Brancaforte. *Giovanni Vailati e Amato Pojero. Epistolario: 1898-1908.* Milano: Angeli 1993; C. Rizza, (ed.) *Benedetto Croce-Giovanni Vailati. Carteggio (1899-1905).* Acireale-Roma: Bonanno, 2006; and R. M. Chisholm and M. Corrado (eds.) "The Brentano-Vailati Correspondence" *Topoi*, 1:3–30, 1982.

[5]See M. De Zan, "I carteggi europei di Vailati," in *Annuario del Centro Studi Vailati*, 2004, pages 19–52, R. Pettoello, "Il Carteggio Pikler-Vailati (1892-1908)," in *Annuario del Centro Studi Vailati*, 2005-06, pages 83–106, and M. De Zan, "Il Carteggio Vailati-Schiaparelli (1897-1900)," ibid., pages 107–118.

polarization of knowledge into "two cultures," based on the idea of certain similarities between their respective languages and argumentation schemes. The variety of Vailati's interests was probably related to his freedom from Academic duties, but was also a result of his defense of the unity of knowledge, and his belief in the fruitfulness of speculative analogies between different fields, including the newborn scientific disciplines of psychology, sociology and economics.

Translator's Notes

C. ARRIGHI

This translation project started while I was working as a research assistant for Patrick Suppes in Stanford, when he asked me to retrieve some material about the pragmatist views of Giovanni Vailati. While working on an article about Bruno de Finetti, he noticed that de Finetti, in *Theory of Probability* (1974), mentions Vailati's writings on pragmatism as a work that he "particularly admires." Given the scarce number of Vailati's writings available in English, I undertook the task of translating his two main articles on pragmatism (chap. 18 and 19 of this volume). Suppes really appreciated them, especially for the prominence of the role played by predictions and conditional expectations in Vailati's pragmatist approach to epistemology. In his recent article about de Finetti, Suppes writes: "It is unfortunate that the work of the Italian pragmatists is not more available in English."[6]

From here came the idea of extending this limited initial project, and the evolution of this idea into this volume has been possible thanks to a grant provided by the *Centro Studi Giovanni Vailati* in Crema and the scholarly collaboration of Mauro De Zan and Paola Cantù, respectively the president and one of the members of the *Centro Studi.*

I translated most of Vailati's articles in this volume, with the assistance of Wendy Hall for extensive corrections of the drafts and the advice of Patrick Suppes regarding technical terminology.[7] The excep-

---

[6] "Some philosophical reflections on de Finetti's thought," in Galavotti 2009, *Bruno de Finetti, Radical Probabilist*, London: College Publications, p. 21.

[7] Several excerpts translated into English by Robert Innis have also proved helpful. See Innis, Robert E. 2002. *Pragmatism and the Forms of Sense: Language,*

tions are the articles "Pragmatism and Mathematical Logic," "A Study of Platonic Terminology," "The Attack on Distinctions," and "On Material Representations of Deductive Processes" (chap. 12, 13, 14, and 15)—these articles were translated and published by contemporaries of Vailati (as indicated at the beginning of each article in this volume), and we are just reprinting them for the reader's convenience.

In Vailati's work we can see an abundance of quotations, many of which are reported in their original languages, including ancient Greek and Latin. Given that the ability to read several foreign languages is not common, we have opted, in general, for quoting the same passages from an English edition, as indicated in a footnote. The original passages in French, German, Italian, Latin and Greek have generally been omitted with some minor exceptions:

- well known passages as the one from Moliére's *The imaginary Invalid*;
- quotations and terms that are relevant for the understanding of Vailati's thesis, as some excerpts from Leibniz, and many words in ancient Greek (especially chap. 7 and 13);
- verses from poems, as in the case of Michelangelo, Dante, Schiller and Berni.

If no English translation is mentioned, then I have translated the passage myself from an Italian edition, with the help of Paola Cantù for some passages in Latin, French, German and ancient Greek. This is also the case for some passages (mainly from Aristotle) that Vailati most likely quoted by memory, and therefore do not correspond exactly to the original text.

At the beginning of every essay by Vailati a footnote indicates where the article was originally published. However, the articles used for the translation are the ones found in the collection of Vailati's writings published after his death (1911). The only exception is "The Difficulties Involved in a Rational Classification of the Sciences," (chap. 4) which Vailati originally wrote in French, and was recently published in Italian by Mario Quaranta in a selection of Vailati's philosophical writings (*Giovanni Vailati. Gli strumenti della ragione*, Il Poligrafo, 2003). This Italian version is the one used for the translation.

The translator's or editors' notes and additions, even when integrating Vailati's own footnotes, are indicated in squared brackets. Regarding the references, the editors have decided to leave in the articles those provided by Vailati himself, to keep the integrity of the original text,

Perception, Technics. University Park, PA: Penn State Press.

though we also have added a list of references at the end of each article, including:

- the references already mentioned in full by Vailati in the text;
- complete references to works mentioned by Vailati, even if we are not sure of the edition he had access to—sometimes we have chosen an edition known to be part of Vailati's personal library, of which we have record;
- references to volumes used to retrieve an English version of a passage quoted by Vailati. In general, this information is included in the bibliography entry of the original work. For example: "France, Anatole. 1885. *Le livre de mon ami*. Paris: Lévy. Engl. transl. by J. Lewis May and B. Miall. *My friend's book*. In *The Works of Anatole France*, vol. 5. London New York: Lane 1908."

To Paola Cantù goes the credit for retrieving many sources of quotations that were not clearly indicated neither in the original text nor in the Italian editions of Vailati's writings, and for organizing and formatting the extensive list of references. Mauro De Zan has collected the additional bibliography found at the end of this volume, to encourage further studies.

One last note on Vailati's style of writing. As Patrick Suppes pointed out in one of our exchanges, "the sometimes impenetrable style of thinking and writing in German philosophy of the 19th century has often been commented on. This tendency was present in more philosophers of the last half of the 19th century than we care to mention, not only those writing in German but also in Italian, French, and English. Vailati was affected by this style of writing, even if much less so in his thinking." As a translator, I necessarily had to make certain decisions about terminology and syntactic structures. I have followed Vailati's writing quite closely, because one of the intentions of the editors was to convey Vailati's style; but at the same time I have tried to ensure that the English would flow as well as possible, given the intrinsic differences between the two languages—sometimes I have opted for a paraphrase of an entire convoluted paragraph, not just because a close translation would have "sounded" wrong, but because it would have introduced ambiguities in the meaning. Notwithstanding these limitations and some inevitable mistakes on my part, I hope that this translation will be of some use.

Acknowledgments

The editors would like to thank the University of Milan, the Philosophy Department and the library staff for facilitating Paola Cantù and Mauro De Zan in their search for manuscripts and texts, and the Vailati Center in Crema for offering Claudia Arrighi a grant that allowed her to translate Vailati's texts into English. We are grateful to Dikran Karagueuzian of CSLI Publications for believing in this project and in particular for his endless patience. A special thanks goes to Wendy Hall for painstakingly correcting the original drafts of translated articles, to Andrew Haigh for revising the English in the first introductory essay, and to Sarah Terman, Daphne Humes, and Maya Juarez for their proofreading. We would also like to warmly thank all colleagues, friends, and family members who helped us with comments and encouragement.

Part I

Introductory Essays

Life and Works of Giovanni Vailati

P. Cantù and M. De Zan

Giovanni Vailati (1863-1909)

Giovanni Vailati was born in Crema in April 1863. Crema is a small, medieval town, situated forty kilometres south-east of Milan, in Lombardy, but which for many years was under the dominion of the Venetian Republic. Vailati's parents belonged to the city's aristocracy, and so followed a typical Venetian lifestyle—spending the winter in a palace in the town center, where they frequented the theatre and the nobles' club ("ridotto dei nobili")—and spending the summer in their villa in Offanengo, where they remained to run the farm estate until the first autumnal mists began to rise up from the many ditches that irrigate the fertile country of Crema (Greenfield, 1934).

It was common for the children of the Lombard and Venetian aristocracy to be sent to renowned religious colleges belonging to secular orders, and so it was that Vailati first attended the Barnabite College (boarding school) in Monza and then the Barnabite Gymnasium in Lodi, where he studied classical humanities and sciences until 1880. Vailati later abandoned religion during his time at university, but maintained friendly relations with his old teachers, to whom he sent copies of his works.

Education and Academic activity in Turin (1880-1899)

In autumn 1880 Vailati moved to Turin, and for two years attended the courses of the Mathematics Faculty. He then passed to the Real School for Engineering, where he got a degree in Civil Engineering in

Logic and Pragmatism. Selected Essays by Giovanni Vailati.
C. Arrighi, P. Cantù, M. De Zan, and P. Suppes.

1885. After that, he did not start working as an engineer but continued his mathematical studies, finally getting a degree in mathematics in 1888.[8] Vailati was interested in continuing his life in Turin, where he got a position in 1892 as the assistant to Giuseppe Peano for his course in Infinitesimal Calculus.[9]

Turin, which had been the capital of the newborn Kingdom of Italy from 1861 to 1865, was becoming a modern industrial town, deeply influenced by a positivist and pragmatic mentality: the development of scientific and experimental laboratories had a great impact on the cultural scene. Among the scientists who were active in Turin at the time were sociologists such as Cesare Lombroso; physiologists such as Jacob Moleschott and Angelo Mosso; natural scientists such as Michele Lessona; psychologists such as Enrico Morselli, and economists such as Salvatore Cognetti de' Martiis. But in the same years Turin was also well-known for its lively cafés, where Nietzsche spent the last intellectually active years of his life (Verrecchia, 1978).

From 1880 onwards, Vailati took the habit of writing down annotations and comments on the books he had read in small notebooks (*quaderni*), some of which (about 130) are now conserved in the Vailati Archive of the Philosophical Institute of the University of Milan. Vailati's interests included ethics, epistemology, economics, statistics, linguistics, and psychology, but were mainly devoted to evolutionist positivism and experimental psychology. He read defenders of social Darwinism, including John Fiske, John Lubbock, and especially Herbert Spencer's *First principles* (1862). But he also read recent results in experimental psychology, including Ludwig Büchner, Théodule Ribot, Francis Galton, Henry Mandsley, Prosper Despine and Cesare Lombroso, since he was driven by an interest in the complex relations between hereditary characters, mental pathologies, special skills, criminal behavior and the subconscious. He shared Lombroso's idea that the investigation of people suffering from mental illnesses could be useful to the inquiry of the human mind.

His deep involvement in anthropology and psychology was accompanied by a growing interest in philosophy, in particular in authors who had developed a non-reductionist description of mankind. Vailati was known among his fellows as the 'philosopher,' spending most of his time in Turin's National Library, reading classics of philosophy. He devoted particular attention to the *Dialogues et fragments philosophiques* by

---

[8]Unfortunately many documents of the University Archive in Turin were lost, so the title, the content, and the name of the supervisor of Vailati's master's thesis are unknown.

[9]For a deeper analysis of Vailati's university years, see De Zan 2009.

Ernest Renan (1876), and, probably through the reading of the former, to the writings of Arthur Schopenhauer, whose aphorisms are often accurately copied in the notes. But he also developed a deep interest in William K. Clifford's writings about the philosophy of science, and in the theory of knowledge—especially the works of Locke, Hume, and John Stuart Mill. Reading Mill's *Examination on the Hamilton's Philosophy* (1865) and the *System of Logic* (1870) at the same time as the *First Principles* of Spencer (1862), Vailati argued against any philosophical attempt at hypostatizing scientific concepts, or at grounding knowledge on *a priori* intuition, thus adhering to Mill's criticism of Hamilton's theory of knowledge in order to develop a criticism of Spencer's metaphysics (De Zan, 2009).

This criticism is related to an anti-Kantian feature of Vailati's thought that is one of the main divergences from Peirce's form of pragmatism. While Peirce often considers Kant's theses in a positive way, tracing the origin of the expression 'pragmatism' to Kant himself,[10] Vailati always criticized any revival of Kant's theory of knowledge, repeatedly opposing Kant to Locke, whose *Essay Concerning Human Understanding* he had read carefully already in 1882. In particular, he praised Locke's criticism of the misuse of language in scientific and philosophical disputes, an issue that motivated his own pragmatism.[11]

Having finished his studies at the university Vailati went back, rather reluctantly it seems, to Crema, where he secured some administrative work for the local municipality, allowing him plenty of time to devote himself to theatre, modern literature, and philosophy. In 1890 he became a member of the *London Society for Psychical Research*, whose aim was—in Vailati's own words—"to promote by any means unprejudiced, and careful investigations, the knowledge of the causes of error in observations, and of the precautions to take against memory's illusions and the tendency of language to put in the description of facts something that was not actually observed."[12]ailati's interest for psychic phenomena, though never accompanied by specific investigations into this field, is evident from the number of writings he devoted to the topic from 1896 to 1900. He participated in the 1896 *International Conference in Psychology* in Munich. In some articles published in Lombroso's "Archivio di Psichiatria" and in "Rivista di Studi Psichici," Vailati criticized Spiritism, but he believed in the possibility of telepathy. He was mainly concerned with the necessity of developing a rigorous method of

---

[10]See Peirce 1905.

[11]See the Inaugural Lecture to the Course in History of Mechanics that Vailati gave at the University of Turin in 1898 (this volume, chapter 2).

[12]V

investigation of psychic phenomena, avoiding both the dogmatic prejudices of Positivists, and the ingenuous approach of many scholars in psychical research. To the latter he recommended the study of the history of science in order to avoid the hypostatization of concepts, an error that in the course of history was repeatedly made, for example in mechanics and in physical sciences.

The collaboration with Peano and the journal "Rivista di matematica"

Vailati's collaboration with Peano's "Rivista di Matematica" started in 1891, and in 1892 he began his academic activity at the Mathematics Faculty of the University of Turin, where he obtained a position as Assistant Lecturer in Infinitesimal Calculus, the course taught by Giuseppe Peano.

In the first two volumes of the *Rivista* (1891-1892) Vailati published three articles on mathematical logic and an article on the foundations of geometry: "Un teorema di logica matematica" [A theorem of mathematical logic] (1891b), "Le proprietà fondamentali delle operazioni della logica deduttiva" [The fundamental properties of the operations of Deductive Logic], "Dipendenza fra le proprietà delle relazioni" [Dependence between the properties of relations], and "Sui principi fondamentali della geometria della retta" [On the fundamental principles of the geometry of the straight line].[13] In the third and fourth volumes (1893-1894) he published some reviews of books in mathematical logic by Nagy (1892) and Burali-Forti (1894), and a presentation of the courses of the Mathematics Faculty of the University of Texas, where Halsted, Macfarlane, and Taylor directed the School of Pure Mathematics, the School of Physics, and the School of Applied Mathematics respectively.[14] In the fifth volume (1895) he wrote two more articles on geometry: "Sulle relazioni di posizione tra punti d'una linea chiusa" [On the relations of position between points of a closed line], and "Sulle proprietà caratteristiche delle varietà a una dimensione" [On the characteristic properties of one-dimensional varieties].[15] In the sixth volume of the journal (1896-99) he published his historical contributions to the *Formulario*,[16] the common project of the Peano school, and some reviews of Hontheim (1895), Perez (1895), and Couturat (1901).[17] There

---

[13]See Vailati 1891a, 1892a, and 1892b.

[14]See Vailati 1893, 1894a, and1894b.

[15]See Vailati 1895b and 1895a.

[16]The *Formulario* had various editions between 1895 and 1908. See in particular Peano 1901a.

[17]See Vailati 1898d, 1896c, and 1901c.

were no more articles from Vailati in the two following volumes of the journal, published between 1900 and 1906, apart from some historical notes added to the *Formulario* (1902a).

After 1896 Vailati would be closer to Vito Volterra, professor at the University of Turin, even if he still had contacts with Peano's group, and particularly with Alessandro Padoa.[18]

Vailati's logical and mathematical writings concern mainly the analysis of relations and operations, both in algebra and in geometry. The essay on the fundamental properties of the operations of deductive logic focuses on the search for a minimal number of "combinatorial properties of an operation or a system of operations that have to be assumed as primitive in order to prove all other combinatorial properties that such an operation or system of operations actually possesses" (Vailati, 1891a, p. 2). This foundational approach is maintained in the mentioned geometrical writings. The interest for the theory of proportions, which goes back to a talk presented in Livorno (1902b), is evident in the historical article "Sulla teoria delle proporzioni" [On the theory of proportions] (1924), strongly influenced by Zeuthen 1896.

Vailati's contribution to the *Formulario* probably concerned mainly the paragraphs on functions and relations of the logical section and some historical notes, as Vailati 1902a. In the 1893 volume of the *Rivista* he added a note to the logical section explaining that it contains a revised presentation of the formulas already contained in the previous edition, and an entirely new paragraph devoted to functions and relations, because "from a certain point of view they belong to logic rather than to mathematics" (Peano, 1893, p. 1).[19]

Vailati also wrote an article on Peano's mathematical logic that was published in the "Revue de Métaphisique et de Morale" (1899b).

---

[18] See the letters from Padoa to Vailati (about thirty letters and postcards written from March 1896 to May 1908) kept in the Vailati Archive at the University of Milan. Most letters inform us about the friendly relations between Vailati and Padoa: a letter from 1898 shows that Padoa recommended Vailati as temporary teacher in Pinerolo during the time he spent in Brussels giving a series of lectures on mathematical logic (Padoa, 1898); several letters from 1900 show that Padoa and Vailati organized together their stay in Paris for the 1900 International Conferences. Some logico-mathematical issues are also addressed, especially in some letters—first published in Cantù (2007)—that Padoa sent to Vailati in 1905 concerning the relation of equality, and in particular the possibility or impossibility of deriving the reflexive property from substitutivity. Note that the derivability of reflexivity from other defining properties of equivalence had been discussed in Vailati 1891a and, with reference to the former text, also in De Amicis 1892.

[19] The only reference added to this paragraph of the logical section is Dedekind 1888.

Vailati's Inaugural Lectures in History of Mechanics

In 1895 Vailati became Assistant Lecturer in Projective Geometry, a course given by Full Professor Luigi Berzolari, and in the following academic years he was demoted to Voluntary Assistant in Mathematics, a position as Lecturer in the Undergraduate Course in Mathematics that was practically unpaid, though it allowed him to freely choose the topic of his lectures. Vailati decided—for the first time in an Italian Faculty of Sciences—to give lectures in History of Mechanics, following a suggestion from Vito Volterra, who held him in high esteem, and encouraged him to publish his works on the history of science (De Zan, 2003). Between 1897 and 1898 Vailati published three essays in "Atti dell'Accademia delle Scienze di Torino" on the center of gravity in Archimedes' statics, on the development of virtual labor from Aristotle to Heron, and on the influence of Benedetti's observations concerning the fall of heavy bodies on Galileo. A fourth essay on Galileo's laws of motion was never finished.[20]

Vailati's inaugural lectures, which he published at his own expense and circulated in Italy and abroad thanks to Volterra's help, were deeply influenced by Ernst Mach, with whom he was in correspondence from 1896 to 1907 (Vailati, 1971, pp. 113-134). Vailati, who reviewed Mach's writings[21] and also promoted an Italian edition of *Die Mechanik* (1883),[22] was interested not only in the historical but also in the philosophical conceptions of Mach: he held Mach's phenomenism in great esteem and saw a similarity between Mach's epistemology and Pragmatism.

The three inaugural lectures already show the dominant interests of Vailati: history and philosophy of science (especially mechanics, economics and psychology), mathematical logic, argumentation theory, philosophy of language, and pragmatism.

On the Importance of the History of Science (1896)

In the first inaugural lecture, held in 1896 (December, 4) on the importance of researches in History of Science[23] Vailati claimed that an analysis of the nature of history of science is necessary, for the latter has become a science in itself that is taught as an autonomous disci-

---

[20]See Vailati 1897a, Vailati 1897b, and Vailati 1898c.

[21]See Vailati 1896a, Vailati 1896b and Vailati 1901b, and Vailati 1905d.

[22]Vailati's intention is reported by Papini in a letter to Prezzolini dated October 21, 1902. Vailati finally wrote the Introduction to the translation into Italian by D. Gambioli (Mach, 1909).

[23]*Sull'importanza delle ricerche relative alla storia delle scienze. Prolusione a un corso sulla storia della meccanica, letta il 4 dicembre 1896 nell'Università di Torino* (Vailati, 1897c).

pline in several universities. Vailati's conception of science here is not yet fully original—Vailati's remarks are still deeply influenced by positivism (Spencer and the positivist psychology in particular), Darwinism, and Mach's epistemology—nor fully coherent, for there is, as we will see, an unresolved tension between continuism and discontinuism.

Nonetheless some original issues are already present: 1) the idea of the development of science as a progressive accumulation of knowledge is tempered by the acknowledgment of the positive function of errors; 2) beyond the Machian application of the metaphor of the economy of nature, a new metaphor of the economy of economics is applied in the analysis of mathematical notations and formalism; 3) in the essay on the Italian mathematician Giovanni Benedetti, Vailati described Galileo's discovery of the laws of motion as a 'scientific revolution.'

1) Vailati argues that what varies in science is not the content but the standard of acceptance of proofs and arguments, which increased in the passage from ancient to contemporary works. As an example he mentions mathematics, and argues that the comparison between Euclid's treatise and modern formulations of mathematics shows that the differences in the content are mainly formal or of minor importance. There is an evident continuism in Vailati's conception of science, whose progress is compared to "a series of explorations of an unknown land, where every exploration corrects or refines the results of previous explorations and makes it easier, for those in the future, to achieve the common goal" (1897c, this volume, p. 6). The history of science—he argues— is "a series of successes, each of which has overtaken and eclipsed the one before it, just as the one before that had done" (ibid.). Darwin's evolutionism, and the analogy between the evolution of species and the evolution of knowledge by means of a fight for survival and the adaptation to the environment, are used to "give a new, and more concrete meaning" to Leibniz's aphorism *the present is child of the past but is also parent to the future* or to Pascal's remark that the succession of human generations in the course of the years has to be considered as the life of a single man *who lives forever and learns continuously.* (this volume, p. 7). This positivist approach is mitigated by the belief that the importance that "various competing trains of thought on a certain field of research are going to acquire or lose at a given time" cannot be formulated by "a scholar, who does not care about anything other than the current state of the science he is studying," just as a geometer cannot "determine the path of a curve from only one point or one linear element." (ibid.)

The positivist conception of the development of sciences as a progressive enterprise is also tempered by Vailati's attention to the positive role of errors in the history of science:

> An erroneous assertion, an inconclusive argument from a scientist of the past can be worthy of consideration as much as a discovery or an ingenious intuition, if they are equally useful in shedding light on the causes that have accelerated or delayed the progress of human knowledge, or in revealing how our intellectual faculties operate. Every error shows us an obstacle to avoid, while not every discovery shows us a path to follow (this volume, p. 5).

2) Darwin's evolutionism is mediated by Mach's comparison of the economy of nature with the economy of thought that is typical of the scientific progress. In *The Origin of Species* (1859) Darwin quotes the construction of hexagonal cells by bees as an example of natural selection. As Vailati recalls, the Alexandrine mathematician Pappus in his work on isoperimetry had already mentioned the fact that bees seem to know that the hexagon can hold more honey than a triangle or a square for the same expenditure of material used in constructing the different figures (Pappus, *Collections*, Book 5). As Darwin defines the cells constructed by bees to contain larvae as constructed with the greatest possible economy of labor and wax, Vailati judges theories that are produced by human thought to contain observational data as made "with a decreasing use of concepts and direct recourse to experience or intuition, with a decreasing need of distinctions and special considerations that vary from case to case, in other words with the maximum possible economy of that most precious of worldly materials, man's thought" (this volume, p. 19). Vailati's reference to Darwin does not imply a strict biological reductionism, but shows his belief in a continuity in the evolution of biological and cultural phenomena.

Another metaphor, this time from economics, is applied in the analysis of mathematical notations and formalism. In modern industries that are based on fixed capital, the replacement of production facilities, though necessary to increase productivity, might not result in an immediate increase in output, for the expenses might require some time to be amortized. Analogously the introduction of a new notation in mathematics, though more efficient in the production of knowledge, might be resisted, or considered as not sufficiently fruitful because it requires time and costs in order to be learned (this volume, p. 15). The balance of gain and costs is the reason why a method might not be abandoned, even if one knows that it is outdated or that it has been surpassed by a new one. A pragmatist element is here clearly delineated: scientific concepts are "instruments which only have value depending on their usefulness in achieving the purpose so defined" (this volume, p. 16). But for Vailati a different method does not introduce novelties of content, but is only a way to produce the same result in a more efficient way.

3) The pragmatic analysis of gain and costs according to the aims of science introduces a discontinuity element in Vailati's epistemology. The history of mechanics, and more generally the history of sciences, is filled with "intellectual confrontations" between opposing ideas in the mind of scientists, where the ideas that can better satisfy the needs and the aims of science at a given historical moment ultimately prevail (this volume, p. 18). Even if the "intellectual confrontations" between different ideas might remind us of Kuhn's thesis on the development of science through successive paradigm changes by means of what he called scientific revolutions (1962), Vailati's intellectual battles are not radical discontinuities, but rather progressive changes in human mind that mirror the natural process of adaptation of living beings to the environment.

Discontinuity is more evident in the characterization of Galileo's theory of dynamics given in "The speculations of Giovanni Benedetti on the movement of heavy bodies" (Vailati, 1898c), where Benedetti is given the merit of having made Galileo's "big, scientific revolution" possible. Vailati introduced—long before Koyré (1939)—the term 'revolution' to designate the relevant change introduced by Galileo's laws of motion.

Benedetti was the point of departure of a scientific revolution because he had a "clear awareness" not only of the insufficiency of the Aristotelian theories in the explanation of new phenomena generated by the introduction of firearms, but also of the "direction into which one should proceed [...] in order to forge better theories that deserve to be substituted to the former."[24] In the inaugural lecture on the deductive method as a research tool (1898a) Vailati insists on the role of the invention of firearms, which contributed to the discovery of the fundamental laws of motion, because it "made new facts available to the observers where the two main determining circumstances of the trajectory of a thrown body were energically surpassing the perturbating influences of the others" (this volume, p. 58). Discontinuism is here connected not to a methodological but to a technological change that allows new kinds of experiments, and thus new kinds of observations: "The sieges and the wars, that afflicted our country in the century that separate the birth of Leonardo from that of Galileo, acted in this respect as real laboratories for experimental mechanics" (this volume, p. 58). The originality of this historical insight of Vailati was appreciated

---

[24]Cf. Vailati 1898c in Vailati 1911, p. 161.

by Mach himself, who thanked him for his "valuable" critical remarks in the preface to *The Science of Mechanics* and gave him the credit for having first understood the connection between the construction of firearms and the development of mechanics.[25]

On the deductive method (1897)

The second inaugural lecture on the deductive method as an instrument of research[26] is entirely devoted to an analysis of Gaileo's method, based on the combination of induction and deduction (*sensate esperienze e certe dimostrazioni*). Vailati argues that modern science is not mainly inductive, but rather based on a new conception and a systematic application of the deductive method.

The reason why induction is not as relevant as deduction in the rise of modern science has nothing to do with a presumed higher grade of certainty of the assertions obtained by deduction; what makes deduction essential is its capacity of being not only a demonstrative means, as it was in Aristotle, but also an heuristic tool, that guides the research of the experimental scientist, as was the case in Galileo's works. Deduction is thus considered as a means to explain and anticipate experience rather than as a means to prove results.[27]

Experimental scientists made use of deduction in those cases in which "the propositions taken as a starting point were considered more in need of proof than the resulting ones, cases where, therefore, the resultant propositions were those which had to pass on, to the initial conjectures, the grade of certainty that they were directly acquiring from a comparison with facts and experimental verifications" (1898a, this volume, p. 31). Deduction does not transfer the certainty of the premises to the conclusions, but rather uses the certainty of the conclusions that can be observed experimentally to ground the plausibility of the conjectures assumed as hypotheses.

In this lecture the historical discontinuity between Aristotle and Galileo is seen as a change that concerns not only the notational apparatus of science, but its theoretical approach. There is a fundamental rupture between Aristotle and modern science, that is not due to new tools (as in the previous metaphor from economics), but rather to a different theoretical use of well known tools: it is the heuristic

---

[25] "As Vailati remarks, the rapid spread of firearms in the fourteenth century gave a distinct impulse to the study of the motion of projectiles, and indirectly to that of mechanics generally" (Mach, 1883, p. 526).

[26] *Il Metodo Deduttivo come Strumento di Ricerca. Prolusione ad un corso libero di Storia della Meccanica, 1897-1898* (Vailati, 1898a).

[27] For an analysis of the pragmatic themes involved in Vailati's conception of deduction as a means of knowing see Innis 2002.

use of deduction made by Galileo that allows him to make the best out of empirical experiments. This change in Vailati's perspective and its originality with respect to the continuist views of other historians of science of the time was probably the reason for the success of this essay, which was translated into Polish by Samuel Dickstein and into French in "Revue de Métaphysique et de Morale" (Vailati, 1898b).

On the role of language in the history of science and culture (1898)

The third inaugural lecture concerns the role of matters of words in the history of science and culture.[28] Vailati claims that the history of science offers many examples of matters of words that are not—contrary to the positivist dictum—useless and unnecessary with respect to matters of fact. An historical analysis of matters of words—either when they gave rise to controversies or when they failed to be noticed—shows that they can be relevant for the development of science, at least inasmuch as they can promote but also hinder its progress. Such an analysis can thus reveal the mechanism of language in the transmission of knowledge, and teach us to detect sophisms, learning to avoid them or to defend ourselves from their consequences. The belief in the fruitfulness and inevitability of errors, together with the refusal of a "clear distinction, established once and for all, between questions which can be the subject of scientific research and others to which such a privilege does not belong" (Vailati, 1899a, this volume, p. 65) are the cornerstones of Vailati's criticism of positivism. But the possibility of tracing such a distinction is not entirely abandoned, and the analysis of matters of words is taken to be most useful in distinguishing between solvable and unsolvable matters, and understanding "which and how many of such [unsolvable] questions get this characteristic from some fundamental flaw in our way of formulating them, or from the fact of being merely fictitious questions, i.e. that there is no corresponding determined sense that could be assigned to the compound of words used to state them." (ibid.).

Vailati remarked that there are cases in which the ordinary language is unable to distinguish the use of an expression as a definition (as a proposition that determines the meaning of a name) or as an assertion (on some real objects). He believed this lack of distinction to be a common source of ambiguities and mistakes in psychology and social sciences, though rarely dangerous in the technical sciences, for if an

---

[28] *Alcune osservazioni sulle Questioni di Parole nella Storia della Scienza e della Cultura. Prolusione ad un corso libero di Storia della Meccanica, 1898-98* (Vailati, 1899a).

assertion is acknowledged as true, it can also be taken as a definition. The lack of a clear distinction between definition and assertion is— according to Vailati's analysis—at the base of the misunderstanding of Berkeley's and Hume's remarks, who aimed at modifying the definition of the expressions 'substance,' 'existence,' and 'cause' rather than negating that there might be substances, causes, or things that exist (this volume, p.75 ff.). Changing the definition of a name might change the objects that fall under the name in its new meaning, because what falls under a concept depends on its definition, as what exists depends on the definition of existence.

Matters of words are analyzed as a source of epistemological illusions that might have negative or positive effects on the development of science. In one case they generate "extremely pessimistic and discouraging theories on the limits that scientific research should impose on itself" (this volume, p. 77). In the other case they favor the progress of knowledge.

As an example of the first case, Vailati considers the notion of primitive propositions and notions. He argues that the distinction between explained and unexplained matters is often taken to coincide with the distinction between knowable and unknowable things, while it rather refers to our capacity or incapacity "to deduce our cognitions from one another and to order them in such a way so that part of them are consequences of those remaining" (ibid.). Just as admitting unexplained propositions does not imply an enlargement of what we do not or cannot know, similarly the acknowledgement of undefined notions does not imply that their meaning should be mysterious: on the contrary it is usually so well-known that we cannot find more familiar concepts. Two classes of phenomena can be explained one by means of the other: the fact that we usually use a class of phenomena to explain another class is just a consequence of our viewpoint, of our being more familiar with certain facts than with others, it is a matter of psychology. There is no place for philosophy as a superior judge of matters of foundations in Vailati's perspective, for if the deduction of classes of phenomena from other classes of phenomena can be symmetric, then there cannot be a unique list of plausible principles and general hypotheses for each science: the choice is rather conventional. If philosophy can play a role in matters of foundations, it cannot play the role of a "Supreme Court of Cassation," but rather the role of a "clearing house" that rules at a meta-level the transactions between different sciences (this volume, p. 79).

As an example of illusions that might have a positive function, Vailati mentions the tendency to believe that one can associate an object with any name, as in the case of definitions by abstraction and in the case of the introduction of ideal ('fictional') elements.

> So, if two objects are in a certain relationship, and such relationship has properties similar to those of the equivalence or similarity, the supposition that they should actually resemble each other in some aspects may lead, and in fact has led in many cases, to the discovery of new properties in the objects in question, and to the realization of which are, among those properties, those whose common possession correlates with, or determine, the existence of their relationship. (this volume, p. 83).

Even when the analogy could not be precisely expressed by a relation of equality, "talking and arguing as if it had in fact been achieved, has often suggested important generalizations, which, notwithstanding their merely verbal and formal character, have provided the occasion and incentive for substantial scientific progress" (this volume, p. 83). Vailati considers several examples, including the introduction of the point at infinity in geometry, irrational numbers in arithmetic, the notion of latent heat in physics.

Defending the heuristic positive role of analogies, Vailati does not condemn the presence of metaphors in mathematics, refusing to take part in the crusade against intuition and impure proofs in mathematics. Vailati acknowledged that scientific technical language, like ordinary language, was actually full of metaphors, and believed they should at least be made explicit, for "even if after long use [they] have stopped reminding us of the image suggested in origin, [they] have not lost their ability to induce us to attribute to the facts that such expressions describe all the properties of the image to which they refer" (this volume, p. 87). The metaphor of 'dead analogies' is further developed in the paper "On material representations of deductive processes" (1905a, this volume, chapter 15), where Vailati shows the presence of several metaphors in the language that is used to describe logical operations and the influence that they have on the way we conceive them (see below, p. xliii).

Vailati's intermediate position between a dogmatic refusal of analogy and a skeptical attitude to logical investigations directed at the elimination of implicit intuitions from mathematics could be interpreted as a stand in the controversy between the Italian school of algebraic geometry, which arrived at many new results without giving rigorous proofs, and the logical school of Peano. Segre (1891) argued that the first way to arrive at a mathematical truth does not usually consist in a satisfactory proof, because the scientific truth is placed at the top of a high mountain that is at first reached by difficult paths between dangerous peaks (safer ways can be traced only afterwards). Peano answered that mathematics is based on logical deduction, and any activity that is not deductive should be considered "poetry, but surely not mathematics" (1891, p. 67). Vailati's position is certainly nearer to Segre than to Peano:

> In contrast with Molière's character who was surprised when he realized he had always spoken in prose without knowing it, we should be surprised to have always spoken in poetry without noticing it. This is not harmful to us, in the same way as it is not harmful to the mathematician, who investigates the properties of functions, to use sentences that refer to, or are taken from, their geometric representation, and in the same way as it is not harmful for the geometer to talk about spaces with n dimensions, or about points in common to lines which do not meet each other (Vailati, 1899a, this volume, p. 87).

The inaugural lecture ends with an appreciation of theories of reasoning and argumentation, which, together with mathematics and linguistics, constitute a means of emancipation from the unconscious slavery of thought from words. An implicit reference to William James occurs again when, after having criticized the Positivists' contempt towards the "imperfect" scientific theories of the past, Vailati mentions the contributions of American experimental psychology and—"last not least"—of mathematical logic to the renewal of interest in history of sciences (this volume, p. 91).

Outside the Academy (1899-1903)

In October 1899 Vailati accepted a position as mathematics teacher in a high school in Syracuse, Sicily, definitively renouncing his academic career. In the following years Vailati would mainly devote himself to issues connected to philosophy of science: from the status of psychology to its connections with logic, philosophy of language and with the issue of determinism in science.

In Sicily Vailati met one of his previous correspondents: Giuseppe Amato Pojero, a member of the Mathematical Circle of Palermo, and founder of the *Società per gli studi filosofici*.[29] Thanks to Amato Pojero, Vailati got to know Franz Brentano, who began a rich correspondence with Vailati (Chisholm and Corrado, 1982) and invited him to Austria in the summer of 1902.

In 1900 Vailati moved from Syracuse to a high school in Bari, Apulia, and then in 1902 to Como, Lombardy, not too far from his native town

---

[29] Antonio Brancaforte has published their correspondence in Vailati and Amato Pojero 1993.

Crema. During his activity as a school teacher, Vailati diversified his researches, describing himself as a mole burrowing a lawn in different directions and running from one to the other gallery advancing a few decimetres in each direction:[30] in these years he mainly wrote reviews and took part in international conferences. In the summer holidays he traveled across Europe, meeting philosophers and scholars with whom he was in correspondence, and who praised him not only for his scientific merits but also for his humanity and whole-heartedness. So wrote Mario Calderoni after their first meeting at the Psychology Conference in Münich in 1896: "I saw him universally celebrated and requested from all intervening scholars; in the streets, in the pubs, in gatherings and meetings he was always in the middle of a group which he fascinated with his simple, whole-hearted, and nonetheless interesting, informative conversation" (Calderoni, 1924).

During these years Vailati continued his 'work' as reviewer that would lead him to write a huge number of reviews. Vailati believed in the philosophical relevance of reviews and had a preference for this 'literary genre':

> My preference for this literary genre that, though not separately considered in rhetoric textbooks, is a true, freestanding genre like madrigal, sonnet, or satire, does not depend only on the fact that I do not have time to write longer works, but from the belief that it is a very useful and too often neglected genre, that is wrongly let at the mercy of those who write only to praise (or blame) the works they are reviewing, rather than to separate what is good from the rest (Rizza, 2006, pp. 74–75).

Among the few essays of this period there are three texts that are strictly related to Vailati's paper presented in 1904 at the Heidelberg International Conference of Mathematicians: Vailati 1903a on Saccheri's *Demonstrative logic*, which he had the merit of rediscovering, an article on Aristotle's theory of definition (1903b, this volume, chapter 7), and Vailati 1902a—a historical contribution to Peano's *Formulario* on the distinctions between real and nominal definitions, and between definitions of classes and individuals and definitions of functions and relations.[31]

International Conferences

During the years he spent as teacher, Vailati also attended and presented papers at several International Conferences on different topics, including Psychology, Philosophy, Mathematics and History.

---

[30]Letter of Vailati to Papini, June 1, 1908 (Vailati, 1971, p. 463 ff.).

[31]See below, page xl, and page xlvii. See also Lolli 1985.

In Paris Vailati took part, together with Padoa and the other members of the Peano school, in the International Philosophy Conference, where Russell was impressed with the clarity of language and reasoning of the Italian group:

> The Congress was a turning point in my intellectual life, because I there met Peano. I already knew him by name and had seen some of his work, but had not taken the trouble to master his notation. In discussions at the Congress I observed that he was always more precise than anyone else, and that he invariably got the better of any argument upon which he embarked. As the days went by, I decided that this must be owing to his mathematical logic. I therefore got him to give me all his works, and as soon as the Congress was over I retired to Fernhurst to study quietly every word written by him and his disciples. It became clear to me that his notation afforded an instrument of logical analysis such as I had been seeking for years, and that by studying him I was acquiring a new and powerful technique for the work that I had long wanted to do (Russell, 1998, p. 147).

At the International Conference of Philosophy Giuseppe Peano presented a paper on definitions (1901b). Padoa presented his best known contribution to logic and the foundation of mathematics (1900), arguing that a logically perfect deductive theory should have a system of irreducible axioms and a system of primitive irreducible symbols, and used the so-called Padoa's definability criterion to verify the latter condition. Vailati did not give a talk on mathematical logic, having abandoned its study some years before, but on the classification of sciences, and especially on an analysis of Comte's classification (1901a).[32]

Like Peano, Padoa, and Volterra, Vailati also attended the International Conference of Mathematicians. Padoa presented two papers: a study on the principles of geometry that was later translated into Italian and into Spanish in the journals "Periodico di matematica" and "El Progreso Mathemático" respectively (1902a), and a paper on the definition of the field of natural numbers by means of two operations: the successor of an integer and the symmetric of an integer (1902b). Volterra presented a paper on the role of Betti, Brioschi and Casorati in the foundation of the Italian school of algebrists (1902b), and a second paper on the equation of Poisson and its transformations (1902a).

---

[32]See below, page xxxvii. It is possible that Vailati had originally planned to discuss this topic in a course of mechanics, given that the structure and the content of this paper are quite similar to those of the three inaugural lectures on the history of mechanics. In this same period Vailati discussed problems connected to the classification of science also in some reviews, especially in Vailati 1899d, Vailati 1900, and Vailati 1902c.

The classification of sciences (Paris 1900)

In "Des difficultés qui s'opposent á une classification rationelle des sciences" [The difficulties involved in a rational classification of the sciences] (1901a) Vailati connected the classification of the different sciences to the differentiation of labor, showing once more his deep interest in sociology and economics. After raising two typically pragmatic objections —most classifications are based on a vague and mistaken notion of what it is to make a classification, and overlook "the practical motivations that have determined the division of intellectual labor"—Vailati discussed the conceptual distinctions introduced by Durand de Gros in *Aperçu de taxinomie générale*[33] and put forward three objections to Comte's classification, which are grounded in historical counterexamples and aim at a rehabilitation of the role of two social sciences: sociology, whose method can be not only inductive but also deductive, and psychology, which deserves to be considered as a science. Apart from showing the need for a conceptual clarification of the notion of classification, that should be taken to be descriptive—and thus historically based—rather than normative, Vailati's remarks were aimed at showing the fruitfulness of an analysis that takes into account the aims of the special sciences and limits itself to the relations between one science and its neighboring disciplines, renouncing the unattainable claim of giving a simultaneous classification of all sciences.

The historical awareness of the complexity of the ways in which sciences had developed prevented him from believing that any ideal scheme might adequately represent the many-sided relations between different sciences. Nonetheless he defended the usefulness of partial, flexible classifications, which might still serve various aims—to compile a bibliographical catalogue, to organize a didactic activity, or to establish an interdisciplinary, historical research project.

> Between the research of a perfect and ideal grouping of the various sciences according to a uniform and necessarily unilateral criterion, and the passive adhesion to the traditional divisions between the areas of research of the different sciences, divisions for which most of the time the historical causes of their origins have long disappeared, there is a large area open for useful and important attempts. If they are unable to order and unify according to new principles the variety of human knowledge, it does not mean that they will be less effective for the progress of science and to better the economy of the efforts that tend to make it grow (Vailati, 1901a, this volume, p. 106).

---

[33] See Durand de Gros 1899 and Vailati 1900.

The classification of mental states (Paris, 1900)

The analysis of Brentano's states of consciousness was the topic of a talk Vailati gave in 1900 at the III International Conference of Psychology in Paris. In "Sulla portata logica della classificazione dei fatti mentali proposta dal prof. Franz Brentano" [On the logical import of the classification of mental facts proposed by Franz Brentano] (1901e) Vailati remarked that Brentano's tripartion of mental facts in representations, expectations and volitions has a logical meaning, for it corresponds to the distinction between definitions or analytic propositions, factual propositions and judgments of value. As in the third inaugural lecture, Vailati argued that the lack of a clear distinction between these different kinds of propositions in the ordinary language has induced epistemological mistakes, as that of believing that one can derive propositions of one category from propositions of another category, for example geometrical propositions from geometrical definitions, or normative propositions from definitions and factual propositions. Against the naïve scientism of some contemporary Positivists, Vailati believed that the inability of science to predict wants or desires was not a weakness of science, but rather a consequence of the fact that one cannot derive predictions on judgments of value from factual propositions alone. "To blame science, or scientists, for their inability in this regard is only slightly less absurd than it is to blame the talent of a painter for the fact that the light of a lamp he has painted is not able to brighten the dark room where the painting is hanging." (this volume, p. 112). Without entering into a detailed discussion of Brentano's classification, Vailati used it to defend science from its opponents, arguing that the distinction "helps us to understand that we are wrong to expect something from science which, due to its own nature, it cannot give us" (this volume, p. 112).

On the concepts of cause and effect in historical sciences (Roma, 1903)

In April 1903 Vailati took part, in Rome, in the International Conference of Historical Sciences, where he gave two talks, one in history of science—"La dimostrazione del principio delle leva data da Archimede" [Archimedes's proof of the principle of the lever] (1904b)[34]—and one in philosophy of science—"Sull'applicabilità dei concetti di causa e di effetto nelle scienze storiche" [On the applicability of the concepts of cause and effect in historical sciences] (1903c, this volume, chapter 6.).

Vailati took part in a debate about the nature of history in which Italian Positivists and neoidealist philosophers were deeply involved.

---

[34]This text is widely discussed in Palmieri 2008.

Vailati argued that history should be considered as a scientific discipline, for physical laws—like historical laws—are not necessary, because they are general but subject to exceptions, and hypothetically valid. First, he claimed that, since the conditions that have to be verified for a physical law to be valid cannot be exhaustively formulated, physical laws—like historical laws —are general, but subject to exceptions, and only hypothetically valid. Secondly, he argued that most scientific laws are obtained by induction and not by deduction, and that even in the case of mathematical physics, which is mainly deductive (see this volume, chapter 2), only the connection between premises and conclusions is necessary, and not the laws themselves.

> Therefore the truth of a law is compatible, in every special case, both when the facts mentioned in it happen or not, because all it affirms is not that such and such a fact *happens* or *does not happen*, but only which are the facts that join it *when it happens*, or with which it would be joined *in the case it should happen* (this volume, p. 116).

Vailati's refusal of the determinism of human will is associated with his refusal of some interpretations of the materialist conception of history. He criticized those views according to which social phenomena are only ideological reflections, and economic conditions the causes of all social transformations.[35] Between economics and society there is not a cause-effect relation, but rather a relationship of mutual dependence. It is the practical restriction to a certain aim and to a certain point of view that induces the researcher to consider certain factors as causes of a given social phenomenon:

> [the researcher] allows himself, more or less consciously, to be induced to limit his attention and to consider as causes only those, among the conditions of a given fact, whose modification he believes would be necessary or useful to provide if we were to generate or prevent the fact in question or others of a similar nature, or to modify them in the way he desires. This kind of partiality should not be considered illegitimate, or confused with that which consists in allowing our passions and our interests to influence the evaluation of the proof of facts and theories (this volume, p. 118).

The notion of mutual dependence between cause and effect, and more generally, the concept of correlative properties was further developed in "La caccia alle Antitesi" [The attack on distinctions]—first published in 1905 in the journal "Leonardo" and translated into English in 1907 (this volume, chapter 14).

---

[35] Vailati's rejection of the common interpretation of the materialist conception of history has to be distinguished from his judgment on Marx's philosophy (this volume, p. 117).

On the meaning of the difference between axioms and postulates in Greek geometry, Heidelberg 1904

In 1904 Vailati participated in the 3ʳᵈ International Conference of Mathematicians in Heidelberg, where he presented a paper in the section on History of Mathematics, in which Cantor, Dickstein, Zeuthen, Tannery, Loria, and many others also participated. Vailati remarked that if axioms are distinguished from postulates on the basis of a higher degree of evidence or intuition, then the traditional distinction between axioms and postulates becomes useless in geometry, for the latter gives "less and less importance to 'intuition' and to the criterion of 'evidence' in choosing fundamental propositions" (1904a, this volume, p. 145).

Quoting Proclus' *Commentary on the first Book of Euclid's Elements* Vailati outlined three possible ways to distinguish between postulates and axioms. The expression 'postulates' might be reserved: 1) for propositions that include some assertion of existence (e.g. the postulate of Archimedes); 2) for propositions that belong to a single science and are not common to several sciences (e.g. the geometric proposition "All right angles are equal"); 3) for propositions that are used as *implicit* definitions of relations or operations, or of classes of entities that satisfy such relations and operations (e.g. "Two quantities equal to a third are equal to each other").[36]

Presenting postulates as propositions that include some assertion of existence, Vailati introduced a distinction between the Principle of Archimedes, which is considered as a postulate, and Dedekind's Continuity, which is considered as a definition, i.e. as one of those propositions which, "even if they are presented, as this one, in the form of assertions of existence, are really used only to extend and generalize the meaning of some locution, making it applicable to a broader field than the one it was previously reserved for" (1904a, this volume, p. 149).

The distinction between direct and indirect definitions (applied to the so-called 'implicit' definitions) is expressed in Vailati's essay "La teoria Aristotelica della definizione" [The Aristotelian theory of definition] (1903b, this volume, p. 7) and in a letter that he sent to Frege on March 17, 1904:

> But I believe that if only Mr Hilbert could make up his mind to renounce his opinion that the axioms represent the 'fundamental facts of intuition' (an opinion whose source is perhaps to be sought in his irrational devotion to Kantian philosophical jargon, which is still de-

---

[36] At this Conference Hilbert defined equality by means of reflexivity and substitutivity. Vailati presumably attended Hilbert's talk (Hilbert, 1905), which might be relevant to the analysis of the correspondence with Padoa in 1905. See above footnote 18 and Cantù 2007.

plorably popular among writers on the philosophy of science), all the rest of his exposition could be given an irreproachable form. When he says that a given group of axioms defines a 'relation' (for example 'between') or a class of objects (for example 'points'), he does not sufficiently distinguish the different nature of the definition in the two cases: 1) To define 'a *relation*' by means of axioms is to enunciate a *condition* (or functional equation) or several conditions which are supposedly satisfied by the relation being defined. 2) To define a *class of objects* by means of axioms is to characterize it as constituted by objects *between which* one can establish the 'relations' that satisfy the conditions enunciated in the axioms. In the first case we have, so to speak, a *direct* definition, and in the second an *indirect* definition (that is, a definition of *a class of objects* by means of other definitions, that is, by means of the definitions of the relations that can supposedly be established between them. (Frege, 1980, pp. 173–74)

Pragmatism, logic and language

In 1904 Vailati was asked to edit the works of Evangelista Torricelli on behalf of the Accademia dei Lincei, and he moved to Florence, where he taught at the Technical Institute "G. Galilei." Here he often met Giovanni Papini and Giuseppe Prezzolini, the founders of the militant journal "Leonardo." Vailati had already been in correspondence with Giovanni Papini since 1902, after having read *On the psychological theory of prevision* (1902), and he remained in contact with him until shortly before his death (the latter postcard is dated January 1909).[37]

The Pragmatism Club in Florence (1904-1905)

During the time he spent in Florence, Vailati, fascinated by the strong personality of Papini and by the opportunity to criticize the cultural backwardness of the Italian universities, started to collaborate on the journal, where he published reviews of recent works by Pierre Duhem, Ernst Mach, Henry Poincaré, Ernst Schröder, Charles S. Peirce, Louis Couturat, Federico Enriques, and William James, as well as several essays on science, language, and philosophy that are included in this volume (see chapters 8,10–14).

The debate on pragmatism in the journal "Leonardo"

At about this time the editorial group of the journal "Leonardo" started a lively debate on the nature of pragmatism, having the aim of transforming the journal into the official organ of Italian Pragmatism. In November Mario Calderoni, a disciple of Vailati, published an essay

---

[37] Vailati's letters to Giovanni Papini have been published by G. Lanaro in Vailati 1971, pp. 323–473.

entitled "Le varietà del Pragmatismo" [The varieties of pragmatism], in which he opposed Peirce's writings, considered as the original nucleus of pragmatism, based on the 'rule,' and James's conception, which he considered as a wider and derivative variant (Calderoni, 1904). Prezzolini, whose adhesion to pragmatism was quite short, replied in "Il mio prammatismo" [My pragmatism] (1905) that there are no profound distinctions between the two conceptions. In the same year, three more articles were published: Calderoni 1905, Schiller 1905, and Papini 1905, which was signed "The Florence Pragmatism Club."[38] Calderoni criticized Prezzolini, and Papini tried to mediate between the different conceptions of pragmatism that were opposing the collaborators to the journal (Casini, 2002).

The common ground was an instrumentalist conception of theories and beliefs and a related pluralist conception of pragmatism as a collection of methods, like the corridor of a hotel with many doors leading to innumerable rooms, a metaphor by Papini that James appreciated:

> As the young Italian pragmatist Papini has well said, it lies in the midst of our theories, like a corridor in a hotel. Innumerable chambers open out of it. In one you may find a man writing an atheistic volume; in the next some one on his knees praying for faith and strength; in a third a chemist investigating a body's properties. In a fourth a system of idealistic metaphysics is being excogitated; in a fifth the impossibility of metaphysics is being shown. But they all own the corridor, and all must pass through it if they want a practicable way of getting into or out of their respective rooms (James, 1908, Lecture 2).

Knowledge and Will

In 1905 Calderoni, Papini and Vailati published in "Leonardo" three talks on the relations between beliefs and will that they had presented at the 5th International Conference of Psychology in Rome: Calderoni's "Intorno a una definizione della volontà" [On a definition of will] is described in the editorial as considering will as an effect of beliefs; Papini's "Influenza della volontà sulla conoscenza" [Influence of will on knowledge] as considering will as the cause of beliefs; and Vailati's "Distinzione tra conoscere e volere" [Distinction between knowledge and will] as considering will as the cause of erroneous beliefs.[39] Calderoni, following Vailati, defined voluntary actions as those actions whose probable outcomes can be reasonably foreseen, arguing that one is juridically and morally responsible for all acts that imply a conscious expectation. Papini on the contrary wrote about the primacy of action and creativity

---

[38]The name of the group was written exactly as it appears here, in English.

[39]See the June-August issue of "Leonardo" 1905, especially p. 125.

on will. Vailati recalled here, as he had already discussed in 1901e (this volume, chapter 5), Brentano's distinction between expectations and volitions, arguing that beliefs and volitions have often been confused because of the linguistic similarities of the propositions that express them, and because of the meaning of the word 'cause' in ordinary language.

At the International Conference in Rome the group of Italian pragmatists met William James, whose talk "On the Notion of Consciousness" was published in an Italian translation in the July-August issue of "Leonardo." James enthusiastically described the meeting in a letter to his wife: "I have been having this afternoon a very good and rather intimate talk with the little band of 'pragmatists,' Papini, Vailati, Calderoni, Amendola, ..." (James, 1969, p. 227) and in a letter to George Santayana dated March 1905:

> "What I really write to you for is to tell you to send (if not sent already) your *Life of Reason* to the *Revue de Philosophie,* [...] and to the editor of "Leonardo" (the great little Florentine philosophical journal) [...]. The most interesting, and in fact genuinely edifying, part of my trip has been meeting this little cénacle, who have taken my own writings, entre autres, au grand sérieux, but who are carrying on their philosophical mission in anything but a technically serious way, inasmuch as "Leonardo" (of which I have hitherto only known a few odd numbers) is devoted to good and lively literary form." (James, 1969, p. 228)

Maybe because Vailati and Calderoni were quite far from the theories he had developed in his latest writings, James became more fond of Papini, with whom he started a regular correspondence and whom he considered to be the most relevant exponent of the Italian pragmatism (James, 1906).

On material representations of deductive processes

An interesting example of Vailati's interest in an analysis of non-deductive parts of the scientific discourse is offered by his writings on the role of metaphors in science. The role of metaphors in science had already been analyzed in the third inaugural lecture, where Vailati had defended the necessity of making such metaphors explicit.

Vailati himself made use of metaphors in his own writings, taking them not only from biological or natural sciences but also, if not especially, from economics, as was the case in the first inaugural lecture, where he compared the introduction of a new notation to the replacement of production facilities in an industry, or in the third inaugural lecture, where he presented philosophy as a clearing house.

In "I tropi della logica" [The tropes of logic]—an article published in "Leonardo" in 1905 and translated into English in the "Journal of Philosophy, Psychology and Scientific Methods" in 1908—Vailati analyzed "the employment of physical metaphors as means of representing mental facts" (1905a, this volume, p. 197) in order to draw "some indications of the means of regulating the play of mental activities" (this volume, p. 198).

In this article, which was quoted in Dewey (1909, chap. 7), Vailati considered the metaphors related to deductive processes, classifying them in three groups:

1. metaphors of supporting or upholding;
2. metaphors of ascending or descending;
3. metaphors of containing or including.

Different metaphors are connected to different conceptions of deduction that Vailati had outlined in the second inaugural lecture. If one considers an assertion as supporting another or as being drawn from another, one considers deduction as a means of proof. If one considers conclusions as being already contained in premises, deduction is considered as a process that cannot produce anything new, while if premises are the simple elements that compose conclusions, deduction is conceived as an analysis.

The most recent definition of mathematics

In accordance with the polemic spirit of the journal, in "La più recente definizione della matematica" [The most recent definition of mathematics] (1904c) Vailati considers a provocative definition attributed to Bertrand Russell: "mathematics is a science where we never need to know if what is said is true, nor do we need to know what we are talking about" (this volume, p. 137). Vailati explains the paradoxical content of the definition by means of two relevant changes in the mathematical discipline: the hypothetic-deductive approach introduced by modern axiomatics, which he describes in Poincaré's words, and the formal approach associated with Peano's mathematical logic and with Peirce's theory of relations.

Vailati argues that mathematics is not mainly interested in truth because it investigates different systems of axioms independently of their conformity to "real" facts. His explanation of the first part of Russell's definition is entirely based on Poincaré (1902): on the one hand different systems might all be compatible with experimental observations (e.g. non-Euclidean geometries) and their mathematical interest does not consist in their being true, but in their being more convenient; on the other hand assuming a false hypothesis might be fruitful, if it artificially simplifies the facts to which it is supposed to refer. As Poincaré had argued both in the analysis of the differences between the properties of the geometrical space and the perceptual spaces, and between the features of the physical and the mathematical continuum, the mathematical models do not correspond to reality as such, but they are artificial constructions used to describe physical facts.

Turning to the second part of Russell's quotation, Vailati argues that the power of a language is proportional to the number of words that are devoid of meaning if taken in isolation. Relying on Max Müller's assertion that language begins where interjections end (Müller, 1891, vol. 1, p. 507), i.e. where the meaning of words is not predetermined but depends on the way they occur in a sentence, Vailati argues that the force of mathematical language depends on the amount of symbols that denote relations, operations, functions.[40] Calling functional symbols meaningless might be misleading, but what Vailati means is that mathematics is interested in the study of uninterpreted relations and operations. Peano's mathematical logic and Peirce's theory of relations are mentioned as the two recent developments that

> emancipate mathematical deductions from any appeal to facts or intuitions with reference to the meaning of the operations, or relations, under consideration. These are defined by the mere simple enunciation of a certain number of fundamental properties that, being able to be common to relations or operations with the most disparate and heterogeneous meanings, are compatible with the most various interpretations of the symbols appearing in their enunciation. (1904c, this volume, p. 141)

Pragmatism and mathematical logic

In the short essay "Pragmatism and Mathematical Logic" (1906b) published in "Leonardo," Vailati enumerates six pragmatic features of logical theories:

1. the value of each assertion is intimately connected to its use in the deduction of consequences: a postulate is a proposition that has the same epistemological status as any other proposition, but it is chosen as a postulate because of its usefulness for the specific aims of the theory;

2. assertions are distinguished on the basis of their relation to facts: possible or essential;

---

[40]The same idea is at the base of *The grammar of algebra* (1908b, see this volume, chapter 16).

3. the recourse to historical analysis of science and language shows the compatibility of some modern theories with ancient theories;

4. the development of the theory of definition—based on the distinction between definitions by abstraction, by operations, by postulates, on the interest for the notion of definability, and on the consideration of implicit and local definitions—shows the importance of contextual considerations;

5. the construction of particular models to prove the consistency of a set of postulates shows the "mysterious ally" between abstract theories and "particular facts";

6. the introduction of the symbolic notation illustrates a tendency to the simplification of theories, which is a condition for their instrumental application.

Apart from the discussion of which of the above mentioned issues should be considered as truly pragmatic in nature, it is interesting to discuss the stance of Vailati on the one hand with regard to the conceptions of Peano and of the members of his school, and on the other hand with regard to the role of history, language, and philosophy in logic.

Notwithstanding relevant differences between the members of the school, which was far from homogeneous, the works of Peano and his disciples were mainly oriented to the search for convenient systems of postulates and of definitions for each mathematical theory (Pieri's axioms for geometry, Peano's axioms for arithmetic and for logic, and so on), rather than to a unified theory. Besides, they were based on the idea, clearly formulated by Vailati, that different interpretations of the same symbols could and should be admitted in order to study the independence of the primitive notions and propositions of a given theory (1904c, this volume, p. 141).

Concerning the role of language in mathematics, Vailati distinguished the mathematical project of expressing the whole of mathematics in a formal language, a project that he repeatedly praised but in which he did not participate, from the philosophical analysis of science, which includes the uncovering of metaphors, the study of the argumentative schemes, the logical analysis of ordinary language.

In "A Study of Platonic Terminology" (1906c) Vailati also mentioned the relevance of linguistic analysis for the work of the historian, who should be aware of the "modifications of technical philosophical language which aim at expressing *new* ideas or *new* distinctions" (Vailati, 1906c, this volume, p. 174).

Vailati's pragmatic and logical interest in definitions

Definition emerges as a logical problem already in Vailati's inquiries on relations and operations. Vailati shares Peano's ideas that definitions are merely conventional: there is not a single definition but several possible definitions of the same concepts, and the choice between them depends on the point of view of the researcher. Vailati's arguments reveal a good knowledge not only of Peano's position, but also of Burali-Forti's and Padoa's results on definitions.[41]

If from a logical point of view different definitions might be equivalent at least in the general sense that they allow, given certain conditions, to derive the same propositions, different definitions might have radically divergent consequences. Different definitions might be heuristically not equivalent, for certain definitions might hinder the progress of science, while others favor it. So, while in the Peano school the analysis of different definitions was mainly a logical and foundational issue—determine which concepts are independent from other concepts or which definitions allow us to reduce the number of primitives—in Vailati's eyes it soon became an historical and epistemological issue: how can different definitions influence the efficiency of a theory or its foreseeing capacity? Which definition is more appropriate to the aims of a science at a given period of time?

Vailati's interest in the history of ideas is thus strictly connected to the analysis of different historically given definitions of the same words, showing how new ways of defining a word might generate new concepts. This was a viewpoint which Vailati acquired gradually over time, probably due to the development of an historical sensibility that drove him progressively away from his earlier positivist approach. In particular, while in the inagurual lecture Vailati still believed that mathematical logic was a difficult but more efficient way to achieve the same results, just as the change of machinery is a costly way to rationalize production, in his last works he became more and more interested in the positive and negative consequences of the adoption of one definition rather than another. Besides, he considered how definitions were obtained, because this could explain the origin of the concept defined, and also its meaning, given that the meaning of a concept is related to its context of use and to the way that it has been introduced. Vailati was thus interested in the *Wirkungsgeschichte* of definitions, even if rather in an instrumentalist rather than hermeneutic way.

The interest in definitions, and in their logico-mathematical origin, might also explain why Vailati's historical essays were mainly devoted

---

[41]See in particular Burali-Forti 1894, and Padoa 1905-06.

to the Socratic and the Aristotelian theory of definition, or to the Euclidean difference between axioms, postulates, and definitions, to the changes determined by the deductive method in the history of modern mechanics, and to the study of classifications of sciences.

The interest in definitions is also dominant in Vailati's approach to Brentano's psychology: he immediately transposes the distinction between different psychological facts on the logico-epistemological domain, interpreting it as a difference between assertions and definitions. So, even the 'pragmatic' distinction between knowledge and will, and its consequences on the analysis of the task of science that should foresee the former but not the latter, is again a matter of the correct definition of the concepts involved and of the role of scientific thought.

Some pragmatic themes that emerge from this collection of Vailati's essays are related to the distinction between matters of words and matters of facts, and especially to the pragmatic allowance of different definitions—depending on their degree of appropriateness to specific aims. The importance of definitions does not consist mainly in their being points of departure of the deduction, as if an agreement on the meaning of words were only a prerequisite of an argumentative practice. It rather consists in their making explicit the conceptual elements that play a significant role in the deduction. For this reason, Vailati's version of pragmatism has a logico-semantic vein that might allow an interesting comparison with the recent approach of Robert Brandom.

But we would like to recall here instead that Moritz Pasch was one of the first authors who insisted on the importance of analyzing scientific propositions in order to free deductions from an implicit or unconscious recourse to intuition. There is an echo of Pasch's epistemology in Vailaiti's approach, even if Vailati mentions him only once as the first "to analyze the fundamental propositions of geometry of position and to determine which notions and entities concerned by it (point, right line, plane, segment, angle, triangle, tetrahedron, and so on) can be considered as primitive, indefinable and such that all other notions and entities can be defined by means of them."[42] Pasch's geometrical results had influenced Peano,[43] but his epistemology influenced other Italian mathematicians, such as Veronese, who recognized the importance of tracing back the abstract mathematical and geometrical notions to their empirical analogues, including the results in a list of empirical observations that, though clearly distinguished from the definitions, might shed some light on the reasons why certain definitions are preferred (Cantù,

---

[42] See Vailati 1899b, repr. in Vailati 1911, p. 239–40.
[43] See for example Gandon 2006.

1999). Veronese had discussed the empirical origin of mathematics in correspondence with Vailati, as the latter had asked for his opinion on the opportunity of including empirical and practical mathematics in the programs for younger pupils (Cantù, 2000).

Definitions are a common ground to Vailati's and Peano's researches. Though never declaring any specific interest in philosophy, Peano shared with Vailati a pluralist, antidogmatic, and antifoundationalist conception of definitions. Defending the plurality of views that emerged in his own school, Peano argued that definitions by abstraction, by a nominal definition, by means of a relation, and by means of an operator are 'equally logic and equally rigorous': the best definition is nothing else but the definition that each teacher prefers (Peano, 1915, p. 409). The emergence of this 'pragmatic' theme shows that Vailati's claim that there were points in common between Peano's mathematical logic and pragmatism was grounded. But it does not show that Vailati's own version of pragmatism might be regarded as the explicit philosophical formulation of Peano's implicit epistemology, nor that the logical issues considered in "Pragmatism and mathematical logic" should faithfully correspond to Peano's conception of logic.

Nonetheless, apart from Vailati's rhetoric, especially in the articles published in "Leonardo," on the simplification of theories by elimination of concepts and words, as if the progress of science should depend more on the elimination of superfluous machinery rather than on the introduction of new, refined conceptual tools, Peano's and Vailati's perspectives on language share a common ground. Peano's project of *latino sine flexione* was also a simplification of the language that should determine

> a minimal number of words, prefixes and suffixes, that are necessary to express any idea, that is to build the *latino minimo*. This method is an application of the Mathematical Logic, which allows to decompose, by means of a series of equalities, a set of mathematical ideas into primitive and derivative ideas (Peano, 1903-04, pp. 279–80).

Educational projects and pedagogical theory (1905-1909)

The edition of Torricelli's works could not be realized, but Vailati asked to remain in Florence in order to continue his studies in the National Library. Instead he was given another appointment from the Public Ministry of Education: he was nominated member of the Royal Commission in charge of the Educational Reform for Secondary Schools. He thus moved to Rome and started a series of trips around Europe to analyze and compare different scholastic systems.

The Italian Commission for the reformation of school

The Italian school system was based at the time on a rigid distinction between humanities and sciences after the first 5 common years: humanities were taught in the 'Ginnasio' (5 years) and 'Liceo' (3 years) that gave access to higher education; sciences were mainly taught in technical schools, which gave access only to some scientific universities. The proposal of the Ministerial Commission was driven by the idea that there should be a unique system lasting 8 years and three curricula in the 'Liceo' (5 years): classical, scientific and linguistic. Vailati agreed on the first part of the proposal but not on the second: he instead suggested a unique kind of liceo, where both humanities and sciences would be taught and where each would be given equal weight. Vailati did not favor the introduction of philosophy in the curricula of the secondary schools; he rather believed in the opportunity of introducing a Philosophy course in every university faculty, but his idea was never realized, and the Italian Academy became more and more divided into two opposed and non-communicating branches: humanities and sciences.

Apart from the General Reform of Secondary School, which in the end was never approved, Vailati was in charge of preparing new programs for the Mathematical Courses. He thus began a correspondence with many contemporary Italian mathematicians, in order to get their critical remarks on the project. Like the Italian geometer Veronese, who had devoted several studies to the problem of teaching mathematics to young pupils, Vailati was favorable to an empirical and practical approach, based on intuition and on concrete experiences. Vailati presented his ideas on the teaching of mathematics in many reviews, but also in "L'insegnamento della matematica nel primo triennio della scuola secondaria superiore" [The teaching of mathematics in the first three years of high school] (1907b).

This article suggested an operative or experimental method to teach geometry to younger students. He refused to call such a method 'intuitive'—as was done in the same years by Veronese—because what distinguishes this method from the 'logical' or 'rational' teaching of geometry (i.e. from the Euclidean style) does not depend on the fact that students restrict themselves to the learning of intuitive truths, but rather on the fact that they learn non-intuitive truths by experiments (Cantù, 2000). The experimental discovery of truths does not exclude the introduction of proofs; on the contrary it is the best way to let the student develop "the desire and the need to understand 'how' and 'why' certain properties subsist, and to induce him to find interest in the learning of (or search for) deductive relations between properties and reasoning that lead him to acknowledge them as being consequences of one another" (Vailati, 1907b, p. 305). These remarks against the rational learning of geometrical proofs at an early age was motivated by a criticism of the mnemonic approach to the learning of definitions and theorems, based on the treatment of students as "recipients to be filled" rather than persons, "fields to be sown, plants to be grown, fires to be lighted." Students, he argued in a review of C. Laisant, should be asked to understand and not just to learn (Vailati, 1899c).

In a review of H. G. Wells's book *Mankind in the making* he did not spare his harsh criticism to the school system:

> Learned man, teachers, pedagogy scholars would refuse with horror the idea of taking part in three lectures a day, were it only for a week and only on topics they are deeply interested in. But they do not see how absurd it is, from an educational but also psychological and even hygienic point of view, to oblige students aged from 10 to 18 to remain riveted at least five hours a day for the whole year, as if there were no other means to attain the goals that should be reached in this way. For the result of this system of intensive culture—so similar to the barbaric nutrition system that is applied in the plain of Lombardy to obtain the exquisite goose liver—comes down to this, to cultivate in the students, especially in the most intelligent ones, such a repugnance for everything that is connected to school, or to what is taught in schools, that one might be glad that a large part of the school programs is not worth being known.[44]

In his review of Wells' book, Vailati argued that notionism was caused by scientific and technological backwardness: he polemically remarked that teaching was still organized as if Gutenberg's printing method "had not yet influenced our school system". In a technologically developed society the traditional lecture given by the teacher facing the students is just one among many different means to teach.[45] Vailati expressed a similar criticism of school didactics in the essay "Sull'arte di interrogare" [The art of asking questions] (1905e, this volume, chap. 10),[46] where he also encouraged teachers to modify the way they ask questions to their students:

> The first formulation under which the question was asked represents, in my opinion rather characteristically, the type of question teachers

---

[44]See Vailati 1906a in Vailati 1911, p. 713.

[45]See Vailati 1906a in Vailati 1911, p. 713.

[46]This essay was influenced by James's *Talks to teachers on psychology: and to students on some of life's ideals* (1899) delivered at Edinburgh in 1901-1902.

should move towards as much as possible, either with the purpose of stimulating the student to reflect, or with the purpose of testing the condition of his knowledge. The best questions, for both purposes, are the ones that refer to the *prediction* of a specific fact, those where, after describing a given situation and a series of specific operations to the student, we ask what he would *expect* to find or to obtain if he were to perform them, or how he would *act* if he wanted to achieve a specific result given the circumstances (this volume, p. 156).

Pupils—he believed—should be left in a condition to learn autonomously, following their own interests and using all possible tools to acquire the cognitions they judge accessible and interesting. Notwithstanding the similarities, Vailati did not mention the laboratory school founded by Dewey in Chicago in 1896.[47] Recalling the criticism made in Papini and Prezzolini 1906, Vailati denounced the bad habit of publishing textbooks containing only pedantic lecture notes "compiled with dreadful uniformity according to the scholastic programs," rather than introductory books containing selected bibliographical references.[48]

Vailati's conception of school as a laboratory where the students participate in a dynamic process of learning does not correspond to the notion of a laboratory of scientific disciplines where the teacher or her assistants show to young students the 'canonical' experiments of modern science, but rather a place to realize the education of critical minds—a place enabling students to solve problems, learn autonomously by abstraction from sensible and concrete elements.[49] For this reason, Vailati insists on the importance of drawing in order to guide students to the learning of abstract geometry but also to the learning of manual work, intended not as an early specialization towards professional activity, but as an effective way to "stimulate and exercise [...] the various faculties of observation, discrimination, attention, and judgment, which are at stake in any kind of work" (Vailati, 1901d).

Vailati's last years (1907-1909)

In the years that preceded his death Vailati's interests ranged over various fields, from history of science to philosophy, from education (he was still involved in the works of the Reform Commission) to religion.

In 1907 and 1908 he published several articles on the history of mechanics, for which he had developed a renewed interest after the publication of *The Origins of the Static* by Pierre Duhem (1905-1906).

---

[47]Vailati mentioned Dewey's pragmatism only in two reviews of James's writings.
[48]See Vailati 1906a in Vailati 1911, p. 715.
[49]Cf. Vailati 1899c.Vailati's conception of the school as a laboratory has been emphasized in De Zan 1996. See also Minazzi 2000.

He also became a member of the scientific board of the Italian Society for the Progress of Sciences, directed by Volterra, who had transformed it from an aristocratic club into a democratic association based on interdisciplinary debate.[50]

A systematic volume on pragmatism

In this same period Vailati developed, together with Calderoni, the project of a systematic book on pragmatism, whose first two chapters "Le origini e l'idea fondamentale del Pragmatismo" [The origins and fundamental idea of pragmatism] (1909b) and "Il Pragmatismo e i vari modi di non dir niente" [Pragmatism and the various ways of saying nothing] (1909a) were published in the journal "Rivista di Psicologia Applicata" in 1909.[51]

Vailati and Calderoni 1909b acknowledged Peirce as the first to introduce the expression 'pragmatism' to denote a methodology that determines and clarifies the meaning of an assertion by indicating "which particular experiences, according to such an assertion, are going to take place, or would take place under specific given circumstances" (this volume, p. 234). After defending 'pragmatism' from the charges of 'utilitarianism' and 'relativism,' Vailati considered the relevance of this methodology to three cornerstones of his own philosophy: 1) the distinction between volitions and expectations; 2) the role of deductive inferences in the determination of the meaning of propositions; 3) the logical rather than psychological aim of the analysis of "predictive elements, that are always implicit in our assertions, even when absent from our present consciousness."

The distinction between volitions and expectations had already been introduced in the paper presented at the International Conference of Psychology in Paris on Brentano's classification of mental states (1901e), and in the article on knowledge published in "Leonardo" (1905c). The consideration of "deduction as an instrument of explanation and anticipation of experience" (this volume, p. 30) was discussed in the second inaugural lecture (1898a). The agent's relevance in the determination of the meaning of words and the importance of giving reasons as part of the meaning of words was hinted at in the third inaugural lecture (1899a). Recalling Sidgwick, Vailati remarked that

---

[50]Volterra's inaugural talk at the first congress of the Italian Society for the Progress of Sciences, held in Parma on September 25th, 1907, has been published in an English translation in the appendix to Goodstein 2007, pages 261-269.

[51]See this volume, chapter 18 and chapter 19. For a deeper discussion of the 'pragmatic' elements contained in these two works, see the essay by M. Caamano and P. Suppes in this volume.

"the advantage of research of this kind, on the sense of words, does not consist so much in the definitions that we find as in the operations that we have to do to find them, and that the fruit of such discussions is not in the conclusions reached, but in the reasons that we must discover and bring forward to justify them" (Vailati, 1899a, this volume, p. 70). An instrumentalist definition of meaning of an assertion as related to its deductive consequences was formulated in the essay on pragmatism and mathematical logic, where he attributed to Peano's mathematical logic and to Peirce's pragmatism "the tendency to regard the value, and even the meaning, of every assertion as being intimately related to the use which can be made, or which it may be desired to make, of it for the deduction and construction of particular consequences or groups of consequences" (1906b, this volume, p. 164).

Finally, the logical interest inherent in the analysis of language (tracing the distinction between assertions and definitions, or between volitions and expectations, classifying fallacies, developing a normative rather than descriptive theory of reasoning), and the opportunity of making unconscious aspects of language become explicit (as in the case of scientific metaphors) were already present in the third inaugural lecture Vailati (1899a), even if further developed in the essay on language as an obstacle to the elimination of illusory contrasts (1908a). Some of these aspects, which were related to the readings of Hume and Berkeley in the first writings, are here connected to Berkeley's *New Theory of Vision* (1732) and to Pikler's analysis of the judgments of existence of space and time in *The Psychology of the Belief in Objective Existence* (1890).

Vailati and Calderoni 1909a goes back to the analysis of the distinctions between assertions and definitions, relating it to the Lockean distinction between verbal (trifling) and real propositions, and with the Kantian distinction between analytic and synthetic judgments.

Definitions are thus once more at the center of Vailati's attention. An issue that was already discussed in the article on Saccheri (1903a), in the paper on the Aristotelian theory of definition (1903b) and in the historical notes to Peano's *Formulario* (1902a), concerns the problem of proving the compatibility of different properties that are assigned to the same object by a complex definition: a problem that can be solved by assuming or proving "the existence or constructability of figures or things that satisfy the conditions posed in the definitions" (1909a, this volume, p. 253).

Vailati also developed a criticism of the use of abstract terms and of useless generalizations in philosophy, praising pragmatism for suggesting the substitution of abstract terms by concrete expressions as a therapy. The abuse of generalization takes place, according to Vailati, when generalization is considered not "as a means to certain logical or practical goals," but as a goal in itself. In "Dal Monismo al Pragmatismo" [From Monism to Pragmatism] (1907a), one finds several examples: the determination of too general classes of concepts of which one has nothing relevant to say, or the tendency to look for causes and explanations of certain facts beyond the point in which one is still capable of ascertaining the facts in questions, or the tendency to give and ask for definitions of what cannot be defined without recourse to other unexplained notions. Vailati's critical target is derived from Papini 1907, which is an attack against monists, and in particular against the philosophy of Enrico Morselli, a Professor of Psychiatry at Genoa University.

The beginning of this essay, as the conclusion of "Pragmatism and mathematical logic," reveals that some positivist elements that Vailati had absorbed in his youth were never really dismissed, notwithstanding the fact that positivism had soon become his main critical target. One of the advantages of pragmatism is described as the possibility of separating meaningful from meaningless propositions, arguing that it makes it easier "to distinguish those that can actually be proved or refuted from the ones that are not subject to any proper proof or refutation. This is because they refer to mind-states of which each individual subject is the only irrevocable judge, and also because these assertions are only apparent, and they are, in fact, sentences with *no meaning*" (1909a, this volume, p. 249).

The goal of the analysis of ordinary language and of the distinction between expressions containing volitions and expressions containing expectations is thus reduced to the mere elimination of trifling matters of words and false questions. Every expression that cannot be proved or refuted is considered as meaningless, and no analysis of its possible grounds is given. If no space is left for an objective evaluation of what falls outside the scientific domain, no rational argumentative practice or critical thinking would be applicable in many cases that Vailati himself had considered in his analyses of ordinary discourse. And the latter would have a very limited scope: banishing what is fallacious, rather than comparing the argumentative rules and schemas applied in different contexts.[52]

---

[52] For an analysis of Vailati's defense of mathematical logic and the ambivalence of his "practical" conception of logic, see Bozzi 2000, especially p. 106 f.

Modernism

Vailati was not himself a believer, but he did not neglect the discussions that animated the catholic milieu of his time, and became interested in what is known as Roman Catholic Modernism. In 1893 he had attended the lectures given by Antonio Fogazzaro, the author of *Little Ancient World* and *Malombra*, on the compatibility of the Darwinian evolutionism with the Christian doctrine.[53] Fogazzaro belonged to a wider group of intellectuals—active between the end of the 19th century and the beginning of the 20th century in Italy, but also in France and in England,—who defended a rationalist interpretation of the Bible, secularism and the conciliation of faith and reason. This movement, that is known as 'modernism' after Pope Pius X introduced the name in the encyclical *Pascendi Dominici gregis*, was condemned by the Roman Catholic Church as the 'synthesis of all heresies': even if the compulsory oath against modernism that had been introduced for bishops and priests was not abolished until 1967, many Italian modernist priests and intellectuals continued to meet, as in the Roman circle organized by Ernesto Buonaiuti (Demofonti, 2003, p. 112) and frequented by Vailati himself.[54]

On the philosophy of language

Buonaiuti had described religion as an innovating movement that breaks up previous institutions, but finally becomes itself a dogmatic institution. In "Il linguaggio come ostacolo alla eliminazione di contrasti illusori" [Language as an obstacle to the elimination of illusory contrasts]—published on the Modernist journal "Rinnovamento" (1908a, this volume, chapter 17)—Vailati considers society as a network of obligations, responsibilities and commitments that individuals have not accepted nor are able to justify, but that impose themselves on everybody's life. Analogously, a language imposes on the speaker a number of classifications and distinctions that the speaker has not herself accepted, and cannot understand. This is—according to Vailati—common to physical and to social sciences, but the branch of philosophy that is devoted to the analysis of concepts should individuate unnecessary or unjustified expressions, as was done by the medieval theory of discourse that had classified fallacious questions—the so-called *exponibilia*.[55] Vailati defended not only the right but also the necessity

---

[53]Fogazzaro's last novels were banned by the Roman Catholic Church in 1905 because of his unorthodox ideas on Darwinism.

[54]Incidentally, Vailati was the only layman frequenting the circle.

[55]Among Vailati's examples there is what modern theorists of argumentation call the "fallacy of the many questions."

for philosophy and science to oppose unjustified crystallizations of concepts, as happened when Galileo criticized the Aristotelian distinction between celestial and terrestrial phenomena. Independence from the language constraint does not consist in the arbitrariness of modifying the terminology used to designate given concepts, provided the meaning of the terms is preliminarily fixed by definition, but rather in the freedom of modifying conceptual distinctions and classifications that are "inappropriate or inadequate to the goals that one has in a given occasion." According to Vailati, modifying the concepts is much more important for philosophical and scientific discussions than modifying only the terms used to denote such concepts.[56]

The grammar of algebra

In 1908 Vailati attended the International Conference in Philosophy in Heidelberg and presented a paper "The grammar of algebra" at the Conference of the Italian Society for the Progress of Sciences (1908b).

In a recent inquiry on Vailati's linguistic analyses, Innis (2002) has rightly claimed that Vailati's approach to language is partly based on a "rhetoric of suspicion" and partly oriented to a descriptive and constructive task. If the previously mentioned article on language as an obstacle to the elimination of illusory contrasts was rather based on a negative conception of language, the essay on the grammar of algebra is based on a different approach, mediated by the comparison between ordinary language and the symbolic language of mathematics.

Vailati distinguished between phonetic and ideographic languages, between positional and non-positional writings, between nomenclatures and languages, and individuated the peculiarity of the algebraic language in being ideographic and positional. He then proceeded to a detailed analysis of the grammar and the syntax of algebraic language, comparing it to ordinary language. Relying on Müller's definition of language as composed of words that do not have a meaning if taken in isolation, Vailati analyzed the distinction between verbs that require to be completed by an object (and that he called 'generally transitive') and verbs that are strictly 'intransitive.'

Recalling Peirce's contributions to the theory of relations, Vailati compared transitive verbs with relative nouns and classified general transitive verbs according to the number of objects they need—a distinction that corresponds in algebra to the number of values of a function. After characterizing the algebraic language as containing only transitive relations—for it is taken to be based on equalities—Vailati discussed the differences between equality and identity, and the nature

---

[56]Vailati 1908a in Vailati, 1911, p. 899.

of definitions by abstraction, remarking that the choice of the kind of definition of a new symbol might depend on the nature of the concepts, but also on matters of convenience, clarity, and intelligibility.

Invoking the attention of philologists on symbolic languages, Vailati wrote another 'apologetic' essay: as in the case of the two essays on the definition of mathematics (this volume, chapter 8) and on the comparison between mathematical logic and pragmatism (this volume, chapter 12), Vailati mentioned other logicians, but discussed only the problems that were familiar to him from the debates with the logical school of Peano. For example, the interest for the debate on the use of one single sign to express different equivalence relations had been mentioned in the Frege-Peano discussion, and again in Burali-Forti and Marcolongo's analysis of vectorial notations, but also in Pieri's writings.[57] The interest for definitions by abstraction and for equality is probably related to his friendship with Padoa, who had published an article on equivalence relations as conditions for the introduction of definitions by abstraction (1905-06).

Vailati's death and the project of the collected works

In the autumn 1908 Vailati planned to go back to his teaching post in Florence, but in December he contracted influenza, from which he failed to recover. Hoping for a milder winter, he moved to Rome, where he was hospitalized in March 1909, suffering from a rheumatic fever with cardiac complications.[58] The onset of tonsillitis led to his death on May 14, 1909. Right up until his death Vailati had hoped to recover,[59] devoting himself to reading: Marcus Aurelius *Meditations* and Spinoza's *Ethics*, as well as novels by Stendhal, Rolland and Maupassant. The official funeral took place in Rome, attended by the Senate vice-president, Blaserna, the senator Volterra and the deputy Torre; several articles and obituaries were published (De Zan, 2000a). Volterra asked Mario Calderoni, Umberto Ricci and Giovanni Vacca to edit a volume of Vailati's collected works (1911), whose costs were paid for by a public subscription. Among the subscribers there were not only Italian intellectuals, but also international scholars, such as Samuel Dickstein, Pierre Duhem, Knud Ferlov, Bèla Fogasari, Daniel and Élie Halévy, Johan Ludwig Heiberg, William James, Adolphe Landry, A. Lasson, Léon Xavier, Bertrand Russell, Victoria Welby, Gyula Pikler,

---

[57] See Frege 1980, Burali-Forti and Marcolongo 1909, and Marchisotto and Smith 2007.

[58] See Orazio Premoli's biography of Vailati in Vailati 1911.

[59] See the letter from Einaudi to Papini, March 6, 1909, in Kühn 1960.

who would later dedicate a book to Vailati,[60] and Vernon Lee (Violet Paget), who would dedicate a work on pragmatism to the memory of the friend Giovanni Vailati, "who better than anyone else, explained the incompatibility between 'willing to believe' and 'making one's ideas clear' (Lee, 1912)."

Conclusion

Vailati's interests were so varied that one can hardly present them all satisfactorily in a single essay: this was surely not the intention of our introduction. We have rather tried to offer a sampling of the variety of topics that he was interested in, while summarizing the main events of his life and introducing the reader to a figure who was not academic, but was strongly connected to the new research waves in philosophy and science and to the social ferment at the beginning of the 20th century.

In the variety, if not serendipity of Vailati's interests, there are some important themes to be traced: one is surely Vailati's adhesion to pragmatism, which is discussed in the following essay by M. Caamano and P. Suppes. Another main theme can be detected in Vailati's interest for the definition of concepts. This 'pragmatist' theme is related to Peano's logical inquiries on the topic, but it is also deeply connected to several aspects of Vailati's own research, and especially to the interpretation of the common features of pragmatism and mathematical logic.

References

Berkeley, George. 1732. *An essay towards a new theory of vision*. London: J. Tonson.

Bozzi, Silvio. 2000. Vailati e la logica. In M. De Zan (2000b), pages 88–111.

Burali-Forti, Cesare. 1894. *Logica Matematica*. Milano: Hoepli.

Burali-Forti, Cesare and Roberto Marcolongo. 1909. Per l'unificazione delle notazioni vettoriali. In G. Castelnuovo, ed., *Atti del IV congresso internazionale dei matematici, Roma 6-11 Aprile 1908*. Roma: Tipografia dell'Accademia dei Lincei. Repr. Nendeln (Liechtenstein): Kraus, 1967.

Calderoni, Mario. 1904. Le varietà del pragmatismo. *Leonardo* 2.

Calderoni, Mario. 1905. Variazioni sul pragmatismo. *Leonardo* pages 15–21.

Calderoni, Mario. 1924. Giovanni Vailati, commemorazione letta a Crema il 20 giugno 1909. In O. Campa, ed., *Scritti*, vol. 2, pages 161–180. Firenze: La Voce.

Cantù, Paola. 1999. *Giuseppe Veronese e i fondamenti della geometria*. Milano: Unicopli.

---

[60]He wrote: "Giovanni Vailati in Freundschaft und Hochachtung zugeeignet" (Pikler, 1908).

Cantù, Paola. 2000. L'insegnamento della geometria nelle scuole medie inferiori. Una lettera inedita di Giuseppe Veronese a Giovanni Vailati. *Il Voltaire* 5:109–118.

Cantù, Paola. 2007. Il carteggio Padoa-Vailati. Un'introduzione alle lettere inviate da Chioggia. *Chioggia. Rivista di Studi e ricerche* 30:45–70.

Casini, Paolo. 2002. *Alle origini del Novecento. Leonardo, 1903-1907.* Bologna: Il Mulino.

Chisholm, R.M. and M. Corrado. 1982. The Brentano-Vailati Correspondence. *Topoi* 1:3–30.

Couturat, Louis. 1901. *La Logique de Leibniz d'après des documents inédits.* Paris: Alcan.

Darwin, Charles. 1859. *The origin of species.* London: Murray.

De Amicis, Enrico. 1892. Dipendenza fra alcune proprietà notevoli delle relazioni fra enti di un medesimo sistema. *Rivista di Matematica* 2:113–127.

De Zan, Mauro. 1996. Attualità di Giovanni Vailati e superamento della classe come struttura base dell'organizzazione scolastica. In D. Generali and F. Minazzi, eds., *La scuola italiana. Tra delusione e utopia*, pages 183–193. Padova: Edizioni Sapere.

De Zan, Mauro. 2000a. Giovanni Vailati letto dai contemporanei. In M. De Zan (2000b), pages 37–49.

De Zan, Mauro, ed. 2000b. *I Mondi di Carta di Giovanni Vailati.* Milano: Angeli.

De Zan, Mauro. 2003. Sul carteggio tra Vito Volterra e Giovanni Vailati. *Annuario del Centro Studi Giovanni Vailati* 1:79–89.

De Zan, Mauro. 2009. *La formazione di Giovanni Vailati.* Lecce: Congedo Editore.

Dedekind, Richard. 1888. *Was sind und was sollen die Zahlen?.* Braunschweig: Vieweg.

Demofonti, Laura. 2003. *La riforma dell'Italia del primo Novecento.* Edizioni di Storia e Letteratura.

Dewey, John. 1909. *How we think.* London: Heath.

Duhem, Pierre. 1905-1906. *L'origines de la Statique.* Paris: Hermann. 2 voll.

Duporcq, Ernest, ed. 1902. *Compte rendu du deuxième Congrès international des mathematiciens tenu à Paris du 6 au 12 août 1900.* Paris: Gauthier-Villars.

Durand de Gros, Pierre-Joseph. 1899. *Aperçus de taxinomie générale.* Paris: Alcan.

Frege, Gottlob. 1980. *Philosophical and Mathematical Correspondence.* Chicago: University of Chicago Press.

Friedlein, Gottfried. 1873. *Procli Diadochi in primum Euclidis Elementorum librum commentarii.* Teubner. Repr. Hildesheim: Olms 1992.

Gandon, Sébastien. 2006. La réception des *Vorlesungen über neure Geometrie* de Pasch par Peano. *Revue d'Histoire des Mathématiques* 12(2):249–290.

Goodstein, Judith R. 2007. *The Volterra chronicles. The life and time of an extraordinary mathematician (1860-1940)*. American Mathematical Society and London Mathematical Society.

Greenfield, Kent Roberts. 1934. *Economics and liberalism in the Risorgimento; a study of nationalism in Lombardy, 1814-1848*. Baltimore: The Johns Hopkins Press.

Hilbert, David. 1905. Über die Grundlagen der Logik und der Arithmetik. In A. Kraser, ed., *Verhandlungen des III. Internationalen Mathematiker Kongresses in Heidelberg 1904*, pages 174–185. Leipzig: Teubner.

Hontheim, J. 1895. *Der logische Algorithmus in seinem Wesen, in seiner Anwendung, und in seiner philosophischen Bedeutung*. Berlin: Verlag von Felix L. Dames. Repr. in Vailati (1911), pages 149–153.

Hultsch, Fridericus. 1875-1878. *Pappi Alexandrini collectionis quae supersunt e libris manu scriptis edidit Latina interpretatione et commentariis*. Berlin: Weidmann.

Innis, Robert E. 2002. Paleo-pragmatism's linguistic turn. Lessons from Giovanni Vailati. In *Pragmatism and the Forms of Sense: Language, Perception, Technics*, pages 99–130. University Park, PA: Penn State Press.

James, William. 1899. *Talks to teachers on psychology: and to students on some of life's ideals*. Longmans, 1901.

James, William. 1906. G. Papini and the Pragmatist Movement in Italy. *Journal of Philosophy, Psychology and Scientific Methods* 3:337–341.

James, William. 1908. *Pragmatism*. New York: Longmans & Green.

James, William. 1969. *The Letters of William James*. Boston: Athlantic Monthly Press.

Koyré, Alexandre. 1939. *Études galiléennes*. Paris: Hermann.

Kühn, Eva. 1960. *Vita con Giovanni Amendola*. Firenze: Parenti.

Kuhn, Thomas Samuel. 1962. *The Structure of Scientific Revolutions*. Chicago: The University of Chicago Press, 1970.

Lee, Vernon. 1912. *Vital lies; studies of some varieties of recent obscurantism*. London, New York: J. Lane.

Lolli, Gabriele. 1985. *Le ragioni fisiche e le dimostrazioni matematiche*. Bologna: Il Mulino.

Mach, Ernst. 1883. *Die Mechanik in ihrer Entwicklung historisch-kritisch dargestellt*. Leipzig: Brockhaus (1889), 2nd edn. Engl. trans. by T.J. McCormack. *The science of mechanics. A critical and historical account of its development*. Open Court Publishing Co.: Chicago, London 1919.

Mach, Ernst. 1909. *I principii della Meccanica esposti criticamente e storicamente nel loro sviluppo*. Roma-Milano: Albrighi Segati. Italian transl. by D. Gambioli.

Marchisotto, Elena A. and James T. Smith. 2007. *The legacy of Mario Pieri in geometry and arithmetic*. Boston, Mass.: Birkhäuser.

Mill, John Stuart. 1865. *An examination of Sir William Hamilton's philosophy, and of the principal philosophical questions discussed in his writings.* London: Longman, Roberts & Green, 1872.

Mill, John Stuart. 1870. *A system of logic, ratiocinative and inductive; being a connected view of the principles of evidence and the methods of scientific investigation.* New York: Harper & Brothers.

Minazzi, Fabio. 2000. Vailati e la scuola italiana. In M. De Zan (2000b), pages 223–251.

Müller, Max F. 1891. *The science of language: founded on lectures delivered at the Royal Institution in 1861 and 1863.* London: Longmans, Green.

Nagy, Albino. 1892. *Principi di logica, esposti secondo le dottrine moderne.* Torino: Loescher.

Padoa, Alessandro. 1898. *Conférences sur la logique mathématique.* Bruxelles: Université nouvelle de Bruxelles.

Padoa, Alessandro. 1900. Essai d'un théorie algébrique des nombres entiers précédé d'une introduction logique à une théorie déductive quelconque. In *Bibliothèque du congrès international de philosophie. Paris 1900*, vol. 3, pages 309–365. Paris: Colin. Engl. transl. in J, van Heijenoort (ed.), *From Frege to Gödel*, Cambridge, Mass.-London: Harvard Univ. Press. 1967, 119-123.

Padoa, Alessandro. 1902a. Un nouveau système des définitions pour la géométrie euclidienne. In Duporcq E., ed., 1902, pages 353–363.

Padoa, Alessandro. 1902b. Un nouveau système irréductible de postulats pour l'algèbre. In Duporcq E., ed., 1902, pages 249–256.

Padoa, Alessandro. 1905-06. Che cosa è una relazione? *Atti della Accademia Reale delle Scienze di Torino* 41:818–826.

Palmieri, Paolo. 2008. The empirical basis of equilibrium: Mach, Vailati, and the lever. *Studies in History and Philosophy of Science* 39:42–53.

Papini, Giovanni. 1902. La teoria psicologica della previsione. *Archivio per l'Antropologia e l'Etnologia* 32(2):351–375.

Papini, Giovanni. 1905. Pragmatismo messo in ordine. *Leonardo* 3(2):45–48.

Papini, Giovanni. 1907. Non bisogna essere monisti. In *Ricerche e Studi di Psichiatria, Nevrologia, Antropologia e Filosofia.* Milano: Vallardi. Repr. in *Sul pragmatismo (Saggi e Ricerche) 1903-1911.* Milano: Libreria Editrice Milanese. 1913, pages 83–102.

Papini, Giovanni and Giuseppe Prezzolini. 1906. *La coltura italiana.* Firenze: Lumachi.

Peano, Giuseppe. 1891. Osservazioni del Direttore (ad una lettera di C. Segre). *Rivista di Matematica* 1:66–69.

Peano, Giuseppe, ed. 1901a. *Formulaire de Mathématiques.* Turin: Bocca-Clausen.

Peano, Giuseppe. 1901b. Les définitions mathématiques. In *Bibliothèque du congrès international de philosophie. Paris 1900*, vol. 3. Logique et Histoire des Sciences, pages 279–288. Paris: Colin.

Peano, Giuseppe. 1903-04. Il latino, quale lingua ausiliare internazionale. *Atti della Reale Accademia delle Scienze di Torino* 39:273–283.

Peano, Giuseppe. 1915. Le definizioni per astrazione. *Bollettino della Mathesis* 7:106–120.

Peano, Giuseppe et al. 1893. Sulla raccolta di formule. *Rivista di Matematica* 3:1.

Peirce, C. S. 1905. What pragmatism is. *The Monist* 15(2):161–181.

Perez, E. 1895. El cultivo de la matemática y la forma deductiva de la inferencia. *Memorias de la Sociedad Científica Antonio Alzate* 8:315–363.

Pikler, Gyula. 1890. *The Psychology of the Belief in Objective Existence*. London: Williams and Norgate.

Pikler, Gyula. 1908. *Über Theodor Lipp's Versuch einer Teorie des Willens. Eine kritische Untersuchung, zugleich in Beitrag zu einer dynamischen Psychologie*. Leipzig: Barth.

Poincaré, Henri. 1902. *La science et l'hypothèse*. Paris: Flammarion. Engl. transl. *Science and hypothesis*. New York: The Science Press, 1905.

Prezzolini, Giuseppe. 1905. Il mio prammatismo. *Leonardo* 3(2):48.

Renan, Ernest. 1876. *Dialogues et fragments philosophiques*. Paris: Calmann-Lévy.

Rizza, Cinzia, ed. 2006. *Benedetto Croce – Giovanni Vailati Carteggio (1899-1905)*. Acireale-Roma: Bonanno.

Russell, Bertrand. 1998. *Autobiography*. London: Routledge.

Schiller, F.C.S. 1905. The definitions of pragmatism. *Leonardo* 3(2):44–45.

Segre, Corrado. 1891. Su alcuni indirizzi nelle investigazioni geometriche. Osservazioni dirette ai miei studenti. *Rivista di matematica* 1:42–66.

Sidgwick, Henry. 1874. *The methods of ethics*. London: Macmillan, 1963.

Spencer, Herbert. 1862. *First principles of a new system of philosophy*. London: Williams and Norgate.

Vailati, Giovanni. 1891a. Le proprietà fondamentali delle operazioni della logica deduttiva studiate dal punto di vista d'una teoria generale dello operazioni. *Rivista di Matematica* 1. Repr. in Vailati (1911), pages 2–8.

Vailati, Giovanni. 1891b. Un teorema di logica matematica. *Rivista di Matematica* 1. Repr. in Vailati (1911), page 1.

Vailati, Giovanni. 1892a. Dipendenza fra le proprietà delle Relazioni. *Rivista di Matematica* 2. Repr. in Vailati (1911), pages 14–17.

Vailati, Giovanni. 1892b. Sui principi fondamentali della geometria della retta. *Rivista di Matematica* 2. Repr. in Vailati (1911), pages 9–13.

Vailati, Giovanni. 1893. Recensione a A. Nagy, Principi di logica esposti secondo le teorie moderne. *Rivista di Matematica* 3. Repr. in Vailati (1911), pages 18–19.

Vailati, Giovanni. 1894a. Recensione a C. Burali-Forti, Logica matematica (Milano, Hoepli, 1894). *Rivista di matematica* Repr. in Vailati (1911), pages 22–25.

Vailati, Giovanni. 1894b. Recensione a Catalogue of University of Texas for 1893-94. *Rivista di Matematica* 4. Repr. in Vailati (1911), pages 20–21.

Vailati, Giovanni. 1895a. Sulle proprietà caratteristiche delle varietà a una dimensione. *Rivista di Matematica* V:183–185. Repr. in Vailati (1911), pages 30–32.

Vailati, Giovanni. 1895b. Sulle relazioni di posizione tra punti d'una linea chiusa. *Rivista di Matematica* 5. Repr. in Vailati (1911), pages 26–29.

Vailati, Giovanni. 1896a. Recensione a E. Mach, Populär-wissenschaftliche Vorlesungen. *Rivista di Studi Psichici* Repr. in Vailati (1911), pages 60–63.

Vailati, Giovanni. 1896b. Recensione a E. Mach, Populär-wissenschaftliche Vorlesungen. *Rivista sperimentale di Freniatria* 22(3). Repr. in Vailati (1911), pages 43–45.

Vailati, Giovanni. 1896c. Recensione a E. Perez, El cultivo de la Matematica y la forma deductiva de la inferencia. *Rivista di Matematica* 6. Repr. in Vailati (1911), pages 33–34.

Vailati, Giovanni. 1897a. Del concetto di Centro di Gravità nella Statica di Archimede. *Atti della Regia Accademia delle Scienze di Torino* 32. Repr. in Vailati (1911), pages 79–90.

Vailati, Giovanni. 1897b. Il principio dei Lavori Virtuali da Aristotele a Erone d'Alessandria. *Atti della Regia Accademia delle Scienze di Torino* 32. Repr. in Vailati (1911), pages 91–106.

Vailati, Giovanni. 1897c. *Sull'importanza delle Ricerche relative alla Storia delle Scienze. Prolusione a un corso sulla Storia della meccanica, letta il 4 dicembre 1896 nell'Università di Torino*. Torino: Roux e Frassati. Repr. in Vailati (1911), pages 64–78. Engl. transl. "On the importance of research regarding the history of science," this volume, chap. 1.

Vailati, Giovanni. 1898a. *Il Metodo Deduttivo come Strumento di Ricerca. Prolusione ad un corso libero di Storia della Meccanica, 1897-1898*. Torino: Roux-Frassati. Repr. in Vailati (1911), pages 118–148. Engl. transl. "The deductive method as an instrument of research," this volume, chap. 2.

Vailati, Giovanni. 1898b. Le méthode déductive comme instrument de recherche. *Revue de Métaphysique et de Morale* 6:667–703.

Vailati, Giovanni. 1898c. Le speculazioni di Giovanni Benedetti sul moto dei gravi. *Atti della Regia Accademia delle Scienze di Torino* 33. Repr. in Vailati (1911), pages 161–178.

Vailati, Giovanni. 1898d. Recensione a Joseph Hontheim, Der Logische Algorithmus in seinem Wesen, in seiner Anwendung und in seiner philosophichen Bedeutung. *Rivista di Matematica* 6. Repr. in Vailati (1911), pages 149–153.

Vailati, Giovanni. 1899a. *Alcune osservazioni sulle Questioni di Parole nella Storia della Scienza e della Cultura. Prolusione ad un corso libero di Storia della Meccanica, 1898-98*. Torino: Bocca. Repr. in Vailati (1911), pages 203–228. Engl. transl. "Some observations on the questions of words in the History of Science and Culture," this volume, chap. 3.

Vailati, Giovanni. 1899b. La logique mathématique et sa nouvelle phase de développement dans les écrits de M. J. Peano. *Revue de Métaphysique et de Morale* 7(1). Repr. in Vailati (1911), pages 229–242.

Vailati, Giovanni. 1899c. Recensione a C. Laisant. La Mathématique: philosophie, enseignement. Paris: Carré et Naud 1898. *Il Nuovo Risorgimento* 9(8). Repr. in Vailati (1911), pages 258–259.

Vailati, Giovanni. 1899d. Recensione a C. Trivero, Classificazione delle Scienze. Hoepli, Milano 1899. *Rivista italiana di Sociologia* 3(4). Repr. in Vailati (1911), pages 249–250.

Vailati, Giovanni. 1900. Recensione a J.P. Durand (De Gros), Aperçus de taxinomie générale, Alcan, Paris 1900. *Rivista di Scienze Biologiche* 1-2. Repr. in Vailati (1911), pages 298–299.

Vailati, Giovanni. 1901a. Des difficultés qui s'opposent à une classification rationelle des sciences. In *Bibliothèque du Congrès international de Philosophie. Paris 1900*, vol. 3. Logique et Histoire des Sciences. Paris: Colin. Repr. in Vailati (1911), pages 324–335. Ital. transl. in Quaranta (2003), pages 179–202. Engl. transl. "The difficulties involved in a rational classification of sciences," this volume, chap. 4.

Vailati, Giovanni. 1901b. Recensione a E. Mach. Analyse der Empfindungen und das Verhältnis des Physischen zum Psychischen. Jena: Fischer 1900. *Rivista di Biologia generale* 1-2. Repr. in Vailati (1911), pages 346–350.

Vailati, Giovanni. 1901c. Recensione a L. Couturat, La logique de Leibniz d'après des documents inédits, Alcan, Paris 1901. *Rivista di matematica* 7. Repr. in Vailati (1987), vol. 2, pages 193–204.

Vailati, Giovanni. 1901d. Recensione a M. Begey *Del lavoro manuale educativo*. torino: Paravia 1900. *Rivista di Biologia generale* 1-2. Repr. in Vailati (1911), pages 343–345.

Vailati, Giovanni. 1901e. Sulla portata logica della classificazione dei fatti mentali proposta dal prof. Franz Brentano (Comunicazione presentata al III Congresso Internazionale di psicologia di Parigi, agosto 1900). *Rivista Filosofica* 2(1). Repr. in Vailati (1911), pages 336–340. Engl. transl. "On the logical import of the classification of mental facts proposed by Franz Brentano," this volume chap. 5.

Vailati, Giovanni. 1902a. Aggiunte alle Note Storiche del Formulario. *Rivista di Matematica* 8(3). Repr. in Vailati (1911), pages 449–453.

Vailati, Giovanni. 1902b. *Di un modo di riattaccare la teoria delle Proporzioni fra segmenti e quella dell'Equivalenza (II Congresso degli Insegnanti di Matematica delle Scuole secondarie, promosso dall'Associazione Mathesis, Livorno 17-22 agosto 1901)*. Livorno: Giusti. Repr. in Vailati (1911), pages 399–402.

Vailati, Giovanni. 1902c. Recensione a A. Naville, Nouvelle classification des sciences. Alcan, Paris 1901. *Rivista di Biologia generale* 3. Repr. in Vailati (1911), pages 429–439.

Vailati, Giovanni. 1903a. Di un'opera dimenticata del P. Gerolamo Saccheri ("Logica Demonstrativa" 1697). *Rivista Filosofica* 4. Repr. in Vailati (1911), pages 477–484.

Vailati, Giovanni. 1903b. La teoria aristotelica della definizione. *Rivista di Filosofia e scienze affini* 2(5). Repr. in Vailati (1911), pages 485–496. Engl. transl. "The Aristotelian theory of definition," this volume, chap. 7.

Vailati, Giovanni. 1903c. Sull'applicabilità dei concetti di causa e di effetto nelle scienze storiche. International Conference of Historical Sciences, Rome, April 1903. *Rivista Italiana di Sociologia* 7(3). Repr. in Vailati (1911), pages 459–464. Engl. transl. "On the applicability of the concepts of cause and effect in historical sciences," this volume, chap. 6.

Vailati, Giovanni. 1904a. Intorno al significato della differenza tra gli assiomi ed i postulati nella geometria greca. In *Verhandlungen des III Internationalen Mathematiker Kongresses in Heidelberg 8–13 aug. 1903*. Leipzig: Teubner, 1905. Repr. in Vailati (1911), pages 547–552. Engl. transl. "On the meaning of the difference between axioms and postulates in Greek geometry," this volume, chap. 9.

Vailati, Giovanni. 1904b. La dimostrazione del principio delle leva data da Archimede nel libro primo sull'equilibrio delle figure piane. In *Atti del Congresso Internazionale di Scienze Storiche, Roma, 1903*, vol. 11. Roma: Lincei. Repr. in Vailati (1911), pages 497–502.

Vailati, Giovanni. 1904c. La più recente definizione della matematica. *Leonardo* pages 7–10. Repr. in Vailati (1911), pages 528–533. Engl. transl. "The most recent definition of mathematics," this volume, chap. 8.

Vailati, Giovanni. 1905a. I tropi della logica. *Leonardo* 3:3–7. Repr. in Vailati (1911), pages 564–571. Engl. transl. "On material representations of deductive processes," *Journal of Philosophy, Psychology and Scientific Methods*, 5(12):309–316, 12 June 1908. Repr. this volume, chap. 15.

Vailati, Giovanni. 1905b. La caccia alle antitesi. *Leonardo* 3:53–57. Engl. trans. The Attack on Distinctions, *Journal of Philosophy, Psychology and Scientific Methods*, 4(26):701–709, December 19, 1907. Repr. this volume, chap. 14.

Vailati, Giovanni. 1905c. La distinzione tra conoscere e volere. *Leonardo* 3. Repr. in Vailati (1911), pages 626–629. Engl. transl. "The Distinction Between Knowledge and Will," this volume, chap. 11.

Vailati, Giovanni. 1905d. Recensione a E. Mach. Erkenntnis und Irrtum. Skizzen zur Psychologie der Forschung. Barth: Leipzig 1905. *Leonardo* pages 193–94. Repr. in Vailati (1911), pages 667–69.

Vailati, Giovanni. 1905e. Sull'arte di interrogare. *Rivista di Psicologia* 1(2). Repr. in Vailati (1911), pages 572–576. Engl. transl. "The art of asking questions," this volume, chap. 10.

Vailati, Giovanni. 1906a. Idee pedagogiche di H.G. Wells. *Rivista di Psicologia applicata alla Pedagogia ed alla Psicopatologia* 2(3). Repr. in Vailati (1911), pages 713–717.

Vailati, Giovanni. 1906b. Il pragmatismo e la logica matematica. *Leonardo* 4(1):16–25. Repr. in Vailati (1911), pages 689–694. Engl. transl. by H. D. Austin "Pragmatism and mathematical logic," *Monist* 16:481–491, 1906. Repr. this volume, chap. 12.

Vailati, Giovanni. 1906c. A study of Platonic terminology. *Mind* 15(60):473–485. Repr. this volume, chap. 13.

Vailati, Giovanni. 1907a. Dal monismo al pragmatismo. *Rivista di Psicologia applicata alla Pedagogia ed alla Psicopatologia* 3(4). Repr. in Vailati (1911), pages 787–790.

Vailati, Giovanni. 1907b. L'insegnamento della matematica nel primo triennio della scuola secondaria. *Bollettino di Matematica* 6(8-9). Repr. in Vailati (1911), pages 805–809.

Vailati, Giovanni. 1908a. Il linguaggio come ostacolo alla eliminazione di contrasti illusori. *Rinnovamento* 2(5-6). Repr. in Vailati (1911), pages 895–99. Engl. transl. "Language as an obstacle to the elimination of illusory contrasts," this volume, chap. 17.

Vailati, Giovanni. 1908b. La grammatica dell'algebra. *Rivista di Psicologia Applicata* 4. Repr. in Vailati (1911), pages 871–889. Engl. transl. "The grammar of algebra," this volume, chap. 16.

Vailati, Giovanni. 1911. *Scritti di G. Vailati, 1863-1909*. Leipzig-Firenze: Barth-Seeber.

Vailati, Giovanni. 1924. Sulla teoria delle proporzioni. In F. Enriques, ed., *Questioni riguardanti le matematiche elementari*, pages 143–191. Bologna: Zanichelli.

Vailati, Giovanni. 1971. *Epistolario, 1891-1909*. Torino: Einaudi. G. Lanaro (ed.).

Vailati, Giovanni and G. Amato Pojero. 1993. *Epistolario: 1898-1908*. Milano: Angeli. A. Brancaforte, ed.

Vailati, Giovanni and Mario Calderoni. 1909a. Il Pragmatismo e i vari modi di non dir niente. *Rivista di Psicologia applicata* 5(9). Repr. in Vailati (1911), pages 933–41. Engl. transl. "Pragmatism and the various ways of saying nothing," this volume, chap. 19.

Vailati, Giovanni and Mario Calderoni. 1909b. Le origini e l'idea fondamentale del Pragmatismo. *Rivista di Psicologia applicata* 5(1). Repr. in Vailati (1911), pages 920–32. Engl. transl. "The origins and fundamental idea of pragmatism," this volume, chap. 18.

Verrecchia, Anacleto. 1978. *La catastrofe di Nietzsche a Torino*. Torino: Einaudi.

Volterra, Vito. 1902a. Betti, Brioschi, Casorati, trois analystes italiens et trois manières d'envisager les questions d'analyse. In Duporcq E., 1902, pages 43–57.

Volterra, Vito. 1902b. Sur les équations aux dérivées partielles. In Duporcq E., ed., 1902, pages 377–378.

Zeuthen, Hieronymus Georg. 1896. *Geschichte der Mathematik im Altertum und Mittelalter*. Kopenhagen: A. F. Höst und Sön.

Reflections on Vailati's Pragmatism

M. Caamano and P. Suppes

Preliminary remarks

The pragmatic project of developing a richer notion of experience

Classical pragmatists made a sustained effort to develop a new conception of experience, free from some simplistic assumptions shared by both traditional rationalists and empiricists, like the idea that experience results from a combination of simple sensations. In his main paper on pragmatism, "The origins and the fundamental idea of pragmatism" (1909b), Giovanni Vailati characterized our experience of permanent, objective existence in terms of a certain kind of conditional expectations, in particular, those which are conditioned to certain deliberate actions of ours being performed. His experiential account of objective existence, based on a systematic relation between deliberate actions and expectations, is a permanent contribution to pragmatic thought, which we analyze and assess. We also consider Vailati's revision of the Peircean pragmatic maxim, the pragmatic evaluation of meaningless assertions, and his vindication of inferential usefulness as a determining factor in both formal systems and empirical theories. Our discussion will as well include a critical analysis of some less satisfactory aspects of Vailati's thought, whose Brentanian conception of mental facts contrasts sharply with James' sophisticated study of the mind in *The Principles of Psychology* (1890). But let us now make some preliminary comments to place Vailati's work within the broader pragmatic tradition. Evans' bibliography (1930) of the references to pragmatism

Logic and Pragmatism. Selected Essays by Giovanni Vailati.
C. Arrighi, P. Cantù, M. De Zan, and P. Suppes.
Copyright © 2009, CSLI Publications.

in the works of Vailati makes evident that we can find no mention of John Dewey in any of them. On the other hand, there are, although mainly critical, numerous references to William James, as well as frequent reference to C. S. Peirce to acknowledge his positive philosophical influence on Vailati's own thought.[1]

Vailati's revision of the Peircean pragmatic maxim

Following Peirce, Vailati understands pragmatism primarily as a method for concept or meaning clarification. His main revision of Peirce's conception of this method consists in restating it more restrictively as a criterion of empirical significance, so that it becomes possible to avoid paradoxes leading to the conclusion that rival hypotheses with the same empirical, experiential consequences would mean the same.[2] According to Vailati, the pragmatic criterion of empirical meaningfulness requires the translatability into assertions about expectations or predictions. The notion of expectation is precisely the crucial one in his approach, as he argues that the only part of an assertion's content that can be confirmed or refuted by experience is that which implies some predictions.

> Any disagreement regarding the personal experience perceived by any of us is an ultimate fact that can be regarded as a datum, but which can never be the subject of controversy.

> The question of truth or falsehood can only be posed when the perception or experience under scrutiny suggests or predicts other perceptions, the latter being not present and actual, but rather future and possible—that is, when and because the immediate perceptions and experiences are connected to *expectations* or *predictions* of any sort (Vailati and Calderoni, 1909b, this volume, p. 236).

---

[1] "To the end, however, he seems to have considered that James frequently made an overstatement of the case which is set forth more compellingly by Peirce—not to mention Socrates, Berkeley, and J. S. Mill" (Evans, 1930, pp. 417–418).

[2] "To concede the possibility that there could be an automaton so perfect that it reacts, to any stimulus, in a way identical to the way a supposedly conscious human would react, is the same as conceding that there is no difference between the hypothesis of the presence of a consciousness or that of an automaton for what concerns the predictions that we can deduce from either hypothesis. If we were to apply the previously mentioned criterion, which pragmatists would like to use to determine whether there is a difference in meaning between two propositions, this would lead to a paradoxical conclusion, i.e. that when we assert the existence of other "conscious" beings other than ourselves, we are not saying anything different from asserting that, instead, such conscious beings do not exist—unless we intend, with the latter assertion, to deny any of those reactions or behaviors which are distinctive features of those bodies that we refuse to think of as having consciousness," (this volume, p. 244).

Consequently, a main goal of Vailati's pragmatism is the logical analysis of the predictive elements always implicit in assertions when we reason or think. By thus restricting the aim of the Peircean pragmatic maxim, he succeeds in eliminating the remaining reductionist, verificationist features of the former, without giving up one of the initial motivations of the pragmatic philosophy, namely, to provide a method that enables us to avoid cognitively useless discussion. The ultimate purpose of his method for analyzing the meaning of an assertion is thus to establish, on the basis of its empirical significance, whether its discussion can be useful.

> [...] pragmatists, with their analysis of meaning of propositions in terms of predictions, are not trying to give a complete description of the contents of all our beliefs—they try instead, as mentioned before, to put focus on *the only part of content whose discussion could be useful* (Vailati and Calderoni, 1909b, this volume, p. 244).

Proceeding in accordance with the pragmatic method involves not taking part in debates unless it is possible to determine which facts should be the case to decide if a given assertion is true or false. For example, the debate on the alternative between the hypotheses of consciousness and that of automaticity to explain the existence of other beings behaving like humans should not be undertaken until it is determined that both hypotheses are able to provide predictions comparable in precision and extension.

Rejection of the Jamesian theses about the will's influence on belief

As was already pointed out, Vailati took a critical stance towards James' approach, specially focusing on the main theses put forward by the latter in "The Will to Believe" (1896), and, on the other hand, hardly considering the ideas presented in *The Principles of Psychology* (1890). Vailati's main objections to the argument from "The Will to Believe" are the following: first, that will can highly influence thought, but not so much beliefs,[3] second, that those rare cases where will, or desires and passions, influence belief formation must be recognized and explained, but they should not be vindicated as useful and logically justified, and third, that science must result from a dispassionate search for truth, as well as from the reluctance to believe on insufficient grounds, which implies that passionate interests cannot be necessary conditions

---

[3] "[there is, in James] [...] a confusion between the power of will over our thoughts (which is great) and over our beliefs (which is not so great)" (Vailati's quote from "Un manuale per i bugiardi: G. Prezzolini, L'arte di persuadere," (Vailati, 1907, p. 774), introduced by Evans (1930) on p. 421).

of religion as much as of science, as James maintains. In order to support his second objection, Vailati distinguishes cases in which human desires affect the objects of belief from others where this does not occur. The first kind of case covers the whole realm of value judgments, including moral judgments or even judgments about our own capacities, but not so religious or scientific judgments, as James thought. In the case of certain kinds of events, like moral actions, their occurrence may depend on our deciding whether to believe something, while in other sorts of events there is no such dependency.

Vailati's opposition to these Jamesian ideas somehow underlies the former's complaint that regarding pragmatism as a utilitarian approach constitutes a serious historical misunderstanding, prompted by the ambiguity of Peirce's assertion that the meaning of a concept consists in its practical consequences.[4]

> First of all, amongst these misunderstandings, we should mention the perception of pragmatism as a sort of "utilitarianism" applied to logic; that is, a doctrine that in order to evaluate the truth or falsehood of beliefs, uses a criterion based on the consequences of such beliefs being more or less useful, or agreeable, etc.

> [...] The methodological rule, as stated by Peirce, does not wish to define the distinction between true and false beliefs as something more arbitrary, more "subjective," more dependent on individual opinions and feelings. In fact its purpose is the exact opposite.

> Such methodological rule is nothing more than [...] a form that would be able to indicate, more clearly, what kind of experiments or observations can and need to be performed, by us or others, to decide whether, and to what extent, our assertions are true (Vailati and Calderoni, 1909b, this volume, p. 234).

To summarize what concerns the connections between Vailati and the classical pragmatists, we must emphasize, on the one hand, his sympathy with Peirce's pragmatic method to clarify meaning by translating any assertion into the conceivable experiential consequences that its truth would imply, and on the other hand, his rejection of James' attempt to question the fact/value dichotomy—an attempt shared by Dewey, whose approach is not discussed by Vailati.

---

[4] "Hence is justified the maxim, belief in which constitutes pragmatism; namely, in order to ascertain the meaning of an intellectual conception one should consider what practical consequences might conceivably result by necessity from the truth of that conception; and the sum of these consequences will constitute the entire meaning of the conception" (Peirce, 1902-1907, p. 158).

Vailati's pragmatic analysis of the concept of objective existence in terms of conditional expectations

The most central concept to which Vailati applies the pragmatic method for concept clarification is that of objective existence. All classical pragmatists (including now Vailati) agree that practice plays a constituent role in experience, which is always active and inferential, shaped by interactions with surroundings and the corresponding habits or expectations. This account of experience is very different from the sense-data conception of experience entertained by empiricists like R. Carnap or B. Russell, and even from the one inherited from rationalists like Descartes.[5] Christopher Hookway, as a specialist in pragmatism of the Peircean trend, gives Dewey much credit for the view that "experience is full of inference,"[6] but we think that it would be fair to trace that merit back to Vailati (with Peirce as a predecessor).

Vailati's vindication of the distinction between appearance and reality on the basis of experience, attempted also by Russell, is more successfully argued by the former because of the central role he assigns to inference (from one experience to the expected one), and his rejection of anything like "hard data." In this conception of experience lies precisely one of the key differences between two empiricist traditions represented by pragmatism and neopositivism. Pragmatists reject any passive conception of experience according to which the latter should be explained in terms of sense-data or some macroscopic, stable objects or properties. By contrast, they developed an active conception of experience where no element or aspect is acknowledged as given, basic, but instead action is regarded as always entering in our experience of the environment. According to Vailati, Peircean pragmatism should not be associated with Protagoras but with Socrates, who opposes the former's subjective, sensory-centered account of knowledge by appealing to the importance of prediction. Vailati includes a long quote from Plato's *Theaetetus* that ends with the following statement by Socrates:

> For any thought we entertain that does not have nor imply any reference to the future, that is, no prediction or expectation, the opinion of

---

[5]This opposition is spelled out by James (1890, ch. IX, pp. 231–33).

[6]Hookway paraphrases Dewey's view on this issue in the following fashion: "We experience all sorts of objects, events and processes, and we should not follow philosophers who seek to impose a distinction between the thin uninterpreted data of experience and the inferential processes which lead us to interpret what we experience as books, people and so on. The dichotomy between the passive given of experience and the rich results of our active conceptualization is not supported by our experience," (Hookway, 2008, sec. 4.3).

any of us cannot be refuted (Vailati and Calderoni, 1909b, this volume, p. 236).

Vailati understands Peirce's methodological rule as establishing that we must examine assertions to identify the part that implies some predictions, since only that part can be confirmed or refuted by experience and thus shown to be meaningful. Predictability is the crucial requirement to determine both truth and meaning. Experience is therefore ascribed a double role (epistemic and semantic): providing the means to verify a theory, as well as those to determine the part of the theory that is meaningful and can therefore be an object of useful discussion. Proceeding in accordance with the pragmatic method involves not taking part in debates unless it is possible to determine which facts should be the case to decide if a given assertion is true or false. As Vailati explains, the key contribution of the pragmatic method consists in enabling us to ascertain what sorts of experiences should occur in order to make an assertion true. Determining the truth or falsehood of an assertion requires, first, ascertaining the predicted experiences that would have to occur for the assertion to be true, and, second, ascertaining whether they have occurred or not. By making it possible to determine what part of the assertions' content implies predictions, pragmatism would enable us to meet a precondition to decide whether a proposition is true or false. The pragmatic method, therefore, does not provide a criterion to decide whether an assertion is true or false, but rather a criterion to determine the part of an assertion's content that is necessary (though not in general sufficient) to decide whether the assertion is true or false. The better the predictions thus implied are in terms of precision, extension, and possibility of refutation, the more profitable the discussion of that theory can be. Since the task of determining meaning is prior to the task of determining truth, Peirce's pragmatic rule helps to apply an objective criterion of truth by providing an objective criterion of meaning. Vailati deplores that pragmatism's later historical development, with its emphasis on rather subjective aspects like practical interests and usefulness, appears to stem from a misunderstanding of the original pragmatic rule.

Predictions based on deliberate actions presented as the criterion to determine objective existence

Despite their common grammatical form in present tense, Vailati notes, assertions about the present always imply a reference to the future. This is so regardless of the kind of thing whose existence is asserted: objects, properties of objects like position and shape, dispositional properties of objects, or something other than objects and their properties, like attitudes, concepts, memories, minds, and events. There are two basic kinds of expectations: proper (or effective) expectations that some event will happen, and conditional expectations, which consist in predictions that some event would happen given other previous conditions. The two kinds of expectations are related in the following way: a conditional expectation whose condition has been satisfied is necessary for a proper expectation. The latter, therefore, depends on the former, more precisely, on the former's condition being verified or waited for. The expectation after this has been verified is not conditional but effective. Given that an expectation is a state, a conditional expectation represents a complex state that may bring about another state, that is, another expectation, if it is verified that its condition has been satisfied.

There are different kinds of conditional expectations depending on the sorts of conditions involved. Relying on J. Pikler's ideas, presented in his book *The Psychology of the Belief in Objective Existence* (1890), Vailati distinguishes between conditions that consist of some deliberate acts of ours and those that do not. Only the former would be essentially involved in judgments about existence or in attribution of properties. These judgments are based on the belief in a necessary connection between experiences produced by a voluntary act of ours and that act, that is, the belief that certain experiences can only be obtained by means of certain deliberate actions on our part. When we believe that this connection is contingent, or we consider that those experiences are rather connected to certain conditions which are not produced by us, then we just form the belief that there is a concatenation between some facts or, at most, that there is a cause-effect relation between them. In short, experiences on the basis of which we assert existence are only obtained by means of certain deliberate actions on our part.

Vailati mentions two examples by Pikler to illustrate how judgments on existence are translatable into judgments on necessary connections between experiences and deliberate actions of ours. The belief in the permanent, objective existence of space would amount to the belief that certain space-presentations are permanently capable of being presented to us through our volition. Similarly, the belief in the objective existence of time would be equated with the belief that, by means of voluntary actions, we can achieve specific experiences of succession and coexistence in correspondence with any of our series of experiences.

Application of Vailati's criterion to different domains of existence

An extremely appealing feature of Vailati's account of objective existence has to do with the fact that it turns out to be easily applicable

lxxvi / M. Caamano and P. Suppes

to many different domains of existence, as well as to the semantic analysis of the corresponding expressions for those domains (like different sorts of general terms). Judgments on existence of something other than objects and their properties, i.e. things like attitudes, concepts, memories, etc., also result from a belief in the connection between some experiences and some actions. For example, we assert the existence of qualities of character, like being irritable, not because the person is angry at some point, but because he would get angry given certain conditions and stimuli that would not make other people angry.

Vailati draws our attention not only to the role of possible experiences but also to that of possible actions that would imply possible resulting experiences. Actions involved in arriving at a certain judgment on existence need not be actual. The possibility of attaining experiences can be relative either to actual dependency on our actions, or to the virtual dependency on actions that would be possible if certain conditions (not dependent on our will) were the case. If certain actions were able to produce certain experiences in the past, or if they can be imagined as able to produce them in the future, then those actions could lead to judgments on existence too.

On this point of view, there would be a gradual movement from possible or probable conditions to impossible or unlikely ones. As an example of the latter, he puts the case of conditions involved in direct verification of scientific hypotheses whose required methods of observation will never be available. As more extreme cases, he mentions both judgments on past events and on someone else's experiences. The conditions of the expectations involved in these judgments are impossible to satisfy, since they would require living in the past, in one case, and being another person, in the other. The ground of the conviction that there are other minds beyond our own is provided by the similarities between my behavior (caused by certain mental states) and the behavior of others. Our knowledge of other minds comes, therefore, from signs like the behavior of certain "things" in certain circumstances. Consequently, assertions about the existence of other conscious beings must be considered as a hypothesis, among other possible ones, to explain some facts about our experience. These judgments thus cannot be verified directly, but they can be verified indirectly by directly verifying other assertions that can be deduced from them. Such process of deduction would be useful in two different respects, which Vailati explains as follows.

In this process of deduction of directly verifiable propositions from others that are not, pragmatists are inclined to see not only a tool to determine the truth or falsehood of these unverifiable propositions, but also a tool to determine their meaning (Vailati and Calderoni, 1909b, this volume, p. 243).

As we have explained before, Vailati avoided the possible paradoxical consequences of equating those two methods, by restricting their use to empirical content determination and without extending them to meaning determination in general.

In Vailati's approach, predictions play a crucial role also in assertions apparently referring to immediate observations and assertions containing general terms. Assertions of the first kind are usually considered to refer to immediate observations and, therefore, to be infallible. Nevertheless possibilities of error may be hidden in what seems to be immediate knowledge. Typical judgments like those about illusory sensations or feelings show that these assertions actually imply predictions that must be taken into account to validate them. The assertion "I am cold," for example, does not imply just an acknowledgment of certain feelings but also predictions about the character or consequences of those feelings, like some behavioral or physiological responses (wrapping up well, shivering, turning pale, etc.). We may only be aware of the predictions when we have to validate the assertions, such as when we confront illusory happiness or apparent tiredness. Pleasure and preferences are immediate, irrefutable things, but assertions about them are usually not only about mental states but about their typical consequences and circumstances. When we make assertions about a person's feelings, we do not try to make an assertion just about mental states, but also about the presence of plans of actions or dispositions to act in specific ways. This issue has been further discussed by Wittgenstein in epigraphs 290–298 of *Philosophical Investigations* (1953), where he, in a similar vein, argues that talking about sensations requires being able to recognize them, which would be only possible by ascertaining the typical consequences that those hypothetical mental states would entail. A controversial point here is to what extent acknowledging the existence of sensations should depend on having an objective criterion for sensation determination. In this respect, Wittgenstein seems more radical than Vailati, who, although emphasizing that talk about sensations or feelings always includes objective aspects, like those behavioral or physiological ones, also accepts that those mental states themselves exist, even if they remain subjective and irrefutable when separated from their objective consequences.

Vailati notices that predictions are also involved in the use of general terms, since the latter require a classification of the designed objects and, therefore, a comparison to recognize similarities and differences, something which calls for the employment of procedures that may be repeated.

According to Vailati, the fact that many predictions are potential, absent from present consciousness, does not pose any problem to pragmatism, since the goals of this approach are logical, rather than psychological. Its focus is on the logical elements or aspects involved in asserting existence, and not on the psychological elements playing a role there. Pragmatism seeks the development of a validity criterion for reasoning and thinking, by providing a criterion for empirical meaningfulness. According to such criterion, assertions must be translatable into certain kinds of expressions that refer to a certain kind of conditional expectations.

Some anticipatory achievements in the development of semantics

Putting aside his analysis of existence assertions, Vailati's study of language is mainly focused on the problem of cognitively meaningless assertions, together with the associated one concerning illusory conceptions prompted by a misleading use of language.[7] These very problems have also been tackled from non-pragmatic approaches, like neopositivism for instance.[8] However, the ideas underlying Vailati's discussion of such issues turn out strikingly valid according to current developments in the philosophy of language. In particular, his account of meaninglessness has two important implications for current debates in this field. First, the characterization of analyticity as a dynamic property, dependent on how the meaning of given expressions evolves according to their use.[9] Second, and more important, the recognition that semantics (meaning) proves dependent on pragmatics (use, context of speech), which represents one of the central issues involved in the development of a pragmatic approach to language,[10] like the in-

---

[7] Vailati devotes his 1908 paper to this latter issue.

[8] Famously in Carnap's (1932/1959), "The Elimination of Metaphysics Through Logical Analysis of Language."

[9] "As previously noted, the fact that sometimes propositions, synthetic to begin with, become analytic, even though their exterior form is unaltered—that is, without this transformation being indicated by any special verbal sign which allows us to recognize it independently from the examination of the context of speech—far from taking away from the importance of the distinction between the two aforementioned kinds, is, on the contrary, one of the reasons why it is important to insist on it" (Vailati and Calderoni, 1909a, this volume, p. 251).

[10] "[...] to determine the meaning of every phrase or abstract proposition by means of the examination of the consequences which are involved in it, or the applications

fluential one suggested in Wittgenstein's *Philosophical Investigations* (1953) or, more recently, in Robert B. Brandom's *Making It Explicit* (1994).

Semantics or meaning regarded as dependent on pragmatics (use, context of speech)

Like the later Wittgenstein and Robert Brandom, Vailati conceived linguistic expressions as dynamic instruments for communication determined by often implicit rules of use and discursive commitments. He indeed rejects, as the later Wittgenstein does, the Augustinian account of language as a class of expressions standing for objects in the outer world. Expressions may convey information of many different kinds, and, as Brandom argues, in order to be able to grasp the meaning of an assertion, we must take into account the speaker's commitments involved in such assertion in a given speech context.[11] Since Vailati was especially interested in the cognitive significance of assertions, his emphasis was placed on their inferential role or usefulness, which would vary as knowledge advanced. The characterization of meaning in terms of deductive or inferential usefulness is regarded by him as a feature common to both mathematical logic and pragmatism:

> [...] their [mathematical logicians' and pragmatists'] common tendency to regard the value, and even the meaning, of every assertion as being intimately related to the use which can be made, or which it may be desired to make, of it for the deduction and construction of particular consequences or groups of consequences (Vailati, 1906a, this volume, p. 164).

This emphasis on the inferential fruitfulness of an assertion, as a key aspect of its meaning, is also noticeable in Vailati's interpretation of Plato's concept of εἶδος (*eidos*). In his view, the notion of *eidos* anticipated the current notion of connotation, referring the term '*eidos*' to those qualities that determine a class due to the importance of their consequences. Those characteristics which are common and exclusive to all the members of a class must be also important to be an *eidos* (Vailati, 1906b, p. 484).

Vailati's account of language also agrees with that by the philosophers just mentioned in highlighting not only the dynamic, purpose-dependent dimension of meaning, but also its pluralistic nature. Indeed,

which are made of it, and to regard two phrases or propositions as equivalent, or as two ways of saying the same thing (Peirce), whenever they are employed, by any one who adopts them, as a means of arriving at the same particular conclusions" (Vailati, 1906b, this volume, p. 175).

[11]See Wittgenstein (1953, epigraph 1–11), and Brandom (1994, chap. 1).

he repeatedly points out that the same expression may have different meanings depending on the discursive contexts in which it appears. The expressive goal of a certain expression, together with its corresponding rule of use and inferential role, may vary from one discursive context to another, even within the same period of time. This point can be illustrated by taking again the example of the word '*eidos*,' whose meaning is elucidated by Vailati through the analysis of those images that Plato used, in different contexts, to clearly draw the distinction between what we now call connotation and denotation:

1. The image of possession: objects are described as sharing or having part in the possession of a certain *eidos*. Vailati draws our attention to the correspondence between this sense of the word '*eidos*' and that of the word 'property' in modern logic.

2. The image of participation or composition: the *eidos* is regarded as being elements or ingredients taking part in the composition of single objects as well as determining the resemblances among them, which explain their being called by the same name.

3. The image of imitation: the *eidos* is described as being models of which all single things would be copies. Resemblance, therefore, occurs not only among objects of the same class, but also between those objects and the *eidos*.

Each of the above images leads to different philosophical notions which, in turn, lead in different understandings of what today we call 'connotation.'

The pragmatic evaluation of meaningless assertions: the problems of becoming analytic and betraying the expressive goals

In his second main work on pragmatism, "Pragmatism and the various ways of saying nothing" (1909a), Vailati applies the pragmatic criterion for empirical meaningfulness to detect meaningless assertions. In pointing out the main reasons why assertions with no meaning may appear meaningful, he employs a dynamic notion of analyticity, remarkably in tune with its current conception, such as the one by Carnap or even the residual one by Quine,[12] according to which analytic statements

---

[12] By "the residual notion of analyticity" in Quine we mean his idea from "Epistemology Naturalized" (1969) that what are usually called 'analytical statements' correspond in his approach to those statements that prompt an unanimous consensus reaction within a linguistic community. Quine maintains, therefore, his thesis from "Two Dogmas of Empiricism" (1951) that there are no analytical statements —i.e. statements which are true or false just by virtue of their meaning—although now he points out a distinctive feature of those statements usually considered ana-

express only convenient linguistic conventions or speakers' agreements that may change depending on the state of knowledge or the different interests underlying the fixing of conventions. The general idea, widely shared from Carnap's discussion of the issue, is that the analyticity of a statement must be understood as relative to the semantic rules of the language containing it. Such a relativistic feature is precisely what underlies Vailati's dynamic notion of analyticity.

Another interesting pragmatic notion that Vailati introduces in this context is that of the logical or practical goals established for certain types of linguistic expressions. With regard to this, he claims that ignoring or confusing the pre-established goal of a certain expression can lead to a meaningless use of the latter. In other words, determining the meaningfulness of an expression requires, first, ascertaining the goals that an expression of that kind has associated, and second, confirming that such goals are met. To different kinds of expressions may correspond, for example, different referential goals, which should not be neglected if those expressions are to be applied in a meaningful way.

Among the main reasons why assertions with no meaning may appear meaningful Vailati mentions the following:

a) Sentences that are or have become analytic (without any verbal sign of this change).[13] Since analytic statements express only linguistic conventions or stipulations, they cannot be employed to assert anything meaningful, that is, cognitively valuable. As an example, Vailati mentions the law of inertia: "a body unsolicited by any force continues to move indefinitely with the same velocity and in the same direction" (Vailati and Calderoni, 1909a, this volume, p. 250). Depending on how we understand the word 'force,' the law of inertia can be considered full of meaning or almost meaningless.

b) Sentences that are or have become analytically false.[14] A main

---

lytic. As for Carnap's account of analyticity, his most influential ideas can be found in "Empiricism, Semantics and Ontology" (1950), and "Meaning postulates" (1952), now in *Meaning and Necessity* (1956).

[13] "One of the most important cases concerns sentences or idioms that were once meaningful, but that, due to changes in meaning of some of the terms that they contain, end up becoming 'true by definition' and in this case they no longer represent an assertion that can be confirmed or refuted through new experiences, but are merely indications or statements relative to the sense in which a certain word is used or we would like it to be used" (Vailati and Calderoni, 1909a, this volume, p. 250).

[14] "It does not appear possible for propositions of this sort—i.e. propositions where the term acting as subject implies, because of its meaning, not the possession but rather the non-possession of the quality, or of some qualities expressed by the predicate—to be regarded by anyone, not even for a moment, as having meaning" (Vailati and Calderoni, 1909a, this volume, p. 254).

cause of contradictions in terms is the tendency to use words referring to some properties or relations as if their meaning were independent of any consideration of reference. An example of this would be to talk about the "absolute" motion of a body, thus applying "absolute" to a property, like motion, that is always relative.

There are also cases of apparent contradictions originated by changes in the meaning of the terms of an assertion. Once an analytic proposition has become synthetic it can be denied without this implying any contradiction in terms. We find this case, for instance, in the extension of the concept of addition to the case of negative numbers, or in Hume's revision of the concept of cause. Here again Vailati's analysis resembles Wittgenstein's, whose characterization of meaning as established use makes it possible to account for category mistakes or nonsensical expressions as something dependent on the established rules of use for every language.

c) Tendency to forget the logical or practical goals of generalization process.[15] This problem corresponds to the more general one which lies in seeking as an end what has been previously sought as a means. In the present case, the epistemic means of generalization are pursued as an end itself thereby becoming epistemically useless. The goal of general concepts is to establish classes of objects about which there is or could be something significant to be asserted or denied (in comparison to what could be asserted or denied of some other classes of objects). However, the generalization process may reach the point where the concept is no longer useful in distinguishing between different things, that is, in achieving the goal for which it had been introduced. The uselessness of the resulting concept would be manifest in the fact that it would render opposite assertions as meaning the same. An example of this would be a sentence like "everything is an illusion" and "nothing is an illusion." If the concept of illusion embraces everything, both sentences could be somehow equivalent, since none of them would make it possible to distinguish what is an illusion from what is not.

d) Consideration of mere mutations in terminology as entailing effectual results.[16] A common case where changes in expression are wrongly

_____

[15] "We can find a third source of questions and assertions with no meaning in the tendency to forget that what is called the 'generalization process' is nothing other than a means to certain logical or practical goals, and that there are limits, surpassing which would entail the impossibility of reaching those goals" (Vailati and Calderoni, 1909a, this volume, p. 256).

[16] "The abovementioned case of processes of generalization is not the only one where our tendency to automatically extend our thought-processes beyond the point where those processes are justified by the goals prefixed, leads us to consider mere mutations in terminology or forms of expression as effectual results" (Vailati and

understood as involving a cognitive difference is that of illusory explanations. In such explanations, the *explanans* is simply re-stating the *explanandum*, instead of asserting sufficient causes of the facts described in the latter. This is also the case in what Comte calls "metaphysical explanations," where the *explanandum* is merely described in abstract terms in the *explanans*, which does not refer to any general law from which the former could be deduced. To illustrate this, Vailati refers to the famous quote from Molière: "*opium facit dormire quia habet virtutem dormitivam*" ("opium makes people sleep because it has a sleeping virtue").

Vailati concludes his examination of meaningless assertions by claiming that the best remedy to all the above problems consists in translating any assertion containing "abstract" words into those containing "concrete" words so that it is possible to make explicit the tacit, unspecified restrictions on which the validity of general propositions always depends. This solution would also imply the employment of particular examples in order to guarantee the independence and compatibility of different assertions, and thus to avoid any implicit contradiction between hypotheses of the same group. Notice that the solution suggested by Vailati does not share the reductionist aspect typical of the partial solution provided by neopositivists,[17] namely, translating theoretical statements into observational ones. Rendering abstract statements into concrete ones, by contrast, does not have any implication concerning reduction to observation statements, it just rather entails the possibility of specifying some concrete cases satisfying what the abstract statement establishes.

Vailati's naturalistic conception of knowledge: cognition understood as a fallible, goal-oriented activity

A step towards the naturalization of metaphysics

As already explained in the second section (The analysis of the concept of objective existence in terms of conditional expectations), Vailati vindicates the distinction between existence and experience, reality and appearance, being and being perceived, as one that can be established in terms of the role played by potential experiences producible by voluntary acts.

Calderoni, 1909a, this volume, p. 258).

[17] As it is well-known, the other neopositivist, partial solution complementing the one mentioned here is to translate every statement into another showing its logical form.

This conclusion is summarized by Berkeley with the sentence "*esse est percipi*," but it could be better expressed by the sentence "*esse est posse percipi*." Far from destroying the distinction between "to be" and "to be perceived," Berkeley instead was clarifying the basis and meaning of such a distinction, showing how the *being or existence of an object is nothing but the "potential being" of certain experiences.* Plato had already acknowledged, up to a certain point, that assertions about the existence of objects can be reduced, in the end, to assertions made on the possibility of certain experiences (Vailati and Calderoni, 1909b, this volume, p. 238).

This account of reality amounts to a first step towards the naturalization of metaphysics, for it entails that metaphysical problems are approachable by means of the pragmatic method. Pragmatism, understood as critical empiricism, does not share the metaphysical agnosticism of the usual positivism.[18] Vailati's standpoint is very close to James with respect to this issue. They share a vindication of a naturalistic metaphysics, which is connected to their common rejection of apriorism and, in general, foundationalist epistemological views. Metaphysical postulates would be valuable as ideals. James states the following: "Metaphysics should take heart from example of physics, simply confessing that hers is the longer task" (1890, Vol. II, Ch. XXVIII, p. 671).

As a result of applying the pragmatic methodology, many classical distinctions have been questioned or reviewed, like that between essential and accidental properties, which are now understood as relative, or the one between categorical and hypothetical general propositions, which has been shown invalid, given the hypothetical character of all general propositions. On the other hand, applying the pragmatic methodology makes also possible the vindication of certain distinctions. To this respect, Vailati claims that philosophers' systematic attempts at destroying distinctions for the sake of generality lead to a result opposite from the one aimed at, namely, to the increase in the number and importance of distinctions (Vailati, 1905a, p. 709, this volume, p. 195). The traditional philosophical tendency to search for the highest generalities, i.e., the universal, had a bearing on the rejection of distinctions, which were typically questioned due to their gradual, overlapping or relative character. Vailati argues for these three types of

---

[18] "Mathematical logic has thus contributed most efficaciously to the defense of the position of the pragmatists against the 'agnostic' prejudice which attributes the impossibility of the resolution of such problems [i.e., those of providing a scholastic definition of the most important words of science and philosophy] to a pretended incapacity of the human mind to penetrate the 'essence' of things" (Vailati, 1906a, this volume, p. 168).

distinctions, showing, through numerous examples, how none of those qualities makes the corresponding distinctions less adequate. By drawing gradual distinctions we can distinguish between different subclasses of properties within the same kind of property. In the case of overlapping distinctions, we are subordinating distinctions or segmentations. Among all successions, only some are relevant for theoretical and practical purposes, namely, those that make it possible to increase the number and scope of predictions and actions. As for the relative distinctions, they are based on relational properties, which are characterized by being dependent on comparisons or other relations between objects.

As an example of a gradual distinction, he mentions the following: the only difference between determinism and indeterminism consists in the estimate of the probability or frequency of divergences in the effects of causes having given degrees of similarity. For, in a strict sense, no facts repeat themselves, which implies that to assert that there is a causal relation amounts to saying "that *effects* which *resemble* one another constantly succeed *causes* which *resemble* one another" (Vailati, 1905a, p. 708, this volume, p. 194). Vailati illustrates the case of an overlapping distinction by pointing out that despite the fact that differences in quantity are ultimately grounded on differences in quality, the fact that the first are only a special case of the latter does not make less important the distinction between them, since quantitative differences, unlike qualitative ones, permit a fixed, successive arrangement of the objects possessing them, and can be compared in detail by using measurement.

Finally, to illustrate the case of a relative distinction, he says the following:

> To say that the motion adopted as "standard" is uniform, without saying *with regard to what other motion* (just as, in the case of points of reference, to say that a body is stationary without saying in regard *to what other bodies*), is as unreasonable as to say that a man is a "contemporary" without saying of what other person (Vailati, 1905a, p. 706, this volume, p. 192).

A moderately instrumentalist conception of science

Like the other traditional pragmatists, Vailati emphasizes the instrumental value of theories,[19] acknowledging at the same time a dependence relation between instrumental success and a certain agreement

---

[19] "Against a similar fatty degeneration of theories pragmatism, likewise, represents an energetic reaction; insisting as it does on the instrumental character of theories—affirming that they are not an *end in themselves*, but *media* and 'organisms' whose efficacy and value is rigorously dependent upon their agility, upon the absence of encumbrances and hindrances to their movements, upon their resem-

with the facts. In this regard, he argues that a common wrong idea is that the law of inertia results just from convention, without corresponding to any real fact. In criticizing this conclusion, he points out that the very possibility of choosing certain conventions to establish time and position depends on the existence of certain facts that make that choice possible and effective.

The instrumental dimension of scientific theories is somehow underlying Vailati's interest in historical research on their development, since he acknowledges that no static account of theories could explain their adaptive characteristics.[20] The above dimension, however, is most obvious if we consider the role that idealizations play in science. The heuristic efficacy of the process of inquiry requires an idealistic and simplifying starting point, which clashes with direct and mere passive observation. The epistemological importance of idealization is stressed by Vailati in the context of discussing the epistemological implications of Plato's argument for the existence of the *eidos*.

> That is, it [the Platonic Theory] manifests itself as an assertion of the heuristic efficacy of that process of inquiry, which, taking as a starting point, idealistic and simplifying concepts and hypotheses, not having any exact counterpart in what is called the reality of things, arrives, precisely by means of deductions from these, and by means of what have been recently called (Mach) "experiments in thought" (*Gedankenexperimente*) at analyzing, comprehending, dominating this reality and discovering in it and under it, independently of recourse to direct experiment, regularity, laws, standards, which direct and passive observation would never have been able to reveal (Vailati, 1906b, this volume, p. 181).

According to Vailati, the role played by the so-called law of causality in the physical sciences basically consists in imagining regularities and uniformities as existing among phenomena, so that it is possible to anticipate the causes or laws that are responsible for a certain effect. Mere empirical generalizations, by contrast, would not suffice to fulfill such a goal. It is interesting to notice how James's and Vailati's views are very closely connected with regard to the role of idealization in science. They both agree that, in order to scientifically explain the

---

blance rather to lions and tigers than to hippopotami and mastodons [...]" (Vailati, 1906a, this volume, p. 170).

[20] "Theories are therein expounded, not as in the ordinary treatment, under their 'static' aspect—as one might express it,—their aspect of repose; but under that of movement and development—not in the conventional attitudes of stuffed animals, with glass eyes; but as organisms, which live, eat, struggle, reproduce: or at least like figures in a cinematograph, with some naturalness of progression and development" (Vailati, 1906a, this volume, p. 166).

phenomena, we need to represent them in a very abstract, idealized and artificial way, so that measurement and mathematical predictions become possible. In James words:

> The order of scientific thought is quite incongruent either with the way in which reality exists or with the way in which it comes before us. Scientific thought goes by selection and emphasis exclusively (1890, Vol. II, Ch. XXVIII, p. 634).

This instrumental aspect of theories, resulting from the heuristic requirement concerning idealization, has been widely discussed in current Philosophy of Science, becoming a classical subject within this field. Indeed, authors like Nancy Cartwright or Arthur Fine have recently stressed, respectively, the idealization process required by the mathematical treatment of empirical phenomena, and the crucial role that theoretical fictions play in the scientific inquiry.

Nevertheless, in contrast to the above contribution, Vailati has also kept some idealistic assumptions about science that would be difficult to maintain today. For example, science must be regarded as not influenced by feelings or particular interests. As we saw earlier, Vailati opposes James' view that passionate interests are necessary conditions of religion as much as of science. Contrary to this, Vailati argues that science must result from a dispassionate search for truth. A second assumption states that science must be considered as continuous and cumulative.[21] Notwithstanding historical changes, theories should continue to express substantially the same facts and to serve the same ends. The diachronic characterization of theories, in presenting them in their dynamic aspect, should make evident that they develop in a consistent, lineal, cumulative way. The apparent incompatibility between different stages in a theory's development are due to the introduction of new methods or notation for processes formerly treated with different procedures and referred to by other names. It is easy to realize how the current, widely shared interpretation of scientific change, which has been greatly influenced by the Kuhnian vindication of a discontinuous development of science, opposes Vailati's approach here. For T. S. Kuhn had emphasized, precisely, how revolutionary theory changes often involved attaching incompatible meanings to the same words such as the term 'mass' in Newtonian and relativistic mechanics.

---

[21] "The logicians as well as the pragmatists have thus contributed to destroy a number of prejudices attributed to supposed incompatibilities between the theories now current and the views of the great scientists or thinkers of antiquity" (Vailati, 1906a, this volume, p. 165).

Cognition understood as a fallible, goal-oriented activity

As for Vailati's fallibilist conception of knowledge, his main point is
that propositions cannot be both irrefutable and instructive. The over-
sight of this incompatibility between analytic and synthetic statements
would have resulted in numerous paralogisms, where the certainty of
an analytical statement would be mistakenly transferred to a synthetic
one. Meaningfulness or cognitive value is conceived as incompatible
with absolute certainty, self-evidence and universality. Many equivocal
argumentations have derived from the fact that sentences that are used
as synthetic truths in ordinary applications are also used as analytic
truths in some other applications, keeping in the first case the character
of certainty that is only ascribable to the second.[22] Put in Vailati's own
words:

> Such a fact is the source of a number of equivocal and illusory argu-
> mentations, among which we must highlight, first of all, those based
> on the apparent character of certainty and evidence that is conferred
> to this kind of assertions, only because they can be interpreted, at
> the same time or in rapid succession, as belonging to one or the other
> of the aforementioned kinds. Therefore, there are propositions that,
> while working in their ordinary applications as true assertions, rela-
> tive to facts which can either be produced or not and would induce
> us to declare such propositions as false, can, at the same time, also be
> presented as propositions whose truth cannot be contested, if not by
> someone who doubts the meaning attributed to some of the words in
> the proposition. Thus, they are exempted, whenever necessary, from
> any need of proof or possibility of confutation (Vailati and Calderoni,
> 1909a, this volume, p. 252).

A similar standpoint could be found already in Aristotle's idea that
"the existence cannot be part of the essence of any thing" (τὸ δεῖναι οὐχ
οὐσία οὐδενί), ch. 7 in *Analytica Posteriora*, this volume, p. 253). The
so called "ontological proof" (i.e., Anselm's demonstration of God's existence) would constitute a clear case of nonobservance of the principle
that we cannot say of anything that it exists by definition. Still another example, this borrowed from Bolzano (*Wissenschaftslehre*, 1837):
the sentence expressing the so-called "principle of causality," i.e. that
"every effect must have a cause," is often regarded as an irrefutable
synthetic statement on the wrong basis that we cannot conceive an

---

[22] "The most frequent form in which these types of paralogisms are seen consists of
saying that such an object has such a property because it is its '*essential*' property
(or inherent to its '*nature*'), because without such a property the object in question
would no longer be what it is—or, in other words, what the thing should be if it
could be given the name we had begun using for it" (Vailati and Calderoni, 1909a,
this volume, p. 252).

effect without a cause. But if we are making a synthetic use of that statement, what we mean is that every fact or event has a cause, which is no longer self-evident.

Vailati's fallibilist conception of cognition is also evident in his resort to cognitive (inferential) usefulness as a criterion for the choice of definitions and postulates. He attempts to broaden the Scholastic theory of definition, so that definitions are understood as propositions justified only by virtue of the importance and utility of the consequences which are derivable from them.

> These [postulates and definitions] appear in their true quality as propositions which possess the function of determining, in view of given ends or application, the various fields of research; that is, as propositions whose sole justification consists in the importance and utility of the *consequences* which it may be possible to deduce therefrom (Vailati, 1906a, this volume, p. 168).

This approach entails an anti-foundationalist and pluralistic conception of both definitions and postulates. According to Vailati's view, there is no ultimate, categorical distinction between postulates and other propositions within the same field. The choice of postulates is not determined by some postulates being more evident than others, but depends on the pre-established end, together with the examination of the relations between postulates and dependent propositions.[23] Requirements like those concerning the minimum number of postulates accepted or the exact determination of their domain of validity or applicability are also connected to the pragmatic understanding of postulates. To illustrate this point, Vailati uses the following example (borrowed from Maxwell, and cited by Roiti (1887)): the proposition "the area of a triangle is given by one half the product of the base by the altitude" would not be true if one took, as unit of measure of areas, the square with base and altitude as unit length, instead of the square having such unit as side.

---

[23] "Instead of conceiving of the difference between postulates and the other propositions which are demonstrated by means of them as consisting in the possession on the part of the former of some special character which renders them *per se* more acceptable, more evident, less disputable, and so on; the mathematical logicians regard postulates as propositions *on a par with all the others*. The choice of such 'postulates' may differ according to the end in view, and must, in any case, depend upon an examination of the relations of dependence or connection which may be established between these 'postulates' and the remaining propositions of a given theory, and upon a comparison with the form into which the treatment as a whole would develop under conditions of varying choices" (Vailati, 1906a, this volume, p. 164).

This fallibilist understanding of knowledge is evident also in Vailati's skepticism about irrefutable assertions concerning perceptions or feelings, as we have already discussed in the subsection "Application of Vailati's criterion to different domains of existence." He argues that typical judgments, like those about illusory sensations or feelings, show that these assertions actually imply predictions that must be taken into account to validate them. The following quotation expresses this idea:

> It is in this same sense that we talk about "false pleasures," "wrong preferences," even though pleasures and our preferences are immediate irrefutable things. What we intend when using these expressions is simply that the individual appreciation would be different, if we were aware of some overlooked consequence, or if we were reminded of some momentarily forgotten facts (Vailati and Calderoni, 1909b, this volume, p. 245).

Mental states and mental capacities: Vailati *versus* James

Pragmatic aspects in Vailati's conception of the mind

Vailati's conception of the mind has some unequivocal pragmatic aspects, although they are combined with some more traditional, Brentanian ones. Among the pragmatic aspects, we can mention the idea that to entertain a belief is to have a certain kind of expectation. This is closely connected with the common characterization of beliefs put forward by traditional pragmatists, who regarded them as habits determining our actions. Vailati complemented this account by carefully specifying the kind of habit that shapes our actions, namely, a habit of expectation.

> To entertain a certain belief instead of another means, for the pragmatist, to have a certain kind of expectation, different from the expectations he would have if he had a different belief (Vailati and Calderoni, 1909b, this volume, p. 237).[24]

Borrowing an example from Berkeley's *Theory of Vision*, 1732, Vailati points out that judgments about distances, shapes and dimensions of objects do not depend on actual perceptions but on expectations that certain experiences (visual perceptions, in this case) would occur, given specific conditions, such as changes of location of the observer with respect to the object.

---

[24]Later in the same paper he writes: "In fact, alongside our beliefs regarding the future, we have an equally significant number of other beliefs that, apparently, only regard facts from the present or the past. Nevertheless, if we look closer at such beliefs we can see that a reference to the future is always an essential part of their meaning" (Vailati and Calderoni, 1909b, this volume, p. 237).

As we have discussed in the subsection "Application of Vailati's criterion to different domains of existence," Vailati extends his analysis of existence in terms of conditional expectations to mental dispositions, claiming that judgments on existence of mental dispositions, i.e., things like attitudes, concepts, memories, etc., also result from a belief in the connection between some experiences and some actions. He illustrates this point by drawing attention to the fact that we assert the existence of qualities of character, like being irritable, not because the person is angry at some point, but because he would get angry given certain conditions and stimuli that would not make other people angry.

> The "internal" world, no less than the "external" one, does not consist only of what is "in act," in a given moment, but it also consists of what is "in potency." Pikler's sentence, "the 'would-be' of presentation is the 'is' of objective existence," can be applied to one as well as the other (Vailati and Calderoni, 1909b, this volume, p. 246).

Like the other traditional pragmatists, Vailati emphasizes the idea that feelings or sensations involve not only mental states, but also dispositions to act in certain ways. It is this behavioral aspect included in the pragmatic conception of feelings and sensations that makes possible to talk meaningfully about fake feelings or illusory sensations.[25] Such behavioral aspects would thus guarantee the possibility of developing objective beliefs about sensations and feelings. We have stressed before how this view closely resembles Wittgenstein's conception of sensations in his *Philosophical Investigations*.

Some ignored lessons from James' *The Principles of Psychology*

Let us turn now to Vailati's most outdated theses about the mind. They basically result from his endorsement of a Brentanian conception of mental states. In "On the Logical Import of the Classification of Mental Facts Proposed by Franz Brentano" (1901), Vailati adopts Brentano's hierarchical tripartition of conscious states: representations (sensations, remembered sensations, ideas...), expectations (beliefs, convictions, hopes), and volitions (desires, preferences). Three kinds of propositions correspond respectively to the three kinds of mental states: analytic propositions, assertions, and propositions expressing evaluations or judgments of value. Vailati argues for a drastic separa-

---

[25] "In cases like these we talk about fake compassion or fake enthusiasm; we say that a person thinks they love, but do not, showing that when we assert that someone is enthusiastic or in love, we do not intend to assert the presence, in this person, of a state of mind, but also the presence of plans of 'actions' or dispositions to act in specific ways" (Vailati and Calderoni, 1909b, this volume, p. 246).

tion between the three mental states, claiming that no judgment of one kind can be used to support a judgment of any of the other kinds. In other words, inferences would only be valid within the same kind of propositions. Accordingly, he rejects naturalist ethics, like utilitarianism. And, in general, as he did in other papers, he criticizes the ambiguity of linguistic expressions with respect to the kind of propositions that they are expressing, as a source of philosophical and scientific misunderstanding. There are at least two points that seem questionable. First, whether, after Quine, analytic and synthetic propositions can be so drastically separated, something which would even conflict with some of the views later adopted by Vailati. Second, whether normative judgments should not be influenced by factual or descriptive judgments—the very possibility of normative naturalism, so akin to pragmatic epistemology, would require this. A further problem is that, in Vailati's latter works, he does not acknowledge any relevant role to be played by representationsin so far as they are not part of a certain class of expectations.

"The Distinction Between Knowledge and Will" (1905b) connects quite closely with the paper about Brentano's classification of mental states, to which Vailati makes reference in this later article. Again, he insists that factual assertions should be kept completely apart from normative or value judgments. The first would always imply some predictions on what would happen if some circumstances were verified, the second, by contrast, would imply our desire that such circumstances were verified, as well as our disposition to produce or prevent them. The principle of non-contradiction would apply only to assertions, not to value judgments. Here also Vailati warns us against possible confusions, due to the fact that propositions of one kind would assume the appearance of those of the other kind (taking the indicative form instead of the imperative one). The confusion would make that differences in taste and aspirations be misunderstood as differences in belief (the inverse case is not mentioned in the paper, although it is quite common too). Consequently, scientists, according to Vailati, should not claim any special authority in deciding the value of scientific results, nor in judging the use that should be made of them. As an example of normative aspects "hidden" under factual ones, he mentions the ordinary concept of cause, which amounts to the concept of constant antecedent of a fact. In analyzing how the constant antecedent is usually recognized, Vailati draws our attention to the fact that our criterion to choose a small group of antecedent events, among all the existing ones, is based on the belief that antecedents within such group are more modifiable or more easily influenced by us. We, therefore, would usually take into account antecedents that suggest responsabilities. It is interesting to notice that here Vailati begins by accepting that will and desires can affect beliefs, an acceptance that is not maintained in other papers, where he points out that they may affect thought but not beliefs, considering the latter at least questionable. Moreover, as we pointed out in the subsection "Rejection of the Jamesian theses about the will's influence on belief," one of his main criticisms against James' pragmatic approach lies in the assumption that the will can highly influence thought, but not so beliefs.

Another problem concerning the above thesis regards the fact that it implies an unjustified separation between thought and belief. While such separation is analytically possible, it is not supported by a phenomenological description of our thoughts, which is the one at issue in Vailati's argument. The rigid, Brentanian classification of mental facts endorsed by Vailati, sharply contrasts with William James' account of mental phenomena from *The Principles of Psychology*, especially Ch. IX on the stream of thought.

We do note that, contrary to James, Vailati explicitly avoids any analysis of experience in psychological terms, rather, he attempts a logical analysis of empirical meaning, as well as of the conditions to assert objective existence. Therefore, their main new ideas are developed from very different perspectives, and could even be regarded as complementary in some respects. Yet, as we have seen, Vailati does explore the nature of the mind in some of his works, resorting to Brentano's approach, and apparently ignoring James' persuasive account.

Proceeding to the main points of interest, it seems that James' criticism against the empiricist account of experience turns out to be much more elaborate than Vailati's. James clearly rejects the idea that experience can be decomposed into simple sensations, which stand for real qualities in the outer world. Although both philosophers would agree that the immediate data of experience are always complex, relational, and inferential, only James emphasizes the idea that they form a unity.[26] When Vailati states that immediate sensations are not reliable, James might simply deny their existence. Furthermore, James did not restrict his criticisms to the empiricist approach but extended them also to the Kantian notion of experience, which Vailati, on the other hand, left quite unexplored. According to James, both empiricists and apriorists share a wrong initial hypothesis, namely, that there

---

[26] "The next point to make clear is that, however complex the object may be, the thought of it is one undivided state of consciousness," (James, 1890, Vol. I, Ch. IX, p. 277). Earlier in the same work James says: "Knowledge about a thing is knowledge of its relations," ibid., p. 260.

are basic units of experience that are combined in our mind. It is not surprising that, in criticizing the thesis of the modularity of the mind put forward by Jerry Fodor, Hilary Putnam stresses the current validity of James' account of mental functions (Putnam, 1992, chap. 3, note 21). The latter would have prevented us repeatedly against the mistake (made by Fodor) consisting in identifying a mental function with the brain mechanism that is necessary for that function. Putnam insists on James' idea that the same brain "marks" can perform many different functions.

We agree with Putnam's remark, but with a qualification we consider fundamental. As in a modern multicore personal computer, the brain as a more subtle system, has a many-many relation between global functions and local computations by various collections of synchronized neurons, a phenomenon we would expect in any rich computational setup. So there is no need to appeal to mental functions to make the point. (We quote a related remark by James, in footnote 28.)

Another interesting aspect from James' philosophy, which is not discussed by Vailati, is the denial that the Lamarckian notion of evolution can account for the structure of human mind. The evolutionary aspects of the mind, which Peirce had already emphasized in developing the epistemological side of pragmatism, were somehow neglected in Vailati's approach. James, on the contrary, developed an advanced study of how the structure of human mind resulted from evolution. In the 150th anniversary of the *On the Origin of Species* (1859) and the 200th anniversary of Darwin's birth (1809), it is interesting to notice James' decided resort to the Darwinian notion of evolution. He explains mental structure (whose existence he does acknowledge) on that basis, mainly as the result of genetic, accidental variations becoming naturally selected. Even scientific conjectures would be, in the first place, "a 'spontaneous variation' in some one's brain." On the other hand, the notion of accidental or spontaneous variation has no place in Vailati's analysis of experience. In considering the zoological distinction between two modes of origin of brain structure—one by way of adaptation, the other by way of accidental variation—James clearly commits to the second as the one which promotes a more stable, hereditary mental structure:

> In zoological evolution we have two modes in which an animal race may grow to be a better match for its environment. First, the so-called way of 'adaptation,' in which the environment may itself modify its inhabitant by exercising, hardening, and habituating him to certain sequences, and these habits may, it is often maintained, become hereditary. The second, the way of 'accidental variation,' as Mr. Darwin

termed it, in which certain young are born with peculiarities that help them and their progeny to survive. That variation of this sort tend to become hereditary, no one doubts (James, 1890, Vol. II, Ch. XXVIII, p. 627).[27]

Maybe due to this commitment, the question of whether or to what extent the mind has representational capacities is better clarified within the approach offered by James. According to him, the brain structure obtained from adaptation corresponds to the kind of structure the outer world impresses on us, that resulting from accidental variation, on the other hand, does not mirror the relations in the natural environment. To put it in James' terminology: each kind of origin of mental structure involves "wholly disparate natural cycles of causation" (1890, Vol. II, Ch. XXVIII, p. 628). The role of accidental variations in generating inward relations among our objects of thought, rather than reproductions of the outer order, would equate scientific beliefs with ethical and aesthetic ones, the main important difference between them being the requirement that scientific beliefs be congruent with the time-space relations of the outer world.

There is, however, a substantial affinity between James and Vailati concerning their interest in characterizing objective existence, and vindicating the distinction between appearance and reality by appealing to the experiential conditions that would support our belief that some object, quality or relation has objective existence. Both stress the importance of certain experiences being repeatable, as well as intersubjectively acknowledged.[28] Although, in this respect, we think that Vailati is the one introducing some novel and clarifying ideas, in particular, his view that any assertion of objective existence requires successful manipulation of phenomena, that is, the recurrent satisfaction of certain conditional expectations determined by the stable effects of our actions. By contrast, the notion of expectation is not so central in James' account of objective existence, whose determination would be instead more dependent on the role of selective attention and the stability of outer relations: "Apart from purpose, of course, no realities ever are absolutely and exactly the same" (1890, Vol. II, Ch. XXVIII,

---

[27]The argument against the hereditary nature of adaptive, non-accidental variations is more convincingly developed in the section of "The Origin of Instincts," (1890, Vol. II, Ch. XXVIII, pp. 679–688).

[28]"[...] there is no proof that the same bodily sensation is ever got by us twice. What is got twice is the same object," (James, 1890, Vol. I, Ch. IX, p. 232). Further in this work, we find the following: "For and identical sensation to recur it would have to occur the second time in an unmodified brain. But as this, strictly speaking, is a physiological impossibility, so is an unmodified feeling an impossibility," (ibid., pp. 233–234). "Knowledge about a thing is knowledge of it relations," (ibid., p. 260).

p. 650, n. 15).

The philosophical proximity between James and Vailati becomes manifest also in their discussion of other subjects, like those of *a priori* knowledge, nonsense or meaningless expressions, naturalistic metaphysics, or the role of idealization in science. With regard to *a priori* knowledge, both deny that it can provide a foundation for empirical knowledge, and insist that analytical, necessary, *a priori* truths do not carry any information about the world, but just about our language (Vailati) or mental categories (James). Interestingly enough, only the latter emphasizes the invariable character of our elementary mental categories for long evolutionary periods, consequently, agreeing with the apriorists in the description of our current mental categories, although disagreeing with them as to the origin of those categories, which is natural, according to James. Those fixed mental categories are responsible for the necessary character of analytic truths, which seems stronger than that mere necessity derived from the structure of language. Because of such categories being invariable in a certain sense, and implying certain necessary relations, if they happen to harmonize with the real classes of objects and relations in the world, then any inferred analytic truth would also be empirically true. Yet, James claims that this harmony is not only difficult to ascertain, but even very frequently discarded by experience.

Closing remarks

Vailati's legacy to pragmatism includes, among other contributions, the development of a criterion of empirical meaningfulness, an analysis of the experience of objective existence, a decided acknowledgment of semantics' subordination to pragmatics, as well as a careful examination of the role that inferential usefulness plays both in language, by determining meaning, and in science by determining the choice of postulates. The idea that the empirical meaningfulness of an assertion depends on the predictive elements it involves has been adopted also by neopositivists, but the distinction between proper and conditional expectations can only be found in Vailati's work, and it is that distinction which reveals deliberate actions as the grounds for objectivity. Without manipulations and studied interactions with the environment, the predictions that we could formulate would not suffice to develop beliefs about objective, permanent existence. Vailati also deserves credit for showing that this is so in every domain of existence, i.e. in the domain of physical objects and properties as much as in the domain of psychological dispositions. On the other hand, the double role, semantic and epistemic, that he ascribes to the inferential usefulness of assertions, not only connects with recent developments in the philosophy of language, but also makes it possible to reconcile the traditional features of a pragmatic epistemology: anti-foundationalism, fallibilism, anti-skepticism, and naturalism.[29]

With his own original viewpoint, Vailati managed to refine and further develop some of the main theses from Peirce. In doing so he provided important applications, such as the emphasis on predictions, to clarify the meaning of different controversial assertions coming from both philosophical and scientific fields. We can say that he not only refined pragmatic methods, but also tried to make sure they worked well.

References

Bolzano, Bernard. 1837. *Wissenschaftslehre.* Sulzbach: Seidel. Repr. in E. Winter, J. Berg, F. Kambartel, et al. (eds.) *Bernard Bolzano. Gesamtausgabe.* Reihe 1, Schriften. Band 11–13, 1985–1992.

Brandom, Robert. 1994. *Making It Explicit. Reasoning, Representing, and Discursive Commitment.* Cambridge, MA: Harvard University Press, 2000.

Carnap, Rudolf. 1932. Überwindung der Metaphysik durch logische Analyse der Sprache. *Erkenntnis* 2. Engl. transl. *The Elimination of Metaphysics Through Logical Analysis of Language.* In A. J. Ayer (ed.) *Logical Positivism.* New York: Free Press, 1959, pages 60-81.

Carnap, Rudolf. 1950. Empiricism, semantics, and ontology. *Revue Internationale de Philosophie* 4:20–40.

Carnap, Rudolf. 1952. Meaning postulates. *Philosophical Studies* 3:65–73. Reprinted in Carnap (1956), pp. 222-229.

Carnap, Rudolf. 1956. *Meaning and Necessity: A Study in Semantics and Modal Logic.* Chicago: University of Chicago Press, 2nd edn.

Evans, Valmai Burwood. 1930. The Pragmatism of Giovanni Vailati. *International Journal of Ethics* 40(3):416–424.

Haack, Susan. 2006. Introduction. In S. Haack, ed., *Pragmatism, Old and New. Selected Writings*, pages 15–67. New York: Prometheus Books.

Hookway, Christopher. 2008. Pragmatism. In E. N. Zalta, ed., *The Stanford Encyclopedia of Philosophy (Summer 2008 Edition).* URL = http://plato.stanford.edu/entries/pragmatism/.

James, William. 1890. *The Principles of Psychology.* New York: Henry Holt. (Reprinted Bristol: Thoemmes Press, 1999).

James, William. 1896. The will to believe. In *The will to believe, and other essays in popular philosophy.* New York: Longmans, Green, and Co., 1897.

---

[29]These features are the ones usually mentioned in characterizing the epistemological dimension of traditional pragmatism. Cf. Haack (2006, pp. 18–25), and Wiener (1973-74, pp. 551–6).

Peirce, C. S. 1902-1907. Pragmatism and pragmaticism. In S. Haack, ed., *Pragmatism, Old and New. Selected Writings*, pages 151–167. New York: Prometheus Books, 2006.

Pikler, J. 1890. *The Psychology of the Belief in Objective Existence*. London: Williams and Norgate.

Putnam, Hilary. 1992. *Pragmatism. An Open Question*. Oxford: Blackwell, 1995.

Quine, Willard van Orman. 1951. Two dogmas of empiricism. *Philosophical Review* 60(1):20–43.

Quine, Willard van Orman. 1969. Epistemology naturalized. In *Ontological Relativity and other Essays*, pages 69–90. New York: Columbia University Press.

Roiti, Antonio. 1887. *Elementi di fisica*. Firenze: Le Monnier, 1894. 2 voll.

Vailati, Giovanni. 1901. Sulla portata logica della classificazione dei fatti mentali proposta dal prof. Franz Brentano (Comunicazione presentata al III Congresso Internazionale di psicologia di Parigi, agosto 1900). *Rivista Filosofica* II(1). Repr. in Vailati (1911), pages 336-340. Engl. transl. "On the logical import of the classification of mental facts proposed by Franz Brentano," this volume chap. 5.

Vailati, Giovanni. 1905a. La caccia alle antitesi. *Leonardo* 3:53–57. Engl. trans. The Attack on Distinctions, *Journal of Philosophy, Psychology and Scientific Methods*, 4(25), December 5, 1907. Repr. this volume, chap. 14.

Vailati, Giovanni. 1905b. La distinzione tra conoscere e volere. *Leonardo* III. Repr. in Vailati (1911), pages 626-629. Engl. transl. "The Distinction Between Knowledge and Will," this volume, chap. 11.

Vailati, Giovanni. 1906a. Il Pragmatismo e la Logica Matematica. *Leonardo* 4(1):16–25. Repr. in Vailati (1911), pages 689-694. Engl. transl. by H. D. Austin "Pragmatism and mathematical logic," *Monist* 16:481–491, 1906. Repr. this volume, chap. 12.

Vailati, Giovanni. 1906b. A study of Platonic terminology. *Mind* 15(60):473–485. Repr. this volume, chap. 13.

Vailati, Giovanni. 1907. Un manuale per i bugiardi: "G. Prezzolini. L'arte di persuadere." Lumachi, Firenze 1907. *Rivista di Psicologia applicata alla Pedagogia ed alla Psicopatologia* 3(2). Repr. in Vailati (1911), pages 770-76.

Vailati, Giovanni. 1908. Il linguaggio come ostacolo alla eliminazione di contrasti illusori. *Rinnovamento* 2(5-6). Repr. in Vailati (1911), pages 895-99. Engl. transl. "Language as an obstacle to the elimination of illusory contrasts," this volume, chap. 17.

Vailati, Giovanni and Mario Calderoni. 1909a. Il Pragmatismo e i vari modi di non dir niente. *Rivista di Psicologia applicata* 5(9). Repr. in Vailati (1911), pages 933-41. Engl. transl. "Pragmatism and the various ways of saying nothing," this volume, chap. 19.

Vailati, Giovanni and Mario Calderoni. 1909b. Le origini e l'idea fondamentale del Pragmatismo. *Rivista di Psicologia applicata* 5(1). Repr. in Vailati (1911), pages 920-32. Engl. transl. "The origins and fundamental idea of pragmatism," this volume, chap. 18.

Wiener, Philip P. 1973-74. Pragmatism. In P. P. Wiener, ed., *The Dictionary of the History of Ideas: Studies of Selected Pivotal Ideas*, vol. 3, pages 551–570. Charles Scribner's Sons.

Wittgenstein, L. 1953. *Philosophical Investigations*. Oxford: Blackwell. Engl. transl. by G. E. M. Anscombe.

Part II

Giovanni Vailati. Selected Essays

1

On the importance of research regarding the History of Science[†]

Nowadays we are inclined to attribute much more importance to historical research on the progress of human knowledge than we used to in the past. The tendency to consider the history of science as a mere collection of singular and humorous anecdotes, with no other purpose than that of satisfying the natural curiosity around everything related to life events or the personal qualities of the great scientists of the past, has by no means completely disappeared. Sometimes arguments are still heard in defense of this tendency, that differ only in form from the famous witty remark of the dear illustrious Cartesian philosopher Malebranche. Malebranche wanted to prove that a real scientist should not give any importance to the acquisition of historical knowledge by mentioning the fact that, according to the Sacred Scriptures before tasting the Forbidden Fruit, Adam was in perfect possession of all scientific knowledge, a knowledge that his descendants would have to regain gradually; nevertheless he had no historical knowledge, because such a subject did not yet exist.[1]

[†]First published as *Sull'importanza delle ricerche relative alla storia delle scienze*, Turin, Roux e Frassati, 1897 (Vailati, 1897). Inaugural lecture to a course on the History of Mechanics, read on December 4th 1896 at the University of Turin. Repr. in Vailati (1911), pages 64-78.

[1]Amongst the philosophical schools of Ancient Greece, the one that assumed this same attitude towards historical studies in the most characteristic way was the Epicurean school. Diogenes Laertius narrates that, in the 300 volumes (κύλινδροι) of Epicurus' works, not a single quotation or hint to opinions other than those of the author could be found: "in the whole of them there is not one citation from other sources, but they are filled wholly with the sentiments of Epicurus himself" (*De vitis*

Logic and Pragmatism. Selected Essays by Giovanni Vailati.
C. Arrighi, P. Cantù, M. De Zan, and P. Suppes.
Copyright © 2009, CSLI Publications.

However, this kind of disdain for historical research of the development of human knowledge is ever less in harmony with our ways of thinking about the relationship between the science of the past and the science of the present. I think one would not be too far from showing the real cause of such disdain and its stubborn persistence if one recognized in such disdain the product of mental habits handed down by tradition, which go back to the time when the great initiators of modern scientific methods had the right to resort, almost for legitimate defense, to this extreme measure in their struggles against the abuse of authority in matters of science and experience.

In this regard, I shall mention a typical passage from the *Dialogue Concerning the Two Chief World Systems*. When Simplicio asks which guide is to be followed if they are to abandon Aristotle, Galileo bids Salviati give this answer:[2]

> We need guides in forests and in unknown lands, but on plains and in open places only the blind need guides. It is better for such people to stay at home, but anyone with eyes in his head and his wits about him could serve as a guide for them. In saying this, I do not mean that a person should not listen to Aristotle; indeed, I applaud the reading and careful study of his works, and I reproach only those who give themselves up as slaves to him in such a way as to subscribe blindly to everything he says and take it as an inviolable decree without looking for any other reasons. This abuse carries with it another profound disorder, that other people do not try harder to comprehend the strength of his demonstrations. And what is more revolting in a public dispute, when someone is dealing with demonstrable conclusions, than to hear him interrupted by a text (often written to some quite different purpose) thrown into his teeth by an opponent? If, indeed, you wish to continue in this method of studying, then put aside the name of philosophers and call yourselves historians, or memory experts; for it is not proper that those who never philosophize should usurp the honorable title of philosopher. But we had better get back to shore, lest we enter into a boundless ocean and not get out of it all day. So put forward the arguments and demonstrations, Simplicio—either yours or Aristotle's—but not just texts and bare authorities, because our discourses must relate to the sensible world and not to one [of] paper.[3]

---

philosophorum, B. X, Ch. I, XVII). [In Greek in the original. English translation by C. D. Yonge from Yonge 1853, p. 433.]

[2] At the beginning of *Second Day*. Here Salviati also says: *It is the followers of Aristotle who have crowned him with authority, not he who has usurped or appropriated it to himself.* [English translation by Stillman Drake from Galilei 1632, p. 112.]

[3] [English translation by Stillman Drake from Galilei 1632, pp. 112–13.]

From another perspective this *world of paper* of which Galileo speaks with such contempt, the world of ideas and human imagination, is neither less real, nor less sensible or less deserving of being studied and diligently observed than that other world, which he investigated by dedicating, with so much success, the activity of his mind. Opinions, either true or false, are nevertheless *facts*, and for this reason they deserve and demand to be taken as the object of inquiry, verification, comparison, interpretation, and explanation, in exactly the same way as any other order of facts, and for the same purpose—the purpose, that is, of discerning, as far as we can, amongst their variety, their complexity, their transformations, their constant elements, the uniformities and the laws, that regulate their succession. An erroneous assertion, an inconclusive argument from a scientist of the past can be worthy of consideration as much as a discovery or an ingenious intuition, if they are equally useful in shedding light on the causes that have accelerated or delayed the progress of human knowledge, or in revealing how our intellectual faculties operate. Every error shows us an obstacle to avoid, while not every discovery shows us a path to follow.

Nobody can argue against Galileo's observation when he says that

> there are heated quarrels and arguments on the interpretation of someone's will because the testator is dead, otherwise, if he were alive, it would be a mistake to rely on others instead of himself to determine the meaning of what he had written. In the same way, it is simple minded to look for the meanings of questions of nature among the papers of this or that philosopher rather than in nature's work, which is still alive and always stands working before our eyes, truthful and immutable in all its parts.[4]

But on the other hand it is no less true to say that it is unreasonable to refuse to examine and study the opinions of the scientists of past times just because they used to be revered with superstition as something of superior value to any experience or demonstration; as if an astronomer were to refuse to observe the path of the stars or a naturalist were to refuse to study the habits of birds merely because the Babylonian priests or the Etruscan augurs claimed to be able to predict, without fail, the future of human events by observing the position of the stars or the mood of chickens.

If I were to express briefly that which, in my opinion, characterizes the spirit which continues to give shape to historical investigations about the development of knowledge, I would say that the history of science tends to become a science in itself. What is happening to this

---

[4][Galilei 1855, p. 338.]

discipline also happened to the history of languages at the beginning of the century, when, from mere material for amusing erudition and not always serious etymological lucubrations, it rapidly acquired the dignity of an autonomous scientific discipline, leading the way to modern comparative philology. Indeed, nowadays we can see a proper comparative history of various sciences slowly taking shape. A history whose objective is the analysis and consideration, from a general point of view, of the various scientific methodologies, in order to determine what part each of them has played in the growth of the various branches of knowledge. Only in this way will it be possible, on the one hand, to explain the analogies and similarities which present themselves in successive stages of development of various sciences,[5] and on the other, to understand why some methodologies or procedures, which have been useful and proficient when applied to a certain field of research, show themselves to be ineffective and sterile when applied to another.

The history of scientific theories about a given subject is not to be conceived as a history of a series of attempts, all of which being unsuccessful but the last. It is not to be compared, as it has been with more humor than insight, to the series of actions performed by someone who wants to open a door holding a bunch of keys but not knowing which is the right one.

Instead, history presents us with a series of successes, each of which has overtaken and eclipsed the one before it, just as the one before that had done.[6] The order of historical succession of these successes is not casual or arbitrary, nor is it connected to causes which are not related to the nature and predispositions of human intelligence or which lead to different development structures depending on the branch of science in question.

What we have is always, or almost always, a process of subsequent approximations, like a series of explorations of an unknown land, where every exploration corrects or refines the results of previous explorations

---

[5]Comte (*Cours de philosophie positive*, 1835) deserves the merit of having, for the first time, pointed out these analogies and similarities and having based on them a *natural* classification of sciences. His famous law of the three stages (*theological, metaphysical, positive*) represents an attempt—even if imperfect and rudimentary, to state in a definitive form the regularities in the development of the various branches of human knowledge. Both Comte and Spencer, who followed his steps on this subject, were hindered by the lack of precise and extensive knowledge about the laws of development of languages.
Comparative philology and anthropology are now continuously gathering precious material that need just to be put in order and to be utilized.

[6]I have read recently some acute observations on this subject in the second volume, recently published, of *Cours d'Economie politique* by professor Vilfredo Pareto, page 280 (Lausanne, Rouge, 1896).

and makes it easier, for those in the future, to achieve the common goal. If we consider the competence needed to judge the importance that various procedures for research and testing or various competing trains of thought on a certain field of research are going to acquire or lose at a given time, a scholar, who does not care about anything other than the current state of the science he is studying, will find himself in the same position as a geometer who should determine the path of a curve from only one point or one linear element. He will be incapable of providing any concrete justification for his conjectures on the nature and character of the future path of his science and he has no solid basis on which to sustain reliable predictions on the matter.[7]

Very close to this same line of reasoning there is also another set of considerations which, in the same direction, has lately further modified our judgment on the importance of the historical research under discussion. Modern evolutionary theories, which these days are also deeply influencing the branches of scientific activity that are the most distant from those which gave origin to the evolutionary theories themselves, are about to give a new, and I would even say, more concrete meaning, to the famous aphorism by Leibniz: *the present is child of the past but is also parent to the future*. We are ever closer to recognizing how literally true the sublime metaphor by Pascal is, which says that the succession of human generations over the centuries must be considered as the life of a single man "who lives forever and learns continuosly".[8] We can also express the same idea in the more precise fashion chosen by Francis Bacon: "*Antiquitas saeculi juventus mundi* [The age of antiquity is the youth of the world]. These times are the ancient times, when the world is ancient, and not those which we account ancient *ordine retrogrado*, by a computation backward from ourselves."[9] It is not enough for us to deduce from this premise, as Pascal did, that those we call the ancients are instead the *young* in all things and they constitute what can be considered the infancy of mankind, while the antiquity that we mistakenly revere in them is more appropriately attributed to us. It

---

[7]It is appropriate here to quote the eloquent words used by professor [Ernest] Lavisse [1842-1922] of University of Paris during his speech in occasion of the opening of the academic year, when he encouraged the students not to neglect to study the history of science: "If you ignore this history you will not acquire the idea of the movement of the science nor the feeling of progress, which is the mainspring of intellectual life and embellishes it with unlimited hope. To put a science precisely in its place means to get into the philosophical stage necessary to study it and to arise above the dreadful condition of passive docility." [In French in the original]

[8][In French in the original.] *Fragment d'un traité du vide* (Blaise Pascal, *Oeuvres*, published by L. Brunschwigg and P. Boutroux, Paris, 1908, Tome II, p. 139).

[9][In Latin in the original. Quote in English from Bacon 1605, p. 38.]

is not enough for us to conclude with Galileo that "given that for an individual his last judgments seem to be the most cautious and that with age his wisdom also increases, in the same way for all mankind it seems reasonable that his last opinions are closer to truth."[10] Supported by important results recently achieved by the biological sciences, we are able to analyze further that which is presented in these observations as a simple and plausible analogy. We can recognize the action of a fundamental law that is one of the most glorious achievements of contemporary science, the law formulated by Darwin stating that the various phases corresponding to the development of the species of an individual being are represented on a smaller scale and as a kind of summary in the organic development of the individual.

Every day we see evermore substantial contributions which confirm the ingenious intuition of the eminent English scientist, contributions such as the recent studies on child psychology—let me just mention, among the authors of the most recently published, professor Preyer[11] from Wiesbaden (*Die Seele des Kindes*), Sully (*Studies of Childhood*),[12] Baldwin, Perez, Frédéric Queyrat who writes on the development of imagination and the ability to abstract in children—or the results produced by comparative research on the mental attitudes of primitive and savage populations, as a consequence of the impulse given to this field by the fundamental works by Spencer, Lubbock and Tylor.

The reason why succeeding generations are able, to a certain extent, to start where past generations finished does not lie only in the advantage of having the availability of experiences accumulated during the past generations, passed on and rapidly reassimilated by means of imitation, education, tradition or books.

The mind of a modern man does not differ from the mind of a man of the past, with equivalent intellectual skills, just for the larger quantity or the better quality of the range of pieces of knowledge with which it is furnished.

The differences which are much more important and characteristic are the differences related to the acquisition and fixation of new men-

---

[10][Galilei 1855, p. 329.]

[11]A quote from the interesting communication regarding this project presented by professor Preyer at the International Congress of Psychology held in Munich last August [1896]: "As far as regards the formation of organisms, we no longer doubt that the development of an individual is an abbreviated repetition of the development of the species. As far as regards the psyche, according to my observations of children and young animals, the same thing is no less certain. The intellectual development of all mankind is found abbreviated in a child." [In German in the original.]

[12][See Preyer 1895, and Sully 1896.]

tal habits, the respective strengths of the various intellectual faculties, the different orientation of curiosity, admiration or doubt, the different ability to be satisfied by explanations of a certain kind rather than another, or the greater or lesser inclination to approve different kinds of proof or reasoning, and the estimation of their validity; the differences, finally, related to a different idea of evidence, or related to a greater or lesser influence of what physiologists call *inhibitory functions* on the spontaneous impulses of the mind, or related to a different faith in the various criteria of verification or various investigative processes. It is mainly in these kinds of differences and contrasts that we can see the correspondence between the various phases passed through during the development of the intelligence of an individual, and the following stages of development of what can be called collective intelligence, represented by the stage of the various sciences and by the general level of culture at any given age of human progress.

Let us consider someone who analyzes the different character of the questions asked or pondered on, and the answers considered satisfactory by adults or children belonging to the same society, and then let us consider someone who is investigating, for example, why Greek geometers had a strong preference for demonstrations by *reductio ad absurdum*, while modern geometers try very hard to avoid such demonstrations. The former and the latter are both investigating questions of the same line of research, and their solutions require the same method and the same collection of data.

What I have been saying so far seems to me sufficient to provide an explanation and a justification of a tendency that is more and more common in the modern scientific world, and especially in the nations regarded as the most civilized, i.e. the tendency to give more and more importance to the studies related to the history of sciences. Amongst the many signs and the many manifestations typical of such a tendency it will suffice to mention the large and increasing number of courses dedicated to this topic that can be found in the programs of German Universities, which, with their autonomy and flexibility, can very well provide genuine and typical indications on the nature of contemporary ways of thinking.

I found the following information in the official bulletins of Universities in Germany and Austria, showing the courses announced for the current academic year: Berlin University has a course on the History of Chemistry and another on the History of Medicine, Breslau University has also a course on the History of Medicine, then a course on the History of Mathematics and a course on the History of Botany. Königsberg University has a course on the History of Astronomy, and Graz University has a course on the Scientific Literature in Ancient Greece. We find a course on the History of Chemistry also at Wittenberg University and on the History of Medicine there are courses in Tübingen, Bonn, and Wien.[13] In this last University there is a course on the history of a certain branch of physics, i.e. the history of the mechanical theory of heat, consisting in a series of lectures by professor Ernst Mach, who we will soon mention as the author of some valuable work produced on the history of mechanics (*The Science of Mechanics. A Critical and Historical Account of its Development*).[14]

However, the effects of the new ideas that I have just mentioned are not visible only in this tendency of the history of sciences to become the object of study, a tendency that could be seen as one of the many manifestations of the normal process of division of intellectual labor used for the development of modern science. More than this, it is the direct influence of these new ideas on the general tendency of teaching and teaching methodology that I would now like to bring to your attention. Certainly it has not only been in recent times that people have begun to recognize that the main goal and duty of teaching should not be to have the students swallow the largest possible amount of information, and fill their memories with the largest number of notions and pieces of knowledge.[15]

Herbert Spencer was not the first, nor Pestalozzi, Rousseau, Locke or Montaigne, to assert that the main goal of a teacher must be to facilitate a harmonious development of the intellectual faculties, to stimulate and challenge, while at the same time containing and giving direction to the spontaneous impulses of the developing minds and to use at best their instinctive inclinations with the least amount of influence on our part. At this point there is no need, after all that has been said so far, to spend too many words on showing how the new ideas I have mentioned lead to consider the possession of at least a basic knowledge of the main developmental phases of a given science as an indispensable condition, not merely an instrument, for the realization of a teaching system as close as possible to the ideal system just described.

Regarding mathematical studies in particular, I tend to agree with

---

[13] At the University of Turin professor Piero Giacosa has been teaching a class on History of Medicine for some years now.

[14] Professor Mach has published these days another important piece of work of historic nature (*Principles of Heat*) [Mach 1896] that regretfully I did not have time to consult before writing these pages.

[15] "Of what service is it to us to have a bellyful of meat, if it does not digest, if it does not change its form in our bodies, and if it does not nourish and strengthen us?" Montaigne, *Essays*, B. I, ch. 24, "Du pédantisme" [In French in the original. English translation by C. Cotton, Baldwin from Montaigne 1811, vol. I, p. 151.]

those who believe that the best didactic method to explain the various parts of a certain subject is that which presents the material in a way which follows the historical development of said subject very closely.

This is what is now called the *heuristic* method, which is a method of explaining or teaching where the student or the reader ends up learning the notions of a certain branch of a science going through the kind of considerations that guided the scientists who first came up with such notions. This method undoubtedly has advantages if compared to the ordinary method of presentation, a method that disregards any psychological consideration of the difference between teacher and learner regarding mental training and coordinative habits and that tends to immediately present the subject in the fashion that the teacher can see as the most logically connected, the most *up to date*,[16] the fashion, in short, most satisfactory for someone who, like the teacher, already knows the branch of research in question, someone who wants to coordinate and systematize a number of notions that are already familiar. As a scientist, as a thinker or as a writer, a teacher is entitled to aspire to be in the noble rank of *the master of those who know*,[17] but, as a teacher, above all he has the duty of being the master of *those who do not know.*

Nobody who has had occasion to talk in a school, in front of young people, on any subject related to the abstract and theoretical parts of mathematics can have missed the sudden change in the quality of attention and interest of the students at anytime that the presentation, for some reason, leaves the ordinary route of doctrine and deduction to venture into considerations of a historical nature, for example considerations about the kind of problems and difficulties that gave rise to the development of a theory or the introduction of a methodology, about the reasoning behind the adoption of certain concepts or certain conventions, about the different points of view of the people who gave the major contributions to the progress of a scientific treatment of the subject.

It is certainly desirable to make the most of this healthy and typical appetite of young minds, attracted by those parts of the intellectual meals received that they recognize, instinctively, as easy to assimilate and more appropriate to the normal development of their faculties. To use this appetite in a clever way means to make the teaching more profitable and, at the same time, more pleasurable, effective, and invit-

---

[16][In English in the original.]

[17]["vidi'l maestro di color che sanno," Dante, *The Divine Comedy* (Inferno), Canto IV (Durling et al., 1996, p. 77).]

ing.[18]

But it is now time for me to move to the more detailed exposition of the reasons why those studies regarding the history of mathematics—and of the other sciences more closely connected with mathematics, such as astronomy, mechanics, physics—seem to me to be more interesting and to attract more interest than those studies regarding the history of other branches of human knowledge.

The solidarity of present and past, I would say the collaboration with one another, are so deep and such an indispensable knowledge for anyone who wants to penetrate the spirit of the science of mathematics, like for no other line of studies.

The history of the science of mathematics is a unique and admirable example of a continuous process of elaboration and development where each step towards progress has always assumed the condition of previous steps towards progress as indispensable, where every new acquisition relies on and replaces the previous acquisitions and tends to increase, rather than diminish their importance. If Archimedes and Apollonius could come back to life today and be informed of everything that has been discovered or demonstrated from their times until now regarding the objects of their investigations, we could not show them a single proposition that would contradict the conclusions that they reached, and they could not be induced into conceding they had been wrong in any of their affirmations. If Euclid were to listen to a lecture in geometry in one of our High Schools or Technical Schools, it would not be hard for him to recognize that the propositions, the definitions, the theorems, and the demonstrations that are part of the program are still, after all, his own propositions and demonstrations, even though they had sometimes been retouched, and not always for the best. Then, if he wanted to enjoy flicking through any volume of one of our mathematical journals, it would not take long for him to realize that, amidst the merely formal and secondary differences, there

---

[18]That classic lecture on basic geometry that we find in the second part of Plato's *Menonis* is a model, too little followed, of a presentation that satisfies the aforementioned requirements. In this lecture Socrates takes the role, using his favorite image, of a *mid-wife*, facilitating, only using proper questioning, the student to reach, on his own, the discovery and verification of the simple theorem of geometry that was supposed to be taught. Menonis ends up believing that he already knew the theorem and that Socrates just helped him to remember it. The following considerations, offered by Plato in trying to explain this fact, are based on the hypothesis that discovering and learning are nothing but the remembering of things we already knew in previous lives (this is, essentially, his famous theory of *reminiscence*). Such considerations are certainly more different in shape than in substance from the ideas of Spencer about the hereditary nature of *acquired* mental characters.

is a deep identity between the spirit of his research and the spirit that continues to guide and dominate the research of mathematicians today. He would see that *his* rigour is still our rigour, that his starting point is still our starting point and that we cannot even study that kind of geometry that we decided to call *non-Euclidean* without using the procedures we were taught by him.

However, this kind of cooperation, direct and tangible, between the contemporary scholars of mathematical sciences and their predecessors, is not the only possible kind of cooperation that can be seen and that gives impetus to the progress of science. There is another kind of cooperation that we could call automatic or unconscious, and that is no less important. There is a renowned observation by Euler regarding the impression he could not avoid anytime he was induced, by the nature of his work, to use long derivations or transformations of formulas to reach the results he anticipated. It is, he says, like the symbols and the formulas are taking over the thinking and reasoning for him, and that his pencil is more perspicacious than his brain. He kept his trust in his pencil to the point of uttering, faced with an absurd result to which his pencil had led him, the famous sentence: "Indeed this is seen to be less in agreement with the truth; [I] But whatever it shall be, here the calculation rather than our judgement [is] trusted" (*Mechanica*, vol. I, chap. 3, §272).[19] Such an impression and such trust, however odd and unjustifiable at first glance, become perfectly understandable and natural if we think about how many ideas and how many meditations we can find, some of which even go back to past centuries, so to speak, concentrated and stored in those signs and formulas which through force of habit we can handle easily and quickly. In such signs and formulas, in fact, other minds cooperate with us, through the great distance of time, and without this help we would have to repeat all the work that those minds had already accomplished once and for all, right from the beginning.[20]

---

[19] [See English translation by I. Bruce in Euler 1736, p. 114.]

[20] On the inconveniences arising sometimes from this sort of intellectual cooperation we can find interesting observations in a recent volume by L. Dugas (*Le Psittacisme*, Paris, Alcan, 1895). The same topic is also incidentally noted in the beautiful work by Guglielmo Ferrero on *symbols* [Ferrero 1893]. The considerations by the ingenious Italian sociologist on what he calls, with a quite barbaric word, the *ideo-emotional arrest*, even if referring in particular to the psychological relationships between the legislator and the interpreter of the law, are nevertheless applicable also to the case at issue. The excessive trust in *formulas* and the exaggerated respect for *formalities* may have a common source in the human propensity to consider, in the long run, as an end in itself something that was at the beginning only a mean: it is so that the miser comes slowly to desire the possession of wealth (of the *means*) independently from whatever use or goal he could achieve by it.

The Euler case coincides, basically, with that of a calculator who, after executing a long multiplication, first directly and then using logarithms, would find he had obtained two different results. It is clear that it would be reasonable for him to rely more on the correctness of the logarithmic tables than on his personal ability to perform a long calculation without incurring errors.

It has often been observed that the most important and decisive phases in the development of mathematics, especially in modern times, when naturally data on the process is more abundant and accessible, have been manifested not as sudden additions or instant increases in the wealth of cognitions already acquired and possessed by the more eminent scholars of the science, in any given age, but rather as innovations and reforms in the investigative or demonstrative processes, as changes in the point of view from which the knowledge already possessed by the most competent people is looked at and coordinated, sometimes in the modest fashion of the simple introduction of new instruments or artifacts by which we could achieve results more quickly and easily, results that we could have achieved, or had already achieved before. The diligent examination of historical documents also tells us something more: that among the difficulties met by the mathematical sciences during their development and the obstacles they had to overcome on their long journey, there are a good number of difficulties and obstacles which come from the effect that this special character of the development of science evolution has had on the minds of its scholars.

To elucidate what I mean, I shall mention some special facts as examples. There are some documents, in particular the correspondence between Wallis and Leibniz published in the works of the former, that enlighten the historical details of a really important stage in the evolution of mathematical sciences, the beginnings of infinitesimal calculus.

From these documents we can clearly see the nature of the objections brought against the new views of Leibniz and Newton by some of their contemporaries, scientists who are nowadays rightly regarded, with Leibniz and Newton themselves, amongst the greatest mathematicians of their age. Such objections can be summarized in Huygens' opinion, an opinion expressed by Leibniz in the following words: "Surely Huygens, who had deeply analyzed these studies and increased them in many ways, gave small importance to my calculus at first, not having yet seen its usefulness. He believed that one could only express in a new way things that were already known, exactly as Roberval and the others had given small importance to Descartes' calculus of curves."[21]

---

[21][See the letter of Leibniz to Wallis, May 28, 1697 in Wallis 1693, vol. III, p.

In the correspondence Leibniz mentions this analogy again and again between his position and the position where, less than a century before him, Descartes, father of geometric analysis, found himself. What is particularly interesting are the arguments put forward by Leibniz to defend Descartes and himself against the objections by Roberval and Huygens.

Even in this case it is useful to quote his words, directed to Wallis:[22]

> And if one takes into account that the same thing that was expressed by the Cartesian calculus in easier equations of *loci* of curves was somehow already known to the ancients, then what I expressed in my easier differential equations could not have been unknown to you and to other illustrious men. Surely, before such things were reduced to some constant characters of the analytical calculi, even if one had pursued them with all his strength of thought and imagination, one could not have penetrated in the most composite and concealed things. And yet the same things appear as an amusement and as a game, once the calculus has been set up.[23]

The frequency of episodes of this sort[24] in the history of mathematics, and the fact that they are almost a special characteristic of mathematics compared to the history of other sciences, is not so odd, and indeed it seems perfectly natural and understandable if we keep in mind what I have mentioned previously about the special tie between the mathematicians of a certain generation and their predecessors.

Mathematical sciences have manifested something similar to that which happens in the industrial development of those production branches where what the economists call fixed capital predominates on the circulating capital, that is those branches where the value of the tools is far greater than the expenses for raw materials and the work applied.

This analogy does not apply exclusively to circumstances where, in some branches of industry, a big part of what seems to be produced by any single individual must be considered the product of the efforts of

---

678-80.]

[22] [See the letter of Wallis to Leibniz, May 28, 1697 in Wallis 1693, vol. III, p. 678-80.]

[23] Wallis replies: "But if I somewhere suggested that the geometry of indivisibles by Cavalieri was nothing else but a transmission in abbreviated form of the ancient method by exhaustion, one should consider that I said it not to criticize but to defend it." [See the letter of Wallis to Leibniz, April 6, 1697 in Wallis 1693, vol. III, p. 674–76].

[24] "it has been objected that all of extension theory is merely an abbreviated method of notation." Grassmann, Preface to the second edition of *Ausdehnungslehre*. [English translation by C. Lloyd Kannenberg from Grassmann 1862, p. xiv.]

all these others who contributed to produce the tools or the machines which he used in his work. The analogy can be applied much further and so, for example, in factories that use expensive systems we can see that the positive effect of an improvement in the durable equipment is counterbalanced, for some time, by the increase in inherent expenses for the substitution of old equipment with new. This situation is similar to the inconveniences encountered in the history of sciences any time that some progress, which led to new procedures and new methods, made it necessary to adopt new concepts or substitute new means of representation in place of these, to which long standing use had conferred the advantage of seeming more simple and more natural.

Among the observations I have made so far about the special features of the development of mathematical sciences, this above consideration can be seen as particularly applicable to mechanics.

Boltzmann observed, quite rightly, that the dominant ideas on the nature and purpose of mechanical theories, especially regarding their applications to physics, have recently been changing in a direction opposite to the one followed by the recent changes in the prevalent ideas on the function and task of natural sciences. The latter, in fact, which until fifty or so years ago were still considered merely descriptive and classificatory sciences, tend to attribute more and more importance to questions related to the research of causes and the explanation of facts. That heap of information and classifications that, until recently, constituted the content of what was called "Natural History" is now considered simple material to be used in the determination of the developing processes of the organic world and the determination of the role played by different factors and influences in such development. If we observe, instead, the changes that happened, in the same time span, to our concept of what is, and what should be, mechanics, we cannot be blind to the fact that they tend to go in the opposite direction. This opposite direction has found possibly its most authoritative expression in the definition often mentioned by Kirchhoff, that indicates that the only purpose of mechanics must be the description, in the simplest possible terms and minimal use of hypothesis, of the bodies movements as they actually happen in nature.

From this point of view, the concepts used by mechanics and the suppositions upon which it relies clearly assume the character of instruments which only have value depending on their usefulness in achieving the purpose so defined. It is further proof of this that, as frequently noted, in mechanics it is not the principles or theories which prove the facts deduced by them, but rather the conformity of the conclusions achieved with the experiential data which justifies the principles and limits the range of hypothesis from which it is convenient to start.[25]

The previous observation also provides the explanation for another fact that we will often encounter on other occasions: in no other science besides mechanics have considerations regarding what Hertz[26] calls *Zweckmässigkeit*[27] (a word for which I am not able to find the equivalent in Italian, given that the word 'appropriateness' does not suggest exactly the same concept) been so relevant for the greatest progress in theories and fundamental concepts. It is in this field that the most important and decisive battles in the history of mechanics have been fought. To quote a fact to support this assertion, it suffices for me to recall the first reason brought forward by Galileo, in the words of Sagredo, in the *Dialogue Concerning the Two Chief World Systems*, to prefer Copernicus' opinion over Ptolemy's:

> If, throughout the whole variety of effects that could exist in nature as dependent upon these motions, all the same consequences followed indifferently to a hairsbreadth from both positions, still my first general impression of them would be this: I should think that anyone who considered it more reasonable for the whole universe to move in order to let the earth remain fixed would be more irrational than one who should climb to the top of your cupola *just to get a view of the city and its environs*, and then demand that the whole countryside should revolve around him so that he would not have to take the trouble to turn his head. Doubtless there are many and great *advantages* to be drawn from the new theory and not from the previous one (which to my mind is comparable with or even surpasses the above in absurdity), making the former more credible than the latter.[28]

And to mention another example, apparently of a completely different kind, when Lagrange chose the principle of virtual work as the basis of his analytical treatise on mechanics, was he not doing so because of considerations of the same kind? That is, considerations that are not about compatibility or incompatibility of experiential data with the conclusions he would reach starting from that principle, instead of starting from any of the other principles that he mentions as equally legitimate; but rather considerations about the simplicity and convenience of deducing all the known laws of mechanics from a single fun-

---

[25]See Payot, *De la croyance* (Paris, Alcan, 1896), page 88 ff. [Payot 1896].

[26]In the preface of his posthumous work: *Die Prinzipien der Mechanik* (Hertz, 1894).

[27][The word has been translated with "appropriateness" in the English translation by D. E. Jones and J. T. Walley of 1899. The word was also used by Kant and in that context is often translated with "form of finality."]

[28][English translation by Stillman Drake from (Galilei, 1632, p. 115). Italics added by Vailati.]

damental assumption and being able to coordinate and dominate all of them from a single point of view.

We will also have occasion to see that the other attempts at systematizing and perfecting mechanical theories, from Aristotle to Archimedes, from Varignon to d'Alembert, from Poinsot to Grassmann, clearly show traces of similar influences. We will see, for example, that in the long struggles between various principles which, during the progressive phases of the development of statics, have contested the prize and have aspired to be the most general and the most deserving to serve as the starting point for deducing all others, the criterion of immediate evidence or direct testability against experiential data has always been superseded by considerations about the different simplicity and agility which the various principles lent themselves in order to group together the facts and laws gradually collected through observation, as consequences achievable by deduction. The history of mechanics shows us a series of intellectual confrontations, among which the most interesting are not those between scientists, but rather between the different ideas, confronting each other in the mind of any researcher who has contributed to the progress of science.[29] In these confrontations between contentious points of view which tends to prevail is the one more apt to satisfy the kind of requirements I have mentioned. It is the accumulation of the effects of this kind of selection,[30] and the gradual changes and successive adaptations of the structure of theories caused by its influence, that have produced the result before our eyes in the imposing building of modern mechanics.

In this regard I will add one last observation suggested by a curious passage which I happened to notice while consulting the *Collectiones mathematicae* by Pappus of Alexandria, a valuable document on the history of mathematical sciences in Ancient Greece.[31] In the introduction to book V, regarding problems of isoperimetry, Pappus stops with naive satisfaction to consider the geometric skills of bees, which, in the construction of their honeycombs, have been able to solve perfectly a problem of pure geometry.[32] Pappus shows that the hexagonal shape, used for the cells, is the shape that, given a certain thickness of the

---

[29]See Mach, *Die Mechanik* (2nd edition, page 420) [Mach 1883].

[30]It would be stretching too far to assert, as done by the humorous exaggerator of just ideas Anatole France, that "theories are born to serve as targets, to be put out of joint, to be distended, and finally to burst like bubbles." [France 1885, pages 260-261. In French in the original.]

[31][See Hultsch 1875-1878.]

[32]Similar considerations on this same subject can be found in the works of modern mathematicians (for example MacLaurin). See Mach, *Die Mechanik*, p. 426 [Mach 1883, p. 423].

walls, corresponds exactly to the minimum need of wax—given also
the condition of not leaving fissures between cells. Pappus then elo-
quently expresses his astonishment at the skill of geometric intuition of
these clever little animals, by which they achieve almost instinctively
the conclusions that human reasoning can achieve only by mean of
laborious deductions.

It is now interesting to compare these considerations by Pappus with
those dedicated to this same topic by Darwin, in the chapter of the *Origin of Species* concerning the development of instincts. After detailed
observations and careful comparisons between different procedures in
the constructions of honeycombs used by the kind of bees close to our
common bee, Darwin reaches the conclusion that all characters of per-
fection and symmetry observed in the honeycombs must be considered
the result of a slow and continuous developing process due to the progressive prevailing of those kinds of bees whose honeycombs have details
of construction that bring some kind of advantage, even if minimal, for
the economy of the precious material used to build them.[33]

And the history of mechanics teaches us that we should attribute
the coherence, the symmetry, and admirable coordination of modern
theories of mechanics to this kind of influences, and also their aesthetic
character which has impressed more than one great mathematician,
and induced Hamilton to define Lagrange's analytic mechanics *a kind
of scientific poem*.[34] History shows us that what caused the successive progress of this science, and what has induced it to assume its
actual form, has been, in a much greater part than it would appear,
the need to prepare receptacles for the facts that have been distilled
from observations drop by drop and then collected and classified by
empirical laws. Not only should these receptacles satisfy the condition
of collecting these facts and ordering them coherently and in the most
proper fashion for their utilization, but they should also achieve this
result with a decreasing use of concepts and direct recourse to experience or intuition, with a decreasing need of distinctions and special
considerations that vary from case to case, in other words, with the
maximum possible economy of that most precious of worldly materials,
man's thought.

---

[33] Darwin, *Origin of Species*, Ch. VIII ["the motive power of the process of natural
selection having been the construction of cells of due strength and of the proper
size and shape for the larvae, this being effected with the greatest possible economy
of labour and wax" See section "Cell-making instinct of the Hive bee" in Darwin
1859].

[34] ["The beauty of the method so suiting the dignity of the results, as to make his
great work a kind of scientific poem" (Hamilton, 1834, p. 247).]

References

Bacon, Francis. 1605. *The Advancement of Learning.* Clarendon Press, 3rd edn. Wright W.A. (ed.), 1876. 2nd edition, London: Clarendon press.

Comte, Auguste. 1835. *Cours de philosophie positive,* vol. 2. Engl. transl. in G. Lenzer (ed.), *Auguste Comte and Positivism, The Essential Writings,* New York: Harper, 1975.

Darwin, Charles. 1859. *The origin of species.* London: Murray.

Dugas, L. 1895. *Le Psittacisme.* Paris: Alcan.

Durling, Robert M., Ronald L. Martinez, and Robert Turner. 1996. *The divine comedy of Dante Alighieri,* vol. 1. Oxford University Press.

Euler. 1736. *Mechanica sive motus scientia analytice exposita. Auctore Leonhardo Eulero academiae imper. scientiarum membro et matheseos sublimioris professore,* vol. 1. Petropoli: Ex typographia academiae scientarum. Engl. transl. by Ian Bruce, http://www.17centurymaths.com/contents/euler/mechvol1/ch3a.pdf.

Ferrero, Guglielmo. 1893. *I simboli in rapporto alla storia e filosofia del diritto alla psicologia e alla sociologia.* Torino: Bocca.

France, Anatole. 1885. *Le livre de mon ami.* Paris: Lévy. Engl. transl. by J. Lewis May and B. Miall. *My friend's book.* in *The Works of Anatole France,* vol. 5. London New York: Lane 1908.

Galilei, Galileo. 1632. *Dialogo sopra i due massimi sistemi.* Engl. transl. S. Drake (ed.) *Dialogue Concerning the Two Chief World Systems,* University of California Press, 1967.

Galilei, Galileo. 1855. *Le opere di Galileo Galilei. Pensieri vari.* Società Editrice Fiorentina.

Grassmann, Hermann Günther. 1862. *Extension theory.* AMS Bookstore, 2000.

Hamilton, W. R. 1834. On a general method in dynamics. *Philosophical Transactions of the Royal Society* 124:247–308.

Hertz, Heinrich Rudolph. 1894. *Die Prinzipien der Mechanik in neuem zusammenhange dargestellt.* Leipzig: Barth. Engl. transl. by D. E. Jones and J. T. Walley. *The Principles of Mechanics presented in a new form.* London: Macmillan, 1899.

Hultsch, Fridericus. 1875-1878. *Pappi Alexandrini collectionis quae supersunt e libris manu scriptis edidit Latina interpretatione et commentariis.* Berlin: Weidmann.

Mach, Ernst. 1883. *Die Mechanik in ihrer Entwicklung historisch-kritisch dargestellt.* Leipzig: Brockhaus (1889), 2nd edn. Engl. trans. by T.J. McCormack. *The science of mechanics. A critical and historical account of its development.* Open Court Publishing Co.: Chicago, London 1919.

Mach, Ernst. 1896. *Principles of the theory of heat: historically and critically elucidated.* Dordrecht-Boston: Reidel, 1986.

Montaigne, Michel. 1811. *The essays of Michael de Montaigne,* vol. 1. London: Baldwin.

Pareto, Vilfredo. 1896. *Cours d'Economie politique*. Lausanne: Rouge.

Pascal, Blaise. 1908. *Oeuvres*, vol. 2. Paris: Hachette.

Payot, J. 1896. *De la croyance*. Paris: Alcan.

Preyer, William Thierry. 1895. *Die Seele des Kindes. Beobachtungen über die geistige Entwicklungen des Menschen in den ersten Lebensjahren*. Leipzig: Grieben.

Sully, James. 1896. *Studies of Childhood*. New York: Appleton.

Vailati, Giovanni. 1897. *Sull'importanza delle Ricerche relative alla Storia delle Scienze. Prolusione a un corso sulla Storia della meccanica, letta il 4 dicembre 1896 nell'Università di Torino*. Torino: Roux e Frassati. Repr. in Vailati (1911), pages 64-78.

Vailati, Giovanni. 1911. *Scritti di G. Vailati, 1863-1909*. Leipzig-Firenze: Barth.

Wallis, J. 1693. *Opera Mathematica*. Oxoniae: Theatro Sheldoniano.

Yonge, Charles Duke, ed. 1853. *(Diogenes Laertius) The Lives and Opinions of Eminent Philosophers*. London: George Bell & Sons.

2

The Deductive Method as an Instrument of Research[†]

Eyes and ears are bad witnesses for men,
since their souls lack understanding.[1]

Among the issues that the studies of the history of science are suited to enlighten, and on the resolving of which it is to be expected that they will give the maximum contribution, are to be counted, firstly, those regarding the different methods of research and proof, the causes of their different power and fruitfulness, and the limits of their useful application in the various fields of scientific activity. It is easy to understand the reason for this. As long as, in treating these sorts of questions, we limit ourselves to deriving our data from the observation of the results obtained from the individual sciences, by means of the methods and procedures currently adopted as convenient for those sciences, it would be impossible to have a sufficient number of facts available to

---

[†]First published as *Il metodo deduttivo come strumento di ricerca*, Turin, Roux Frassati, 1898 (Vailati, 1898a). Inaugural lecture to the course on History of Mechanics at the University of Turin, year 1897-98. Repr. in Vailati (1911), pages 118-148.

[1][Eraclitus, fragment. English translation by Arthur Fairbanks, in *The First Philosophers of Greece*, 1898, London, Kegan Paul, Trench, Trubner & Co., p. 25. In Greek in the original.]

Logic and Pragmatism. Selected Essays by Giovanni Vailati.
C. Arrighi, P. Cantù, M. De Zan, and P. Suppes.
Copyright © 2009, CSLI Publications.

establish, from among the different ways the same method works in different fields and the different methods used in one single field, those comparisons needed mainly to guide us in the determination of the circumstances on which their different applicability and effectiveness depend in any single case. The examination and analysis of all those cases where a given method has actually been tested, including those where it had to be abandoned as misleading or unproductive, is becoming more and more difficult because of the very nature of the progress in science itself, which gradually leads to the adoption of methods evermore perfected, and evermore suitable for their respective branches of research, through a continuous process of selection and elimination of methods that in any of these branches is recognized as less suitable and less powerful.

It is on an issue of this very kind that now I intend to make some observations, as suggested to me by some facts I stumbled upon during my research on the History of Mechanics. The question is about one of the most fundamental distinctions that can be established among the procedures of scientific research, the distinction, that is, commonly expressed by contrasting *reasoning* with *experience, argumentation* with *generalization*, the *deductive method* with the *inductive method*. I will make an effort to define and specify the nature and importance of this distinction, mentioning the different forms in which it has been conceived and formulated and trying to highlight the fundamental characters on which it is based. Moving on then to consider the deductive method in particular, I will make some observations, on the one hand regarding what can be called its "state of service" in the history of science, and on the other regarding the various opinions advanced on its value and its purpose, both as an instrument for research and explanation and as a means for demonstration and verification. I will analyze the possible causes of the peculiar contrast between its triumphs and conquests in some areas of investigation, as for example in Mathematics and some of the most important branches of Physics, and its impotency and humiliating failures in other areas of research. I will be examining whether and how much these failures are due to some inherent incapability, or rather to premature or clumsy application, and to an insufficient elaboration, or hasty choice, of the axioms and the hypotheses constituting its essential starting point. Finally I will present the possible reasons for thinking that the deductive method tends to extend its sphere of action more and more and to increase its efficacy and fruitfulness with the increase in the wealth of human cognitions and with their growth in accuracy and multiplicity. I will mention the reasons why the extension of the domain of the deductive method is not only to be considered useful and desirable, but it can justly be considered amongst the most important ideal purposes of scientific research.

I.

We can see that the distinction between the processes of *induction* or *generalization* and those of *deduction* and *demonstration* is already clearly acknowledged in the work of Greek philosophers, who may have made the first attempts at analysis and systematic classification of the processes and artifices used by the human mind in proceeding from the unknown to the known. The collection of Aristotelian writings usually referred to by the collective title *Organum*, i.e. *instrument*, contains, according to the explicit assertion of Aristotle himself, the first essay ever attempted which subjects the latter of the two abovementioned processes to general and fixed norms, and reduces its various types to patterns and formulas (similar to those of modern algebra) with the purpose of avoiding the misunderstandings and illusions caused by imperfections of ordinary language and facilitating the necessary control to guarantee the correctness of operations in the most difficult cases. In the various parts of the *Organum* the distinction between the two kinds of processes is repeatedly indicated as fundamental[2] and it is characterized in terms not much different from those we would still use today. Induction (ἐπαγωγή) is defined by Aristotle as that form of reasoning by means of which, from the examination and comparison of a series of particular cases, we arrive at a general proposition which contemplates not just the observed cases, but also an indeterminate number of other cases, which have a certain relation of similarity with the former cases. He refers to deduction (ἀπόδειξις), on the other hand, as any form of reasoning that can be reduced to the kind he has designated as syllogism (συλλογισμός), which, as we know, consists of the following: starting with two propositions, where one affirms a given property of an entire class of objects, and the other states that one or more objects belong to such a class, we get to a third proposition, where the initial property is also attributed to the aforementioned objects.

The characteristic difference, between the conclusions reached by deduction and those reached by induction, consists, according to Aristotle, of the following: it is not possible to throw any doubt on the truth of the first kind without falling victim to contradiction, unless we are willing to dispute the truth of the propositions taken as a starting point. In the case of induction rather, no contradiction or inconsis-

---

[2]See *Prior Analitics*, II, 25: "In fact, each and every one of our convictions was reached either through a syllogism or by starting with induction."

tency would be incurred by one who, even while conceding the truth of the facts in the premise, were to deny the truth of the generalization that we were trying to base those facts on. This special character of the deductive reasoning is indicated by Aristotle by saying that it leads to *necessary* (ἐξ ἀνάγκης) or forced (βιαία) conclusions, and by using these terms he is far from intending to mean, as he was taken to mean by his followers, that the conclusions reached by deduction are worthwhile, precisely for this reason, to be trusted more than those conclusions reached by induction.[3] The only *necessity* he has in mind is that which would be experienced by a participant in a dispute, who has to concede the truth of a proposition if he has conceded the truth of other propositions from which the first could be deduced.[4] To dispel any doubts about the opinion of Aristotle on this matter, it will suffice to mention that impressive passage in his *Physics* (Book II, at the end), where, by means of an analogy to clarify the meaning he gives to the word *necessity* in the case considered above and to justify its use, he compares it to the other senses the word possesses in ordinary language, and he observes that "when we say that in order to make a saw it is *necessary* to have some iron, we do not intend to deny that the saw could also be made of some other material, but we intend to say merely that in such a case it would not serve the purpose for which it has been made; in the same way, when mathematicians say that the sum of the angles of a triangle is *necessarily* equal to two right angles, they do not intend to say that we are not allowed to doubt this proposition, but simply that they are forced to admit it if they want to continue to consider the propositions on which they intend to base their demonstrations as true." (*Physics*, book II, ch. 9.)[5] No less numerous and explicit are the passages, in Aristotle's works, where he insists on how unreasonable or even absurd it is to believe that deduction could be the only source of certainty. Here he asserts that the fundamental principles, on which we need to rely sooner or later if we do not want to indefinitely extend the series of deductions and syllogisms, cannot have any warranty of truthfulness if not that which comes from induction

---

[3] See *Pr. Anal.*, I, 33.

[4] "Geometers [...] whose claim is that they do not persuade but convince" (Cicero, *Acad.*, II, 116) [In Latin in the text. English translation by H. Rackham from Rackham 1972, pp. 615-17]. "The proofs offered by geometers are not only persuasive but convincing" (Seneca, *Nat. Quest.*, I, 4) [In Latin in the text. English translation (modified) by T.H. Corcoran from Corcoran 1971, Vol. 1, p. 43].

[5] [This and the following passages from Aristotle seem to be more a paraphrase than an exact quote from a specific edition—probably Vailati's own loose translation from the Greek. The passages in English are a translation of Vailati's Italian version (unless otherwise noted).]

or from the direct witnessing by our senses.[6] Regarding this subject, on which subsequently his opinions had been so altered and misunderstood, especially by those who professed themselves his followers and supporters, it will not be superfluous to quote his words exactly.

"The task" he says "of providing the principles on which the deductions are based belongs, for every science, to the observation of the particular facts which constitute its field of research. Therefore in the case of astronomy such a task belongs to astronomical observations, because only when the celestial phenomena have been sufficiently analyzed and understood, will it be possible to establish some deductions in relation to them. And the same can be said for all the other sciences or arts, where demonstrations can also be found soon enough, once the facts to which they refer have been sufficiently studied. If our observations have been so diligent that none of the relevant facts have been missed, we will be able to find demonstrations in all those cases where it is possible, and we will also understand why this is not possible in those other cases where, for the very nature of the question, it is not possible to reduce the exposition in a deductive form." (*Pr. Anal.*, I, 30).

Besides this we should also note that when Aristotle affirms the inductive origin of the principles or axioms on which the sciences of a deductive type rely, he does not intend to exclude the axioms of Geometry from this assertion. He firmly fights the opinion (entertained, apparently, by some mathematicians contemporary to himself) that a science can be founded on mere definitions. "A geometer" he says "indicates the meaning of the word triangle by means of a definition, but the fact that a triangle exists or that it is possible to build one, and that therefore it is allowed to derive consequences from the fact that we built it, is a truth that is neither asserted nor proved by means of a definition, and it must be assumed and demonstrated separately."[7]

He never tires of indicating the use of words that are ambiguous or without a determined meaning as the main cause among the causes of error, which can impair the conclusions reached by deduction and of teaching the suitability and necessity of taking precautions for this reason. It is worthwhile quoting the following passage from the *Sophistical Refutations* on this issue, where, after asserting that the most abun-

---

[6]See *Posterior Analitics*, I, 18: "However, it is not possible to reach universal propositions if not through induction; on the other hand it is impossible that one who does not possess sensations could be guided by induction." And also in book II, ch. 15: "It is therefore evidently necessary that we acquire knowledge of the primary elements through induction." [Both quotes were in Greek in the original.]

[7][This passage seems to refer to *Post. Anal.* II, 7.]

dant source of illusory deductions is the abuse of words, he adds the following observation:

> Given that it is impossible to take all the facts discussed with us and keep them available and that we must use words as though they were tiles so that they may represent them to us, we are in the same situation as those who count money by means of tokens. We are actually in a worse situation, because facts are infinite, while words and signs are of a relatively small number. Therefore, it is unavoidable that sometimes the same name is applied to things which are very different from each other, and for this reason we are induced to mistake for relations and properties what are, in truth, relations and conformities between other things which represent them. And this is one of the circumstances which those who have the purpose, not to be wise, but to appear wise without really being so, should take advantage of. (Ch. I, 5, 6.)

But let us not insist any longer on that part of Aristotle's views about the nature and purpose of the deductive method, that results in perfect conformity with what everyone agrees upon these days, or at least should agree upon. For the present purpose, I find it more important to focus on the differences that can be found between Aristotle's concept of how the application of deduction can be properly used in the constitution and progress of the sciences and the opinions expressed and adopted on this subject by modern scientists, from Galileo onward.

Aristotle's belief on this subject seems to have been determined mainly by the observation of how deduction works in the only two fields where scientists who were contemporaries or his predecessors had been able to use it proficiently, i.e. on the one hand *Geometry*, and on the other *Rhetoric*, meaning the ancient sense of theoretics, the art of changing the opinions of others by means of words. These are the two kinds of application that he has under constant observation during his considerations about the purpose and usefulness of deduction, even when he seems to be completely abstracting from them. It is for this reason that he is inclined to consider the purpose, not just the main purpose but the only purpose, of deductive argumentation to be the increase of certainty, the reduction of what is arguable to what is unarguable, of what is doubtful to what is evident. Deduction is, for him, first of all an instrument apt to guarantee the truth of propositions that were only probable and plausible, reconnecting them to others more certain and less debatable[8] and making them participate

---

[8] The same opinion is also expressed in the philosophical treatises by Galen, which represent the latest stage of development achieved by the ideas of the peripatetic school about scientific methods: "one has to admit that the principle of any proof derives from more evident things." Verification is considered by him as useful for

2. The Deductive Method / 29

in some way in their solidity and evidence, in the same way as we do precisely in geometrical demonstrations or in forensic argumentations, where everyone tries to corroborate his own assertions by supporting them with axioms or laws that are not disputable.

Even if he does not neglect considering the case of deductions made starting from propositions that are not only uncertain but are also expressly recognized as false, Aristotle does not attribute any other purpose to these reasonings other than that of a *reductio ad absurdum* in mathematics or, at most, that of taking advantage, in a dispute, of our adversary's opinions, even if false, to induce him to concede some other fact, true or false, of which we are trying to persuade him (*ad hominem* arguments).

I would not be able to highlight any better the existing contrast in this regard between Aristotle's views and the views of modern science, if not by comparing his own explicit assertion on the inanity of deducing one proposition from another when the latter is not more certain and evident than the first one, with the following passage by Descartes (*Discours de la Méthode*). Here, in his *Dioptrics*, he defends himself for taking propositions more in need of proof than the ones he was deducing from them as a starting point for his reasoning:

> If some of the matters of which I have spoken in the beginning of the Dioptrics and Meteorics should offend at first sight, because I call them hypotheses and seem indifferent about giving proof of them, I request a patient and attentive reading of the whole, from which I hope those hesitating will derive satisfaction; for it appears to me that the reasonings are so mutually connected in these Treatises, that, as the last are demonstrated by the first which are their causes, the first are in their turn demonstrated by the last which are their effects. Nor must it be imagined that I here commit the fallacy which the logicians call a circle; for since experience renders the majority of these effects most certain, the causes from which I deduce them do not serve so much to *establish* their reality as to *explain* their existence; but on the

the ignorant ("the test is evident even to laymen") or at most for those who have not yet learned how to make deductions properly ("the analytical method"). [The quotations are in Greek in the original. See the following passages from Galen, *The affections and errors of the soul*: "Now (I began), it is generally agreed that any logical demonstration should begin with the clearest possible facts. The possibility of making a transition from these to facts which are not evident, while it is not allowed by the Academics and Sceptics, is a point on which the rest of us agree with each other; and we believe that we can find a position superior to their despair of knowledge" (Singer, 2001, p. 144-5). "Logical enquiry employing the analytical method will also lead us to the correct design of the water-clock. Again, the confirmation of its correctness is something apparent even to the layman" (ibid., p. 140).]

contrary, the reality of the causes is established by the reality of the effects.[9]

A similar observation has been made by Gassendi in reply to those who, against some statements by Galileo on the motion of bodies, raised the objection that such statements were based on principles less evident than the conclusions they led to:

> When Galileo made the assumption that the degrees of velocities of a body moving on planes of different inclinations are the same when the elevation of such planes is the same, did not consider it as demonstrated (though Torricelli later provided a demonstration) but as *probable in so far as the conclusions deduced from such assumption were to be coherent with experience.* (*Exercitationes paradoxicae*, book IV.)[10]

The characteristic difference between Aristotle's ideas and those of the founders of modern science about the function of deduction in scientific research lies precisely in how little importance has been given to deduction as an instrument of explanation and anticipation of experience, compared to the large amount of trust put in it as a mean of proof and ascertainment. His arguments about natural phenomena, even in those cases where, instead of being used to demonstrate the conclusions they led to, are used to test the premises on which they are founded, aim to reach this purpose more by showing the contradictions and inconsistencies among the various statements, or by showing that they cannot be affirmed simultaneously, rather than by venturing to conclusions never before suspected, whose verification would have been able to give rise to new observations, which would have contributed to a better clarification on the matter at issue.

The documents that have been left to us on the theories of physics of the Greeks show, moreover, that this trait, far from being especially distinctive of the peripatetic school, was common to all the various speculative branches which for a long time competed in the field of

---

[9][Descartes 1637. Quoted in French by Vailati. English translation by J. Veitch, from Veitch 1850, p. 116. Italics added by Vailati.]

[10][Vailati's original quotation in Latin is taken from the Index (Epistolarum Summulae) of *Exercitationes Paradoxicae* (Gassendi, 1964, p. 35).] Another characteristic trait of this same mental attitude is provided by the answer that had supposedly been given by d'Alembert to one of his students, who was complaining of not finding the fundamental propositions of the infinitesimal calculus clear and evident enough: *Just go on... and faith will soon return* [Davis and Hersh 1981, p. 253]. If Archimedes had been in agreement with this, the infinitesimal calculus would have been born eighteen centuries before Newton and Leibniz. As was so well put by Zeuthen (*Kgl. danske videnskabernes Selskabs Forhandlingen*, 1897, n. 6): "Kepler is the first one who had the *courage* to directly submit, without using a demonstration by exhaustion, the infinitely small quantities to calculation" [Quoted in French in the original].

physics research, including also the branch represented by Democritus and successively by the Epicureans, even though this branch is in many other ways closer to the others, in shape rather than substance, than to the concepts and the theories of modern science. To give an idea of the nature of the questions and the problems whose solutions were considered by the Greeks as the purpose of research in physics, I will quote one of the famous arguments by which Zeno deduced the impossibility of motion from the hypothesis that time consists of a series of moments or instants (ἄτομοι) which are indivisible. "In order for motion, being a change in position from instant to instant, to take place, at least two instants corresponding to two different positions are required. Therefore if we consider the body in a specific instant, we cannot say that *in that* instant it moves: and given that we can repeat this reasoning for all the successive instants, we have the case where the body is not moving in any of them, and as a consequence not even during the interval of time that such instants taken together constitute. Therefore motion is only a deception of the senses."

Setting aside any consideration about the weight or the legitimacy of this argumentation, what is immediately evident when examining it, regarding its ability to teach us something about nature and the laws of motion, is its complete inadequacy in suggesting any experimental verification or in redirecting our attention to some fact that we could not have thought about before building such argumentation. By means of this, the mind of the researcher, using a comparison that Schopenhauer half-seriously applied to some arguments made by geometers, find itself in the same position as a cat which keeps following its tail, believing it to be a foreign object running away from it, without noticing that, turning around as much as it wants, it will always find itself in the same situation.

Going back to what I was saying before, the history of science clearly shows us that, amongst the causes which gradually led to the substitution of the modern experimental methods in place of the ancient methods of mere *passive observation*, the application of deduction[11] has to be included as one of the most important, even in those cases where the propositions taken as a starting point were considered more in need of proof than the resulting ones, cases where, therefore, the resultant propositions were those which had to pass on, to the initial conjectures, the grade of certainty that they were directly acquiring from a comparison with facts and experimental verifications. The im-

---

[11] Pasteur has appropriately defined the *experiment* as an observation guided by preconceptions, that is, in other words, an observation preceded and guided by deductive processes.

possibility of finding proper material among the facts spontaneously present at the observation to verify the conclusions produced by deductions which, even if correct and rigorous, are not based on premises that are recognized as worthy in themselves of unconditional trust, as is the case with mathematical premises, led to the desire and need to artificially increase the sphere of facts to be used in checking theories, and contributed, more than any other circumstance, to the rise of the systematic use of the observation of facts artificially produced with the intent of observing them, i.e. what constitutes an experiment in the strict sense of the word. In other words, ancient physicists were not inclined to experiment, mostly because they were busier making sure of the certainty of the starting propositions than of the truthfulness of those that were deducted by them, and therefore they did not have any reason to question what happens in cases different from those that, presenting themselves spontaneously to their observations, immediately suggested the generalizations on which their arguments were based.[12] Therefore it can be assumed that, in a sense, the increasingly widespread and systematic application of deduction to the study of natural phenomena provided the first stimulus to the development of modern experimental methods, and it is not by chance that the first eminent initiators of such methods were also at the same time the greatest founders and advocates of the application of that powerful tool of deduction, mathematics, to the sciences of physics.

That mental quality, so justly designated as the most precious and necessary for good observation, namely the inclination to be suitably amazed, requires, as an indispensable condition for its development, the disposition to compare preconceptions, even the remotest and most elaborated of all the consequences of our preconceptions, with facts. Without such a disposition we are not able to distinguish, among the enormous chaos of facts available to our explorations, which ones are those whose examination or acknowledgment can determine some important changes in our beliefs (the *experimenta crucis* by Bacon), or can really enlarge the sphere of our knowledge.

Maybe it has not been mentioned enough, by those who dealt with the history of mechanics, that the first and most decisive experiences to determine the advancement of this science beyond the point where the Greeks had brought it, were considered, by those who undertook them,

---

[12]Such generalizations appeared to be sufficiently guaranteed by facts whenever they were able to say, using the technical expression by Lucretius, *De rerum natura*, II, 865: "Nor do manifest facts refute this, *things plainly known to us*, nor do they contradict [...]". [English translation by W. H. D. Rouse from Smith 1932, p. 163. Italics added by Vailati.]

not as *inquiries* towards nature, but rather as challenges, some kind of *cimenti*,[13] to use the word which has now become classic, to which nature was subjected in order to challenge it to answer differently from how it *should have* answered.[14] In fact, for a great number of the most important cases, the experiences turned out to be mere verifications of conclusions that had already been reached independently by the experimenters. They would have been really astonished if the *answers* of nature had not conformed to their anticipations, and such a lack of conformity, when it actually did occur, led them to wonder why the experiments had not worked, rather than immediately doubting the legitimacy of their assumptions. Moreover, sometimes they appeared to be drawn to the experiment more as a way of convincing others than as a way to convince themselves, because for them appealing to facts was, in a way, the line of least resistance in penetrating the stubborn minds of their adversaries, not being able to counter their preconceptions with their own, without basing such preconceptions on some less subjective basis than their own personal convictions.

It is useful to quote here some concrete facts supporting these considerations. Amongst the many that the history of mechanics could provide for me for this purpose, I have chosen the following, which also has the advantage of showing the contrast between induction and deduction in a clear light, as conceived and expressed by Galileo. In the notes to the book *Esercitazioni filosofiche di Antonio Rocco, filosofo peripatetico*,[15] Galileo, contrasting the opinion of the Aristotelians that the velocities of two falling bodies are proportional to their weights, opposing his own, that such velocities do not depend on weight, writes the following:

> It remains for me to provide the *reasons* which, besides the *experience*, confirm my proposition, even though in order to reassure the intellect, whatever the *experience* has reached there is no need for *reason*, which I will provide anyway for your benefit, and because I was *first persuaded by reason than reassured by senses*. [...] I formulated an axiom, which could not be doubted by anyone, and I *supposed* that any descending body has a certain degree of velocity in its motion, limited by nature and prefixed in such a way that, if we want to change it by increasing or decreasing the velocity, we could not do it without interfering with it to delay or accelerate its limited natural course. Once

---

[13]["Trials by ordeal" - "*Cimento*" is the word commonly used by Galileo to indicate an experiment.]

[14]As a typical example of experiences of this kind we can mention that used by Pascal to state that the level of mercury in the barometer is dependent from the height to which the instrument was taken.

[15][See Galilei 1897, pp. 712–750]

this was established, I imagined two bodies of equal size and weight, like two bricks, which leave from the same height at the same moment. We cannot doubt that they will descend with the same velocity, that which is assigned to them by nature, and if such velocity were to be increased by some other moving body, it is necessary for it to move with greater velocity. However, if we imagine that the bricks, while descending, become attached to one another, which one is going to add impetus to the other, doubling its velocity, considering that such velocity cannot be increased by another moving object, unless it is moving with greater velocity? Therefore we should admit that the compound of two bricks is not going to change their first velocity.[16]

From this Galileo arrived at the purely deductive conclusion that if two bodies of the same material and different weights fall at different velocities, this cannot depend on the different weights, but at the most on their differences in shape, which causes the medium through which they are falling to oppose different resistance to their fall.[17]

The discovery of the law of inertia provides us with another no less instructive example of a conquest of science achieved by the predominant use of deduction. The impossibility of reaching it by means of simple inductions based on direct observation is recognized by Galileo himself, who speaks his mind about the matter with the following words:

I say that nothing moves with straight motion. Let us analyze while we are talking. The motion of all heavenly bodies is circular; ships, carts, horses, birds are all moving in a circular motion around the terrestrial globe. The motions of the parts of animals is all circular, and over all we are reduced to not finding anything else but *gravia deorsum et [levia] sursum* which seem to be moving in a straight line. However, we cannot be sure of those either, unless we first demonstrate that the terrestrial globe is motionless. (*Dialogo sopra i due massimi sistemi,* "Seconda giornata.")[18]

It is well-known that to make plausible his hypothesis that the horizon-

---

[16][Ibid., p. 731. Italics added by Vailati.]

[17]From a historical point of view, it is important to note that this same conclusion was also reached, by means of an essentially identical argument, by Benedetti, in his *Diversarum speculationum mathematicarum at physicarum liber*, published in Turin in 1585 [Benedetti 1585]. In this same category of arguments are also included most of those mental processes which Mach has designated by the name *thought experiments* [Gedankenexperimente] (*Zeitschrift. f. Phys. u. chem. Unterricht*, Januar 1897 [Mach 1896-97]) and in particular the argument followed by Mayer to reach the discovery of the mechanical equivalent of heat.

[18][This passage appears as a footnote in Besoni and Helping 1997, pp. 257–58, but it is not present in the English translation by S. Drake, edition 1967. The phrase in Latin in this quote was incorrectly reported in previous publications of Vailati's work as "*gravia deorsum et gravia sursum.*"]

tal component of a body thrown horizontally is constant, Galileo often employs the concept of a horizontal plane as the common limit of two series of planes inclined in opposite directions, where, therefore, a ball thrown in a given direction would tend evidently to move at a respectively increasing or decreasing speed, depending on the inclination of the planes. From this he concludes that such a ball, when thrown on a horizontal plane, would move at a neither increasing nor decreasing speed.

However, he is far from having any illusions about the proof value of this ideal experience if it were to be used in proving the law now known as *the law of inertia*. He actually concedes with no hesitation that, given that such a horizontal plane could not be physically distinguished from a portion of the earth's surface, which had been accepted as spherical even by the Aristotelians, the uniform motion of the ball on it (within the limits of possible observations) conforms perfectly with both the hypothesis successively formulated by Newton as the first of laws of motion, and with the Aristotelian principle of the persistence of circular and uniform motion, and of the dependency of velocities of bodies from their moving away or approaching the point towards which they tend to move.[19]

The law of inertia, as well as that of universal attraction, would probably still be unknown to men, at least in its whole general scope, if, in order to analyze and explain the phenomena where the law manifests itself, they had not had any other method than observation available, or direct measurement or simple experimental findings, however diverse and accurate. The conquest of such important truths could have not been achieved without employing mental activities that are far more abstract and complex than the processes of direct comparison or generalization based on the discovery of analogies, for the retrieval of which the support of deduction is not necessary.

Greek thinkers seem to have had nothing but some vague notion of the power of deduction in this case, a power of which we are provided with classic examples by the application of mathematics to the description and explanation of natural phenomena, and of the extraordinary improvement, deriving from the appropriate use of deduction, of our ability to perceive uniformity in behavior and intimate analogies among phenomena apparently different and unsuitable for reduction and subjection to the same laws. The method that the Greeks applied to the

---

[19]For more details on this regard, see the excellent study by Wohlwill on the discovery of the law of inertia (*Die Entdeckung des Beharrungs-Gesetzes*), published since 1884 in the *Zeitschrift für Völkerpsychologie und Sprachwissenschaft* by Lazarus and Steinthal [Wohlwill 1884].

research of analogies on which they based their explanation of mechanical and physical phenomena was similar in substance to that which is now followed in the purely descriptive and comparative sciences (as for example anatomy, linguistics, botany) if we abstract, of course, from a lesser grade of diligence in the comparisons and distinctions, and most of all from the deficiency in criticism in the interpretation of testimonies and information, which are characteristics that do not touch the substance of the method, but which have their roots in the imperfect coordination and division of scientific labor, and in the difficulties encountered in those times in the transmission and accumulation of results obtained by several isolated observers.

What was considered an explanation of a given phenomenon by the Greek scientists was not its analysis and decomposition into elementary parts, or the determination of the laws of its production, as much as its comparison or identification with other more common and familiar phenomena, which, only for this reason, did not excite that special kind of amazement and wonder in the scientist that induces one to wonder why they happen. Confronted by a strange and unexplained fact, their main preoccupation was to recognize some trait in it that would allow them to refer it to some class of phenomena less able to surprise given their higher frequency of occurrence, and this reference was made by directly comparing the fact in question with some other similar and more familiar fact, and by stripping both facts of their accessory features which were masking their essential identity. Useful examples of explanations of this kind could be those given by Aristotle, in his *Mechanical Problems*,[20] of simpler mechanisms, reducing them or trying to reduce them to the case of the lever. The stimulus or incentive for this operation was expressly indicated by them to be the desire of freeing themselves from the uneasiness, and sometimes (as for example in the case of meteorological phenomena, which occupied a great part of the physical speculations made by the Greeks) also the desire of emancipation from the worries caused by the happening of phenomena too different from those that were subjected to their control. Therefore an explanation that would satisfy these conditions would be, for them, just a sufficient explanation.

And this is not the last of the causes for the lack of accuracy that characterizes their speculations on the causes of natural phenomena. They were really far from requiring from their speculations that attitude to predict still unknown facts and to anticipate, in a way, the experience, that for us represents such an essential condition for the

---

[20][The attribution of "Mechanical Problems" to Aristotle has been disputed.]

trust we have in scientific explanations. In most of the cases their arguments are able to produce, in a mind educated to the rigorous methods of modern science, the irresistible impression that, even if the fact to be explained were to be totally different, they would have not been at all embarrassed in adapting them to the same or a similar explanation with total nonchalance. The physical theories of the Epicurean school, as we find them reported in the fragments conserved by Diogenes Laertius, in his *Lives of the Philosophers*, and in Lucretius' poem, provide us with remarkable examples of this difference between the Greeks and ourselves in how to appreciate the acceptability and sufficiency of given explanations. We can mention, for example, that Epicurus, talking about the causes of eclipses, gives a series of distinct and contradictory explanations, among which, of course, there is also the true one, presenting them all as equally deserving of attention and equally justified, being equally incompatible with the superstitious popular beliefs,[21] according to which such phenomena were to be dreaded as foreboding disasters or as signs of divine anger. While any of us has had occasion to hear quoted several times that verse by Virgil in the *Georgics*:

Happy he who hath availed to know the causes of things,

it is not that often that we happen to see quoted the following two verses, where for this happiness to be attributed to the knowledge of causes the poet gives a reason which conforms but little to the one that would be given nowadays to support the same thesis, and where the only advantage that he attributes to the knowledge of causes is that which enables us to disdain the vulgar opinions about the fate of the souls of the dead and about their sad stay on the shores of the Acheron:

and hath laid all fears and immitigable Fate
and the roar of hungry Acheron under his feet.[22]

There are mental processes that are the most essential part of the

---

[21] "But we ought, above all things, to be on our guard against fables, and this one will easily be, if one follows faithfully the sensible phenomena in the explanation of these things, which are not perceived, except indirectly." And talking in general of the various ways to explain heavenly phenomena: "we may give very different explanations on this subject, equally agreeing with the impression of the senses." (Letter to Pythocle by Epicurus, on meteors. In Diogenes Laertius, book X, ch. I). [English translation by C.D. Yonge from Yonge 1853, p. 462, 455.]

[22] [Virgil, *Georgics* (II, 490). Quoted in Latin by Vailati. English translation by J. W. MacKail from Mackail 1915, pp. 75–76.] And likewise Seneca, talking about earthquakes "It is necessary to find solace for distressed people and to remove their great fear." (*Nat. Quest.*, book VI). [English translation by T. H. Corcoran from Corcoran 1971, Vol. 2, p. 129. In Latin in the text.]

modern methods of explanation and of scientific research, as for example taking theories to their ultimate consequences by means of deduction, with the intention of confronting them with some fact, known or which may become known, which may be incompatible with them; using every known law to the greatest extent to see up to what point it suffices to give an account of all the details encountered in the facts in which its action is manifested and to establish what unexplained residuum it still leaves open to our further investigation; combining several laws with the intention of using them in the analysis of a complicated single phenomenon; but all these operations, no one of which is possible without using deduction, appear to have been completely foreign to the spirit of those first investigators. And these are other characteristics connected to the same difference, that is, the difference between the old methods and those to which are due the instances of rapid progress of the physical sciences in the last three centuries: the aversion to deduction in all the cases in which it is of no use in *proving* something which was uncertain; the inability to use it as a means of securing ourselves against hasty generalizations,[23] increasing in a certain way the points of contact between each theory and the facts from which it can await confirmation or contradiction; the lack of patience, and I would say, as it were, the lack of abnegation, necessary for accurately tracking down the consequences of hypotheses or principles less intuitive and less solid than those of geometry, with the risk of obtaining as the only result of one's own efforts the conviction of having started from poorly grounded suppositions and of having to redo the same work by taking a different starting point; the fact of not being satisfied with vague analogies, but requiring that the agreement, among the phenomena being compared, is verified down to the most minute details accessible to our senses or to the control of instruments and measurements.

The commonly accepted opinion, according to which this difference consists of the simple substitution of a new method, based on experiment and observation, instead of a supposed ancient method proceeding from *a priori* statements and by pure deduction, far from including and exhausting the truly essential traits of distinction between new and ancient research processes, seems to me to be leaving out of consideration

---

[23] Even in the research based purely on induction (statistics), the intervention of deduction is indispensable in that part of the process of research consisting of separating the fortuitos coincidences from those that can lead to the determination of laws that regulates the phenomena studied. It seems as though the Greeks ignored the most basic concepts of probability. They are found perhaps for the first time in Galileo.

precisely those traits that can be regarded as the most fundamental, and of which the remaining traits are just mere consequences. Inquiring into the causes that have contributed to create this opinion so contrary to the positive data offered by the history of science would mean digressing too far from the topic that I have decided to address. We certainly cannot deny that the wonderful results achieved by the Greeks, by means of deduction, in the field of Geometry and the consequent fact of it becoming the science par excellence (as indicated by its name,) on the model of which all others have had to be organized,[24] have contributed powerfully to the creation of damaging prejudices or exaggerated appreciations of the effectiveness of deductive reasoning, both as a means of proof and as a tool for research, and to lead to its immature and improvident application to other sciences, whose nature or stage of development did not yet allow their proficient use. The signs of such an influence are evident in the writings of Aristotle and even more in those of Plato, of whom it will suffice to recall here the eloquent and enthusiastic words used, in the sixth book of the *Republic*, proclaiming the superiority of geometry over all the sciences, and denying to whoever does not know Geometry the right to deal with theoretical research on any subject. It is said of Plato that he answered, to a young man ignorant of mathematics who was asking to be taught by him, as follows: "I cannot dye you, if you do not get degreased first." And when another in the same situation, asked to be admitted to his school, he rejected his request by saying: "How can I take you, if you are like an amphora without handles?"[25]

It has often been the case that these great thinkers have been accused of abusing the deductive method, blaming them for the aberrations reached by those who, in the following centuries, used their statements as a basis on which to build, exactly by means of deduction, mystical or fantasy theories, like the Neoplatonics did, or to design dialectic argumentations in defense of their own preconceptions, as the Scholastic philosophers did. However, this accusation is as far from the truth as saying that in the Bible or in the Penal Code the deductive method is abused, because it is from these that theologians and lawyers take the premises of their syllogisms and make use, exactly by means of

---

[24]The observation is by Locke (*Essay*, book IV, ch. 12, 2): "One thing which might probably give an occasion to this way of proceeding by deduction from axiomatic principles in other sciences was, as I suppose, the good success it seemed to have in mathematics, wherein men being observed to attain a great certainty of knowledge, these sciences came by preeminence to be called μαθήματα or μάθησις, that is learning." [Locke 1690. In English in the original.]

[25]Both these anecdotes are reported by Stobaeus (*Eclogae*) [Meineke 1860].

deduction, of those writings to secure the kind of certainty and indis-
putability that are needed for their conclusions in order to silence their
opponents or to convince whoever has to pronounce the sentence.

Regarding the predominantly deductive nature of Scholastic philosophy, it is easy to understand how and why, in a cultural age intellectually characterized by the tendency to accept or to force others
to accept, with no discussion, doctrines provided by tradition and authority, as though they were beyond any proof, the favorite reasoning
method was that which allowed getting the maximum possible benefit from the dogmatic principles accepted by everyone, or at least that
everyone was not supposed to challenge. It is natural in these circumstances that the mental processes that were most used and reputed
were those which made it possible to extend as far as possible the area
of competence and the scope of the limited *supply* of statements and
norms that were supposed to be sufficient for the systematization of
the beliefs and behavior. These methods were also supposed to automatically achieve such extension of competence and scope, without the
intervention of individual evaluations or criteria, with no dissipation or
attenuation of certainty or reliability, because, as we have seen before,
one of the characteristic properties of deduction is that of being, so to
speak, a *good conductor* of evidence and certainty, and of passing on
untouched, to the conclusions achieved by means of it, all the credibility
and authority possessed by the corresponding premises.

Given that the deductive method had, so to speak, joined forces with
the tendency to excessively respect tradition, and with the aversion to
letting doubts and examinations arise above certain fixed limits, it is
not surprising that, as a consequence, the first attempts to reform and
improve research methods took the shape of protests against the abuse
of deduction and vindications in favor of induction. The mere fact of resorting to induction was already, in itself, a manifestation of insufficient
trust in those principles that were not supposed to be questioned. The
declarations made by Bacon on the sterility of dialectics and against
the syllogistics of Aristotle would have been far less violent and ruthless, had he not been forced, as the popular saying goes, to talk to the
daughter-in-law in order for the mother-in-law to understand, that is,
if he could have completely separated his objections to the abuse of
syllogism from his criticism against all the prejudices and the mistakes
that were, by means of deduction, capable of forming a formidable pha-
lanx against any attempt at progress and the advancement of sciences
beyond the herculean columns designated by incompetent authorities.
In this regard, the position in which Bacon and the other contemporary innovators found themselves facing the representatives of the

old ideas, and the fact that they found themselves forced to consider their own teachers as adversaries, reminds me of those heroic defenders of that medieval town who, during the siege to which they were subjected by Frederick Barbarossa, were forced to defend themselves by firing their shots against their own fellow citizens, as the emperor had ordered his soldiers to plaster with the prisoners the walls of the machines and shields behind which they were moving forwards towards the city walls.[26]

It is not to be believed that the false appreciations, generated in that way by reaction, of the respective importance of deduction and of experiment in scientific research, have generated some detrimental influence on the development of sciences. They have certainly impaired much more the philosophical theories, or the speculative opinions, enunciated by the scientists about general questions on method, rather than the actual procedure that they follow in their research. In this respect, practice has been further ahead compared to theory, and the damage to the progress of knowledge would have been serious if this had not been the case. The great influence that works like the *Novum Organum* by Bacon, the *Discours de la Mèthode* by Descartes or the *Essay on Human Understanding* by Locke undoubtedly had on the progress of science must be attributed much more to their work of demolition and criticism, by means of which they cleared out the terrain to prepare it for the new buildings, rather than to the fact that these works contained correct or exhaustive analyses, or something more than some vague divinations, of the processes of research from which modern science rose.

Jevons rightly observed that the chapter of the great work by Newton dedicated to the enunciation of the fundamental norms of scientific research (*regulae philosophandi*, as he calls them) is really deficient if it is to be considered an attempt to formulate and codify the norms that he follows in the rest of his work, without even mentioning them. Even if similar observations cannot be repeated for all the great scientists (suffice to mention Galileo's case), however, it can be said that, like the systematic application of the deductive method in geometry, probably started by the Pythagoreans, has preceded by some centuries the Aristotelian formulation of the theory of syllogism, in the same way the theoretical speculations on the modern methods of research could

---

[26][Vailati is referring to a well known episode from the history of his hometown, Crema. In 1159, Crema was besieged, stormed and destroyed by the Emperor Frederick Barbarossa. It is said that during the siege the Germans hung some prisoners from Crema on their machines, hoping the defenders would not fire against their fellows. However, this expedient did not work, and turned into a slaughter.]

not find an independent and proper exposition until a long time after the first and most decisive conquests to which they led. Of course this should not encourage any negative assumption about the theoretical or practical value of the general research on scientific method. Such assumptions would be as unwarranted as those of someone who would doubt the importance or usefulness of Archimedes' speculations on the lever just because the use of the lever as an instrument and the acquisition of the necessary knowledge to use it had preceded, by who knows how many centuries, the research by Archimedes on the equilibrium of planes, and are not even an exclusive property of the human species. If someone had asked Galileo or Newton to write down a general scheme coherent with the norms that they had, consciously or instinctively, followed in the progress of their research, they would have given an answer similar to that said to have been given by [Joseph] Fraunhofer when asked for explanations about how a new lens that he had built for his telescope worked: "I built it not to look at it, but as a means to look at other things."

Therefore, even if general observations on the research processes and suggestions regarding the method are not rare in the works of great scientists, by which such new processes and methods were started, nevertheless in these works we do not find a coherent and explicit treatment of the questions related to the classification and analysis of the mental activities involved. Therefore, for example, regarding fundamental concepts such as *cause, agent, explanation, attitude*, etc., we can say that only in the writings of David Hume can we find these concepts as objects of a psychological analysis deep enough to make it possible to use them as the basis of a systematic and coordinated exposition of the research methods used in the physical sciences, such as that of John Herschel in his famous *Discourse on the Study of Natural Philosophy*.[27] As regards the function of hypotheses as an instrument of research, we can say that it is only in the aforementioned work by Herschel and in Comte's writings, published almost simultaneously, that such a question was discussed from a general point of view and with a level of accuracy corresponding to the importance and difficulty of the topic.

II.

The subject left for me to discuss concerns the *conditions on which the different applicability and fertility of the deductive method in the various research fields depend.* Even in this case it has not been possible to bring theory to the same level as practice until later on, and even then

---

[27] [See Herschel 1830.]

maybe not completely, and to make the former able not merely to justify the latter, but also to be a guide for organizing the instinctive and
habitual procedures in a system of norms that go back to a few general principles, by which they would be summarized and coordinated.
Among the works where this task of coordination and organization has
been developed the most and has become more deliberate, the *System
of Logic* by John Stuart Mill seems to be the best suited on which to
base the exposition that I am about to make on the present state of
such questions. The best way to present the relevant part of Stuart
Mill's views seems to me to be by mentioning his discussion of one of
the most common objections moved against the use of syllogism as a
means of proof, an objection whose origin is usually attributed to Bacon. It actually goes back much further and it is appropriate for me to
express it with the words which have already been stated in that curious hotchpotch of slanders against human reason and against science,
the *Pyrrhonic Sketches* by Sextus Empiricus, a work where precious
remains of the scientific theories of Greek philosophers have been preserved amongst much rhetorical debris, judged from the point of view
of the school called skeptical (that is, *observing*), founded by Pyrrho
and then continued by the New Academics Arcesilaus, Carneades, and
Clitomachus, all philosophers who lived in the third century before the
vulgar era. It should be noted that Sextus Empiricus is also the author of a book entitled *Against Mathematicians*, in which, among other
things, he scolds the geometers for being too naive in believing they are
able to avoid all those difficulties which can be brought against their axioms and their fundamental concepts, by resorting to the heroic means
of qualifying them as simple suppositions or arbitrary conventions.

Here there are the words of Sextus Empiricus in his chapter against
Aristotle's logic: "When they say: *Every man is a mortal. Socrates
is a man. Therefore, Socrates is a mortal*, intending to infer the last
proposition from the first one and given that they also agree that any
certainty attributed to the first one is a consequence of induction from
particular cases such as the one stated in the last, they fall into a
circular argument (εἰς τὸν δι' ἀλλήλων ἐμπίπτουσιν) In fact, if when we
state the general proposition *Every man is a mortal* we were not already
convinced of the truthfulness of all the particulars that it includes, we
would not have any reason to believe it to be true."[28] From this he
concludes that no syllogism or series of syllogisms can ever be suited to
giving us any knowledge of something beyond what we already knew
before, and that deduction, far from being the typical and most correct

---

[28] [See Sext. Emp., *Pyrr. Hyp.*, I, 164 ff. in Bekker 1842, pp. 94–95.]

form of reasoning, is nothing but a sophistic artifice used to hide our ignorance from our own or others' eyes, or to make our own opinions, expressed in a different way, look like proof of our same own opinions.

The position taken by John Stuart Mill on this objection can be briefly characterized as follows: He concedes, first of all, how such objection is completely founded and indisputable in the case of syllogisms of the kind mentioned above, that is syllogisms where one of the premises consists of the enunciation of a law or general proposition, while the other premise affirms that, in a certain case, the conditions that make such a law applicable are verified. So, taking the previous example, it cannot be denied that the proposition *Socrates is mortal* must already be considered true before it is possible to state the general proposition where we assert the mortality of all men, and we cannot say we are sure of the truth of it, if we have not made sure of its applicability in all the cases it contemplates. Therefore any doubt we can have left on the mortality of one man is for this reason also a doubt left on the truth of the proposition where the mortality of all men is affirmed.

Therefore it cannot be denied that, if by reasoning we mean a mental operation that allows us to go from the known to the unknown and widens the field of our cognitions, then the syllogisms like the one mentioned before do not have any right to be called reasoning at all. We use them at most, simply to interpret and apply, in a given circumstance, the result of some reasoning made before, by ourselves or made for us by others, that is those results that memory or tradition preserves for us under the shape of general propositions, also preserving or not the memory of the factual proof or reasons that induced us to accept them and believe them as true. Such general propositions, to use a quote from Schopenhauer, do not represent for us a field where our cognitions sprout and grow, but rather a barn where they lie in a heap and are saved from bad weather and kept ready for our needs. The purpose for the syllogisms of the aforementioned kind is, in summary, only that of enabling us to take advantage of past experience, our own or that of others, without having to refer directly to every single fact or the entire series of particular observations of which such an experience is actually made. This also allow us, up to a certain point, to completely forget such experiences, without giving up the advantage of being guided by them in adjusting our judgments and our expectations regarding facts that have not yet happened, or are still unknown. The real reasoning, the passage, that is, from assertions on known facts to assertions on still unknown facts, is not represented here by the syllogism, but rather by those previous inductions that induced us to accept as true the general proposition that, by means of syllogism, we are using with profit.

Therefore syllogism does not correspond to a phase in the process of researching and ascertainment of truth, but is simply a mechanism suited to facilitating the use and transmission of the truth already known.

But if this is completely true for the kind of syllogisms under discussion so far, we would make a huge mistake if we were to believe that the same considerations can be applied to syllogisms of any kind. If the natural tendency towards too hasty generalizations would induce us, even for a moment, to embrace such an opinion, to be made aware of the deceit of which we are victims, it would suffice to think about the repeated triumphs that, from the Greeks to us, syllogism has had, and is still providing in the field of Mathematical Sciences, where it represents the only kind of reasoning and proof allowed. The most superficial glance at the glorious collection of discoveries that the history of Mechanics shows to us as the results of deductive reasoning would suffice. There are deductions and syllogisms where something more and different is done than merely applying a general rule to a special case, a special case where it is possible to directly recognize the presence of the characters that make the general rule applicable. There are syllogisms where both premises are general propositions, and where the conclusion is a new general proposition that would not have been able to be proved by induction, without resorting to *observation or experiences that would be completely different from those by which the corresponding premises have been, or could have been, proved.*

To have a good characterization of this class of syllogisms, rather than making general observations, it would be useful to give an example, taken from the history of Mechanics. The reasoning that led Huygens to the discovery of the fundamental properties of the centers of oscillation, and to state for the first time, under a general form, the *principle of live forces*, is basically a syllogism of which these are the two premises:

I). "If a pendulum composed of several weights and set in motion from rest, completes any part of its full oscillation, and from that point onwards, the individual weights, with their common connexions dissolved, change their acquired velocities upwards and ascend as far as they can, the common center of gravity of all will be carried up to the same altitude with that which it occupied before the beginning of the oscillation." [29]

II). The angular velocity ω, moving the pendulum when its center of gravity is in a certain position, so that the weights that compose it

---

[29] [C. Huygens, *Horologium oscillatorium*, Part IV *De centro oscillationis*, Prop. VI. (Huygens, 1673). Quoted in Latin by Vailati. English translation by P. E. B. Jourdain from Jourdain 1911, p. 29.]

go up independently of each other and are able to raise their common center of gravity to a given height h from the original level, is tied to the height by this relation:

$$h \sum m = \sum m \frac{(r\omega)^2}{2g}$$

that is

$$2gh = \omega^2 \frac{\sum mr^2}{\sum m}$$

where m represents the masses corresponding to the weights the pendulum is made up of, and r are the respective mean distances of these from the rotation axis. This second premise is nothing but the enunciation, in a convenient form for the present argumentation, of the law discovered by Galileo that connects the velocity of a body in a given instant with the height to which such a velocity would be able to make it raise again.

From these two premises Huygens concludes that the relation in the second which is affirmed to exist between the angular velocity of the pendulum, when in its descent it passes from that position, and the height that could be reached, by virtue of it, by the center of gravity of the weights that compose it, if they were to ascend independently of each other, shall also hold between such angular velocity and the height where the center of gravity of the pendulum was, before the pendulum started to move. This conclusion immediately provides the rule to determine the length of the simple pendulum, whose oscillations are isochronous to those of a compound pendulum.

In this syllogism, and in the others of the same kind, it is clear that the conclusion reached is not only far from being already known and accepted when the premises are known, but even if it were previously known by direct experience, still it is not even remotely suitable to be used in support or as proof for either of the two premises, unless the mental operation, represented by the syllogism that connects them, has been performed in one way or another.

In general, anytime we come to know with certainty that a given phenomenon A is constantly connected with the phenomenon B, not through a generalization directly based on the examination of the facts where we can see the connection between the two mentioned phenomena, but instead through our previous knowledge of a connection between A and a third phenomenon C, and moreover of a connection between C and B, the syllogism that represents this mental operation really provides a growth of our knowledge. It is, in fact, only *after* the connection between A and B has been determined in this way, by means of their individual connections with C, that we are able to see, in those facts where such connections hold, some simple special cases to be classified together with the cases where we observe the connections stated in the premises. And in this way, because of the effect of deduction, we become able to discover, among facts apparently different, some intimate analogies, that immediate observation would have not been able to show us.

The example we have mentioned, even though the premises appear to be complex, is not to be considered among the more complicated examples of reasoning that can be found in the exposition of a deductive science. The case most often encountered is the one where a conclusion that we want to reach is not the asserting of a connection between a given circumstance or phenomenon A and another circumstance or phenomenon B, but rather a group of circumstances or conditions and another group of circumstances or effects. In this case it is often necessary to combine together not just two but a much higher number of laws or connections, already known and demonstrated to hold among single circumstances in the first group and single circumstances in the second, in a way that creates not just a *chain*, but rather a real *net* or *tissue* of arguments connected in multiple ways one with another. And I do not even need to mention that each proposition that has been used in this process could in turn have been reached, not through direct observation, but as the conclusion of other similar processes, based on other general propositions, which in turn can be of the same sort and so on.

There are sciences where this task of choosing and concatenating propositions that are already known, or accepted as true, is a much safer and more effective tool for research than direct experience or observation, even when done in a diligent way and with the aid of instruments. Moreover, in these sciences this could be the only tool used, not just for verification, but also for the discovery of new laws and new relations among the studied phenomena.[30] And we do not need to point out that these branches of science, far from being stationary and unprogressive, are instead precisely those where the advance of knowledge is the fastest and the results are the most wonderful. To say that, in the syllogisms used in dealing with these sciences, as for instance

---

[30] In these sciences the use of the Socratic method of teaching, or by dialogue and repeated questioning, discharges the student from this work of choice and concatenation of the propositions through which he reaches new conclusions, and it gives him the impression that they are much easier to reach than that which they really are. From this, it obtains its stimulating effectiveness.

in Geometry, what is asserted in the conclusions is already *implicitly included* in the premises, is simply to affirm, by means of a poor and not really appropriate metaphor, the simple fact, that nobody denies, that the propositions chosen as fundamental are perfectly sufficient to prove all the conclusions based on them, with no need of supplementary aid from experience. Intended as such, the sentence above points out not a flaw, but an advantage of the process of deduction compared to induction, and it is not a valid objection against the use of syllogism, no more than it would be a valid objection against the value of the sculptor's art to say, as Michelangelo did,[31] that a beautiful statue is already included in the boulder from which the artist wants to carve it, and that the job of the sculptor is merely to remove the superfluous parts from the block of marble, which prevent the observer from seeing inside.

After what I have said so far, there will be no need to spend too many words on indicating the circumstances on which the greater or lesser applicability of the deductive method in the various fields of research depends.

If the propositions reached directly by induction from the facts observed for a given science were of this kind: the property A is always joint with property B, property C with property D, the E with F, etc., without ever having the case where the same property appears at the same time in two different propositions, where in each one its connection with two different properties is respectively stated, it is clear that the deductive process would be completely inapplicable. In this situation it would not be possible to determine or discover a law or connection between two properties, relying only on experimental data that guarantees the connection of every property with a third, and this is exactly what constitutes reasoning by deduction. The only kind of explanation applicable to phenomena belonging to such a field would be where we recognized it as characteristic of the inferior stages of scientific development, that is that consisting of the immediate comparison of a fact in question with other facts, among those already known that are more similar, so that the new fact can fall, if possible, in the domain of some

---

[31] Michelangelo Buonarroti, *Rime*, Sonnet I.
"Non ha l'ottimo artista alcun concetto
Che un marmo solo in s'e non circoscriva
Col suo soperchio, e solo a quello arriva
La man che obbedisce all'intelletto."
("Nothing the greatest can conceive/ That every marble block doth not confine/ Within itself: and only its design/ The hand that follows intellect can achieve.")
[See Biagioli 1821, p. 1. English translation by H. W. Longfellow, from Longfellow 1883, p. 392.]

existing generalization or, if this is not possible, we would record the fact aside, waiting for other similar facts that could, one day, lead by means of induction to the discovery of some still unknown law. The sum of independent and unconnected truths that can be reached this way is designated with the name of *empirical laws*. A science consisting only of this kind of laws would have a catalogue of general propositions, each one proved by distinctive sets of observations and experiments, and none of them would be suited for use as a control for the others, or to communicate to the remaining the higher grade of certainty or reliability that it may possess.

Even though most sciences, especially the physical sciences, are far from this extreme case, nevertheless it is evident the they differ from it in different grades, and they differ more in parallel to the frequency of propositions in them suitable for pairing so that they form syllogisms in the way that we have seen. The sciences where this condition is satisfied in a way that no proposition appears in them as isolated or abandoned—unsuitable, that is, for connection to the others as indicated above—tend, for this reason, to become organized, I would actually say to become crystallized, in the form of a system of consequences that can be deducted by appropriately chosen groups of fundamental propositions.

It is not surprising, then, that for centuries deduction has already established its exclusive and absolute dominion on Geometry and on the Mathematical Sciences in general, which are really the only ones where deduction has been able to completely and apparently definitively surpass any direct interference from induction, especially if we observe how, for the axioms and the fundamental relations always used in Mathematics, the conditions that we have recognized as necessary and sufficient for the application of deduction are satisfied. In fact the relations between quantities or between figures that we designate with the words "*equal to*," "*greater or lesser than*," "*coinciding with*," "*function of*," etc., "*to tend to the same limit*," "*equivalence*," "*projectivity*," etc., are all relations of the kind that, if they exist between one quantity or figure and another quantity or figure, and also between the latter and a third one, it is possible to conclude, *independently from any direct observation*, that they exist between the first and the third.[32]

---

[32]The kind of reasoning known to mathematicians under the name of complete induction, as has been well highlighted by Poincaré, consists, in the end, of demonstrating the possibility, in a given case, of executing an indefinite series of deductions, all of which have a common premise, and in each of them appears, as another premise, the conclusion obtained by the previous deduction. In order for this reasoning to be able to demonstrate that a given property is possessed by a class of

It would not be appropriate to go into more detail on this important subject. However, some interesting considerations in this regard can be found scattered in the writings by De Morgan, Mach, and Grassmann. Also, Helmholtz dedicates some observations on it in his memoirs (*Zählen und Messen*) [1887] to which we refer anyone interested in the topic.

From what I have said so far we can see how is it possible that the discovery of new laws, related to a new class of phenomena, makes the use of the deductive method more accessible for the study of such phenomena. Such is seen, for example, in Chemistry in the discovery of the law of definite proportions, which allows the prediction of the proportions of the combination of two substances when we know the proportions in which each of them may be combined with a third. Just for this reason, this discovery has opened a way to reasoning by means of deduction, modifying in part the structure of the science, even without losing the predominantly inductive character that it still has.

Among the discoveries that have contributed and still contribute most effectively to enlarging the area of application of deduction, we should count those that consist of recognising how, in the production of phenomena of a given class, the action of several agent causes taken together can, without altering the effect, substitute the action of a single cause or of a smaller number of causes, on condition that these are connected with the former by a certain constant relation. We can see this happening, for example, when several forces act on the same point, whose cumulative effect, as stated by the laws discovered by Galileo, does not change if they are substituted by a single force, obtained from those by a simple geometrical construction, which is always the same and is executed on the segments that represent those forces of direction and intensity. Statics gives us several characteristic examples of the influence of discoveries of this kind on the constitution of new theories of the deductive kind. So, regarding the simplest case of equilibrium that can be considered, that of a lever from which several weights hang at different distances from the axis of rotation, the method followed by Euclid and Archimedes to determine, by means of deductive reasoning, the conditions on which such equilibrium depends, consists basically in verifying and using repeatedly the following property: if a lever is in equilibrium under the action of these weights, the equilibrium is not perturbed if any of these weights is substituted by two of them

---

objects, such objects need to be able to be ordered in a way where each of them is obtained by the preceding one, in the same way as from that we can obtain the next. See the article by Poincaré: *Sur la nature du raisonnement mathématique*, in "Revue de Métaphysique et de Morale," 1894, pp. 371–84 [Poincaré 1894].

equal to the half of the first one, and if their points of suspension are equidistant from the original suspension point (Archimedes), or by two weights, each equal to the original one, whose suspension points are situated between the fulcrum and the original suspension point, one distant from it as the other is from the fulcrum (Euclid).[33]

One of the most effective means, even if unfortunately not always applicable, of reaching similar results, i.e., of discovering the relations that must exist among several groups of causes, suited to cooperating in the production of a given phenomenon, in order for one group to be substituted for another without altering the effect, is that of studying in isolation the way of action of each of the causes in question, trying to determine what is invariable and common in their behavior when they act separately and when each of them acts together with the others instead. It is precisely in following this procedure that Galileo, as already mentioned, reached the greatest of his discoveries, that which made the creation of Dynamics possible as a deductive science: the discovery, that is, of that fundamental law of motion that can be stated by saying: if several forces concur in determining a certain movement, because they concur, they do not cease to produce, each on its own, the same effects that they would produce if they were acting alone, contrary to previously commonly accepted belief, according to which, for example, the action of the weight of a thrown body was thought to be suspended for some time, or at least radically modified, simply for the reason of it being associated with the other cause of motion, represented by the impact or push, by which the body was thrown. Before this law was discovered and clearly formulated, the mechanical theorist who would attempt to determine the motion produced by the simultaneous action of several forces, where the behavior for each of them was also perfectly known, found himself facing the same difficulties that today would be faced by a chemist, attempting to determine *a priori* the properties of a compound, using only his knowledge of the properties of the components.

III.

What I have said so far on the conditions on which the different applicability and fruitfulness of the deductive method in the various fields of research depends, easily allows us to have an idea of the nature of

---

[33]The reader can find more clarifications regarding the method followed by Euclid in my article: *Di una dimostrazione del Principio della Leva attribuita ad Euclide* [On a demonstration on the principle of the lever that is attributed to Euclid] in an Arabic manuscript at the National Library in Paris. (*Bollettino di Storia e Bibliografia Matematica*, November-December 1897) [Vailati 1897a].

the *advantages that its use brings* in all those cases where possible, and to understand the reasons for the opinion, commonly and almost instinctively accepted, according to which the extension of the field of action of deductive reasoning is to be considered desirable and which corresponds to the actual progress of the sciences where it happens.

Among these advantages there is one on which I have already had occasion to insist while mentioning Aristotle's opinions on the function of deduction as an instrument of proof, therefore I will linger on it just long enough to distinguish it from the others. This advantage consists in the mutual control that propositions, tied by means of deduction, are able to exercise on one another, and in the mutual support that they provide each other in this way, in a manner of speaking, bringing together the cumulative strength of all the facts and all the verifications that each of them has available individually. Just as in a well-ordered state, an injustice suffered by the last of the citizens is felt with undiminished intensity and repaired with undiminished strength as if it had been suffered by the most influent or affluent of people, in the same way in a science ordered by deduction, any proposition, however complex and laboriously reached, is no less protected against doubt and objections than the more evident and primitive propositions appearing in the exposition of such science, provided, of course, that we abstract from the occasional material error in calculation, the probability of which can easily be decreased by any grade that can be practically assigned. In such sciences no fact or innovation can be considered sufficient enough to invalidate the truth of a demonstrated proposition, if that fact or that innovation does not have enough importance not just to be able to shake the trust in the propositions that they seem to contradict, but also to force us to modify or abandon as unsupported at least one of the fundamental propositions that we could use to demonstrate it.

Even if this advantage of the use of deduction seems to be great, and even if, as we have seen, it is considered to be the only one deserving of consideration by philosophers and scientists,[34] nevertheless it is far from being indicated as the main one among those which cooperate in making the extension of the deductive treatment desirable to all cases where it is applicable. There are others which are much more important, and whose importance is not merely evermore recognized with the progress of analyses of research methods, but actually also

---

[34]This does not mean that, in some branches of research, and especially in Astronomy, they would not use deduction much more as a means of representation and coordination of facts rather than as a simple means of proof and verification. It is remarkable, in this regard, a fragment from Pappus, reported by Hultsch from a Vatican Greek code (Hultsch, Pappi *Collect.*, III, praef.) [Hultsch 1875-1878].

grows with the development of sciences and with the growth of the patrimony of human knowledge. Such advantages are those related to the ability of deduction to simplify and facilitate the description and the characterization of the behavior of phenomena analyzed in a certain study, allowing us to represent the laws that regulate them in our minds, by means of a minimal number of general propositions, each including the most comprehensive set of particular facts and special cases, which in appearance are heterogeneous.

In order to understand how deduction can be used to this purpose, a tangible example of how this happens in the simplest and most elementary kind of deductive reasoning will suffice, the one where, in given circumstances, the connection between two phenomena A and B depends on the previously independently observed fact, that in given circumstances, phenomenon A is constantly conjoint with a third phenomenon C, and that C is also constantly conjoint with B. It is evident that in this case any of the conditions or circumstances on which one of the connections expressed in one of the premises depends, must also be included among the circumstances on which the connection stated in the conclusion depends, while among the circumstances on which the latter depends, there could be some that are not required for the connection asserted in one of the premises. In fact, for the validity of the conclusion, we need not just have the satisfaction of the conditions on which one of the premises depends, but also those on which the other depends; and these two groups of conditions can also be completely distinct and independent from one another. In order to explain myself with an example, we can think of a chain, which can be broken by any cause that would break one of the rings, but the inverse proposition would not be true; that is, any cause known to be able to determine the break of the chain would not be considered able to produce the break of a specific ring. From this it follows that in the case of the chain, the conditions that must be verified in order for the chain not to break are many more than those which should be verified for one specific ring not to break. Similarly, in the case of the above-mentioned syllogism, the conditions and restrictions that must be satisfied in order for one of the premises to be true are in general far fewer, and therefore more likely to show up together or be present at the same time in a wider range of cases, than the entire group of those whose concurrence is needed for the proposition obtained from them by deduction. That is the same as saying, in other words, that the premises are more general, and they include and dominate a greater number of particular facts than those included and dominated by the proposition that has been deduced from them.[35] The same or similar considerations clearly also apply to other more complex kinds of deductive reasoning, and it is clear that they actually acquire more importance as the series of propositions through which a given conclusion is reached becomes longer. It is this reduction of a fact, or of a law, to other more general laws or facts that constitutes what we call *scientific explanation*, and it is important to note how the advantages inherent in this process do not depend at all on the circumstances that the facts or the laws, upon which a given explanation is grounded, are presented to our minds as more familiar or more evident in themselves than those that we are explaining by their means. Applied in such a way, deduction as a means of explanation allows us to embrace a variety and multiplicity of facts in one glance and with one single act of the mind; the consideration of such a variety of facts would otherwise require a considerably greater number of operations and distinct intellectual efforts. With its aid we manage to put ourselves at a point of view from which the analogies, the relations,

---

[35]This effectiveness of deduction, as a means of generalization, is always present, even when there is no real case, or it is not known, in which the conditions required for the truth of one or the other of the premises are verified, without also verifying, at the same time, all the others that are in addition required for the truth of both of them, and therefore for the truth of the conclusion deduced from them as well. To explain through an example, even if Kepler's laws corresponded to the actual movements of the stars no less exactly than the results obtained by deduction from Newton's laws, the substitution of the latter for the former would have represented, nevertheless, a step towards a wider generalization, because while Kepler's laws only refer to the motion that the planets *actually undergo*, Newton's laws (even abstracting from the fact that they also include the case of the motion of bodies on the earth's surface) also tell us something about the motion that they *would have*, or *would have had* if the initial distribution of masses and velocity had been different.

In the sciences that have a relation with practice, which refer, that is, to facts partially subject to the control of human will, the conjectures related to what *would happen*, if some conditions held that which they have never held before, often have much more importance than the cognitions about what happens, or has always happened, in the absence of such new conditions.

It is for this reason that we should attribute to deduction a function much more important as a means for *invention* rather than a means for *discovery*. The part that it plays in mechanical inventions is well highlighted by Reulaux (*Kinematics*, p. 22 in the Italian translation by Professor Colombo). [See Reulaux 1875. Vailati quotes from Reulaux 1876.] One can also consult the works by Kapp (*Philosophie der Technik*) and by Espinas (*Technologie des Grecs*). [See Kapp 1877 and Espinas 1897.] Similar considerations can perhaps explain the fact, often acknowledged, that regarding the study of social phenomena, the boldest inventors and creators of the outlines of reforms, and the most ruthless critics of the theories justifying the actual institutions and social rules, are exactly those researchers that distinguish themselves for having a greater tendency towards the use, or abuse, of deduction (for example Rousseau or Marx—nn).

and the connections among the phenomena that we are investigating are explained to our intellect just as the topographical details of a region are offered to the view of one who contemplates them from high ground. In this way deduction multiplies our abilites to perceive order, uniformity and constant laws in the midst of a tumultuous succession of facts and events, or, to express the same thing with a sentence from Plato (*Republic*, book 7,) it puts us in a position to *discern the one in the many* (τὸ ἓν ἐν πολλοῖς ὁρᾶν) and to discover with the mind's eyes the immutable poles around which turn the chaos and the perpetual procession of phenomena and of sensations.

To sum up, if we intend as the purpose of scentific research the construction of a group of theories and mental images whose correspondence with the facts represented is more and more perfect, and such as to allow us evermore reliable, more precise predictions with a further grasp of its long term behavior and a more effective control of the means available to us in order to make things instrumental to the satisfaction of our needs or to the realization of our aspirations, we shall recognize, as the main purpose of deduction, that of making us able to reach these goals by simpler means and reducing the mental operations and the number of facts and experiences required for the task to a minimum.

It could seem paradoxical to say that the power of deduction in this regard is such that through it we come to discover not only the more general and elementary properties that we study, but even get to force them to be reproduced in our minds as if the laws that regulate them and the properties they possess were far more simple and general than they actually are. Nevertheless, this is literally true. So, for example, the fact that there are no perfectly rigid bodies or absolutely incompressible fluids does not prevent the physicist from studying and determining which properties they *should have* if they were to exist, or by means of deduction come to analyze them, connect them, and recognize them as independent from one another, exactly as though they were properties of bodies which actually existed. In this way we obtain conclusions that are still applicable to bodies that are not perfectly rigid or absolutely incompressible, provided that, of course, their lack of rigidity or incompressibility is not such so as to make the difference between their actual behaviour and that of their ideal fictitious models so great that it generates errors or inconveniences that are not compensated by the advantages provided by the performed simplification. Perfectly similar to this is the procedure that had to be followed by those who started the study of shapes and figures of bodies, emancipating it from any consideration of the other properties of the bodies themselves or the matter from which the figures were made.

This simple process of abstraction that made at the same time both possible and necessary the application of deduction to the research of properties of space, seems to us so simple and natural that we almost cannot conceive that it required any labor or intellectual effort. Instead we go as far as qualifying it as *mystic* or *metaphysical*, in the negative sense of the word, the way in which Plato expressed himself, when he describes this mental process, saying that it consists in substituting the inane pursuit of the fleeting and ephemeral images offered by the senses, for the consideration of their prototypes or models that are inalterable and perpetual, and the contemplation of the eternal forms (εἴδη) or ideas of things, ideas or models to which the real objects, which correspond to them, are in the same relationship as the shadows with the bodies that produce them. The fact that we now feel induced to invert this metaphor and instead see our theories and abstractions as the shadows of things, rather than considering things and real objects as the shadows of our concepts and our abstractions, should not prevent us from recognizing the piece of truth embedded in that renowned and poetic Platonic myth, where men, entangled in sensations, and unable to abstract, are compared to people seated in an almost dark cave with their shoulders facing the entrance, from which a scarce light enters, and they have to observe, instead of the objects passing in front of the cave, the faint and deformed shadows that such objects project on the uneven and cavernous cave walls.

Plato would have probably expressed himself differently, if he had had other examples before his eyes, besides those provided by Geometry and Astronomy, of this procedure of simplifying idealization that is an indispensable prerequisite for any application of deduction to the study of natural phenomena. So, for example, he would certainly have been disgusted to see an ideal model of the real man in that abstract kind of *Homo aeconomicus*, as it has been called, which was forged for the same identical purpose by Adam Smith during his research on the laws of production and distribution of wealth. After all, like the physicists denote with the name of *perfect fluids* or *ideal gasses* those that they imagine equipped with properties appropriately chosen to be able to study their behavior deductively and with the help of calculations, in the same way the economists can qualify with the name *perfect* or *ideal man* (independently, of course, from any moral appreciation) the kind of man who is selfish and indifferent to any other desire than that of earning as much as possible with as little work as possible, a kind of man that they have forged in order to put him at the base of their arguments, and that has been so useful in tracing, with the help of deduction, some of the most important laws of social economics unknown to the ancients, among which we may mention the theory of income by Ricardo, his discoveries on the impact of taxes, and his analysis of the determining causes of international exchanges.

It should be noted, and is clearly seen from the examples I have already provided before the process of simplification in question, that its application can be made possible and convenient only by the fact that phenomena which actually exist, whose behavior is not far from that which they would have if the suppositions, by means of which the properties of the ideal models corresponding to them were determined, were exactly verified. This happens only when, among the causes that actually determine the behavior of the phenomena in question, we can identify some of them as the most influential and in so being that, comparing to them, other causes can be seen as simply perturbing circumstances. The insufficient realization of this condition may constitute the most formidable obstacle opposing the kind of discoveries that we have indicated as the most effective and actually decisive in determining the applicability of the deductive method to new fields of research. Let us think, for example, about the insuperable difficulties that would have been posed by the discovery of the law of universal attraction, if the positions and masses of the planets had not been such so as to allow the neglect, in a first approximation, of their mutual actions, with respect to the preponderant action of the sun on each of them, or of the earth on the moon. Astronomers, as it is observed in this regard by Schiaparelli, would have found themselves in a position similar to the position where meteorologists still find themselves. It would have been impossible for them to use the Roman tactic of *divide et impera*, consisting in facing one enemy at a time, a tactic poetically symbolized in the story of the Orazi and Curiazi. In the same way, taking another example from Mechanics, the fact that the action of friction is harder to separate from the other causes determining equilibrium and movement is likely to be the reason why the problem of the equilibrium of a body on an inclined plane, even though no less simple and basic than the one in the equilibrium of the lever, found a solution much later. The difficulties against the solution of this and other similar questions (for example that of the behavior of the wedge and the screw) can be compared to the difficulties that Archimedes would have encountered in his research into hydrostatics, if he had been able to observe only floating bodies of such a small size that the effects of their weight would have been completely masked by the action of capillarity.[36]

---

[36]This same example is used by Crookes (*Presidential Address to the Society for*

These observations indicate how much influence can be exercised, in pushing a certain branch of a science to be deductively organized, by the highlighting of the artificial production of new experiences, in which some of the causes that usually cooperate in the production of the studied phenomena assume more importance with respect to the others, and in which these other causes take secondary position and, even without being suppressed, they end up being, in a sense, "withered." So, for example, a contribution to the invention of firearms, which made new facts available to the observers where the two main determining circumstances of the trajectory of a thrown body were energically surpassing the perturbating influences of the others, was provided, more than we may believe, by the discovery of the fundamental laws of motion, those laws that made the constitution of Dynamics possible as a deductive science through the work of Galileo, Huygens, and Newton. The sieges and the wars, which afflicted our country in the century that separate the birth of Leonardo from that of Galileo, acted in this respect as real laboratories for experimental mechanics. It is enough simply to read the first chapter of Newton's work on the system of the world (*Liber de Systemate Mundi*,)[37] where he summarizes the considerations through which he reached the discovery of the law of universal attraction, to be persuaded that, instead of the legendary apple to which tradition attributes the undeserved honor of leading Newton to conceive the real cause of the motion of the moon, it would be closer to the historical truth to give the honor to a cannon ball.

I would like to add one last observation related to what I said previously about the usefulness of simplifying idealizations in the study of complex phenomena, which are caused by many, heterogeneous causes.

The ease with which such simplifications are suited in leading to new conclusions by means of purely mental operations and independently of any direct examination of the concrete facts to which they refer and the absolute uselessness of any appeal to these to guarantee the correctness of the deductions themselves, leads us sometimes to lose sight of the fact that the application to real cases of the obtained results must be preceded by the research required to establish whether, in these real cases, the conditions that the theory supposes are truly present, that is whether, for these cases, the influence of all those causes that the

---

Psychical Research, 1895) to show up to which point our knowledge or ignorance of the laws of nature can depend on circumstances completely subjective and not at all connected with the higher or lower actual complexity of the phenomena to which the laws refer. [Crookes's Presidential Address was given on January 29, 1897. See Crookes 1897, p. 93 and Vailati 1897b.]

[37] [Newton 1728.]

theory has not taken into account is really negligible.

A direct consequence of this is that the attention of the researcher tends to focus too exclusively on the development and the further elaboration of the more remote consequences of suppositions adopted simply for the reason that they appeared first, instead giving too little importance to the considerations and the analyses that can be used as guides in determining the suppositions themselves in the most convenient way to make the theories based on them, suited to reaching the purposes to which they are dedicated.

The scholar, as observed by Descartes, is then in danger of finding himself in the same situation as that of the servant who was so solicitous in executing the orders of his master that, trying not to waste time, he was starting to walk even before his master had finished giving him his orders and had indicated where the servant was supposed to go.

We should interpret the well known motto by Newton, *hypotheses non fingo*, as a protest against this behavior and there is a piece of advice that tends to warn against this danger, repeated many times and in many ways in the writings of the Greek philosophers, that theories have duties towards facts, while facts have no duties towards theories: "men ought not to seek for things in words, but for words in things."[38]

References

Bacon, Francis. 1620. *Novum Organum*. London: Billium.

Bekker, ed. 1842. *Sextus Empiricus*. Engl. trans. by P. M. Mills, *Sextus Empiricus and Greek scepticism*, Cambridge: D. Bell, 1899.

Benedetti, Giovanni. 1585. *Diversarum speculationum mathematicarum at physicarum liber*. Turin.

Besoni, Ottavio and Mario Helping, eds. 1997. *(Galilei) Dialogo sopra i due massimi sistemi del mondo, tolemaico e copernicano*, vol. 1. Roma: Antenore.

Biagioli, Nicolò Giosafatte, ed. 1821. *(Michelangelo Buonarroti) Rime*. Milano: Silvestri.

---

[38]See Diogenes Laertius, I, 9, Myson. [Yonge 1853, p. 50. In Greek in the original.] It is curious to see how this reproach (being, that is, more inclined to deform the facts to adapt them to theories than to modify their theories to adapt them to the facts) is made by Aristotle (*De Coelo*, II, 13) against the Pythagoreans, whose astronomical ideas were, as it is known, much closer to the modern ones than Aristotle's ideas. He characterizes them as "those who do not research theories and causes in order to give an account of the observed facts, but instead solicit the facts to make them fit some theories and opinions that are their own and in which they try to accommodate them." How can we find a better confirmation of the ideas that I have exposed above, on what constitutes in reality the characteristic difference between the research methods followed by Aristotle and those followed by Copernicus and Galileo?

Cooke, Harold P. and Hugh Tredennick, eds. 1955. *(Aristotle), The Organon*. London, (Cambridge, Massachussets): Harvard University Press.

Corcoran, Thomas H., ed. 1971. *(Seneca) Naturales quaestiones*, vol. 1-2. Cambridge (Mass.): Harvard university press.

Crookes, William. 1897. Presidential address to the Society for Psychical Research. January 29th, 1897. In *Presidential addresses to the Society for Psychical Research, 1882-1911*, pages 86–103. Bristol, U.K.: Thoemmes Press (1996).

Davis, P. J. and R. Hersh. 1981. *The Mathematical Experience*. Boston: Birkhäuser.

Descartes. 1637. *Discours de la méthode*.

Espinas, Alfred. 1897. *Les origines de la technologie: étude sociologique*. Paris: Alcan. First appeared in *Revue philosophique*, 1890-1891, *Archiv für Geschichte der Philosophie*, VI-VII, and *Annales de la Faculté des lettres de Bordeaux*, 1893.

Fairbanks, A. 1898. *The first philosophers of Greece*. London: K. Paul, Trench, Trübner & co.

Galilei, Galileo. 1632. *Dialogo sopra i due massimi sistemi*. Engl. transl. S. Drake (ed.) *Dialogue Concerning the Two Chief World Systems*, University of California Press, 1967.

Galilei, Galileo. 1897. *Le opere di Galileo Galilei*, vol. 7. Firenze: Barbera.

Gassendi, Petrus. 1964. *Opera omnia*, vol. 3. Stuttgart-Bad Cannstatt: Frommann Holzboog.

Helmholtz, Hermann von. 1887. Zählen und Messen, erkenntnistheoretisch betrachtet. In *Philosophische Aufsätze, Eduard Zeller zu seinem Fünfzigjährigen Doctorjubiläum gewidmet*, pages 17–52. Leipzig: Fues.

Herschel, John Frederick William. 1830. *A preliminary discourse on the study of Natural Philosophy*. London: Longman, Rees, Orme, Brown & Green. Repr. London: Routledge-Thoemmes, 1996.

Hultsch, Fridericus. 1875-1878. *Pappi Alexandrini collectionis quae supersunt e libris manu scriptis edidit Latina interpretatione et commentariis*. Berlin: Weidmann.

Huygens, C. 1673. *Horologium oscillatorium, sive De motu pendulorum ad horologia aptato demonstrationes geometricæ*. Muguet.

Jourdain, Philip E. B., ed. 1911. *(Mach, Ernst) History and Root of the Principle of the Conservation of Energy*. The Open Court.

Kapp, Ernst. 1877. *Grundlinien einer Philosophie der Technik: zur Entstehungsgeschichte der Cultur aus neunen Gesichtspunkten*. Braunschweig: Westermann.

Locke, John. 1690. *An Essay Concerning Human Understanding*. London: Tegg, 1841, 29th edn.

Longfellow, Henry Wadsworth. 1883. *The poetical works of Henry Wadsworth Longfellow*. Boston: Houghton, Mifflin and company.

Mach, Ernst. 1896-97. Über Gedankenexperimente. *Zeitschrift für den physikalischen und chemischen Unterricht* 10:1–5. Engl. transl. by S. Kripsky and W.D. Price in "On Thought Experiments", *Philosophical Forum* 4(3): 446-457, 1973.

Mackail, John William. 1915. *The Eclogues and Georgics of Virgil.* London: Longmans, Green, and Co.

Meineke, August. 1860. *Ioannis Stobaei Eclogarum physicarum et ethicarum libri duo.* Leipzig: Teubner.

Mill, John Stuart. 1870. *A system of logic, ratiocinative and inductive; being a connected view of the principles of evidence and the methods of scientific investigation.* New York: Harper & Brothers.

Newton, Isaac. 1728. *De mundi systemate Liber Isaaci Newtoni.* London: Tonson, Osborn and Longman.

Poincaré, Henri. 1894. Sur la mathématique. *Revue de Métaphysique et de Morale* pages 371–84. Repr. as Chap. 1 of *La science et l'hypothèse*, Paris: Flammarion, 1902. Engl. transl. "On the nature of mathematical reasoning," in P. Benacerraf and H. Putnam (eds.), *Philosophy of mathematics: Selected radings*, Cambridge, 1983, 2nd edn, pp. 394-402.

Rackham, H., ed. 1972. *(Cicero) De natura deorum; Academica.* Cambridge, Mass.-London: Harvard University Press-Heinemann.

Reulaux, Franz. 1875. *Theoretische Kinematik. Grundzüge einer Theorie des Maschinenwesens.* Braunschweig: F. Vieweg und Sohn. Engl. transl. by Alex. B.W. Kennedy, *The kinematics of machinery. Outlines of a theory of machines*, London: Macmillan, 1876.

Reulaux, Franz. 1876. *Cinematica teorica : principi fondamentali di una teoria generale della macchine, traduzione autorizzata di Giuseppe Colombo.* Milano: Hoepli.

Shorey, Paul, ed. 1982-1987. *(Plato) The Republic.* Cambridge (Mass.): Harvard University Press.

Singer, Peter N., ed. 2001. *(Galen) Selected Works.* Oxford: Oxford University Press.

Smith, Martin Ferguson, ed. 1932. *(Lucretius) De rerum natura.* Cambridge, Mass. / London: Harvard University Press / Heinemann, 2nd edn.

Vailati, Giovanni. 1897a. Di una dimostrazione del principio della leva attribuita ad Euclide. *Bollettino di Storia e Bibliografia Matematica* . Repr. in Vailati (1911), pp. 115–17.

Vailati, Giovanni. 1897b. Il pensiero di Crookes sulle Ricerche Psichiche. *Archivio di Psichiatria, Scienze Penali ed Antropologia criminale* 18(4). Repr. in Vailati (1911), pages 112–114.

Vailati, Giovanni. 1898a. Il metodo deduttivo come strumento di ricerca. *Prolusione ad un corso libero di Storia della Meccanica, 1897-1898*. Torino: Roux-Frassati. Repr. in Vailati (1911), pages 118-148.

Vailati, Giovanni. 1898b. Recensione a G. Schiaparelli, Studio comparativo tra le forme organiche naturali e le forme geometriche pure, Hoepli, Milano 1898. *Archivio di Psichiatria, Scienze Penali ed Antropologia criminale* 19(4). Repr. in Vailati (1911), pages 192–197.

Vailati, Giovanni. 1911. *Scritti di G. Vailati, 1863-1909.* Leipzig / Firenze: Barth.

Veitch, John, ed. 1850. *(Descartes) Discourse on the method.* Sutherland & Knox.

Wohlwill, Hans Emil. 1884. Die Entdeckung des Beharrungs-Gesetzes. *Zeitschrift für Völkerpsychologie und Sprachwissenschaft* 14:131–135.

Yonge, Charles Duke, ed. 1853. *(Diogenes Laertius) The Lives and Opinions of Eminent Philosophers.* London: George Bell & Sons.

Zeuthen, Hieronymus Georg. 1897. Notes sur l'histoire des mathématiques (suite) VII. Barrow, le maître de Newton. *Kgl. danske videnskabernes Selskabs Forhandlinger* (6):565–606.

3

Some Observations on the Questions of Words in the History of Science and Culture[†]

3.1

The distinction between questions regarding the truth or credibility of a certain opinion and those regarding, instead, the convenience of expressing it in one way rather than another, begin to gain, rather than lose, prominence and importance when we acquire a more intimate knowledge of the various transformations through which the scientific theories have developed, and of the various meanings that the same verbal form has assumed in succession before its present meaning was attributed to it. This renders even more peculiar and in need of explanation the fact that, in the history of sciences, there is a frequent occurrence of facts that contradict, or at least seem to contradict, the commonly received opinion that the "questions of words" should be considered idle and futile when compared to the "questions of facts," and that time and efforts expended on these are basically wasted, at least with regard to the actual advancement of knowledge.

Above all it is not rare at all to find the case of important and decisive scientific advancements that seem to be determined or, in any case, provoked by the explanation of controversies that seem to refer only to

[†]First published as *Alcune osservazioni su questioni di parole nella storia della scienza e della cultura*, Turin, Bocca, 1899 (Vailati, 1899). Inaugural lecture for the open course on the History of Mechanics, read on December 12th 1898 at the University of Turin. Repr. in Vailati (1911), pages 203–228.

the meaning that was or was not supposed to be given to a certain sentence or word: controversies, that is, that would not have happened, or that would have been resolved immediately if those who were part of them had, from the beginning, taken the time to properly define the terms used, in this way making impossible any misunderstanding on the real weight of their respective assertions. Moreover, we see how very frequently mistakes have been made, and acquiring new cognitions has been delayed, due, if not entirely at least mainly, to the fact that indispensable "questions of words," in given circumstances, were not addressed, and could not be discussed, and certain confused and ambiguous notions were not subject to analysis and criticism because of excessive respect towards the verbal casing that protected them.

I intend to point out, using examples taken in particular from the history of Mechanics, how helpful the examination of facts of this sort can be, not just to enlighten us on the intimate mechanism of language and the way it works, both as a means of representation as well as transmission of ideas and knowledge, but also to guide us in instituting a correct diagnosis and characterization of the illusions and sophisms that imperfections of language can generate, and to suggest the best suited means to remedy these imperfections, or at least to mitigate the effects and to prepare us against their influence.[1]

Maybe we are too inclined to believe that the causes of mistakes and obscurities, which have never ceased to be fertile, to a greater or lesser extent, at any stage of scientific development before ours, have now, for some reason or set of reasons, completely ceased to exercise their damaging action. That such causes will not induce us to make the same mistakes made by our predecessors is very natural, but it is not a sufficient enough reason to conclude that they cannot lead to other mistakes of the same kind, of which it is also natural to be unaware of... otherwise we would not make them.

We should also not forget that even if we can consider ourselves immune to many of the illusions that at times have delayed, and at others have accelerated, the course of ancient science, that is not because we have recognized the causes that produced them, but rather because we have stopped dealing, at least scientifically, with a large part of the questions whose handling is more suited to exposure to the dangers that can arise from such questions.

This prudent tactic, which in our century has even had the honor of

---

[1] "We must not just say the truth, but also the cause of the error. This contributes, in fact, to the reliability. Because when we can see rationally the reason why it appears to be true what is not, this makes us believe more in the truth." Aristotle, *Nicomachean Ethics*, B. VII, ch. 14. [In Greek in the text.]

being elevated to the dignified level of philosophical system under the name of positivism, even if fully justified from a practical point of view, is subject to serious objections, especially when it claims to be based on a clear distinction, established once and for all, between questions which can be the subject of scientific research and others to which such a privilege does not belong.

Objection is rightly raised that establishing to which of these two categories a given question belongs is, in its turn, a question that is not easily solved, and which can even be considered as less definitely solved simply because all attempts so far to solve the question have been fruitless, unless we want to assert that all so far unresolved questions must be considered unresolvable.

It does not seem possible to find an adequate answer for these objections, and others of the same sort, without relying on research, or at least conjectures, on the causes upon which the solubility or insolubility in general of a given question depends, or in other words, without making some attempt to determine the circumstances, or the common traits, that distinguish the questions considered accessible to investigation from those about which it is pointless to deceive ourselves about ever arriving at reliable conclusions.

It has not escaped the attention of the most competent people who dealt with this topic how, among the cognitions that can be most helpful in such determination, those related to the structure and development of language and to the nature of functions that language performs must be considered first. In fact it is only by means of these that, while considering the questions that may qualify as insoluble, we are able to judge which and how many of such questions get this characteristic from some fundamental flaw in our way of formulating them, or from the fact of being merely fictitious questions, i.e. that there is no corresponding determined sense that could be assigned to the compound of words used to state them.

It should be noted that in such cases, and especially in the latter, where our inability to find a solution finds its complete explanation in the fact that there is no question to be solved, our instinctive tendency to place the problem among those to which the scientific investigation is not applicable becomes definitely justified, totally independently from any opinion or preconception about the greater or lesser convenience of widening the field of scientific investigation in one direction rather than another, or about the greater or lesser power of the means of investigation available.

After these premises, directed to point out on the one hand the practical interest, so to speak, presented by the topic I am going to address, and on the other the close connection between such a topic and the studies on the history of science, I move to summarizing briefly some fundamental considerations on the mechanism of language, which we have to keep in mind in order to understand the following treatise well.

3.2

One of the most obvious features that distinguishes technical language from ordinary language, and in general evolved languages from primitive languages, seems to me to consist, in the latter, in the greater difficulty of the exact determination of the meaning of words by means of definitions, that is by means of other words that are useful, in a way, in decomposing such meaning in the individual elements composing it.

Such a feature is connected to a fundamental difference of which we may form a clear and distinct idea even by simply examining the contrast between the usage of the same language by a child or an adult man, or by an ignorant man or a competent man about a certain topic.

So, taken to extreme cases, the child who applies an already familiar denomination to a given object is trying to express, in most cases, merely his sometimes really vague impression of a resemblance between such an object and others to which he is already used to applying the same designation—on the other hand, only in exceptional cases does the scientist classify objects together, applying the same name to them, without having first determined which are the conditions that he requires to be satisfied in order to be able to apply the given designation to a given object. In other words, any time a scientist refers to a number of objects with the same name, he is asserting, not just that those objects resemble one another, but that they resemble one another in something, i.e. they have certain common characteristics, which could be enumerated and designated, and which together constitute what is commonly called the "meaning" of the name in consideration.

It is useful to immediately note how, while the characters constituting the meaning of a given name must be common to all the objects to which the name is applicable, such objects are usually far from exhausting all the known or unknown characteristics they possess in common. They represent only a group of those, chosen for reasons of convenience, or of tradition, among the many other groups of characteristics that could have equally been used to outline the same class of objects. Therefore it could easily happen that two names, even though having completely different meanings, could each apply to all the objects to which the other applies, and only to those objects—that is, as is common expression, they have the same sphere of application.

However it is evident that, the larger the number of characteristics whose possession is required in order to be able to apply a given name to a given object, the more the sphere of application of such a name becomes smaller, while, on the contrary, the greater the number of objects to which a given name is applicable, the less the name itself will be meaningful, that is the smaller the amount of information that we would give on a given object when we apply such a name to it.[2]

The propositions, where it is asserted that the objects designated with a given name have other specific characteristics in common beside those that are part of the constitution of the meaning of the name applied to them, are those that are ordinarily called general propositions. With them we assert, substantially, that any time an object presents certain characteristics, it also presents others, or in the same way, that certain specific facts or phenomena present themselves or tend to present themselves constantly together or tend to coexist or to invariably succeed each other.

It is not appropriate to linger on the processes through which we reach the knowledge and the ascertainment of these propositions. It is instead appropriate for our present purpose to direct our attention to the radical contrast between these propositions and those, instead, by which we express our intention whether to include a given characteristic among those that are part of the meaning of a given name.

With these we do not state any evaluation that can be held true or false, i.e. conforming or not to the facts to which it refers, but we express only our deliberate intention of using a given word in a given sense and our desire to make our intention known to others; that is, in using them we simply state norms which we declare to follow in expressing our opinion by means of language, norms that cannot be judged as true or false, but only as appropriate or inappropriate, suited or not suited to the particular purpose that we have in mind.

A very important fact to be noted from our point of view is the following: ordinary language is completely lacking (unless one resorts to circumlocutions) in any external verbal signs to distinguish, independently from the speech context, whether a given proposition belongs to

---

[2]Schopenhauer, *Die Welt als Wille und Vorstellung*, book II, ch. 6. "For the most special concept is almost the individual and thus almost real; and the most universal concept, e.g., Being (the infinitive of the copula) is scarcely anything but a word. Therefore philosophical systems, keeping within such very universal concepts without descending to the real, are scarcely anything but a mere idle display of words." [In German in the original. English translation from Schopenhauer 1819, p. 64.]

one or the other of the two categories mentioned above.[3] In fact if we indicate with A and B any two generic names, the sentence "the As are Bs" can be used both to express our belief that anytime the conditions are verified in order for A to be applicable to a given object, the other conditions that make the name B applicable are also verified, and to indicate that among those conditions that we need satisfied in order for A to be applicable, we can also find those conditions that need to be satisfied in order to apply the name B.

The reason for such imperfection of language lies, on the one hand, in the following, that the assertions, where the meaning of a word gets decomposed in its elements, did not start to be formulated and recognized as different from the others, if not in a very advanced state of intellectual development, when the fundamental structure of the language had already been formed. On the other hand, the reason lies in the fact that the distinction between those and the general propositions, in the strict sense of the term, has no practical importance, given that, any time one of the latter is recognized as true, for this reason alone it becomes convenient, or at least not damaging, to adopt the norm or convention that we express with exactly the same sentence. In fact, when all the objects that possess a certain property also possess another property, what kind of inconveniences can arise from indicating, with the same sign, not just the possession of the first, but also that of the second property?

3.3

The first scientific research where the necessity arose to clearly distinguish the propositions that only have the purpose to determine the meaning of terms used from those that contain assertions or suppositions regarding the real object under consideration, was, very likely, seen in geometry research.

In the practical field the questions related to the meaning of words appeared to be too intimately connected to the questions of interpretation of another's will (for example the legislator, the testator, the contracting party, etc.) because their contrast with questions of fact, in the strict sense of the term, could have the prominence needed to

---

[3] The different pairs of technical terms, used in what follows to designate respectively these two species of propositions, reflect in a characteristic way the variation of opinion regarding their relative importance. The same distinction established by the Scholastic philosophy between "essential" propositions and "accidental" propositions, reappears in Locke as a distinction between "trifling" propositions and "real" propositions, and in Kant as the distinction between "analytic" propositions and "synthetic" propositions.

reach a clear concept of the special functions of the ones and the others, and moreover to consider the imposition of a given meaning to a given name as something independent from customs and tradition and as a question of convenience that is subject, in part, to the individual will.

What gives the importance of a unique document in the history of human thought to Plato's dialogues is the fact that in them we have the first example of a series of methodic attempts directed towards analyzing and specifying the meaning of the general terms of current use, such as those referring to human actions and social and political relationships, and which serve as the basis of the enunciation of moral evaluations or of principles related to conduct.

Aristotle[4] attributes the merit of having recognized and proclaimed the practical importance of investigations of this kind to Socrates, and also that of having found an adequate method to strip those who disputed with him of their false persuasions produced in them by the naive usage of words without a determined meaning.

Such a method consisted in gradually leading the interlocutor, by means of questions in succession, to concede that for any definition that he was able to propose for the term in question, special cases could always be mentioned where the term was applied by him without the presence of all the characteristics that, by virtue of the definition chosen, were supposed to be present, or cases where the term mentioned was not applied even if all the characteristics were present. With this sort of *reductio ad absurdum* of all the definitions that the interlocutor was step by step induced to propose in succession for the term in question, Socrates led him to confess, in the end, that he did not know exactly which characteristics were supposed to be possessed by an object or a person so that the term in question could be applicable to it. This is a form of confessing, in other words, that the sentences where he was applying the term to special cases, even if such sentences were commonly used and accepted by everybody as true and indisputable, were after all lacking in any sense, determined or determinable, and, not being able to give any real information on the objects or people to which they referred, could not be considered either true or false, but simply empty verbal formulas indicating at most the fact that the application of the same name to things not having any common character had the stigma of vulgar use.

This constituted the destructive part, so to speak, of the Socratic

---

[4] *Metaphysics*, B. XII, ch. 4: "Two are the things that can be justly attributed to Socrates, the inductive reasoning and the definition of the universal." See also ibid., B. I, ch. 6: "Socrates looked for the universal and he was the first to direct his thinking towards definitions." [Both quotations are in Greek in the text.]

method, where the interlocutor was forced to recognize his own ignorance, or at least to renounce his too high opinion of his own wisdom.
This was followed by the constructive part, where Socrates joined him
in order to reach together a determination of the necessary delimita-
tions for the field of application of the name in the best possible way, so
that it was possible to use it with a univocal and determined meaning,
that actually corresponds to common characters in all the objects to
which it is applied, and to those only. Such common characters were
put in evidence by means of the examination in succession of a certain
number of special cases, from which, by means of a process of generalization or induction, we finally extract the definition we were looking
for.

This is, in its general traits, the process represented and adorned by
the most splendid artistic form of Plato's dialogues, in most of which
the common thread consists exactly in the purpose of determining the
meaning of such words.

So, for example, in Phaedrus and Gorgias the matter is to define
what rhetoric is, in Meno what virtue is, in the Republic what justice
is, in Lysis what friendship is, in Laches what courage is, in Charmides
what self-control is, in the Symposium what love is, in Rival Lovers
what philosophy is and in the Statesman what a statesmen is.

It is not besides the point to mention how Sidgwick's observation
is applicable to such dialogues, some of which are numbered with very
good reason among the most sublime masterpieces of literature of any
time and country. He observes that the advantage of research of this
kind, on the sense of words, does not consist so much in the definitions
that we find as in the operations that we have to do to find them,
and that the fruit of such discussions is not in the conclusions reached,
but in the reasons that we must discover and bring forward to justify
them.[5]

3.4

Let us go back now to the distinction, on which I have insisted before,
between the propositions where is asserted that all the objects of a given
class possess a given property and the others where we indicate that we
intend to designate, with a certain name, the objects that possess an
assigned property. I will now try and show how the previously noted

---

[5]See Welby, "Sense, meaning and interpretation," in *Mind* (April 1896), p. 194.
In the first part of this article, Lady Welby makes the following observation, very
appropriately: "that it is through the very instinct which prompts even the most
futile 'verbal' dispute, that language has gained that degree of efficiency which it
already possesses."

fact that these two kinds of propositions are not ordinarily distinct from each other by any exterior verbal sign constitutes a most fruitful source of ambiguity and illusory argumentation.

Sometimes the slightest uncertainty about the meaning of a word is enough to make it impossible to decide whether a given proposition, where such a word appears, is able to give us any information, true or false, about the facts to which it refers, or is rather destined only to indicate what the relationship is between the meaning that we want to give to the word itself and the one that is given to other words, by us or other people.

To clarify this distinction, I will use an example taken from mechanics.

The term "momentum" of two forces, or two weights, was introduced for the first time by Galileo, to express the variation of effectiveness that the same force, or the same weight, tends to have in moving a certain mechanism, with the variation of the point on the mechanism where they are applied, or of the direction of action, or, in general, with the variation of any condition to which their action is subjected, both because of the limits of the system, and because of the properties of the medium where the movement take place. Thus a given weight has more or less "momentum" depending on the inclination of the plane along which it descends, or depending on the greater or lesser density of a liquid where it finds itself immersed.

Therefore Galileo affirmed that two different forces or weights had the same momentum with respect to a given device, on given points where they were applied, when, notwithstanding their different intensity or direction, they exercised an identical action to move it or, in other words, when they could be applied in such a way that one would balance the other, if directed in opposite directions.

Now, if we consider, for example, the proposition: "Two forces, applied to a rigid body revolving around an axis, are in equilibrium when their momenti, with respect to the axis, are equal and of opposite sign," it is evident that the simple inspection of the sentence does not allow us to understand whether the speaker intends to assert something on the conditions of equilibrium of a rigid body in those circumstances, or whether instead he merely intends to indicate his intention in using the word "momentum" in the sense that we have seen before, instead of the sense that we would give to the word ordinarily.

If such were the intention of the speaker, the sentence "are of equal momentum" could be substituted with the other less ambiguous "they are called of equal momentum," so that we could see clearly that he is giving us absolutely no information on the laws of equilibrium.

In the same way, to take another example from Mechanics, the proposition: "A point exposed to a constant force is subject in equal intervals of time to equal increases in velocity" can be used, when we give the word "force" the meaning that it has in Galileo's works, to state a fundamental law of Dynamics that he discovered, but if with the word "force" we intend, instead, the product of mass and acceleration, it becomes a simple fragment of definition, an assertion, that is, that does not say anything at all about the circumstances that produce the constancy in acceleration, but it simply informs us about the fact that, by virtue of conventions made about the meaning of the word "force," to say that "such a point is subject to a constant force" is the same as saying that such a point, in equal intervals of time, is subject to equal increases in velocity.

But the examples taken from the history of physical sciences, even though they have the advantage of giving an exact idea of the distinction I am referring to, are for this same reason little suited to making us aware of the danger to which we may be exposed by the lack of proper means to decide in which of the two categories mentioned above we should enlist a given assertion, and the inconveniences that arise from mistaking one assertion for another that sometimes can hide under an identical verbal form.

In these sciences the meaning of technical terms, even though subject to great variations in time, is nevertheless sufficiently precise and determined in each age so that any doubt is dispelled whether a given proposition must be considered as "true by definition," or rather as the enunciation of a principle to be adopted, a theorem to be demonstrated, or a law to be explained. Therefore it is quite rare in these sciences to have the case, as so frequently seen in the psychological or social sciences (and even more so in the theoretical discussions of any kind among people who use a technical language related to a topic on which they are not competent), that questions of words are discussed without being aware of them, and quite rare too is the case that for some kinds of considerations to be mistaken for important discussion, or for satisfactory explanations, the kind of considerations, that is, that deserve to be classified with those that have made immortal the name of Monsieur de la Palisse.[6]

---

[6]French Marshal who fought under Francis I in Pavia. Among other things, the following famous song:

Il mourut le vendredi
le dernier jour de son âge.
S'il fût mort le samedi,
il eût vécu d'avantage.

3.5

However, this does not prevent the ambiguity considered above from appearing in other forms, even in the mathematical and physical sciences. So, for example, this is not the only cause that originally contributed to create the still very widespread idea that the principles of Arithmetic and Geometry must be considered as superior truth, independent of any experience, and possessing a certainty, not only of a higher grade, but in a way of a nature and origin different from those possessed by all the other truths known to us. However it is evident that this same cause, if not the only one, is to be counted among the causes that have mostly acted and still act in fuelling prejudice and in preventing the proof on which it is founded from being recognized as illegitimate.

It is easy to see how its action is exercised in this respect. In Geometry, as in any other deductive science, we are forced to take as a starting point some suppositions that cannot find their perfect realization in any concrete case, but represent instead some ideal simplifications of the forms and processes presented to us by experience. As a consequence, the fundamental propositions of science assume the appearance not only of assertions related to the properties possessed, or supposed to be possessed, by the things we talk about, but rather of conventions by means of which we specify concepts and we delimit the sphere inside which we intend to make our considerations. The result is that such fundamental suppositions can be shaped as definitions, without inconvenience, provided that some "postulates" are added to them which are required to demonstrate, in every single case, that some entities, corresponding to the single definitions we state, are "possible" or "constructable." When the basis of a science is presented this way, any objection which can be raised against a fundamental proposition begins to appear not only perhaps baseless, but actually absurd. For example, if someone were to express the doubt that a "straight line" does not possess all the fundamental properties that are attributed to it in the ordinary exposition of Geometry, we could answer him that this cannot be, because in this case it would not be a "straight line" anymore. In doing so we are not saying anything more than this: that if that were the case, then it should be called by another name, because in the end it is simply a question of vocabulary.

The Greek geometers who first adopted this form of exposition were,

(He died on a Friday/ the last day of his age./ Had he died on the Saturday,/ he would have lived longer.) It is not an exaggeration to say that 80% of the propositions present in an ordinary treatise of Philosophy or Science of Law is part of this class of irrefutable truths, whose practical and didactic importance is, on the other end, not always negligible.

moreover, perfectly aware of the fact that, in order to be able to deduce conclusions from simple definitions that were not purely verbal or illusory, it is necessary either to implicitly suppose, or postulate, or demonstrate by means of previously assumed axioms, the existence or the constructability of entities which satisfy the conditions stated in the definitions themselves.

Aristotle's writings in Logic represent in a certain way a codification of the processes followed by the founders of Geometry as a deductive science and he did not miss pointing out the distinction discussed above in the most explicit and general terms. In chapter VII of the second book of the Posterior Analytics he warns against the confusion and sophisms that can arise from losing sight of such a distinction, with the following sentence: Nothing can be affirmed to exist by definition (τὸ δ' εἶναι οὐκ οὐσία οὐδενί) and the history of Scholastic philosophy stands to demonstrate that this wise warning was far from superfluous.

This kind of ambiguity often leads to paralogisms, where a special character of evidence and certainty is attributed to certain assertions by making them appear like consequences of mere definitions. The classical way to justify such paralogisms consists in saying that a certain object possesses a certain property because it is its "essential" property, or it is inherent to its "nature," without which it would cease to be what it is (i.e., what it should be if the name that we have been using for it is really applicable to it).

A characteristic example of this kind of reasoning is provided by the notorious demonstration of the existence of God, devised by Anselm of Canterbury and adopted with some slight modification even by Descartes, a demonstration known to the scholars of History of Philosophy as the "ontological proof."

Besides it is not necessary to move so far back from our times nor from our special field of study to find other characteristic examples of arguments of the same nature. It will suffice, for example, to examine the considerations related to the principles of Mechanics offered in the writings of some of the more eminent representatives of contemporary "positivism," such as Spencer, Taine, Wundt.

It is difficult, in fact, to bring back to any other origin the idea presented in Spencer's *First Principles* [1862], that the inertia law and the law of conservation of energy, which humankind came to know through a long series of intellectual efforts, are truths as evident in themselves as the axioms of Arithmetic, and as such cannot be imagined as not true. He seems to have reached this strange conclusion on the basis of the opinion (that few will contest) that, if the ancients had reached a concept of "force" similar to the one that such a word conveys in modern Mechanics, they could not have done anything but believe in the truth of the inertia law. But is this not simply proof of the fact that in order to reach such a concept of "force" it is necessary to already have been in possession of the knowledge that brings acceptance to the inertia law? It was the possession of this knowledge that gave the name "force" the meaning that it now has, and it is not this meaning that lead to the acquisition of that knowledge.

It is only for people who already have this knowledge that the definition presently given to "force" in Mechanics treatises represents something more than an arbitrary change in the sense that this word has in ordinary language, a change that could be seen as more suited to producing misunderstanding rather than giving information on the causes or laws of motion.

3.6

Another form, under which verbal illusions due to the cause in question often appear, consists in mistaking the attempts to analyze and decompose the meaning of a given name into its elements, for arguments intended to show the non-existence of the objects to which such a name would be applicable. The same tendency, which leads us to see an assertion in the enunciation of a definition on the existence of the defined object, also induces us to mistake the refusal to accept a given definition for the refusal to accept the existence of objects to which the name that was being defined could be applied, for which we want a new, more precise or appropriate definition.

In this way, to take an example that was a watershed in the history of modern thought, the classical research made by Berkeley on the concept of "substance" and of "reality"[7] was regarded as intending to negate the existence of matter and the reality of the external world, only because they wanted to demonstrate that when we say "this object really exists," we may only mean what follows: that we believe that, if we or other beings similar to us, were to find themselves in certain conditions, they would feel certain sensations.

Against this opinion it was objected, and by many still is, that it is incompatible with the common belief in the existence of something

---

[7]An important contribution on this kind of research has been recently provided by professor Gyula Pikler from Budapest University in his work: *The Psychology of the Belief in Objective Existence* (London, Williams and Norgate, 1890) [Pikler 1890]. The same subject has also been addressed by Jaurès (renowned socialist member of Parliament) in his pamphlet: *La réalité du monde sensible* [1891]. See also a curious thought by Pascal on this topic: *Pensées* [1670], art. XX, 13. (Garnier, Paris, p. 248.)

"outside ourselves," and that, if such opinion is adopted, it would imply the denial of any distinction between appearance and reality, between sensation and hallucination; on the contrary, it actually represents a perfectly legitimate attempt to clarify of what exactly such a distinction consists, and to determine on what characteristics it is founded and which constitute the practical and theoretical importance.

Far from taking away meaning from the sentences where the existence or the reality of material objects is asserted, Berkeley's opinion makes what we mean when we utter them clear and makes us more aware of the misunderstanding generated by the multiplicity of different senses that the words "existence," "reality," etc. have assumed in the common language.[8]

Observations of great similarity to those mentioned so far can be repeated regarding the objections that were raised against the deep analysis made by David Hume on the concept of "cause," and against his assertion that we can intend the cause of a phenomenon only to be the sum of circumstances whose presence is necessary and sufficient in order for the phenomenon to take place. It should not seem strange that this assertion has been considered as equivalent to negating the existence, or at least the knowability, of "true causes" if we think how, even at the present time, eminent scientists express their judgment on the purpose of scientific research saying that its goal is not the determination of the "causes," but that it should be limited to investigating the laws regulating the succession of phenomena, as though one thing were different from another and as though to "discover the causes of a phenomenon" could mean something more or different from determining the circumstances from which it is constantly preceded, whose presence is sufficient in order for it to take place.[9]

A concrete example of this kind of misunderstanding is provided by the sentence that is now become almost banal: that the object of Me-

[8]Boltzmann justly observes: "What exists depends on the definition of existence." ("Ueber die Methoden der theoretischen Physik," in W. Dyck *Katalog mathematischer und mathematisch-physikalischer Modelle, Apparate und Instrumente*, München, 1892, pp. 87–98. [See Dyck 1892. Cf. "Indeed, it depends on the definition of existence whether bodies, or their kinetic energy or even their qualities exist, so that one day we might well simply define away our own existence." Engl. transl. by Paul Folkes in (Boltzmann, 1892, p. 5).]) On this subject see also the memoir recently presented by the same author under the title: *Ueber die Frage nach der objectiven Existenz der Vorgänge in der unbelebten Natur* (1898) [Boltzmann 1897].

[9]A concise and clear development of this topic can be found in the work of professor Angelo Brofferio, *Le Specie dell'Esperienza* [The Kinds of Experience] (ch. V), work that, even if honored by a prize from the Accademia dei Lincei (1884), does not seem to me to have been appreciated enough by the Italian public. A reason for this may have been the premature death of its author.

chanics is not that of explaining, but that of describing in the simplest way possible the phenomena of motion. With this sentence we establish a contrast between description and explanation, without realizing that explaining is, after all, simply a special kind of describing, characterized by the fact that in explaining we make greater use, on the one hand, of processes of comparison and on the other, of deductive argumentation by means of which we manage to gather together in the same category, and to consider as particular cases of the same law, phenomena which, when examined superficially, appear completely different and with no connection to one another. Now, we could say that there is no other science where this way of describing, which we have designated with the name of explanation, is brought forward so far and applied in such a systematic way as in Mechanics. Denying, then, that the arguments we find in this science constitute explanations of the phenomena studied, it is not simply a use of the word 'explanation' that would make it inapplicable to any other process or reasoning found in any other science, but moreover (and this is even worse) it means using it in such a way so as to attribute to it any possible meaning, because we could not establish which characters must be present in the arguments found in a given science for it to be allowed to say that by means of them we give "explanations" of the facts to which they refer.

3.7

The misunderstandings of the kind we are now going to discuss, inducing us to formulate questions for which we cannot even imagine the possibility of finding solutions, are suited to providing fuel for extremely pessimistic and discouraging theories on the limits that scientific research should impose on itself.[10]

Any expansion of our cognitions, it is said, is merely an expansion and extension of our surface of contact with the unknown and the inexplicable, and our explanations do nothing but substitute one "mystery" for another. It would be much truer, and also more useful, instead to observe that the distinction between those things "explained" and those things "unexplained" does not refer to any intrinsic difference in their certainty or "knowability," but only to our ability to deduce our cogni-

---

[10]There are traces now, in more than one direction, of reactions against this intellectual pusillanimity. In the philosophical field I am pleased to mention, as a characteristic example, the recent volume by Guastella, *Saggi sulla teoria della conoscenza* (Palermo, Sandron 1898) ["Essays on the theory of knowledge," Guastella 1898], a work that under many aspects deserves to be pointed out to the scholars of philosophy. I had occasion to talk about this work in *Nuovo Risorgimento* (issue September-October 1898) [Vailati 1898].

tions from one another and to order them in such a way so that part of them are consequences of those remaining.

Sometimes, as a consequence of a discovery or an ingenious intuition, we come to recognize an analogy between two classes of phenomena, which at first glance seemed to have no connection with one another, and the analogy is so intimate it allows us to deduce their behavior from the same group of general laws, which before we thought applicable only to phenomena of one of the classes. In this case we say we have found an "explanation" of a class of phenomena by means of those of another class.

We would be equally right in saying that such a result constitutes an "explanation" of the facts of the latter class by means of those of the former: to say one thing or the other depends on the point of view we look from or, to put it more correctly, depends on the fact that the facts of one class are more familiar to us than those of the other, and it was the observation of those that led us for the first time to the knowledge of those laws which later, due to more investigations, we have come to recognize as applicable also to the facts of the other class.

Now it is evident that this fact, despite its consideration being important from an historical or psychological point of view, definitely cannot lead to any fundamental distinction between the two classes of phenomena; and it should not prevent us from recognizing that the phenomena of which we give an explanation and those by means of which the explanation is given enter into the processes of "explanation" in a symmetrical way, so to speak, just as it happens in the processes of comparison, where there is no substantial difference between the act of comparing one thing with another and comparing the latter thing with the former.

It is not necessary to say anything more to show the superficiality and the pointlessness of these sentences which we have already mentioned, where the processes of scientific explanation are represented as relying inevitably on the admission of primordial laws or facts, which are in their turn even more mysterious and inexplicable than those to whose explanations they are applied.

If what we mean by these sentences was merely that, going back in the series of deductions by means of which we connect our pieces of knowledge, we should end up (if we wish to avoid getting into a "circular argument," as the logicians call it) with principles or hypotheses that we take for granted without being able to deduce them from others, then these sentences would hardly express a deficiency or a limitation of human intellect, because they would be reproaching the intellect of not being able to deduce "something" without starting from "something"—

and this is not only far from being an ideal, reachable or not, but it is not even a requirement to which we can attribute any sense.

To this same mistaken concept of the role of deduction in scientific research may be related the opinion that, as is often also found expressed in different ways by contemporary scientists,[11] the discussions regarding the proof, or the legitimacy of the principles and the more general hypotheses of any particular science, and the final decision of the relative controversies, go far beyond the competence of the specialist scientists, to fall instead under the competence of the scholars of what is called "philosophy," which would then be assigned the dangerous role of Supreme Court of the intellectual field. It would be better if we were to attribute to it the role of clearing house before the sciences in the strict sense of the term.

3.8

A mistake of the same kind as those mentioned so far is that which can be seen in the opinion that all the words to which a definition cannot be given should be considered, only for this reason, as having a less defined sense, or, in a way, a more mysterious one than those that can be defined; not considering that, in order to define the latter, it is necessary, in the end, to use the former, and not considering that any indeterminacy or mysteriousness that can be attributed to the undefined words would also have to be attributed, even more so, to all the other words that we define precisely by using the undefined ones.

What is frequently missed is that our inability to answer the question, "What is this thing?" is not always and only due to the fact that we do not know enough about the thing in question, but, on the contrary, can depend on the fact that in many cases we know that thing too well, so much so that we are unable to find another thing that we know better and that therefore we could use to define the former.

This is the same explanation given by Newton, in the introduction to his book *Philosophiae naturalis principia mathematica*, for not defining the words "time," "space," "motion": "I do not define time, space, place and motion, as being known to all."[12]

This observation does not deny, of course, that it could be convenient, and for certain purposes even necessary, to analyze further the notions of "time," "space," and "motion," both in order to reduce them to other even more elementary notions apprehended in more immediate

---

[11] For example, see Poincaré in the preface to his treatise on optics and electricity [Poincaré 1891].

[12] [I. Definitions, Scholium. Engl. transl. by A. Motte from Newton 1687, Vol. 1, p. 6.]

ways, and to investigate the psychological origin and the condition of development in the individual or in the race.

The opinion that not being able to say what this or that thing is equals a confession of ignorance is an opinion that is probably related to that habit, acquired when we were children, of conceiving any new information as the answer to a question of the type: "What is this?," questions that are inspired in the child because he is frequently in the position of someone who has to make sure that a given object, to him new and strange, has already been observed and noted and, so to speak, classified by those people from whom he is used to get the directives that he needs or desires. For him, to know what a thing is called is like having a key in his hand to acquire all the knowledge he may need regarding that thing. In this way not only is the idea born in him that having such information is the same as knowing what is most important about the thing in question, but he is also induced to imagine that everything has, in a way, its own "natural" name, in the same way that bodies have a taste, a color, their own weight, independent of any convention or will of man.

3.9

Strictly connected to the aforementioned, and no less susceptible to giving rise to illusory problems and imaginary difficulties, is the tendency to believe that, for any name that we use, it is possible to assign a thing of which it is the name, as if it were not possible or necessary to have names that express only "relations" between several objects, or in other words, some properties of such objects that refer to the possible way they behave in relation to each other under specific circumstances.

Thus, taking an obvious example from the technical language of physics, the sentence: "body A has the same temperature as body B," has a perfectly defined meaning even though we are unaware of what the particular conditions of the parts of a given body constituting its state of temperature are. Such a sentence, for the physicist, simply expresses the fact that body A, put in contact with body B (under specific circumstances), never varies in volume, and it will not stop meaning this, even if the bodies that we declare to be of the same temperature had not any other common property if not that of maintaining the same volume when put in contact with one another.

Similarly the question "What is value?" is a question to which an economist can afford not to answer, given that he clearly indicates what is, for him, the sense of the sentence: "a certain quantity of a certain commodity has the same value as another quantity of this other commodity." If he manages to determine, in a given stage of social organization, the causes or the conditions on which depends the fact that two given quantities of different commodities are able to be obtained in exchange one with the other, it will be of little damage to him not being able to give a definition of the word "value" taken in itself.

Rather than mentioning more examples of this kind, it will be useful to indicate the general framework.

Anytime a condition, which can be satisfied or not by some given pairs of objects of a specific class, is such that it possesses the following two properties:

1. That the two objects are symmetrically present in its enunciation, such that they can be put one in the place of the other (without affecting the relation between them, if it previously existed);
2. That if the condition exists for a pair A and B and also for another pair B and C, that have an element in common with the first, it also exists between A and C;

then we have the convenience[13] of creating a word, which I indicate with x for brevity, whose sense, even if not directly assigned by means of a definition, is determined by the meaning attributed to the sentence "a certain object has the same x as another object." It is convenient, that is, to indicate with this sentence, or with a similar sentence, the fact that two such objects satisfy the condition in question.

So, for example, instead of saying that two straight lines are parallel, it is useful to say that the two straight lines have the same direction; instead of saying that the four numbers a, b, c, d, are such that the equimultiples of a and c stay inferior or superior or equal to the equimultiples of b and d, we will say that the first has the same ratio with the second as the third has with the fourth (Euclid); and these conventions would be perfectly legitimate even if we were not at all able to answer the questions: "What is the direction of a straight line?" "What is the ratio between two numbers?"

The convenience of adopting these conventions consists of this, that in this way in order to express propositions and arguments in connection with the relationship at issue, we can use all the expressions and the deductive rules that we already have available to us to express the corresponding propositions in relation to the equalities in the strict sense of the term. We can deal with such relationships as if they were actually equivalences, because they possess the same fundamental

---

[13]In this regard, see *Manuale di Logica Matematica* by professor Burali-Forti (Milan, Hoepli, 1893) in the chapter dedicated to the various kinds of definitions [Burali Forti 1893].

properties.

In the same way, when between two objects of a given class it is possible to define a relationship that possesses the same properties as those indicated by the phrases "greater than," "lesser than," like for example, going back to a case already mentioned, that consisting of the property possessed by bodies of different temperatures, of increasing or decreasing in volume for the only reason of being put in contact, it could be convenient to express the existence of such a relationship by giving a sense to the sentences like the following: "body A has a greater temperature than body B," "the temperature of body B is less than that of body A," etc., independent of any sense that the word temperature may have by itself.

Just like, to take an example from Mechanics in the sentence: "the mass of body A is equal, or greater, or a multiple according to a given number, than the mass of another body B," we can give a complete and thorough definition with no need to answer the question: What is the mass of a body? And such a definition would make sense even if we were to concede that the "difference in mass" between one body and another is not connected to any other physical property besides that consisting in the constancy of ratios between the accelerations that they transmit to each other when they interact.

3.10

The examples mentioned are also enough to show in what sense, and for what reason, the illusions produced by the tendency to believe that any name which is part of a sentence with meaning, should, only for this reason, be the name of "something," are sometimes advantageous to scientific research.

The desire of establishing in any way the meaning of the name in question has often led to wonder whether it were possible to define the corresponding relation in a way that such a name would acquire meaning, if it did not possess it before; and therefore this same desire has led to build some hypotheses about the conditions on which the verification of the relation itself depends, hypotheses susceptible of provoking experiences and leading to new discoveries.

So, if two objects are in a certain relationship, and such relationship has properties similar to those of the equivalence or similarity, the supposition that they should actually resemble each other in some aspects may lead, and in fact has led in many cases, to the discovery of new properties in the objects in question, and to the realization of which are, among those properties, those whose common possession correlates with, or determine, the existence of their relationship.

Even when this goal could not be completely achieved, talking and arguing as if it had in fact been achieved has often suggested important generalizations, which, notwithstanding their merely verbal and formal character, have provided the occasion and incentive for substantial scientific progress. Let us consider, for example, the influence made on the development of modern Geometry by the introduction of the concept of "point at infinity," or, to take a far more ancient example from another branch of Mathematics, let us observe how important has been the introduction of the concept of an "irrational number" for the progress of Arithmetic, or, in other words, the convention of denoting and treating the relations and operations regarding the various ways and processes that lead to the division of the series of rational numbers in contiguous classes not separated by any rational number, as if they were relations or operations on numbers in the strict sense of the word (integer and fractional).

The history of Physics provides classic examples of similar introductions of fictitious entities, and of the various kinds of advantages and inconveniences which such introductions can generate. So, for example, the idea that the temperature of the bodies was determined by how much they were filled by an unfathomable liquid, on the initial distribution of which their behavior and their exchanges of heat when put in contact with one another depended, and the belief that bodies of equal temperature were to be compared, in a way, to vessels where a liquid has been poured in such proportions to reach the same level in both (Dalton), had a great role in leading to the first experiments and measurements of the thermal capacity of different substances,[14] and in anticipating that the sum of products of such a capacity and their respective temperatures was supposed to remain constant when more bodies of the same temperature are put in contact with each other.

Also, from the opinion that this sum was actually measuring the quantity of fluid that can be transferred from one body to another, but not be subject to increase or decrease, Black was induced to suspect that the variations of that quantity, whenever some of the bodies that exchange heat also change their physical state, were determined in such a way that any increase or decrease of heat generated by a change of state should correspond to equivalent increases or decreases, when the

---

[14]It is proof of this the fact that at the beginning it was supposed that the thermal capacity were proportional to the volume. A technical error was initially made also for the mass, which also was reputed to be equal for bodies of equal volumes, even when they were of different specific weight (by Benedetti, and also by Galileo in his youthful writings).

body is subject to the inverse change of state going back to its primitive condition.

The denomination "latent heat," which was used for a long time to designate the quantity of heat which disappeared and was able to reappear, is left as a witness of the kind of ideas which drove those first investigators of the facts to which it refers, and makes us consider as perfectly natural, and in principle, actually perfectly legitimate, the hypothesis used at the beginning by the physicists to make sense of such facts, the hypothesis, that is, that the changes of physical state generated variations in the thermal capacity of the bodies which undergo them, so that the variations of temperature corresponding to those changes were similar to the variations of level in a liquid in a tube where the section were to vary when the pressure of the liquid on the walls of the tube reaches a certain degree.

It is known how useful, but at the same time how detrimental, this same analogy between the transmission of heat from a body to another of lesser temperature and the flowing of liquid from a vessel to another at a lower level was for Carnot. In fact, while this analogy allowed him to have a representation of the work generated by this heat transmission, as determined only by the quantity of heat transmitted and by the difference of the two temperatures, exactly like the job of a mill depends on the quantity of water and the differences in level available, this same idea for a long time prevented him from realizing that, for every production of work obtained this way one finds not only a heat transmission, but also the disappearance of part of it, which makes itself, in a way, latent exactly like in the cases considered by Black.[15]

Besides, as we know, Mayer managed to calculate for the first time the value of the constant ratio between the heat disappearing and the work that it generates by means of attempts made in order to understand the reason for the difference between the thermal capacity of a gas that expands at constant pressure and that of a gas that maintains a constant volume.

In this regard, Mach observes that Mayer was induced to assume the constancy of this ratio, not from the idea that the heat was a kind of movement, but from the persuasion that the "quantity of heat" was something similar to a material substance, not subject to being destroyed or created by men, but able only to transform and temporarily disappear, to reappear unaltered when we repeat the process in the opposite sense.

---

[15] An analogous example of the bad influence of the materialistic metaphor, generated by a verbal ambiguity, is offered by the so called theory of value by Marx (see Kautsky, *Il Socialismo*, ch. I, Turin, Bocca, 1898) [Kautsky 1898].

3.11

We also find many examples of a similar kind in the history of Mechanics in the strict sense of the term.

For example, the research on the laws of collision and communication of motion from one body to another was given a great impulse by the assumption that, if two bodies in motion, colliding against a third body, all else being equal, produce equal effects, that is equal variations of velocity, then such two bodies must possess equal amounts of something which was called "live force," to distinguish it from the "dead force" represented instead by the tension or pressure that a body at rest exercises by virtue of its own weight.

To this something properties were attributed by Descartes similar to those of a material substance, and primarily the property of not being subject to increases or decreases, but only transformations and transmission from one body to another. The effect of this was that the problem of evaluating the amount of this something, contained in a body of a given weight and a given velocity, became equal to the following question: find a function of weight and velocity, with the property that the sum of its values, corresponding to two or more bodies colliding, maintains the same value before and after the collision.

The idea, embraced first by Descartes, that the function possessing such property was the product of the mass times the velocity (which he called quantity of motion for the same reason why, as in the case seen before, the product of the thermal capacity times the temperature was called quantity of heat), led him to conclusions that did not conform to the experience, for the reason that, considering such a product as a representation of a substance, he was able contemplate only the absolute value, and he had to deny that the disappearance of a quantity of motion could be compensated by the disappearance of an equal quantity of the opposite sign. Huygens' research is connected to these unfruitful attempts to overcome this difficulty. He finally managed to prove that in reality there exists only one way to evaluate the live force by which the property realized by Descartes is completely verified, and such a way consists of considering not the products of the velocities times the respective masses, but rather the products of the masses times the squares of the velocities.

The fact that any variation in the value of the sum of such products, for the bodies of a system, is constantly conjoint with a proportional variation of another function whose value depends only on the position of the bodies themselves and by the intensity and direction of the forces to which they are subjected, is stated even in our times with a sentence that suggests the conservation of "something." There is in fact no reason to call two things as different as those respectively indicated by the value of the two functions mentioned above (i.e. live force and potential) by the same name (energy), if not that of being able to express the fact that their sum is constant, with a sentence similar to that which we would use if we were dealing with a substance that, even assuming different shapes, remains of an invariable quantity.

It is clear that any other relation between natural phenomena, which is able to be formulated as the maintaining constant of the sum of two or more functions each containing a special number of parameters, can, with the same verbal artifice, be presented as a law of conservation of "something." The only important thing, in any way, is the existence of a fixed relation between the aforementioned parameters, however we consider appropriate to express the permanence of the relation itself.

3.12

The considerations made so far and the facts mentioned to explain and support them, although not enough to give an idea of the many ways in which language can contribute, sometimes without us noticing, in suggesting analogies and therefore in inducing us to imagine hypotheses and build experiences, seem to me nevertheless sufficient to show how this very feature constitutes the main cause of the influence that has had, and still has, on the progress of a scientific theory, namely the mere fact that such a theory is expressed in one certain way rather than another.

It is the different degrees in the ability to be evocative that can belong to the various ways of representing and formulating a certain theory, and the different directions in which we are led by each of them in generalizing, in deducing, in comparing, in experimenting, that imply that the invention of new ways of formulating and expressing what we already know must sometimes be considered as no less an important contribution to the progress of science than the acquisition of new factual knowledge or the discovery of new laws.

And it is for the same reason that many times some very serious obstacles to the progress of knowledge have been created by the fact that the knowledge already acquired on a certain topic was prematurely schematized and represented in a way detrimental to the results of further investigation, or in a way that created suppositions leading to the investigation of a false trail, preventing a sufficient amount of attention from being directed in the proper direction.

These actions due to language are even more deserving of consideration given that most of them act in a somewhat automatic way[16] and without the minimum intervention of our consciousness and will. So it happens frequently that some arguments or conclusions, of which we would immediately sense the precariousness and temporariness if we were clearly aware of the vague and superficial analogies at their basis, acquire instead the appearance of evident and indisputable truths only because the intervention of language is hiding their real foundations.

The technical scientific language, no less than the ordinary language, is full of metaphorical sentences and expressions that, even if after long use have stopped reminding us of the image suggested in origin, have not lost their ability to induce us to attribute to the facts that such expressions describe all the properties of the image to which they refer.

We would recognize in our own languages, and in similar languages, the same poetic and imaginative character that impresses us in languages which are very different from ours (for example Oriental languages), if we did not have the ability to use the images of our language and the metaphors contained in it, without seeing them for what they are, an ability due to long standing habit (in conformity with a psychological law well known to the scholar of comparative philology).

In contrast with Molière's character who was surprised when he realized he had always spoken in prose without knowing it, we should be surprised to have always spoken in poetry without noticing it.

This is not harmful to us, in the same way as it is not harmful to the mathematician, who investigates the properties of functions, to use sentences that refer to, or are taken from, their geometric representation, and in the same way as it is not harmful for the geometer to talk about spaces with n dimensions, or about points in common to lines which do not meet each other.

Leibniz has justly noted how even Scholastic terminology is completely characterized by the most coarse analogies between mental phenomena and phenomena of the physical world, although considered to be typically arid and stripped as much as possible of any rhetoric blandishment, and from which, as it is known, we have inherited most of our technical abstract terms referring to intellectual operations and to the fundamental concepts of science.

For example, let us think about the importance assumed by it in terms such as the following: "impressio," "dependere," "emanare," "influere," "inhaerere," "fundamentum," "infundere," "transmittere," etc. Having assumed a new abstract sense does not prevent the fact that

---

[16] "Not even those, who know the ambiguity of a term, are always proof against the confusion which it tends to generate." G. C. Lewis, *Use and abuse of political terms* [1832]. See Welby, *Grains of sense* (London, Dent, 1897), p. 9 [Welby 1897].

on some occasions they may suggest ideas which refer only to their concrete and material sense, and they may generate or give persuasive strength to arguments that would not have any strength or plausibility, independent of their primitive interpretation.[17]

The power of words is so strong and the fascination that they exercise on the minds of men, including those of philosophers and scientists, is so great, that, because of them, more than one theory, dead and buried for many centuries, can continue to be used unconsciously to support any of its remotest consequences, finding itself in the position of that knight, as was sung by the poet:

> The poor man, not knowing how much he'd bled,
> Kept on fighting when in fact he was dead.[18]

3.13

What I have said so far certainly falls short of being a complete enumeration of the various ways in which the unconscious enslavement of our thinking to words is manifest in the various fields of intellectual activity. But I flatter myself in thinking that it could suffice in order to understand just how far from the truth we are if we believe that, to be free from such slavery, the mere wish for emancipation from it will suffice.

There may be no other mental characteristic that generates so many differences and levels among men of healthy intellect, as the greater or smaller susceptibility of being victims of the traps of language. Nevertheless this does not prevent such attitude and susceptibility from being extremely subject to alterations and modifications, depending on the intellectual discipline to which anyone can be submitted.

---

[17] We should add to this the characteristic abuse of prepositions implying spatial relations (sub, super, inter, extra, trans.) In this regard it is noteworthy an observation by J. Stuart Mill (*Examination of Sir William Hamilton's Philosophy*, ch. XX): "If there is a recommendation I would inculcate on every one who commences the study of philosophy, it is to be always sure what he means by his particles. A large portion of all that perplexes and confuses metaphysical thought came from a vague use of those small words." [Stuart Mill 1865, p. 438. In English in the original. Vailati had in his own library a copy of the 3rd edition (London, 1867).]

[18] [Vailati quotes: "Il poverin, che non se n'era accorto/ Andava combattendo ed era morto." The original quotation is "Cosí colui, del colpo non accorto,/ Andava combattendo ed era morto"; see *Orlando innamorato* [Orlando in love], Bojardo and Berni 1541, vol. 4, LIII.60, p. 323.] The influence of the imperfections of language on the formation of myths and legends has started only recently to attract the attention of the philologists and the folklorists. We are inclined to see most of those beliefs of primitive populations, previously attributed to a supposed tendency to "personification" of natural phenomena, as effects of successive literal interpretations of metaphoric or symbolic expressions, originally due to the poverty of language.

It is an age-old opinion that the study of physical and mathematical sciences constitutes one of the best ways to educate and fortify the mind in this regard, perhaps as ancient as the institution of schools where the basics of the more ancient branches of such sciences (like Geometry and Astronomy) were taught to young students destined to liberal professions. Opinions are instead much more discordant regarding the effectiveness, which for this same purpose is attributed to a doctrinal exposition directly devoted to describing, classifying, and analyzing the different species of verbal illusions which tend to infect any single form of reasoning or of argumentation.

On this topic there is actually a noticeable contrast between those ideas dominant in the philosophical schools of ancient Greece and those prevailing among the modern scientists and educators. That is, while the latter tend to almost completely deny any effectiveness and practicality of any theoretical exposition dedicated to the examination and analysis of the various reasoning processes and to the characterization of the corresponding causes of error, the Greeks gave extreme importance to this branch of teaching in their plan of intellectual education. They were firmly persuaded that both the arts of deceiving with words and of not being deceived by them were able to be learnt just as we learn Arithmetic or Geometry or any other science, and that a theoretical exposition which would serve as a foundation was an indispensable element of the intellectual education of any well educated person.

As far as the spirit and the way in which this topic was taught are concerned, we have an idea from the precious writings of Aristotle, *Topics* and *Sophistical Refutations*, the only survivors of a large series of "handbooks" dedicated to the same purpose, of which only the titles have survived to the present day.[19]

The time and topic constraints of the present work do not allow me to linger as much as I would like to in showing some of the typical traits of the development of contemporary culture, which seem to justify a new examination of the aforementioned controversy, and tend to welcome views on the topic which are far more similar to those of the Greek philosophers than those that modern science has received as heritage from the thinkers of the last century.

I must be content to list the most significant of these traits, and first of all to raise and impose the development that the new science of lan-

---

[19]It is extremely deplorable that we have lost a writing by Euclid, by the title *Pseudaria* [*Fallacies*], where were collected and classified the main kinds of sophisms and illegitimate arguments that were, or had been, current among the geometers who were his contemporaries or his predecessors. A noteworthy modern book of this kind is the *Budget of paradoxes* by A. De Morgan [1872].

guage, comparative philology, has had in our century, and the tendency which begins to appear in it ascending from merely phonetic questions and related to the transformation of sounds, to those instead related to the intimate structure of language and the phenomena presented by its successive adaptation to its many functions.[20]

The study of the laws regulating the variations in meaning of words and of inflections, for which Breal has recently coined a new word, *la Semantique*, is attracting the attention of glottologists more and more.

We have evidence of this at our University, in a recent publication by our professor Domenico Pezzi, included in the Memorie dell'Accademia delle Scienze di Torino, of the title: "Saggio di un indice sistematico per lo studio della espressione metaforica dei concetti psicologici."

Allow me to note, in passing, how the recognition of the educative importance of this new branch of scientific investigation should have an influence in determining the final outcome of the discussion among the opponents of the teaching of classical languages in high school and those who would like these languages to be taught in a way that can actually deliver the results that can justify its preservation and expansion.[21]

An ever greater increase in the studies related to the history of science and of culture seems to me to be going in the same direction, where the tight psychological and genealogical connection between the beliefs in which the science of our time consist is more and more evident.

To consider the philosophical systems and the imperfect scientific construction of the past centuries as intellectual aberrations, or as monstrosities, would be as ridiculous as though a geologist were to take seriously the idea expressed by Voltaire, that the traces of shells found in some alpine rocks are due to the passage of pilgrims coming back from the journey to the Holy Land.

To complete the list of circumstances that conspire to give back a larger part to the historic and philosophical culture in the intellectual education of the young people who dedicate themselves to the study of sciences, I should still mention the impulse that has been given, in these years, to the research done on the mental faculties by the institution of the laboratories of Experimental Psychology, which thrives in the American Universities, and, last not least,[22] the recent development of

---

[20]I do not want to miss quoting in this regard the recent work by professor Jespersen of the University of Copenaghen, *Progress in Language* (London, 1897) [Jespersen 1894].

[21]Some arguments of utilitarian nature, that the former bring forward often, remind of the utilitarianism of those mandarins who were opposed to the introduction of the railway in the Celestial Empire, saying that they took out too long strips of land from agricultural use.

[22][In English in the original.]

Mathematical Logic.

But it is time to conclude, and I do so wishing that the action of these numerous influences will lead in time to modify, at least in part, the attitude of unappreciation and indifference that over here most scientists feel towards philosophical studies, in which they see only a collection of unfruitful and vain struggles with words.

Let us allow them to quote the renowned sentence spoken by the great scientist and philosopher Pascal, "to scorn philosophy is truly to philosophize,"[23] but then it must be allowed for us to observe that among all the species of philosophy, the one that is most worthy of 'being scorned'[24] is that which believes that the accumulation of knowledge from generation to generation is sufficient reason for each of this generation to believe itself intellectually superior to all those preceding it, that the great minds of the past were speaking and writing only for their contemporaries, and that we do not have anything to learn anymore by studying their works, only because on many "matters of fact" they reasoned less correctly than us and they ignored many things that now must not be ignored by a junior student.

References

Bojardo, Matteo and Francesco Berni. 1541. *Orlando innamorato*. Firenze: Tipografia de' classici italiani, 1828.

Boltzmann, Ludwig. 1892. Über die Methoden der theoretischen Physik. In W. Dyck, ed., *Katalog mathematischer und mathematisch-physikalischer Modelle, Apparate und Instrumente*, pages 87–98. München: C. Wolf und Sohn. Engl. Translation in B. McGuinness 1974, pages 5–12.

Boltzmann, Ludwig. 1897. Über die Frage nach der objectiven Existenz der Vorgänge in der unbelebten Natur. *Sitzungsberichte der Kaiserlichen Akademie der Wissenschaften. Mathematisch-Naturwissenschaftliche Classe* 106(2):83–112. Engl. Translation in B. McGuinness 1974, pages 57–76.

Brofferio, Angelo. 1884. *La specie dell'esperienza*. Milano: Dumolard.

Burali Forti, C. 1893. *Manuale di Logica Matematica*. Milano: Hoepli.

de Morgan, Augustus. 1872. *A budget of paradoxes*. London: Longmans, Green, and co.

Dyck, Walther. 1892. *Katalog mathematischer und mathematisch-physikalischer Modelle, Apparate und Instrumente*. München: C. Wolf & Sohn.

Guastella, C. 1898. *Saggi sulla Teoria della Conoscenza*. Palermo: Sandron.

---

[23] [In French in the original. Pascal 1670, I, IX, 36. Engl. transl. by O. W. Wight, p. 241.]

[24] [The words in quotation marks are in French in the original.]

Jaurès, Jean. 1891. *La realité du monde sensible*. Paris: Felix Alcan.

Jespersen, Otto. 1894. *Progress in language; with special reference to English*. London: S. Sonnenschein & co., Macmillan & co.

Kautsky, K. 1898. *Il Socialismo*. Torino: Bocca.

Lewis, G. C. 1832. *Use and abuse of political terms*. Oxford: Clarendon Press (1898), 2nd edn.

McGuinness, Brian, ed. 1974. *(L. Boltzmann) Theoretical physics and philosophical problems*. Dordrecht-Boston: Reidel.

Newton, Isaac. 1687. *Philosophiae naturalis principia mathematica*. Engl. transl. by A. Motte *The Mathematical Principles of Natural Philosophy*, London: H. D. Symonds, 1803.

Pascal, Blaise. 1670. *Pensées de Pascal sur la religion et sur quelques autres sujets. Nouvelle édition, conforme au véritable texte de l'auteur et contenant les additions de Port-Royal*. Paris: Garnier (1867). Engl. transl. by O. W. Wight, *The thoughts, letters and opuscules*, New York: Debry 1861.

Pikler, Gyula. 1890. *The psychology of the belief in objective existence*. London: Williams & Norgate.

Poincaré, Henri. 1891. *Cours de physique mathématique. Electricité et optique*. Paris: Carré.

Schopenhauer, Arthur. 1819. *Die Welt als Wille und Vorstellung*. Engl. transl. E. F. J. Payne (ed.), *The world as will and representation*, Courier Dover Publications, 1966.

Spencer, Herbert. 1862. *First principles of a new system of philosophy*. London: Williams and Norgate.

Stuart Mill, J. 1865. *An examination of Sir William Hamilton's philosophy, and of the principal philosophical questions discussed in his writings*. London: Longman, Roberts & Green, 1872.

Vailati, Giovanni. 1898. Recensione a C. Guastella, Saggi sulla Teoria della Conoscenza. *Il Nuovo Risorgimento* 8(9-10). Repr. in Vailati (1911), pages 198–201.

Vailati, Giovanni. 1899. *Alcune osservazioni sulle Questioni di Parole nella Storia della Scienza e della Cultura. Prolusione ad un corso libero di Storia della Meccanica, 1898-98*. Torino: Bocca. Repr. in Vailati (1911), pages 203-228.

Vailati, Giovanni. 1911. *Scritti di G. Vailati, 1863-1909*. Leipzig-Firenze: Barth.

Welby, Victoria. 1897. *Grains of sense*. London: J.M. Dent & Co.

4

The Difficulties Involved in a Rational Classification of the Sciences[†]

I. The effects of the division of labor

The progressive tendency towards the division of labor and towards what is called the specialization of functions should perhaps be regarded as the most fundamental of the characters in common to all the processes of development in human cooperation, in the various fields in which such a cooperation is manifested.We can already find a clear awareness of the existence of such a tendency and of the importance of researching its causes and consequences among the more ancient thinkers, who reflected on the conditions of stability and development of states and societies. In many important passages of the *Republic*, Plato points out the complete subdivision of the different jobs and functions among the social classes and the citizens as a necessary condition of the vitality and longevity of any form of human association. He also describes the inherent advantages of a political organization that allows every member of the society to exercise their activity in the direction and in the amount determined by their specific inclinations. As we know, he also insisted on the analogies of this law in the phys-

---

[†] "Des difficultés qui s'opposent á une Classification rationelle des Sciences." Communication presented at the First International Congress of Philosophy in Paris (August 1900), first published in *Bibliothèque du Congrès international de philosophie*, III, Logique et histoire des sciences, Paris, Colin, 1901. Repr. in Vailati 1911, pages 324-335. Italian translation "Difficoltà che si oppongono ad una classificazione razionale delle scienze" in Quaranta 2003, pages 179–194. (Vailati, 1901).

Logic and Pragmatism. Selected Essays by Giovanni Vailati.
C. Arrighi, P. Cantù, M. De Zan, and P. Suppes.
Copyright © 2009, CSLI Publications.

iological field, giving an example of the advantage that we can enjoy, in this regard, by comparing the social organism and the organisms in the strict sense of the word, used for the study of its composition and of the mutual relations among the different parts of which the social organism is composed.

In Aristotle's *Politics*, the advantages and the social importance of the division of labor are often objects of consideration, and he manifests a tendency to regard it as something more than a characteristic property of any society, human or animal, and to recognize in it instead a general law embracing all the products of organic nature.[1]

As far as regards material production or the exchange and distribution of wealth, the research of the conditions and the effects of the division of labor has already led to the birth of a special science which, after Adam Smith, never stopped acquiring more and more importance, both theoretical and practical. However, on the other hand, the facts of similar nature referring to other forms of collective activity, such as science, art, language, family institutions, etc. have only recently started to be taken into consideration and to be analyzed from the same standpoint, especially under the influence of the theory of evolution. Besides lesser direct interest in the latter kind of studies, the cause of this delay has undoubtedly been the greater complexity of the related problems compared with purely economic questions, and the consequent necessity, in these other fields, to have any attempt at synthesis or generalization preceded by greater analytical and descriptive research intended to choose and elaborate the material brought by the progress of historic and philological sciences, which are ever on the increase both in quantity and quality.

Among the many topics suited at the moment to research of this kind, the most interesting seems to be that regarding the development and the gradual differentiation of the different branches of scientific research; it is on this topic that I am going to make some brief observations, intended to highlight its intimate relationship with theoretical and practical questions concerning the classification of sciences.

---

[1]See for example *Polit.*, 1253 *b* (B. I, chap. I): "Now nature has distinguished between the female and the slave. For she is not niggardly, like the smith who fashions the Delphian knife for many uses; she makes each thing for a single use, and every instrument is best made when intended for one and not for many uses." [English translation by B. Jowett from Jowett and Davis 1916, p. 26.]

II. The first difficulty encountered in forming a classification

What has been said so far was necessary in order to justify the method and the form of exposition that I want to use in this study, and to make clear that my intent is not that of providing some new outline of classification to be added to all those others that have been proposed so far, but rather that of examining and characterizing some of the difficulties preventing a satisfactory solution to this problem and to attract interest in the probable causes of the fact that such difficulties have not yet been totally overcome.

One of the main causes has already been mentioned, namely the belief that the research of the best way to order and classify human knowledge could be separated by any consideration about the practical motivations that have determined the division of intellectual labor, about what aspect such motivations may actually assume, and about how they have developed, both in the organization of professions and the transformation of those educational institutes dedicated to preparing the young for the different functions of social life. In other words, not enough attention has been paid, in this matter (as in other similar matters), to the fact that, in order for the research of *what-should-be* to reach valid solutions, it has to be preceded by the careful analysis of *what-is* and of *what-has-been*, i.e. the exact knowledge of the factors contributing to the development of the studied phenomena, in the way in which they have actually developed. In our case we should expect that any research of a perfect and ideal way of distinguishing and then grouping the various kinds of knowledge together which does not take into consideration the actual, historical distinctions and the causes of their origin and their course, would lead to conclusions which are no less fantastic and utopian than those regarding the search for an imaginary kind of perfect society or an ideal form of government, which would have been reached independently by any study of the positive conditions and the laws that dominate the development and the life of societies that have lived in the past, as history shows.

III. Second difficulty

Even though the history of civilization in its different stages constitutes a necessary prerequisite in guiding the study of the aforementioned question, we cannot rely on it being sufficient on its own in eliminating all the difficulties encountered during such a study.

In fact, among these difficulties there are some that do not depend so much on the scarcity of factual data or on the complexity of the topic, but rather on radical defects in the way that the problem to be solved has been conceived and formulated, and on the fact that the problem is stated in a too restrictive way, which may suggest irrational requirements or some conditions that cannot be satisfied simultaneously.

It seems to me that, against this second cause of difficulty and misunderstanding, whose main origins lie in a bundle of erroneous and vague conceptions, regarding the nature and the purpose of the process of "classification" in general, we could not react better than submitting such conceptions, as well as the mental operations to which they are connected, to a more rigorous and precise analysis. Only by applying the results of such analysis to the problem will we be able to separate with confidence the solvable parts from the unsolvable, and the questions for which it is worthwhile finding a solution from those which cannot accept any kind of answer; and afterwards we will be able to proceed in making a particular kind of research that will be perfectly determined and able to lead to conclusions of a certain practical purpose.

IV. Analysis of the classification by Durand (de Gros)

Regarding this stage that is, so to speak, preliminary to the question, it is quite useful to be able to base the following considerations on the general views recently presented by Durand (de Gros) in his magisterial work on the nature and purpose of scientific classifications.[2] His research, inspired mostly by the desire to specify and deepen the concept of natural classification, which has had so much importance in the development of biological sciences, has lead Durand (de Gros) to establish some fundamental distinctions between the various kinds of classification, characterized by the different criteria used in each of them, to determine the position and method of composition of the groups of objects to be classified.

First of all, there are those he defines as "classifications by order of generality," which are those whose objects are distributed in groups determined by the fact that they do or do not possess certain characteristics of similarity or some common properties. Classifications of this kind, the only ones, it could be said, taken into any consideration by traditional Logic, are characterized by the fact that to each of the object classified many different denominations can be applied, which can be ever more general depending on how many successive operations of subdivision have to be performed in order to obtain the smallest of the

---

[2]J.P. Durand (de Gros), *Aperçus de taxinomie generale*, vol. I, Paris, Alcan, 1899 p. 265 [Durand de Gros 1899].

classes that contain it; denominations which, applied to an object, are able to indicate that it possesses some properties or characters common to the other objects to which the same denomination is applied.

The case of classifications of the second kind studied by Durand, which he called "classification by order of composition," is completely different. In these the position and the distribution of the objects in groups are not regulated by considerations related to their greater or lesser similitude, or to the number and the importance of their common characters, but only to the fact of whether they are a part of other objects, which are in turn distributed in classes according to the same criterion, i.e. according to the place they occupy in the composition of other more complex objects, and so on.

We can see this is the case, for example, when we compose a machine with its different parts in our thoughts, and in each of these parts we can distinguish the different bodies that constitute it, until we break down to these latter, in turn, into their elementary parts.

It is not superfluous to underline that in classifications of this second kind, unlikely those of the first kind, every denomination adopted to design each group corresponds to an object no less "real" and concrete than those corresponding to the names of the different parts of which the group itself is composed; nevertheless it is not possible to apply the name that designs the group to any of the parts of which the group consists, as instead we can do in the classification of the first kind.

Therefore, in order to clarify this with an example taken from our topic, if in a classification of the sciences "by order of generality" we have the category "historical sciences," including, for example, the history of religions, comparative statistics, linguistics, etc., the denomination "historical science," which also applies in particular to each of these sciences, must be considered simply as the expression of the fact that they possess a certain group of common characters. If, on the other hand, adopting a classification "by order of composition," we ended up establishing a group of studies related to social phenomena, designating it, for example, with the name sociology, and distinguishing in it, as integral parts, the different disciplines that have as their object some social aspect, or political aspect, or anthropological aspect, etc., then not only would we have allowed the application of the name Sociology to each of the sciences that deals with these different aspects, but also this term would be considered as designating a discipline no less real and concrete than each of those that are its subordinates, given that it has a special task that none of the others could have, and to which any of these partial sciences must contribute in the measure that is due.

In the kind of "classifications by composition" that we have considered, the different subordinate groups, corresponding to the different branches of the tree that represents the distribution of the classified object, represent the different parts into which the object corresponding to the trunk is broken down. Besides the kind just mentioned, there is another where the opposite procedure is followed, that is where the branches represent the compound objects, and the trunk or trunks correspond to elements which are part of their composition. Such is the case of the classifications in chemistry and mineralogy where, taking the simple bodies as a starting point, they are then subordinated to the related compounds and these, in turn, are subordinated to the more complex different products that derive from them. For the purposes of our study it is interesting to note that the analogy between this second kind of classification and the classifications by order of generality is one of the main causes of the manner of conceiving the nature of abstract ideas, that in the history of philosophy carries the name of "realism" (as opposed to "nominalism"). In fact, lacking a clear notion of the essential differences between these two kinds of classification, some people believed they could apply all the properties of the latter to the former, even to the point of admitting, in particular, that in the classification by order of generality also, the ever more abstract and general names designating the different groups must actually correspond to some "entity," "inherent" in a specific way to each of the objects to which the same general name is applied in the same way as in Chemistry, for example, the name "carbonate" expresses the presence of a given component element in all the bodies to which it is applied.

The other kinds of classification, respectively called "hierarchical classification" and "genealogical classification" by Durand, present a greater analogy with the type of classification by composition than with the type of classification by order of generality. The genealogical classification, as indicated by the name, is applicable only to those objects which can be considered derivatives of one another, both for generalization in the strict sense of the term, or by progressive transformation and differentiation, as is the case, for example, in languages and social institutions; it consists of distributing such objects in groups depending on their genetic affinity. The main difference between this kind of classification and those preceding it is the fact that, in this case, the name which is in the mind, so to speak, of each group of individuals, instead of expressing the sum constituted by their union, indicates another individual which has a separate existence and from which they derive, in the same way that from these derive in turn other individuals which constitute new groups and so on.

Something similar to this happens in the case of classifications by hierarchy, where on top of each group an individual also appears, which occupies a privileged position with respect to the group; as for example, in the case of an army, the general with respect to his subordinates or, in astronomy, the sun with respect to the planets, and these in turn with respect to their satellites.

V. Variety of criteria of classification

These four types of classification are surely far from including and exhausting all the varieties of outlines and processes used to group together and order a given set of objects. However, what we have said about their distinctive characters are enough to provide an idea of the variety of criteria that can and must guide us in choosing suitable classifications, when the objects to be classified are of such a nature as to be grouped together, as in our case, under a multitude of heterogeneous and complex relations, each of which requires its own amount of attention.

In my view, it is exactly this situation which can be considered as one of the main reasons why, among the many frequent attempts throughout the history of civilization to build an ideal outline of distribution of the different branches of knowledge, which could represent in one single picture the relationships and fundamental similarities between them, there are none that completely reached their purpose beyond any objection. All of those who have attempted it have been struggling between two kinds of requirements which are difficult to reconcile, on the one hand, the intent of basing their classification as much as possible on simple and uniform criteria, and on the other hand, the desire to build the classification in a way that the multiple kinds of connections and relationships existing between the sciences can be reflected and represented in the most complete and adequate way.

VI. Analysis of Comte's classification

It is appropriate now to leave these general assertions and examine some concrete classification with which to verify the conclusions to which the considerations made so far have led. For this purpose Comte's well known classification is well suited because it stands out among those seen so far, precisely for the reason that its author was above all concerned with and aware of the necessity to find in some way a compromise between the two aforementioned requirements, and because of the systematic efforts he has made in order to be able to keep both simultaneously under consideration.

In fact most of the arguments used by Comte to prove the plausibility of a classification of sciences according to the "hierarchical series" that he proposes, tend to show the intimate connection and the interdependency of the various heterogeneous criteria that he uses separately to determine such a classification, and they also tend to convince us that it is enough to allow one of these criteria to guide us in order to be led to solutions that conform to the requirements that would be imposed by applying the other criteria. In this way Comte observes that the hierarchy he has established between sciences at the same time corresponds to the order of their historical development and to the "decreasing generality" of the properties and of the laws that such sciences study. However, he also makes the point of observing that even if these two criteria end up justifying the same classification, this fact is very far from being due to a simple accidental coincidence. This happens, in his opinion, because the more the phenomena studied in a science correspond to general properties common to very heterogeneous objects,[3] the more the related laws and uniformities present themselves spontaneously to observation, because they happen to be in a larger area of our experience and can be recognized and noted before those others that are more hidden and less frequently verifiable.

Conforming to this observation, in Comte's opinion the reason why, for example, Geometry developed and became a science earlier than biology, is mostly due to the fact that the studies involved in the former refer to a property common to all bodies—that of having extension and of having determined shape and proportions—while the studies of the biologist refer to a particular kind of bodies, those which, besides the properties pertaining to Geometry, possess other specific properties, from which the geometer, as a geometer, can and actually must abstract, that is those bodies which are subject, *not only* to those laws expressing the properties of space or those of inorganic matter, *but also* to other more complex laws, which the biologist has the task of finding and formulating. Comte is again forced to resort to similar considerations when he wants to demonstrate that the two aforementioned criteria (i.e. the historical order of development and "decreasing generality") are not the only ones at the basis of his classification, but that his classification also takes into consideration the greater or lesser similarity that the various fundamental sciences present, from the point of view of *method* and the point of view of what can be defined as *logical* structure.

For this reason, as an example, he makes an effort to prove that the

---

[3]Such as, for example, the properties studied by arithmetic or algebra, which are verified in any order of phenomena in so far as they are at least able to be counted and measured.

preponderance of deductive processes in mechanics, in the strict sense of the term, compared to the greater importance of the inductive and experimental method in the different branches of physics, is simply due to the fact that the fundamental laws of the former are characterized, with respect to those of the latter, by a lesser "complexity," given that, merely for the fact that they extend to a larger group of phenomena, they must correspond to a greater degree of abstraction from the concrete and complicated data of experience.

In the same category we find included the considerations that Comte makes to point out that his classification in series of the fundamental sciences also agrees with the order in which we should put them if we want each of them to be preceded by all those whose knowledge is a prerequisite, that is, all those whose study constitutes an integral part of the intellectual preparation that such a science requires.

VII. First criticism of Comte

Although it is not possible to dispute either the depth or the importance of such observations, or of other similar observations on the topic at issue, it is not difficult to recognize that the direct and simultaneous application of such observations made by Comte to justify his system of classifications implies the supposition that a great quantity of particular and preliminary problems in the mutual relations among sciences has been resolved. A sufficiently deepened examination of such problems would lead to very different conclusions from those reached by the vague and general assertions that we have mentioned.

So, for example, believing that the chronological order of the development of the different sciences could be mainly determined by the greater or lesser extension of the matter subject to the laws studied by such sciences, is equal to disregarding an entire group of circumstances which, as shown by the history of the sciences, have had a decisive influence on their constitution and their development, connections which more or less directly tie or have tied together any order of knowledge to the practical needs and the needs of the economical and social life in the successive stages of development of civilization. And even abstracting from this, it is one of the most constantly observed and noted facts, for everyone who has dealt with comparative research on the development of the intellectual faculties in primitive races or on the development of infant curiosity, that the frequency with which a given phenomenon presents itself as a possible object of experience, far from being a cause attracting attention to it, is rather an obstacle to the desire of knowing how it is produced and to which laws it obeys.

In fact, while the first attempts made to observe, with a certain degree of precision, a phenomenon as common and usual as that of a weight falling freely or along a surface that creates friction, do not go back more than three centuries ago, we can see how ancient are the statistics and the calculations used to empirically determine the periods regulating the production of such rare and extraordinary facts such as eclipses.

VIII. Second criticism of Comte

Another part of Comte's theory is subject to even more serious objections, namely the one regarding the conditions on which the greater or lesser applicability of the deductive method in certain areas of scientific research depends. The tendency to establish a direct connection between such applicability and the degree of "generality" (in the sense explained above) of the properties and the laws constituting the object of each science, led Comte to some of his less justified conclusions on the logical character and the method of each of the fundamental sciences. It is hard to find another cause for the characteristic aversion, which he tried to acknowledge, to the fact that the use of deduction can, to some extent, contribute to solve some questions related to social phenomena; an aversion which, besides inducing him to judge with unfair severity the applicability of probability to sociological research, has led him to completely deny the logical character of that part of economic science whose objective is the determination of the consequences resulting from the free play of a certain group of human movements, if their action could be isolated from the other movements that can have an influence on the action of humans in a given social environment. He would not have missed the close affinity in method and the remarkable similarity in the structure of this important branch of social science with those parts of mechanical physics where the principles and the theories of mechanics find their most simple and direct application, if he had been less subject to the prejudice of a direct connection between the extension of the area of validity of the most general laws of a science and the degree of applicability of deductive procedure to such science. The persuasion that such applicability should, with no exceptions, decrease from one science to another, i.e. in the successive place in the hierarchical order he established, from mathematics to sociology, has induced him to categorically deny that among the different specific branches of this last science, one could exist which is more suited (as political economics is) to have the function, with respect to the others, that mechanics has with respect to the physical sciences. Such a function consists in calculating separately the consequences of those properties of objects and phenomena in question which, for their greater simplicity and measurability, are more easily accessible by a deductive treatment, and more suited to being the starting point for the analysis and the subsequent determination of the different causes which, in each concrete case, concur and overlap their effects in such a way that it is difficult to recognize directly by induction the laws that regulate their behavior.

IX. Third criticism of Comte

Another example of the poor consequences that can be reached by the abstract research of a systematic classification of the different sciences is provided by the position and role assigned, in Comte's picture, to psychology. The fact that it appears as a simple chapter or appendix to biology cannot simply be attributed to the idea that Comte had on the importance of the research on the physiological facts correlated to the facts of consciousness, or to the scarce value he attributed to psychological research, starting from introspection, in the strict sense of the term, to the interpretation and the comparative analysis of products and the exterior manifestations of moral and intellectual activity. In greater part, certainly a great contribution has been seen in the desire to avoid the perturbation that would have been caused in the harmony of the system adopted by the inappropriate inclusion of a new fundamental science which would have taken position between biology and sociology, even though it has relationships with each of these sciences and others of a heterogeneous nature, with respect to those that were chosen in the beginning as the ordering criteria of the classification.

The tight connection, which links the part of psychology which researches the genesis, development and action of intellectual faculties with any kind of studies, which under one name or another refers to the analysis of the methods and procedures of scientific research or to the determination of the different causes of error or illusion and the means of preventing them, was not one of those relationships that can be neglected as meaningless in a system like that of Comte, which tends to regard philosophy as a general methodology of sciences, and clearly distinguished from the previous systems mainly because it has a basis of historical and empirical generalization of an essentially psychological nature, like the "law of the three stages."

A theory of knowledge and a logic (as well as an ethics and a theory of purposes and human ideals) which does not have a corresponding organized and independent group of scientific investigations, having the same relationship with these as that of biology with medicine, or the mechanical and physical sciences with the industrial applications, should have appeared to him as lacking the first necessary condition for their constitution and their progress.

The fact that such consideration was not sufficient for Comte to include psychology in the series of the fundamental sciences can be explained, I believe, by the fear of introducing an element of inconsistency into the hierarchy of sciences which he built. Just as in the Trojan horse, some trap could be hidden inside psychology which could disarrange the very fundamentals of his organization of the sciences, and create a breach in such an organization through which the much feared "metaphysics" could enter.

To understand that such a fear was not completely unjustified, we can think about the ever growing competence that we tend to attribute to psychology, and especially to comparative psychology, in all those questions regarding the criticism of the notions and the principles at the basis of each science, including mathematics and mechanics, and to the ever growing need they have to carefully examine and break down into their most simple elements fundamental concepts and processes that they use. We realize ever more that the questions related to their legitimacy and to the limits of their validity and their applicability cannot be separated from the research which revolves around their origins, the different forms they have assumed in history, and the causes or the conditions that have determined their development and modifications.

It is natural that a position no less characteristic and singular in any classification of science which wishes to take into consideration the most organic and fundamental links that tie them together, must correspond to the singular and original function assumed by Psychology with respect to other sciences, as an indispensable intermediary between them and any attempt to rise to a synthetic conception of the world and of life.[4]

X. Functions and limits of an "ideal" classification

I do not believed that the apparently merely critical an negative considerations that we have seen so far can be accused of not leading to any positive and practical conclusion.

First of all they tend to show that the research of an ideal and

---

[4]I mean psychology in the broader sense, as including not only individual psychology in the strict sense of the term, but also social psychology, in all their branches, from the psychology of infancy to psychiatry, from the history of religions to that of inventions and discoveries, from the study of the needs and cooperation of economics to the research on hypnotism and the so called psychic phenomena, from the comparative philology to "semantics" and "folklore," etc.

perfect classification of the sciences belongs to an important kind of research, whose value does not depend as much on the greater or lesser probability of reaching their purpose, but rather on the importance of the special problems that such research implies, on the questions asked and whose solution they produce and prepare.

Secondly, assuming that the critical observations shown above are sufficient to make the construction of a scheme of distribution of the sciences, capable of representing their many relationships in a proper way, appear utopian and unrealizable, on the other hand, such observations, far from discouraging it, incite the elaboration of some schemes with a more specialized and determined scope, adequate for one or another of the particular purposes that a classification may have. Depending on the purpose, like that of compiling a bibliographic catalogue, organizing a didactic institute, establishing a historical work plan, or preparing the material for a comparative study of methods, procedures or mental attitudes of each science, it is natural that, given that the criteria of distribution or grouping are different, the results to which they lead are also different, and this difference in the results has no inconveniences, either practical or theoretical.

Finally we can draw one last consequence from the previous considerations concerning the relationships between the questions on the classification of sciences and those related to the organization and the division of labor among scientists. We can assert that, while the general purpose of classifications is the simultaneous representation, as in a picture, of the existing relationships, from a certain point of view, between each of the objects to be classified and *all* the others, in the present case; on the contrary, the most important thing, in practice and in theory, is the specification and the *criticism* of the criteria which can lead to justifying and confirming, or rather modifying and suppressing, the boundaries for each science which limit the field with respect to *two or three* other sciences that can be taken into consideration, in one way or another, as bordering or as able to dispute the possession of the contested fields.

Between the research of a perfect and ideal grouping of the various sciences according to a uniform and necessarily unilateral criterion, and the passive adhesion to the traditional divisions between the areas of research of the different sciences, divisions for which, most of the time, the historical causes of their origins have long disappeared, there is a large area open for useful and important attempts. If they are unable to order and unify according to new principles the variety of human knowledge, it does not mean that they will be less effective for the progress of science and to better the economy of the efforts that tend to make it grow.

References

Durand de Gros, Pierre-Joseph. 1899. *Aperçus de taxinomie générale*. Paris: Alcan.

Jowett, B. and H.W.C Davis. 1916. *Aristotle's Politics*. Oxford: Clarendon Press. Translated by Benjamin Jowett, with introduction, analysis and index by H.W.C. Davis.

Quaranta, Mario. 2003. *Giovanni Vailati. Gli strumenti della ragione*. Il Poligrafo.

Vailati, Giovanni. 1901. Des difficultés qui s'opposent á une classification rationelle des sciences. In *Bibliothèque du Congrès international de Philosophie (Paris 1900) III. Logique et Histoire des Sciences*. Paris: Colin, 1901. Repr. in Vailati 1911, pages 324-335. Italian transl. in Vailati 1987, vol. 1, pages 121–133.

Vailati, Giovanni. 1911. *Scritti di G. Vailati, 1863-1909*. Leipzig-Firenze: Barth.

5

On the Logical Import of the Classification of Mental Facts Proposed by Franz Brentano[†]

The classification of the states of conciousness, proposed by professor Franz Brentano, several years ago in his psychology treatise (*Psychologie vom empirischen Standpunkte*, Vol. I, Leipzig, 1874) and which he continued to support in his following publications (particularly in the pamphlet *Vom Ursprung sittlicher Erkenntnis*, Leipzig, 1899), seems to me to have advantages worth mentioning from a "logical" point of view, that is, regarding the application of psychology to the analysis and critical control of intellectual processes.

These advantages depend above all on the fact that the distinctions and relations between mental facts, which are highlighted by this classification, are precisely those whose exact determination is the most necessary in order to avoid the misunderstandings and confusion that are so easily encountered in treatises on the origin and the nature of the proofs of our most *intuitive* pieces of knowledge and our most instinctive and spontaneous judgments.

The classification by Brentano is first of all characterized by this: the states of conciousness, which imply mental attitudes of *expectation* or *prediction*, in all of their variety and shades (conviction, doubt, hope, fear, trust, etc.), are grouped together in one category that is at the

---

[†] "Sulla portata logica della classificazione dei fatti mentali proposta dal prof. Franz Brentano." Communication presented at the III International Congress on Psychology in Paris, August 1900. Published in *Rivista Filosofica*, year II, issue I, January–February 1901, repr. in Vailati (1911), pages 336-340 (Vailati, 1901).

same time coordinated to and opposed by, on the one hand, the category of simple *representations* (including sensations in the strict sense of the term, remembered sensations, mental images, ideas, etc.) and on the other hand, the category of phenomena of *volition* and voluntary impulse or inhibition. The distinction between these three fundamental categories (*"representations," "expectations,"* and *"volition"*) is mainly justified, in Brentano's opinion, by the possibility, or rather by the necessity, of establishing among them that which could be called a hierarchical order, because, on the one hand, every *"expectation"* (πρόληπσις, belief, judgment), being a belief *about something*, presupposes a more or less clear *representation* of what is believed, while on the other hand every *voluntary* act also presupposes (together with a more or less defined representation of at least a part of the process that it tends to realize) some kind of belief, or opinion, regarding the efficacy of the means to be used in order to reach the intended goal.

Now it seems interesting to me to point out, from the point of view of the application of psychology to practical and normative logic, the intimate correspondence existing between this tripartition of the states of consciousness and the most fundamental distinctions that logicians are induced to establish between the different kinds of propositions, when they want to classify them according to their *meaning*, or according to what is called, by the English scholars, their *"import."* [1]

Corresponding to professor Brentano's first category, that is the category of simple *representations*, are those propositions that have the mere purpose of clarifying or analyzing the meaning of a word or phrase that we intend to use. This class includes the propositions that, in Kantian terminology, would be called *analytic judgments*, that is, in general, all those propositions that we use to determine our concepts by means of each other, decomposing them into simpler terms—in other words, all the propositions with the characteristics of *definitions*, in the broader sense of this word.

To the second category (the category of *expectations*) belong the assertions in the strict sense of the term, that is those expressing the degree of our assent, or of our doubt, when confronted with opinions related to matters of fact—i.e. opinions that are true or false independent of any human convention concerning the way to express them. [2]

---

[1] [In English in the original.]

[2] The word *"expectations,"* which we use here because of the lack of a more appropriate term, must be intended in a sense that includes not only judgments about the future (as would be suggested by the etymology of the word) but also those about the past or present. For example, the knowledge that an astronomer may have of the position that a given star will assume *in many years*, and his

It is even more important to take into consideration the contrast between these two types of propositions, which could be designated respectively, adopting the terms used by John Stuart Mill, as *verbal* propositions and *real* propositions, if we consider that the imperfections of language do not always allow us to distinguish, at first glance, to which of the two categories a given proposition refers to. In many cases, in fact, the same form of utterance can, without any exterior modification, be applied to express either a proposition of the first kind or of the second kind.

For example, if we find the following sentence in a treatise on geometry: "*the straight line is the shortest path between two points*," it will be necessary to examine the context before being able to decide whether the author intended, with such a sentence, to give a definition of the term "straight line" or whether, instead, having already determined before, by other means, the meaning of such term, he intends now to assert that the "straight line," which has already been otherwise defined, possesses, or he thinks it possesses, this further property expressed by the aforementioned sentence.

The ambiguity of the word "*is*" (which, in the former case, could be substituted by the words "is called" or "means," but not in the latter) is present, as we can see, even in the technical language of mathematicians, who are justly supposed to have the greatest needs in terms of precision of language. Finally there is a third category of propositions, no less important than the first two, which corresponds to Brentano's third category of psychological facts, i.e. the category of voluntary actions.

This third category consists of the propositions used not to express beliefs regarding what is or what happens (or happened or will happen), but rather to express *evaluations* or "judgments of value" (*Werth-Urtheile*). Even the propositions of this third category, however different they may be from the propositions belonging to the first two categories, may often be confused with the others because of their exterior similarities.

For example, when we say that "*the function of government is to protect citizens in exercising their rights*" we can wonder whether, when uttering this assertion, we intend to merely give information on what usually happens or tends to happen, or whether we want to express our ideal conception about the relationships that *must* exist between government and individuals. To take another example, the same could

---

opinion on the position that that star had *many years ago*, are, from a psychological perspective, two mental facts belonging to the same category, even though the latter would not be called, ordinarily, an *expectation*.

be said of the sentence: "*All citizens are equal before the law*," where the word *are* can, at the same time, be interpreted as expressing what in fact is, or what *should* be. A typical example of the disastrous consequences brought about by losing sight of such an apparently obvious distinction is provided by the all-too famous theory of value by Karl Marx, where the sentence "*two commodities have the same value when their production requires the same amount of normal working hours*" is intended in some cases as a definition of the exchange value, in other cases as an assertion regarding the circumstances on which the reason of the exchange of the two commodities depends, and yet in others, finally, as an assertion regarding a criterion that *should be* adopted in determining the proportions to be followed in the exchange of the commodities in a society where every individual has the right to the "whole product" of his work.

An observation that should be made, regarding these three categories of propositions, is the following: if we take, as a starting point, only those propositions belonging to one or another of the three categories, it could never be possible, by means of any effort of reason or deduction, to obtain, as a conclusion, a proposition belonging to a category different from the category of the propositions we started from.

The illusion that consists of believing in such a possibility has been, and partly still is, the source of many flawed metaphysical speculations, or of idle arguments with no meaning.

This illusion would probably never have taken place without the help of those ambiguities of language that we have mentioned. For example, no mathematician would have thought of conceiving the entire framework of geometry on the basis of a set of simple *definitions* (without adding any axioms or postulates regarding the structure and the properties of the space, real or imagined), if he were not induced by the aforementioned imperfections of language to consider as simple definitions, propositions which, even though similar to definitions in their exterior form, contain *real* assertions, i.e. regarding matters of fact or hypotheses about matters of fact.

So, pronouncing the following sentence "The parallel line to a straight line drawn through a given point is a straight line that goes through the point and never intersects the given straight line, even if they are on the same plane" we may believe that we have merely given the *definition* of the term "parallel line," while in fact we have stated, implicitly, two assertions, not regarding the meaning of that or some other term, but regarding properties possessed, or thought to be possessed, by the straight lines, or points, at issue. We have stated, in fact, first of all that through a certain point taken outside of a straight line, we can draw other straight lines that do not meet it and, secondly, that among those straight lines there is only one that lies on the same plane as the given one. As is known to anyone who has any familiarity with modern research on "non-Euclidean" geometry, these two assertions are not only less manifest and irrefutable as they could seem at first glance, but they could actually even be false without any loss of value, either practical or theoretical, to the original framework of geometry.

The illusion, consisting of the belief that the propositions of the first category defined above can be enough to deduce propositions of the second category, finds its perfect counterpart in another no less common illusion, according to which, propositions belonging to the third category in question (that is, *normative* propositions or *judgments of value* (Werth-Urtheile) could be deduced by propositions of the first two categories, that is they would be based either on simple definitions or on assertions and factual acknowledgments.

The impossibility of building a moral system without supporting it with any *"categorical imperative"* of any kind is a conclusion that has been reached, from disparate starting points, by the more subtle contemporary investigators of the fundamentals of ethics, such as Sidgwick, in his classical volume *Methods of Ethics*, or Nietzsche in *Jenseits von Gut und Böse* and in *Zur Genealogie der Moral.*[3]

It should be noted that those who are affected by the misunderstandings contributing to the opposite opinion are not only supporters of the *"natural"* ethics, nor are those who abuse the double meaning (scientific and normative) of the word *"law."*

Supporters of the utilitarian ethics also forget, and often willingly, that any effort they make, in order to justify some conduct rules relying on considerations about the ensuing social consequences, or those that would ensue, from observing or upholding such rules, cannot result in concrete conclusions unless they can rely on an actual preceding determination of the goals of life, social or individual, and of their respective degree of importance (in other words, unless they rely on what Nietzsche calls a given *table of values*), a determination that requires something more than mere judgments of acknowledgment, and exceeds the competence of "pure" intellect, leading into that of will and human choice. The observation of facts and reasonings, deductive or inductive, can only lead us to *predict* the results of our eventual behavior, and to determine the *means* that can lead us to a certain goal. The conclusions we reach by them can all be phrased in the following fashion: " *Whether we do or do not want that this or that thing happens, we must act in*

---

[3][See Sidgwick 1874, Nietzsche 1886 and Nietzsche 1887.]

this or that way." But there is no effort of dialectic alchemy which can lead by itself to this kind of conclusion: "*We must or we must not want, or desire, this or that to happen.*" And such inability should not be considered as a temporary insufficiency of "science," nor should it be attributed to some kind of obstacle that could be overcome during some successive phase of intellectual progress. The distinction, justly stressed by Brentano, between mental facts of the second and third categories that he has established, helps us to understand that we are wrong to expect something from science which, due to its own nature, it cannot give us. To blame science, or scientists, for their inability in this regard is only slightly less absurd than it is to blame the talent of a painter for the fact that the light of a lamp he has painted is not able to brighten the dark room where the painting is hanging.

Paris, August 22, 1900.

References

Brentano, Franz. 1874. *Psychologie vom empirischen Standpunkte*, vol. 1. Leipzig: Dunker & Humboldt.

Brentano, Franz. 1889. *Vom Ursprung sittlicher Erkenntnis.* Leipzig: Duncker & Humblot.

Nietzsche, Friedrich. 1886. *Jenseits von Gut und Böse. Vorspiel einer Philosophie der Zukunft.* Leipzig: Naumann.

Nietzsche, Friedrich. 1887. *Zur Genealogie der Moral.* Leipzig: Naumann.

Sidgwick, Henry. 1874. *The methods of ethics.* London: Macmillan, 1963.

Vailati, Giovanni. 1901. Sulla portata logica della classificazione dei fatti mentali proposta dal prof. Franz Brentano (Comunicazione presentata al III Congresso Internazionale di psicologia di Parigi, agosto 1900). *Rivista Filosofica* 2(1). Repr. in Vailati (1911), pages 336–340.

Vailati, Giovanni. 1911. *Scritti di G. Vailati, 1863-1909.* Leipzig-Firenze: Barth.

6

On the Applicability of the Concepts of Cause and Effect in Historical Sciences[†]

A beautiful analogy made by Francis Bacon compares the scientist to a reaper, forced to interrupt his work every so often in order to hone and whet his scythe, which is periodically made unable to serve its purpose by its very usage.

Such operations of readjustment and sharpening of the tools of the trade are represented, for scientists, precisely by the discussions related to the methods in the scientific fields in which they practice, and to the critical analysis of the concepts and the means of representation used in such fields.

The most useful shape these discussions can take is, in my opinion, that consisting of the determination of analogies and contrasts presented in this regard by the different branches of science, and in examining whether, and up to which point, such analogies or differences have any justification in the diversity of the matter studied. In this way we can, in a sense, put to work the experience acquired by the scholars of other sciences in their own fields, in favor of any specific science.

An appropriate occasion for some useful observations of this kind is offered by the ever re-emerging disagreements on the characteristics

---

[†] "Sull'applicabilitá dei concetti di causa e di effetto nelle scienze storiche." Communication read at the International Conference of Historical Sciences, section II (Methodology), on April 3rd, 1903. First published in *Rivista Italiana di Sociologia*, year VII, issue 3, May–June 1903, repr. in Vailati (1911), pages 459-464 (Vailati, 1903).

that distinguish the historical sciences, and in general those sciences which have as their subject of study the life of society and the development of culture, from the strictly physical or natural sciences.

In this regard, here I will just highlight some points on which the exchange of ideas and the agreement between the scholars of the former and those of the latter would be particularly desirable.

These notes refer mainly to the restrictions and precautions which should accompany, in the historical and social sciences, the use of the concepts of "law" and of "cause and effect," as they are used in the natural sciences.

It is still frequently debated whether we can speak of "historical laws" in the same sense as we speak, for example, of physical or chemical laws, and whether to research them is the task of the historian, or whether a historian should keep to simple description and documentation of facts and to the critique of the respective testimonies.

A large part of the opposing opinions on the matter seems to me to depend on, more than anything else, the lack of a sufficiently clear concept of what is actually intended by 'law' in the physical and mathematical sciences, and on the tendency to attribute to the laws considered by these sciences, characteristics which they are far from possessing.

So, for example, it is common to contrast the regularities and the analogies offered by the observation of social facts with the laws existing in the physical world, saying that the latter are invariably true, with no exceptions, while this does not happen for the former.

Nothing could better contribute to revealing the inconsistency of such a contrast than examining closer with which procedure, and at what price, the laws of physics and chemistry, and even more the laws of the other natural sciences, acquire the character of being unexceptionable which is attributed to them.

To give an example, used by Pareto in his work *Systèmes Socialistes* [1902], when we say that water freezes at 0 degrees, we affirm something that can be true or false depending on the pressure to which the water in question is subject. Even if we include this restriction within the enunciation of the law, and we say that water, at the pressure of 760 mm., freezes at 0 degrees, we are still far from being able to say we have formulated a law that does not have exceptions, because (even without considering that the solidification point of water can change depending on the substances contained in the solution), it is known that, with certain precautions, it is possible to bring even chemically pure water below 0 degrees, at the pressure of 760 mm., without it freezing.

To what else can we reduce the aforementioned law, then, if not saying that water freezes when certain circumstances are verified, among which, in the present state of our knowledge, there may be some that we are not able to determine or state exactly?

And when this is the case, that is when a physical law cannot be formulated in such a way that in it appears the complete enunciation of all the conditions that have to be present in order for the law to be verified, in what does it differ from a general assertion, true in a large number of cases and subject, in other cases, to momentarily inexplicable exceptions?

In what does it differ, then, from those analogies and regularities that are also encountered in the course of social phenomena like any other order of facts? The other kind of contrast, in my opinion no more founded than the previous mentioned, is the one commonly established between such regularities and the scientific laws in the strict sense of the term by attributing to the latter a special character of "necessity," which would distinguish them from the former even when both were to be constantly true and free from exceptions.

It is not so easy to determine what is meant by those who apply the appellative *necessary* to natural laws and assert that not only do they not have, but that they could not have any exceptions. This idea seems to be suggested to them by considering those physical laws that, being susceptible to being explained or deduced by means of other more general laws, present themselves in the shape of conclusions that cannot be anything else but true if the corresponding premises are true. So, for example, the trajectory of a planet is *necessary* in the sense that it could not be different from what it is, unless the general laws of mechanics, from which it is deduced, were not true.

But is it not evident that this process of deduction of one law from another has to start from some of those which cannot be deduced from others, and which will not be able to be called *necessary* in the above mentioned sense?

Besides, is it not true that every branch of the natural sciences offers an example of laws obtained by direct induction, which cannot possibly be obtained by deduction from other more general laws?

Is this not the most ordinary case in all the sciences that study natural phenomena, with the only exception of the most advanced parts of mathematical physics? Therefore the *absence of necessity*, in the above mentioned sense, not less than the *absence of objections*, is far from being a characteristic that distinguishes the uniformities and regularities found in social phenomena from those which in the physical sciences are called laws.[1]

---

[1] I am glad to be able to mention, in support of the thesis here advanced, the

There is, nevertheless, another circumstance, completely different from the one just mentioned, that contributes in having the "necessity" of physical laws considered as a quality that does not belong to the analogies and uniformities of behavior observed in the facts studied by History. The fact about the influence that, in certain limits, the will of humans can exert on the events and structure of the society which they are part of, is by many regarded as incompatible with the admission that historical events and the transformations of social institutions are subject to norms that have the same grade of inflexibility and rigidity attributed to the laws of the physical world.

What is strange is that those who assert such incompatibility do not realize that, if it were to exist for the historical and social sciences, it should also exist for the physical sciences, for which they actually concede that it does not. In fact, do they see some incompatibility between the laws of hydrostatics and the fact that the path of a river can be changed and regulated by works executed by humans for that purpose?

Is it not the knowledge of the laws of hydrostatics that allows humankind to effectively influence the modification of the course of phenomena for which that laws exist?

Even here, again, as in the previous case, we are dealing with nothing but a misunderstanding, which stems from the lack of a sufficiently clear concept of what is meant by law in the physical sciences.

As was very well expressed by A. Naville in his recent essay on the classification of sciences,[2] any scientific law expressing nothing other than the constant association of certain phenomena with others is always susceptible of being stated under the following shape: if and whenever a certain fact happens or has happened, another fact or group of facts also happens or will happen too.

Therefore the truth of a law is compatible, in every special case, both when the facts mentioned in it happen or not, because all it affirms is not that such and such a fact *happens* or *does not happen*, but only which are the facts that join it *when it happens*, or with which it would be joined *in the case it should happen*.

To use an analogy to clarify this concept, which is maybe a little too abstract, we could say that the existence of a certain number of natural laws for a certain order of phenomena is far from being incompatible with a limited dependency of such phenomena on human will, in the same way as, for example, the existence of a railway network is far from

___

opinion of a historian like G. Salvemini, to whose article, published last year in this same journal, I have permitted myself to refer the reader [Salvemini 1902].

[2][See Naville 1901 and Vailati 1902.]

determining in an univocal way the movement of the trains that transit on it. The existence of the railway network forces the trains to transit on certain lines when they are moving, but it does not imply that they have to move on a certain track rather than another, or that they have to leave at a certain time rather than another, or travel at such and such a speed, or even that they have to move at all.

Moreover it is appropriate to note that the question of whether human will can or cannot contribute in determining the behavior of a certain class of phenomena (as has been well pointed out by Mario Calderoni in his recent essay: *Diritto Penale e Scienza Positiva* [1901]), is completely different from the other question: whether will is, in turn, determined by or dependent, according to laws, on the circumstances that have influence on it.

Many seem to believe that a positive answer given to this last question is the equivalent of denying human will any semblance of determining cause, because the only real causes would be those from which will is in turn determined.

But it is strange that those who think like this do not realize that, if we were also to reason in the same fashion on the physical sciences, we could not talk anymore about causes and effects even in their regard. In fact, if in order to be able to assert that one certain fact is the cause of another we would need to prove that the former, in turn, is not an effect of any other fact, which would be a fact that, even in the physical sciences, can be called the cause of another, given that in such sciences it is accepted that any fact is in turn a product of previous causes?

And if this circumstance does not prevent, in the physical sciences, the qualifying of a certain fact as the cause of another, there is no reason to consider such a circumstance an obstacle when dealing with human will.

The prejudice that we are discussing frequently assumes another shape, which is the common way of interpreting what is called the *materialist conception of history*. Many believe this to consist of considering economic conditions as the only effective factors in development and social transformations, and in characterizing all the other manifestations of collective life, in particular the more lofty, as mere superstructures or ideological reflections, voided of any effectiveness or directive impulse per se.

We can also point out, against the supporters of this theory, that, as in the previous case, to acknowledge the preponderant influence of economic relationships in the formation and development of the individual species of activities arising from human coexistence, does not imply that the latter cannot, in turn, act as modifying causes of the structure and economic life of the society in which they manifest them-selves. Rather than a relationship of cause and effect, we deal here, as pointed out mostly by the economists of the mathematical school, with a relationship of mutual dependence, similar to the one that would ex-ist, for example, between the positions of two heavy spheres sustained by a concave surface, each of which can be regarded as the cause of the position of the other, meaning that each of them forces the other to assume a different position from the position it would assume if it were alone.

However, there are some reasons that could, within limit, justify our tendency to apply the characterization of *cause* to one rather than the other of two mutually dependent facts. Such reasons are precisely the same as those used when, before a set of conditions that contribute together to produce a certain effect, we are induced to choose only a part of those and apply to them, with exclusion of the remaining others, the name of "causes."

In fact, not all the conditions on whose cooperation depends the verification of a certain fact are interesting to us in the same way, and even in this case the example of physical sciences is useful to clarify the motivation and the criteria on which such a difference in interest is determined.

The distinction between cause and effect, and this is even more true for the social and historical sciences than for the physical sciences, is a distinction essentially of a practical nature, in a way more or less directly related to the representation that we have of the way and order in which we should, or we would like, to proceed in modifying the course of the facts in question, and to adapt them to our purposes and desires.

It is for this reason that, as observed by Hobbes, *"One does not seek the causes of what exists but of what may be."*[3] And this is also the reason why in historical and social sciences research into causes tends to lead to very different consequences, depending on the political and ethical feelings or worries of the researcher.

He allows himself, more or less consciously, to be induced to limit his attention and to consider as causes only those, among the conditions of a given fact, whose modification he believes would be necessary or useful to provide if we were to generate or prevent the fact in question or others of a similar nature, or to modify them in the way he desires.

This kind of partiality should not be considered illegitimate, or con-fused with that which consists in allowing our passions and our interests

---

[3] [In Latin in the original.]

to influence the evaluation of the proof of facts and theories. While this second kind of partiality is radically incompatible with the scientific character of any kind of research, the other is perfectly legitimate, in the historical sciences no less than in the natural sciences. And from this point of view, hearing about, for example, one volume of socialist history being in contrast with another of conservative history, should not appear stranger than hearing about one chemical handbook for dyers being completely different from another chemical handbook for pharmacists or agronomists.

The truth is but one, but there are many *truths*, and many are the purposes that we can reach and to which our knowledge can eventually be applied. And to be dealing with one rather than the other of such purposes is, in the historical sciences as in any other branch of investigation, completely compatible with the most serene impartiality in the appreciation of proof and evidence.

References

Calderoni, Mario. 1901. *I postulati della scienza positiva ed il diritto penale*. Firenze: G. Ramella e C.

Naville, Adrien. 1901. *Nouvelle classification des sciences. Étude philosophique*. Paris: Alcan.

Pareto, Vilfredo. 1902. *Les Systèmes Socialistes*, vol. 1-2. Paris: Giarde et Brière.

Salvemini, Gaetano. 1902. La storia considerata come scienza. *Rivista italiana di sociologia* 6:17–54.

Vailati, Giovanni. 1902. Recensione a A. Naville, Nouvelle classification des sciences. Alcan, Paris 1901. *Rivista di Biologia generale* 3.

Vailati, Giovanni. 1903. Sull'applicabilità dei concetti di causa e di effetto nelle scienze storiche. International Conference of Historical Sciences, April 1903. *Rivista Italiana di Sociologia* 7(3). Repr. in Vailati (1911), pages 459–464.

Vailati, Giovanni. 1911. *Scritti di G. Vailati, 1863-1909*. Leipzig-Firenze: Barth.

7

The Aristotelian Theory of Definition[†]

In the early stages of the development of our intelligence the ordinary way followed to understand the *meaning* of the sentences or words used by the people we live with, consists in thinking about the similarities between single facts and objects that are present, or are indicated to us, when we hear them uttered.

To induce us to use, in turn, such sentences or words to designate some new object or event of which we acquire the experience, we need nothing more than an impression, sometimes even very vague, of a similarity between such a new object, or event, and those that we are used to hearing indicated by those given sentences or words.

Only gradually does the application of the same name to more objects start to be consciously used as a means of expressing, not simply the fact that they are similar, but the fact that they are similar to each other *in some respect*, that is, the fact that they have certain characters in common able to be considered and designated on their own.

The more we enrich our verbal patrimony, the more frequent is the case of words for which such circumstances happen, that is, for which we are able to define, *by means of other words*, which are the characteristics or the properties whose presence in the objects is indicated by such words.

In this way we have a second procedure available that can be used

---

[†] "La Teoria Aristotelica della Definizione." First published in *Rivista di Filosofia e scienze affini*, vol. II, year V, issue 5, November-December 1903, repr. in Vailati (1911), pages 485-496 (Vailati, 1903b).

to inform others of the sense that we give to given words, or to learn from them the sense that they give to the words used by them.

This procedure, clearly different from the one mentioned before (the one which consists in simply giving a certain number of examples or special cases properly chosen among those to which the word or sentence in question is usually applied by others or ourselves) is the one indicated by the name *definition.*

The difference between these two ways to define the sense of a sentence or of a word, even if it may look obvious or of little importance, is nevertheless one of those differences whose clear acknowledgment has marked an era in the history of human thinking.

The systematic application of one or the other to the philosophical research and discussions is considered by Aristotle the most important contribution given by Socrates to the progress of philosophy: "For there are two improvements in science which one might justly ascribe to Socrates; now, I allude to his employment of inductive arguments and his definition of the universal" (*Metaphysics*, book XII, ch. 4).[1]

Indeed, what gives to Plato's dialogues the character of a unique document in the history of culture is the fact that in them he presents the first example of a series of attempts directed towards the application of both of the two procedures mentioned before to the critique of traditional opinions and of the principles of current morality, and also to the treatment of the more general and fundamental questions related to science and conduct.[2]

The method that appears to be used by Socrates in such dialogues in order to convince those disputing with him of the scarce foundation of their opinions, and to strip them of the illusion of knowing what they do not know, consists, as is well known, in gradually leading the interlocutor, by means of skillful and pressing questioning, to admit that, for any definition that he was able to propose for this or that word appearing in the thesis that he supported, it was always possible to

---

[1] [In Greek in the text, as always in the following quotations. Book XII is indicated as Book XIII in some editions of *Metaphysics.* Cf. *Met.* 1078b77-79. English translation by J. H. MacMahon, in MacMahon 1896, p. 359.]

[2] Among the many passages by Plato, where the two procedures are explicitly put in contrast, it will suffice here to mention the characteristic one from the *Theaetetus*, where, regarding the definition of *science* (τί ποτ' ἔστιν ἐπιστήμη), Socrates declares to be unsatisfied by Theaetetus' answers, who was listing and indicating the subjects, and the characters, of various single sciences: "But that, Theaetetus, was not the point of my question: we wanted to know not the subjects, nor yet the number of the arts or sciences, for we were not going to count them, but we wanted to know the nature of knowledge in the abstract."—147, A. [English translation by B. Jowett, in Jowett 1892, p. 199.]

mention examples, or special cases, where that same word was applied by him without the presence of *all* those characters which, according to the definition provided by him, should have been present, or where the word was regarded as not applicable *even if* all those characters were present. With this kind of experimental confutation of all the successive definitions that the interlocutor was forced to propose for the word in question, Socrates was pushing him to confess in the end that he did not really know the meaning that he intended in using it, or, in other words, to confess that no precise and determined meaning could be attributed to the sentences where such a word appeared.

This was, so to speak, the destructive part of the Socratic method, during which the interlocutor was led to acknowledge his own ignorance in relation to the subject he was discussing, or at least to renounce the too-high opinion he initially had regarding the accuracy, or certainty, of his own cognitions on the matter. Following this part there was the "reconstructive" part, where Socrates joined the interlocutor in reaching together the determination, in the best possible way, of the restrictions or the modifications necessary for the vulgar use of the word in question, so that it could be effectively used to indicate some common characteristics in all the objects to which the word was applied, and not possessed at the same time by any other object than those.

Such characteristics were revealed by means of a comparison of a certain number of particular cases, from which, in the end, following a process of generalization, the desired definition could be obtained.

The process we have just described is lucidly summarized in all its essential phases by Aristotle with the following example:

> For instance, to define magnanimity, we should examine what quality is common to a set of persons known to possess the attribute of magnanimity. Alcibiades, Achilles, and Ajax were magnanimous: in what did they agree? In impatience of dishonour; which made one a traitor, roused another's wrath, and drove another to self-slaughter. Again, in what did a different set, Lysander and Socrates, agree? In equanimity in adversity and prosperity. What element is common to these characters, equanimity in vicissitudes, and impatience under dishonour? If there is nothing in common, there are two distinct kinds of magnanimity (*Posterior Analytics*, II, 12).[3]

In the further elaboration of the technique of the philosophical disputations made by Aristotle, the considerations of the definitions, their role in the demonstrations, and the way of finding and correcting the

---

[3][Chapter 12 is indicated as chapter 13 in some editions of the *Posterior Analytics*. See *An. Post.* 97b16-26. English translation by E. Poste, in Poste 1850, p. 120.]

defects, become more precise and rigorous, generating an entire group of distinctions and technical terms, whose introduction has had an influence on the development of philosophical speculation that is not inferior to the influence that can be attributed to any other part of Aristotle's doctrine.

A distinction that has been given maximum salience in Aristotle's writings is precisely the one between the propositions used to state a definition, or a part of a definition (i.e. the propositions used when we intend to declare or clarify the sense we want to give to a given word), and the propositions used instead to assert that the objects designated by us with a given name (the meaning of which we supposed our interlocutors already knew) present this or that other trait, *not included* in those that are already attributed to them for the only reason of being called with the name in question.

A fact that could seem strange at first glance is that, in our ordinary language, as also in the ordinary language of the Greeks, the propositions of both of the aforementioned two categories are mostly expressed in a way that does not distinguish one from the other independently of the context.

In fact, if we indicate with A and B two names of which we suppose to have determined the meaning (so that we know what is intended when it is asserted that a given object is an A, or is a B), the sentence "The As are Bs" can be used both ways: to indicate that, *between* the properties whose possession in a given object is indicated by saying that it is an A, we can find *all* the properties whose possession in a given object is indicated by saying that it is a B; or to express our persuasion that any object that is an A (that is, it has traits or properties whose possession in a given object is indicated by saying that it is an A) is *also* a B (that is, *moreover* it also has the traits and the properties whose possession in a given object is indicated by saying that it is a B).

Yet in the first case we are simply giving information on the meaning that is attributed to a given word by us or by others, and we do not express any opinion related to anything more than the use we intend to make of such a word in our speeches. In the second case, on the other hand, we assert something that could be true or false independently from any convention, whether ours or others, on the use of language. We assert, for example, that all those objects presenting given characteristics (that is, those indicated by the name that in the proposition in question appears as the subject), *also* present other characteristics (indicated by the name that in the proposition appears as the predicate); in other words we assert that some given properties, or given facts, tend to appear at the same time, or exist together, or follow one another in a given way.

It is not possible to believe that the need for technical terms to characterize such a fundamental distinction was not felt before Aristotle and that he was the first to introduce some in the philosophical language,[4] especially if we consider the importance to which such a distinction must have been attributed by the scholars of the two branches of speculation whose methodical elaboration is due to Greek philosophers, Aristotle's predecessors, that is on the one side Geometry and on the other Rhetoric, the latter intended in the ancient sense, as the art of persuading and prevailing in disputes.

Nevertheless, it is only in the writings of Aristotle that we find a systematic exposition of the topic, and we can think that Aristotle is referring to this exposition, as much as to the theory of syllogism, when he uses the sentence, in the last chapter of the *Sophistical Refutations*, which expresses the concept that he had of the importance of his own work compared to that of his predecessors:

> Of our present inquiry, however, it is not true to say that it had already been partly elaborated and partly not; nay, it did not exist at all.[5]

In fact it is in the *Topics*, a work in which the book of the *Sophistical Refutations* represents just an appendix, that the distinction in question is established in the most clear and coherent way. It actually represents the basis of the classification of the various kinds of propositions adopted by him, for each of which he addresses the determination of the different forms of argumentation (τόποι) that can be used to support them (κατασκευάζειν) or confute them (ἀνασκευάζειν).

The propositions where it is asserted that the objects to which we designate a given name possess a given property, or a group of properties, are first of all distinguished by Aristotle in two classes, depending on whether the property (or group of properties) in question is possessed *only* by the object indicated by the name or is *also* possessed by other objects beside them:

for necessarily, whenever one thing is predicated of another, it either

---

[4] I am not referring to those who attribute the merit to Kant, induced to do so by the fact that he introduced a new nomenclature (*analytic judgments, synthetic judgments*) to characterize the two mentioned kinds of assertions. We have here a good example of a danger, to which are exposed especially the historians of philosophy, i.e. the one of taking the introduction of new names for the introduction of new concepts or the discovery of new truths.

[5] [*De Soph. El.*, 34, 183b34-36. English translation by E. S. Forster in Forster and Furley 1965, p. 155.]

counterpredicates with the subject or it does not (*Topics*, I, 8).[6]

In the first class we find, on the one hand, the definitions, and on the other hand the propositions where it is asserted that a given property, *even if not included among those appearing in the definition of a given name*, is nevertheless possessed by all the objects corresponding to such a definition and by those objects *alone*:

> And if it does counterpredicate, then it must be a definition or a proprium (for if it signifies what it is to be something it is a definition, while if it does not it is a proprium [...]) (*Topics*, I, 8).[7]

A similar distinction is present in the second class, constituted by those propositions where the property (or group of properties) said to be possessed by the objects indicated by the name appearing as the object of the proposition, is not possessed exclusively by them.

Otherwise we may have the case of a property appearing among those included in the definition (accepted by the speaker) of the name that is the subject of the proposition, and in this case we have a proposition which, although not a complete definition, is *true by definition* (that is, it can be denied only by contradicting the given definition); or, if this is not the case, we have the most ordinary kind of general propositions, which is that of propositions where it is asserted that all those individuals indicated by a given name possess some further property which is not included among those appearing in the definition of the name itself, and which is not possessed *only* by the objects indicated by such a name:

> But if it does not counterpredicate with the subject, then either it is among the things stated in the definition of the subject or it is not. If it is among the things stated in the definition, then it must be a genus or a differentia, since a definition is composed of a genus and differentiae (*Topics*, I, 8).[8]

In this way we have four kinds[9] of propositions, which are respec-

---

[6] [For this and the two following quotes Vailati refers to *Topics*, book I, ch. 6, but we found the quotes in ch. 8. See *Top*. 103b7-9. English translation by R. Smith, in Smith 1997, p. 7–8.]

[7] [*Top*. 103b9-11. Engl transl. by R. Smith in Smith 1997, p. 8, partially modified.]

[8] [*Top*. 103b12-16. Engl. transl. by R. Smith in Smith 1997, p. 8.]

[9] Or, in the way he calls them: "four differences" (*Topics*, I, 7). The same name is also used by him before (*Topics*, I, 3) [we found it in ch. 4 instead: *Top*. 101b24-26]: "From what has been said, it turns out clearly that according to the present division they [the differences] are four in all: either definition, proprium, genus or accident." [Engl. transl. by R. Smith, modif. in Smith 1997, p. 8.] The 'difference' is constantly considered by him to be a particular case of the 'genus'. [Here, and in the following, single Greek words used by Vailati and translated into English will appear in single quotation marks.]

tively characterized by Aristotle when he says in the first two cases, we affirm the 'definition' or a 'proprium' of the subject, and in the other two its 'genus' or an 'accident'.

It is useful to point out right away that this classification established by Aristotle coincides only partially with that which ended up being adopted by the Scholastic tradition as a genuine part of the Aristotelian doctrine, due particularly to the elaboration by Porphyry (in the 'Isagoge').

The main inconvenience presented by Porphyry's classification, compared with the original by Aristotle as it is preserved in *Topics*,[10] consists in the following: while in the latter we can clearly find the fundamental distinctions, in the former by Porphyry, instead, such fundamental distinctions are, so to speak, masked and dimmed by adding many accessory considerations, in particular those on the relationships between genus, species and individuals (γένος, εἶδος, ἄτομα) and those on the concept of "specific difference" (διαφορά εἰδοποιητική),considerations which besides depriving the classification of its original character of symmetry and simplicity, tend to distract from the main purpose and the philosophical importance.

Regarding the successive variations in meaning of the aforementioned technical terms of Aristotelian logic, which happened while passing from the Scholastic to the modern philosophical nomenclature, we should note that the word "genus" (together, of course, with the corresponding words in any modern cultured language) has lost almost any trace of the particular technical sense that Aristotle tried to attribute to it. Such a word, as well as the related "species" (εἶδος), is now applied without discrimination in every case where we are indicating the inclusion in one class or the other, without distinguishing whether such an inclusion depends on the fact that the property (or the group of properties), which constitutes the definition of the second class, appears among those constituting the definition of the first, or on the fact that the two properties (or the two groups of properties), which respectively constitute the definitions of the two classes in question, go constantly together in a way in which any object that possesses the first also possesses the second.

Even the distinction between ἴδιον (*proprium*) and συμβεβηκός (*accidens*) has ceased to be able to be expressed in a modern language with the words corresponding to those used by Aristotle to indicate it.

---

[10]See also *Prior Analitics*, I, 27 [43b7-9]: "The terms which follow the subject must also be divided into those which are predicated of it essentially, those which are peculiar to it, and those which are predicated incidentally." [English translation by R. Smith, in Smith 1997, p. 42.] See also the immediately preceding passage.

When the "property" of a given object, or a given class of objects, is used, whatever quality it or they may possess is in fact intended, without any regard for the fact that such properties are or are not *also* possessed by the other objects, which are different from the ones considered, or not included in the class in question.

Let us go back to Aristotle's classification and the more fundamental of the distinctions found in it, that is, the distinction between the propositions where all (as in the case of the 'definition') or part of (as in the case of the 'genus') the qualities of the subject possessed *by definition*, and the propositions are stated where, instead, (it being exclusive, 'proprium', or not, 'accident') some quality which *does not* appear among those possessed by definition is stated. We should note that the way in which Aristotle characterizes the former is by saying that with them we answer questions of the kind: "*What is this thing?*" (τί εστι τί;) or, as he often expresses himself, with a very effective sentence even though it may sound a little strange: "*What is (or would be) to be this thing?*" (τί ἦν εἶναι;):[11]

"A *definition* is a phrase which signifies the what-it-is-to-be" (*Topics*, I, 4).[12]

"For a definition is a description which signifies the what-it-is-to-be of a thing." (*Topics*, I, 4)[13]

Another sentence used by Aristotle to express the same concept is that which states that the propositions whose predicate is a 'definition' or a 'genus' inform us about the essence (οὐσία) of the subject in question.[14] By saying so he means that what is asserted by them about the thing in question could not cease to be true without it ceasing to be *what it is* (that is, without it ceasing to be what we have supposed it to be by calling it by the name that is the subject of the proposition enunciated). Even for the variations of meaning in this important technical term of the Aristotelian logic we should repeat observations similar to those already made for the other technical terms considered

---

[11] That is, what we intend to say about a given thing by calling it with a certain name. See *Categoriae*, I, I.

[12] [*Top.* I, 5.101b39-102a.1. Engl transl. by R. Smith, in Smith 1997, p. 4.]

[13] [See *Top.* I, 5.154a32-33.]

[14] See *Topics*, V, 2 [130b26-27], where 'definition' is addressed as an 'expression which signifies the essence'. And regarding the 'genus' see also *Topics*, VI, I [139a31], where it is said that it 'is generally regarded as signifying the essence". The same word 'essence' (οὐσία) is also repeatedly used by Plato as a technical term, and with the precise mentioned sense. Therefore in Euthyphro the research of the definition of "sacred" is indicated as τὴν οὐσίαν αὐτοῦ δηλῶσαι. See also the passage from Meno (72, B: εἴ μου ἐρομένου μελίττης περὶ οὐσίας ὅ τι ποτ' ἔστι...) whose importance is justly marked by Lutoslavski (*Origin and growth of Plato's Logic* [1897]).

before, meanwhile to those others, no less than to the word "essence," we can apply the observation made by Stuart Mill (in one of the first chapters of his *Logic* [1870]) regarding the inability of the more abstract terms of the philosophical language in preserving their original sense intact and regarding their tendency to go into the common language acquiring rough and coarse meanings.[15]

One of the more salient and typical traits of the Aristotelian theory of demonstration, as is developed in the two books named *Analytica Posteriora*, can be said to consist in the preoccupation of correctly distinguishing propositions by answering the question: *What is a given thing?* (τί ἐστι;) from those instead answering the question: *Does this given thing exist or not?* (εἴ τι ἐστι ἢ οὔ;)

This distinction is at the basis of Aristotle's concept of a "demonstrative science" (ἀποδεικτικὴ ἐπιστήμη), and with this name, as is known, he means any branch of knowledge that, similarly to Geometry, can assume the shape of a system of conclusions reached, through successive syllogisms, starting from a certain number of fundamental premises.

Here I would like to bring back your attention to the role assigned by Aristotle, among these fundamental premises, to definitions.

He starts by observing that definitions, for the reason that they assert nothing but our intention or purpose of attributing a given meaning to a given word, cannot be properly qualified as true or false:

> Definitions are distinct from Hypotheses, for they make no assertion of existence or not existence (*Posterior Analitics*, I, 10).[16]

Therefore the definitions do not need to be demonstrated, nor would they be able to be demonstrated ("there is no syllogism nor demonstration for a definition" *Post. An.*, II, 8 [II. 93b16-17]).[17] It is enough that they are *understood* ("Definition needs only be understood, and this is not Hypothesis, unless sensation is Hypothesis," *Post. An.*, I, 10 [I.76b37-39, p. 55]).

But even if Aristotle asserts this about definitions, he is still far

---

[15] In this regard it is very curious to note that successive changes in meaning, which gradually led a word with a very abstract meaning like *"essence"* to mean something so concrete that it can be enclosed in a bottle, have a perfect counterpart in the changes that led the words "genus" and "species" (the second under its archaic shape, *"spezie"*) to appear even on the signs of groceries and pharmacies. [Grocery shops in Italy used to have a sign to say they were selling *"generi alimentari"* and pharmacists used to be called *"speziali."*]

[16] [*An. Post.* I. 76b35-36. English translation (modified) by E. Poste, in Poste 1850, p. 55. For the following quotes taken from this edition in English we added the pages at the end of Vailati's reference, in brackets.]

[17] "The signification of a word cannot be evinced by demonstration or definition" (*Post. An.*, II, 7).

from believing that the same can be said about propositions where the existence of what is defined is asserted. The difference between such propositions and definitions is something on which he insists repeatedly:

> To say what a man is and to say that a man exists are not the same thing. When we define we do not demonstrate existence (*Post. An.*, II, 7 [Cf. II.92b4-6,16-17]).

> To unfold the essence of a unit is not the same as to affirm its existence (*Post. An.*, I, 2 [I.72a24-25, transl. modif. p. 42]).

> Definitions neither evince the possibility of their objects' existence, nor that they belong to the object professedly defined (*Post. An.*, II, 7 [II.92b23-25, p. 106]).

> The geometer assumes the conception of Triangle, but demonstrate its existence (Ibid. [II.92b16-17, p.106]).

Among those propositions where the existence of what is being defined or has been defined is asserted, the only ones he thinks should be accepted without demonstration are those referring to fundamental concepts (ἀρχαί) of the science in question.

In this case they must be classified among the hypotheses (ὑποθέσεις) or the postulates (αἰτήματα) that are assumed by such a science.

In all other cases we must require a demonstration, like any other proposition that is not included among such hypotheses and postulates.

> Regarding what is defined, we establish the first principles and those following from them. Instead, regarding what exists, it is necessary to assume the fundamental concepts and then demonstrate the others (*Post. An.*, I, 10 [76a33-35]).

In this way, for example, in Geometry the existence of points and straight lines is postulated: "Of these (points and lines) [arithmetic and geometry] assume the existence and the existence as being such (τό εἶναι καί τοδί εἶναι)" (*Post. An.*, I, 10 [I.76b6-7]).

Regarding instead the square, the cube, the incommensurables etc., the respective definitions are accepted, but this does not mean that we do not have to demonstrate their existence:

> They further assume the meaning of the essential attributes—Arithmetic of odd and even, square and cube; Geometry of angular, inclined, incommensurate. The existence of the attributes is demonstrated by the common principles and former conclusions (*Post. An.*, I, 10 [I.76b7-11. Engl. transl. modif., p. 54]).

These last observations, as well as many others among the most notable contained in the Aristotelian writings on Logic, simply correspond to the enunciation, in general terms, of norms that are actually followed by geometers of that age in the exposition of the science;[18] but this does not mean that the fact that such norms are investigated by Aristotle is any less important in a formal way, that is independently from their application to any kind of matter or subject.

In Sophistical Refutations Aristotle also hints at the danger of paralogisms, inherent to the fact of neglecting to observe and consider these norms in philosophical speculations—he does so when, regarding the argument: "If that-which-is-not is an object of opinion, then that-which-is-not is" he observes that *"it is not the same thing 'to be something' and 'to be' absolutely"*—c. 5⁰.[19] This warning about the difference between the sense that must be attributed to the verb "to be" in the propositions where it is simply a copula and the proposition where it is used to assert the existence of the subject in question, is also repeated in *De Interpretatione* (XI), where such a warning is clarified with an example that deserves to be reported: "For example, take 'Homer is something'—'a poet' wil do for our purpose. But can we say also 'he is'?"[20]

The peculiar insistence by Aristotle on this point was far from being superfluous, as it is proved in Scholastic philosophy not only by the frequent presence of illusory arguments having their roots in this kind of misunderstanding, but moreover also in the reproduction of the reasoning subject to this same objection in the works of many fathers, and may I say not minor fathers of modern thought. Let us take just one example, the classic example of the so-called "ontological" demonstration of the existence of God, attributed to Saint Anselm and taken by Descartes as one of the bases of his philosophical system. It consists in fact in an attempt to use a definition as an argument for the existence of what is defined by it: "supposing a triangle to be given, I distinctly perceived that its three angles were necessarily equal to two right angles, but I did not on that account perceive anything which could assure me that any triangle existed: while, on the contrary, recurring to the examination of the idea of a Perfect Being, I found that the existence of the Being was comprised in the idea" (*Discours de la Méthode, 4me Partie*).[21] As already noted by Schopenhauer, there is no better reply

---

[18] Recently Zeuthen, in his research on the History of ancient Geometry, [1896] has brought the attention on the purpose attributed by Geometers to the demonstration of the existence (or possibility) of the figures they were studying.

[19] [*De soph. el.* 5.167a1-3. Engl. transl. by E. S. Forster in Forster and Furley 1965, p. 27.]

[20] [Cat. XI.21a26-27. English translation by H. P. Cooke, in Cooke and Tredennick 1938, p. 155.]

[21] [In French in the text. English translation by R. Veitch in Descartes 1637, p. 79.]

to this reasoning than to quote the exact sentence used by Aristotle (*Post. An.*, II, 7) to assert that 'existence is not essence', given that it is not possible to say about anything that it exists by definition ('for existent is never a genus').[22]

The source of error indicated by Aristotle also had influence in the field of geometrical theories—in order to be convinced of this it would be enough to think about the obstacles it caused, which prevented the many attempts made by the ancient and modern geometers in demonstrating the Euclidean postulate of the parallels, before the work of Gerolamo Saccheri,[23] from taking the direction that, in Saccheri, led to the discovery of non-Euclidean Geometry.

Such influence is indicated by Saccheri himself in that part of his work dedicated to the examination of the unfruitful attempts of his predecessors, starting from Proclus, who, in turn, also preserved information on other prior attempts (by Ptolemy, Posidonius, Geminus.) A common character of the majority of these attempts consists in starting from a definition of parallel lines which, differently from that adopted by Euclid, does not allow demonstration by means of the axioms previously assumed, that some "parallel lines" exist or are constructable.

Let us see how Saccheri defends Euclid's definition against the objections by Borelli, who believed (such as Posidonius did before him) he could solve the question of the indispensability of the Euclidean postulate by defining two parallel lines as two straight lines that, lying on the same plane, respectively have all their points at the same distance from one another:

> But with reverence for so great a man it may be said: Can Euclid be blamed, because (to bring forward one among innumerable examples) he defines a square to be a figure quadrilateral, equilateral, rectangular; when it may be doubted, whether a figure of this sort has place in nature? He could, say I, most justly have been blamed: if, before as a problem demonstrating the construction, he had assumed the aforesaid figure as given.

> But that Euclid is free from this fault follows manifestly from this, that he nowhere assumes the square defined by him, except after Prop. 46 of the First Book, in which in form of a problem he teaches, and demonstrates the description from a given straight line, of the square

---

[22] [An. Post. II.92b13-14. Engl. transl. by E. Poste in Poste 1850, p. 105.]

[23] *Euclides ab omni naevo vindicatus*, Mediolani, 1733 [Saccheri 1733]. The merit of having pointed out the importance of it goes to Eugenio Beltrami (*Rendiconti Accademia dei Lincei*, 1886 [Beltrami 1889]). A recent note by professor Corrado Segre from the University of Turin (*Atti dell'Accademia delle Scienze*, 1902 [Segre 1902-03]) investigates the influence that Lambert, Bolyai, and Lobatchevski had on the further research.

as defined by him.

> In the same way therefore Euclid ought not to be blamed, because he defined parallel straight lines in this manner [as lines that lie in the same plane and do not not concur on either side, if they be produced in infinitum], since he nowhere assumes them as given for the construction of any problem, except after Prop. 31 of the First Book, in which as a problem he demonstrates, how should be drawn from a given point without a given straight line a straight line parallel to this, and indeed according to the definition of parallel lines given by him, so that produced indeed into the infinite on neither side do they meet one another. And what is more; he demonstrates this without any dependence from the postulate here controverted (*Euclides vindicatus*, p. 32).[24]

And going back to the same argument (on page 99–100), he adds:

> I have said: not without a great sin against rigid logic two equidistant straight lines have been assumed by some as given [...] unless either to assume; that every line equidistant in the same plane from a certain supposed straight line [is itself also a straight line]

> Wherefore to define two *parallel* straight lines under this relation of mutual *equidistance* is the fallacy, which in my aforesaid Logica [demonstrativa] I call *definitionis complexae*, in connection with which every advance toward attaining truth absolutely such is ineffectual.[25]

The chapter on the *"Logica Demonstrativa,"*[26] to which the previously quoted passage refers, is that where Saccheri introduces and characterizes the distinction between the propositions that he calls *definitiones quid nominis*, or *nominales*, and those that he calls *definitiones quid rei*, or *reales*: with this distinction he wants to compare the propositions which are merely establishing the meaning attributed to a given word, and those where moreover the existence of what is defined is asserted.[27]

---

[24] [This and the following quotations from *Euclides vindicatus* are in Latin in the text. English translation (modified) by F. Steinhardt from Saccheri 1733, p. 87–89.]

[25] [English translation by F. Steinhardt from Saccheri 1733, p. 237–239.]

[26] *Logica Demonstrativa*, Augustae Taurinorum, 1697 [Saccheri 1697]. I write about the historical and philosophical importance of this work, an importance that in my view is no more minor than that of *"Logique de Port Royal,"* which just preceded it, in an article about to be printed in *Rivista Filosofica* by Cantoni [Vailati 1903a].

[27] On the topic here addressed, the conformity between the aforementioned ideas by Saccheri and those expressed, almost at the same time, by Leibniz, whose writings on the topic happened to be not available for almost two centuries for the attention of the scholars of Logic is remarkable. An edition of this material was made only this year by Couturat (*Opuscles et fragments inèdits de Leibniz*, Paris, Alcan, 1903 [Couturat 1903]), from the manuscripts of the Library of Hannover. The merit of

The *definitio quid nominis* becomes a *definitio quid rei* by means of a *postulate*, or when we come to the question whether the thing exists and it is answered affirmatively (*Logica demonstrativa*, p. 187).[28]

Regarding the use and the purpose of one or the other of these two kinds of propositions inside the demonstrative sciences, while Saccheri clearly affirms that *"no quid nominis definition can become the object of a dispute, or at most it can become the object of a historical dispute"* (like for example when we discuss whether a given definition has or has not been adopted by a given author, or in a given work), on the other hand he insists on considering the definitions *quid rei* as in need of demonstration, in all cases where the existence of what is defined does not appear among the *hypotheses* or the postulates expressly assumed by the science in question, as it happens, for example, in Geometry, in the case of the straight line or the circle, that are assumed as constructable, provided the tools (ruler, a pair of compasses) needed for their construction are at hand.

In the most ordinary way the *quid rei* definitions are then obtained as the result of a long series of deductions (*"fructum plerumque post longam seriem demonstrationum"*), and if we use them before reaching them through this process we are exposed to the danger of assuming the existence or the constructability of figures which by means of postulates previously assumed, *could be* demonstrated as non-existant or not constructable—such is the case, to mention Leibniz' favorite example, of the "regular polyhedron with ten faces," the impossibility of which is not apparent at first glance.

The fallacy called by Saccheri *"complex definition"* consists, in fact, in thinking that the definitions where the thing being defined is attributed with the simultaneous possession of several properties (as in the case mentioned before of the definition of "parallel line" proposed by Borelli, the property of being a straight line and that of being *moreover* the collection of points on a plane that are equidistant from another straight line) could also be used in demonstrations, independently from the ascertainment of the compatibility of such properties.

In fact, in the case where such compatibility does not exist, that is in the case of the existence of an object that possesses the properties in question at the same time could be demonstrated impossible (by means, of course, of the other hypotheses already included as the

---

being the first to remark on the importance of these writings goes to one of the most distinguished scholars of the History of Science, G. Vacca from Genoa. (*Formulaire de Mathèmatiques*, 1901. [Peano 1901])

[28] [See Saccheri 1697. The English translation is taken from the introduction to Saccheri 1733, p. xviii.]

basis of the demonstrative science in question), any reasoning including among its premises such definition combined with the mentioned hypotheses, would prevent it from having value being based on contradictory premises.

The close connection between these considerations, so decisively important in the history of modern geometry, and the Aristotelian doctrine of definition, as seen in the previously quoted passages, has not been noted, until now, as far as I know, by the scholars of history of philosophy or logic, nor by the scholars of the history of mathematics. We have confirmation of such a connection from the recurrent observations, similar to those seen before by Saccheri, which can be found in the work of the other great initiator of research of non-Euclidean Geometry, I. H. Lambert (1728-77). See in particular his letter to Kant (February 1766) where on the subject of Wolff, he objects to his way of doing philosophy by saying that he "assumed nominal definitions and, without noticing it, shoved aside or concealed all diffiulties in them."[29]

References

Beltrami, Eugenio. 1889. Un precursore italiano di Legendre e di Lobatschewski. *Rendiconti della R. Accademia dei Lincei* 5.

Cooke, H. P. and H. Tredennick, eds. 1938. *(Aristotle) The Categories on Interpretation. Prior Analytics.* Cambridge, Mass.-London: Harvard University Press-Heinemann, 1983.

Couturat, Louis. 1903. *Opuscules et fragments inédits de Leibniz: extraits des manuscrits de la Bibliothèque royale de Hanovre.* Paris: Alcan. Repr. Hildesheim-Zürich-New York: G. Olms, 1988.

Descartes. 1637. *Discours de la méthode.* Engl. Transl. in R. Veitch, J. (ed.) *Discourse on the method.* Sutherland & Knox, 1850.

Forster, E.S. and D.J. Furley, eds. 1965. *(Aristotle). On sophistical refutations. On coming-to-be and passing-away.* Cambridge, Mass.-London: Harvard University Press-Heinemann, 1992.

Jowett, B., ed. 1892. *The dialogues of Plato: Parmenides. Theaetetus. Sophist. State man. Philebus,* vol. 4. New York: Macmillian and Co., 3rd edn.

Lutoslavski, Wincenty. 1897. *The origin and growth of Plato's logic; with an account of Plato's style and of the chronology of his writings.* London, New York [etc.]: Longmans, Green and co.

MacMahon, J. H., ed. 1896. *The Metaphysics of Aristotle.* London: G. Bell and sons.

Mill, John Stuart. 1870. *A system of logic, ratiocinative and inductive; being a connected view of the principles of evidence and the methods of scientific investigation.* New York: Harper & Brothers.

---

[29]English translation by A. Zweig from Zweig 1999, p. 85.

Peano, Giuseppe, ed. 1901. *Formulaire de Mathématiques*, vol. 3. Turin: Bocca-Clausen.

Poste, E., ed. 1850. *The logic of science: a translation of the Posterior Analytics of Aristotle.* Oxford: Francis MacPherson.

Saccheri, Gerolamo. 1697. *Logica Demonstrativa.* Augustae Taurinorum.

Saccheri, Gerolamo. 1733. *Euclides ab omni nævo vindicatus; sive conatus Geometricus quo stabiliuntur geometriæ principia.* Milan.

Segre, Corrado. 1902-03. Congetture intorno all'influenza di Girolamo Saccheri sulla formazione delle geometrie non euclidee. *Atti della Reale Accademia delle Scienze di Torino* 38:535–547.

Smith, R., ed. 1997. *(Aristotle) Topics.* Oxford University Press.

Vailati, Giovanni. 1903a. Di un'opera dimenticata del P. Gerolamo Saccheri ("Logica Demonstrativa" 1697). *Rivista Filosofica* 4. Repr. in Vailati (1911), pages 477–484.

Vailati, Giovanni. 1903b. La teoria aristotelica della definizione. *Rivista di Filosofia e scienze affini* 2(5). Repr. in Vailati (1911), pages 485–496.

Vailati, Giovanni. 1911. *Scritti di G. Vailati, 1863-1909.* Leipzig-Firenze: Barth.

Zeuthen, Hieronymus Georg. 1896. *Geschichte der Mathematik im Altertum und Mittelalter.* Kopenhagen: A. F. Höst und Sön. French translation by Jean Mascart *Histoire des mathématiques dans l'antiquité et le moyen âge*, Paris: Gauthier-Villars, 1902.

Zweig, Arnulf. 1999. *Correspondence.* The Cambridge edition of the works of Immanuel Kant. Cambridge: Cambridge University Press.

8

The Most Recent Definition of Mathematics[†]

The most recent definition of mathematics was given by Bertrand Russell (*International Monthly*, IV, issue I, p. 84)[1] and consists of saying that mathematics is a science where we never need to know if what is said is true, nor do we need to know what we are talking about. It definitely seems a paradox and moreover an enigma. Therefore it is even more interesting to show how such a definition corresponds in the most exact way to the concept of mathematics entertained by those, among its present-day scholars, who took the trouble of wondering how it differs from the other sciences.

This is a fact that does not lack a somewhat humorous aspect: while philosophers from different schools of thought continue to discuss *the nature* of mathematical concepts more than ever, whether they are "*a priori*" or "*a posteriori*," whether they are "*necessary*" or "*contingent truths*," "*analytic*" or "*synthetic*" etc., the mathematicians, for their part, are not only completely uninterested in these kinds of questions, but are also evermore induced to reconsider the question itself of the truth or falsity of their assertions as a question utterly foreign to the sphere of their attributions; as a question on which the interest or importance that they attribute to their research does not depend at all. They tend more and more to make the purpose of their research

---

[†] "La più recente definizione della matematica." First published in *Leonardo*, year II, June 1904, repr. in Vailati (1911), pages 528-533 (Vailati, 1904).

[1] Found quoted by L. Couturat in the first of two articles dedicated to the analysis of Russell's work: *Principles of mathematics* [1903], published recently in *Revue de Métaphysique* (January-April 1904) [Couturat 1904].

Logic and Pragmatism. Selected Essays by Giovanni Vailati.
C. Arrighi, P. Cantù, M. De Zan, and P. Suppes.
Copyright © 2009, CSLI Publications.

not the determination of which of the assertions they are considering *were* true or false, but the research of which of them *should be true* if others were true, or because others would be true; in other words, the determination of which suppositions would be needed, or would suffice, to reach such and such conclusions, and which kind of conclusions we would reach if we were to accept such and such suppositions.

Whether the latter were, in the end, true or false, whether they corresponded more or less to "*reality*," is a matter to which the mathematicians are willing to attribute less and less importance. They do not deny, of course, that such a matter may have its role in deciding which suppositions have consequences that *are worth* treating. However, they do not regard it as the only, nor the principal matter that has to be taken into consideration in such regard. Most of all, they are far from believing that its presence is indispensable in order to make a set of suppositions able to be the starting point of a scientific theory.

For its own same requirements which are imposed by its application to physical and mechanical sciences, mathematics is enriched everyday with new hypotheses or premises which, even if suggested by observation or experiments, correspond to true deformations, or falsifications, of the real facts, which have been made exactly with the purpose of making the study of such facts accessible to the powerful tools of calculation and geometric representation. And such deformations and falsifications, far from being considered exceptional expedients, needed because of some limitation intrinsic to the exercise of our intellectual faculties, are becoming more and more recognized as normal and indispensable conditions for any kind of rational activity.

That same method, called "*successive approximations*," consisting of gradually correcting the results of theoretical investigations, taking into account an ever increasing number of circumstances which complicate the phenomenon under study, presupposes as an indispensable precondition an inverse process, instead consisting of artificially simplifying the facts we want to study, stripping them of most of the characteristics they actually present and trying to determine how they *should behave* if they were as we suppose them to be, that is, if they were different from what they are.

Not only do the hypotheses built in this way stop being acceptable as false, on the contrary they present themselves as all the more apt to serve the purpose the less they are true, i.e. the larger the number of characteristics that they manage to neglect in the conventional or schematic representation that they provide of the facts to which they refer.

Cases of this kind are not the only ones where the preference for a given mathematical hypothesis is determined and justified for reasons that do not have any relationship with the truth, or for reasons related to a better or worse conformity to *"real"* facts.

In this regard the case presented by the new researchers of so-called *non-Euclidean geometry* is no less instructive. It is well known, in fact, how the development of such research has lead to the recognition that at least some of the *axioms* at the base of traditional geometry could be substituted by others which asserted precisely the opposite, without making it any less possible to build a theoretical edifice as coherent and harmonious in all its parts as one built on ancient foundations, and no less compatible with experimental observations, given the narrow limits within which they are inevitably confined.

"One geometry can not be more true than another, can only be more convenient" (Poincaré, *Science et hypothèse*, p. 67).[2] This phrase recently repeated by Poincaré, has by now become banal; that is, that wondering whether the Euclidean geometry is true or not, compared to other geometries which could be built and adopted in its place, has as little sense as wondering whether the metric system or one of the old measuring systems is *more true.*

It will be less easy to justify and clarify the other part of the definition related by Russell, namely, the part which describes mathematics as a science where we do not need to know what we are talking about.

It is necessary, here, to start from a different area of considerations. Let us look at the famous sentence used by Max Müller to try and specify what constitutes the real characteristic feature of a real *language*, as opposed to other less perfect forms of instinctive demonstrations of feelings through sounds, as we can also find in the inferior developmental stages of animal life. *"Language,"* he says, *"begins where interjections end."*[3]

If we wonder as well how the the interjections differ from what the grammarians call the other *"parts of speech,"* we realize immediately that they are the only words that, even when uttered on their own, suffice for themselves to express some kind of feeling or opinion of the person who uttered them, while other kinds of terms, for example nouns or verbs, do not serve such purposes if not grouped together in a string of words (a sentence, a proposition) that has some meaning.

When we utter, for example, the sound *"brr"* or the sound *"sst"*, we do not need to add anything else to make it understood that we are feeling cold or that we desire silence. If instead we say, for example, the

---

[2] [Quoted in French in the original. English translation from Poincaré 1902, p. 39.]
[3] [English translation from Müller 1891, vol. 1, p. 507.]

name of an object without accompanying it with some other word (or gesture) to indicate what we mean by it, or at least explaining if we are asserting that we are seeing it, desiring it or waiting for its appearance etc., we are not expressing an opinion of ours at all, nor the way we feel, but simply at most, that we are thinking about that object without saying anything else about *what we think about it.*[4]

It follows that interjections can be considered those words among others in our language that make *more sense* than all others and which, in some way, are the only ones that make sense, while others are only capable *of acquiring some sense,* in the case where they are elected to be part of a sentence that *makes some sense.*

The above mentioned sentence quoted by Max Müller is equivalent to saying that real language begins with the first introduction of words, which taken by themselves, have no meaning, and that a language is more perfect the greater is the number of words in it that make sense *per se,* as opposed to those that, even when pronounced on their own, express some opinion or state of mind of the person who uttered them.

This is so true that the words that have the least meaning among all the others, namely those to which we need to add the largest number of other words to get a sentence that communicates something, are precisely those that appear later, both in the historical development of languages and in the individual process of their acquisition.[5] Belonging to this kind in particular are the *prepositions,* in so far as they have the task of distinguishing between the various kinds of relations that can exist between the objects considered. In fact they do not, precisely for this reason, indicate absolutely anything if they are not accompanied by the words which denote the objects between which the relationship at issue is intended to exist. So if we pronounce the words "*beside*" or "*above*" or "*below,*" without saying anything more about which are the

---

[4] Just in exceptional cases a name, due to the circumstances of its pronunciation or writing, acquires, just as interjections do, the value of an entire proposition; like, for example, when on a bottle is indicated the name of the content, or when we are calling a person or an animal pronouncing the name.

[5] This is in agreement with the observations by Paola Lombroso (*La vita dei bambini,* Torino, 1904, pp. 88-9 [Carrara Lombroso 1904]) and with the others, by Bergson and Croce, related by Giuliano il Sofista [aka Giuseppe Prezzolini] (*Il linguaggio come causa d'errore,* Firenze, Spinelli, 1904, p. 21 [Prezzolini 1904]). The child understand the sense of sentences before that of words. And even the scientist, on the other hand, finds himself often in the condition of using sentences to which he attributes a determined and precise meaning even if they are composed of words of whose meaning he is not concerned about, even confessing that they could also have none. So for example a physicist can have a very clear idea of what he intends when he says that "*two bodies have masses, one twice that of the other,*" even if he considers idle, or even without meaning, the question *what is the mass.*

things we intend to state that *"one is beside the other"* or *"one is above or below the other,"* we are not communicating to the listener any more information about what we think or believe, than if we were uttering sounds without meaning.

Now we should notice that the most important and essential part of mathematical language consists of signs indicating relations (equality, inequality, relationships of position, of direction, of dimension, etc.), and in this same category signs expressing *functions* and *operations* are also included because even these cannot express any fact or determine assertions if they are not followed or accompanied by other signs indicating the objects or the quantities on which the operation is intended to be executed.

On the other hand, the indication of the objects or the value of the quantities on which one is working is exactly what mathematics tends to avoid as much as possible.

Its progresses, as can be seen confronting arithmetic and algebra, consist exactly of making its conclusions independent to the highest degree, from the assignment of any particular value to the quantities and objects among which the relations considered exist.

And this is not the furthest limit to which one of the characteristic aspirations of mathematics tends, namely the aspiration to *strip*, or (to express the same thing with an opposite metaphor, and maybe more appropriately) to *empty*, the words that it uses of as much meaning as possible.

Much further ahead in this direction we go into the most abstract and speculative regions of its domain.

I would like to hint at the new branches of research represented, on the one hand, by the so-called *theory of relations*, as conceived in the writings of Charles S. Peirce, and on the other by *mathematical logic*, especially under the form that it has recently assumed, by hand of the Italian school led by Peano.

A common characteristic of both these branches is precisely the tendency to emancipate mathematical deductions from any appeal to facts or intuitions with reference to the *meaning* of the operations, or relations, under consideration. These are defined by the mere simple enunciation of a certain number of fundamental properties that, being able to be common to relations or operations with the most disparate and heterogeneous meanings, are compatible with the most various interpretations of the symbols appearing in their enunciation.[6]

---

[6]So, for example, when I state the following proposition: "If event A happened before event B, and event B happened before event C, then event A, also happened

Given a certain group of relations or operations defined in this way, that is they are supposed to possess a certain number of properties arbitrarily determined, the only purpose of the mathematician is that of determining which other properties they must or may possess given the initial suppositions.

To include in such a process any concept derived or suggested by one or another of the many particular meanings that such relations and operations under consideration could assume, as long as they are compatible with the initial suppositions made about them, is bound to be, as a consequence, as illicit as it would be in algebra, for example, to substitute a letter with a specific value or quantity in a formula that is to be demonstrated. This would be the same as taking away any legitimacy and value from the conclusions reached, which would maintain, instead, the greater capacity and generality the more, in reaching them, we have been abstracting from the meanings that could be assigned to the relation or operation signs appearing in them.

It is in this sense that the theory becomes even more perfect and it moves all the more closer to its ideal the more it becomes susceptible to development independent of any reference to the objects or relations the theory deals with; that is, whoever is building it is able to look at it as a mere creation of his own will. The question of the existence or lack thereof of relations or operations that satisfy the initial hypotheses he made, that is the question whether the world we live in presents examples of relations possessing the properties about which he is investigating the possibility and mutual dependency or not, is a question about which the mathematician cares very little, as a musician cares very little about whether a given chord and a given melody correspond to some sound or noise that can be found in nature.

This characteristic of mathematical speculation on the one hand constitutes the main trait that distinguishes it from any other kind of scientific research, and on the other reveals the intimate and fundamental affinity between itself and the creative activity of an artist.

Como, May 6, 1904

---

before event C," the assertion just uttered is such that it would not stop being true if in it, instead of the word "*before*" I were to substitute, in all three instances, the word "*after*," or the word "*contemporarily*." Therefore I have stated a property that is common to the relations indicated by any of these words: a property whose consequences I can research even without indicating or deciding which of the given relations I am talking about. My conclusion will then be valid for *any* relation that has such a property. And if ordinary language does not provide a name general enough for me, (that is, *with enough lack of meaning*) to designate them all at the same time, it will allow me to introduce one and to use it as when necessary and suitable.

References

Carrara Lombroso, Paola. 1904. *La vita dei bambini*. Torino: Bocca.

Couturat, Louis. 1904. Les principes des mathématiques. *Revue de Metaphysique et de Morale* 12:19–50, 211–40.

Müller, Max F. 1891. *The science of language: founded on lectures delivered at the Royal Institution in 1861 and 1863*. London: Longmans, Green.

Poincaré, Henri. 1902. *La science et l'hypothèse*. Paris: Flammarion. Engl. transl. *Science and hypothesis*. New York: The Science Press, 1905.

Prezzolini, Giuseppe. 1904. *Il linguaggio come causa d'errore*. Firenze: Tip. Spinelli.

Russell, Bertrand. 1903. *The Principles of Mathematics*. Cambridge University Press.

Vailati, Giovanni. 1904. La più recente definizione della matematica. *Leonardo* pages 7–10. Repr. in Vailati (1911), pages 528–533.

Vailati, Giovanni. 1911. *Scritti di G. Vailati, 1863-1909*. Leipzig-Firenze: Barth.

9

On the Meaning of the Difference Between Axioms and Postulates in Greek Geometry[†]

The traditional distinction between *postulates* (αἰτήματα) and *axioms* (ἀξιώματα or κοιναὶ ἔννοιαι) is usually thought of as not having any other justification than the lesser grade of evidence of postulates compared to axioms; it is considered, in other words, a consequence of the simple fact that the propositions that form the basis of geometry do not all have, to the same degree, the qualities that induce us to admit such propositions without demonstration.

Given this interpretation of the aforementioned distinction, it is natural that the recent research on the principles of geometry, which has the tendency to give less and less importance to "intuition" and the criterion of "evidence" in choosing fundamental propositions, seems to favor the opinion that the aforementioned difference should be regarded as something negligible, moreover, as something foreign to the field on which the geometer should concentrate his attention.

Therefore it becomes even more interesting to research whether different degrees of evidence actually constitute the *only* criterion on whose basis we can justify the distinction between axioms and postulates, and whether the Greek geometers who introduced this distinction were not guided to it by some other kind of consideration of a different

[†] "Intorno al significato della differenza tra gli Assiomi ed i Postulati nella Geometria Greca." First published in *Verhandlungen des III Internationalen Mathematiker Kongresses in Heidelberg 8–13 Aug. 1904*, Leipzig, Teubner, 1905, repr. in Vailati (1911), pages 547-552 (Vailati, 1904).

character and of more fundamental importance.

An interesting document on this matter has luckily been preserved in a passage by Proclus (*Commentarii in primum Euclidis elementorum librum*)[1] and I would like to highlight here the importance of such a passage.

In it Proclus mentions three different meanings that geometers or philosophers of the various schools attribute to the aforementioned distinction.

The first of these meanings, according to Proclus, is the one adopted by Geminus, which states that the difference between axioms and postulates is analogous to the one between *theorems* and *problems*. That is, just as problems refer to the construction of figures satisfying certain conditions, while theorems state some properties (συμπτώματα) of given figures, or which are supposed to be constructable, in the same way postulates state the possibility of some construction (not reducible to others already accepted as executable), while axioms state some properties which are attributed (without demonstration) to some figure whose constructability has already been postulated, or demonstrated.

It is for this reason that, in Euclid's work, the enumeration of postulates precedes the enumeration of axioms.

The difference between problems and theorems is also characterized by Proclus, in another passage of the same work (page 79), by stating that, in the case of problems, the task is to construct a given figure in a way that satisfies some conditions which such a figure *could* satisfy or not, while in the case of theorems we deal with conditions or properties that the figure in question *cannot but* possess, in addition, of course, to those it possesses by definition. Therefore, adds Proclus, whoever considers the following proposition a problem: "Inscribe a right angle in a semicircle," demonstrates a lack of knowledge of geometry, because he suggests that an angle inscribed in a semicircle could also not be a right angle.

In other words, a theorem, just by asserting that if a figure satisfies the conditions of a group A it also satisfies those of another group B, denies the possibility that the construction of a figure that satisfies the two groups of conditions A and B at the same time, constitutes a different problem from the construction of a figure which satisfies the conditions of group A.

The purpose of theorems is therefore to reduce the solution of a problem to the solution of another, i.e. to diminish the number of problems

---

[1] For the quotes used here I refer to the edition by G. Friedlein (Leipzig, Teubner, 1873) [Friedlein (1873)].

that we need to be able to solve or that we need to suppose as solvable. The postulates would be, among the problems, those which no theorem has reduced to other more simple or elementary problems.

While the postulate asserts that it is *possible* to construct a figure in such a way that it does or does not satisfy certain conditions (for example a circle having a given radius and a given center), an axiom asserts that it is *impossible* to construct a figure that does or does not satisfy given conditions (for example that it is impossible to construct two triangles which have two sides and the included angle respectively equal without the other two angles also being respectively equal). According to this interpretation, the difference between axioms and postulates would then be the same as the one the logicians recognize as existing between the general affirmative proposition and the particular negative proposition (or between the general negative propositions like "no A is a B" and the particular affirmative propositions like "some A is a B"), because the general propositions *deny*, while the particular propositions *assert*, the existence of objects contemporarily belonging to two or more classes (Leibniz).

However, we need to notice that the distinction between general propositions and particular propositions should be intended here in a more fundamental sense than is usually attributed to traditional Logic. It is necessary to consider as "particular" propositions not only those where the subject is preceded by the word "*some*" (or some other equivalent word) but in general any proposition which includes, in some form, some "affirmation of existence."

In this sense, for example, even those which should be qualified as "particular propositions," even though they have their subject preceded by the words "every," "all," or some other equivalent word, nevertheless contain, under the form called by grammarians "direct complement," some propositions introducing a name preceded by the word "*some*" (or some other equivalent word).

In order to explain with an example, let us consider the proposition usually designed as Archimedes' postulate, that is: "Every segment, multiplied by some number, can become greater than any other segment."[2]

It definitely has the outline of a general proposition because it asserts that *all* the segments possess the property stated by the proposition. Nonetheless, notwithstanding this, it is a "particular" proposition, in the sense indicated before, because what is asserted exactly in it is

---

[2]This is, as it is known, the same proposition appearing in Euclid among the definitions in the premise to Book V.

that "Given any two segments, *certain numbers always exist* in such a way that, multiplying one of the given segments by them, we obtain a segment greater than the other given segment."

Another point where the distinctions of traditional Scholastic logic do not appear to be precise enough on the topic we are addressing is that of the so-called propositions "of determination," namely those asserting that a given figure is determined in an unique way starting from some condition or group of conditions, for example the proposition: "through two points runs one and only one straight line."

To the question of whether propositions of this kind should be collocated among the axioms or the postulates, we need to answer by distinguishing the two kinds of propositions that any such proposition contains. The parts of them asserting the existence of some figure satisfying the condition under consideration are *postulates*; *axioms* are instead those asserting that no more than one of such figures *can exist*.

Anyway, even in this case, we should warn against another misunderstanding that can arise from the fact that not all the propositionss of geometry presented as assertions of the *unicity* of a figure satisfying given conditions should be considered as *not* containing assertions of existence. In fact there are some where the assertion of existence takes place even if it does not refer to the same object to which the assertion of unicity refers.

This is the case, for example, of the postulate of parallel lines, because in it, even if what is asserted is equivalent to saying that if we take a point outside a straight line we *cannot* draw more than a parallel line through it, it is also equivalent to the assertion that, given three straight lines on a plane, two of which, *a* and *b*, are parallel and the third one *c* crosses one of those, for example *a*, there *does exist* a point in common between the lines *c* and *b*.

Therefore, we cannot agree with Proclus when he affirms that the aforementioned propositions, in case we intend the distinction between axioms and postulates in the sense we are talking about, should be classified among the axioms, or among the theorems, instead of the postulates.[3]

A warning of the opposite nature should be made regarding another

---

[3]Ibid. p. 183 and p. 191: "This ought to be struck from the postulates altogether." But Proclus, considering it demonstrable, would like to include it with the theorems rather than the axioms. Against those who thought that it should be accepted as "evident," he refers to an interesting observation by Geminus where it is recommended that geometers not trust their intuition too much ("we have learned from the very founders of this science not to pay attention to plausible imaginings in determining what propositionss are to be accepted in geometry.") [In Greek in the text. English translation by G. R. Morrow from Morrow 1970, p. 150.]

kind of propositions which, while they have the aspect of propositions containing assertions of existence, are not *postulates*, in the sense defined before, but instead they are simple *definitions*, i.e. propositions with the only purpose of introducing some new locution and to explain the meaning that we want to attribute to it.

A typical example of propositions of this kind is provided by the so-called *postulate of Dedekind*. In fact the possibility of dividing the set of rational numbers into classes that satisfy the conditions mentioned in it does not depend at all on it being true or not. Therefore the only purpose that we can attribute to it is that of introducing an opportune convention to design such classes and to highlight the analogies that exist between their general properties and those possessed by the classes formed by the lower (or higher) numbers of a given rational number. The same observation can also be made for the other propositions which, even if they are presented, as this one, in the form of assertions of existence, are really used only to extend and generalize the meaning of some locution, making it applicable to a broader field than the one it was previously reserved for. Such are, for example, the propositions where, by means of the concept of "limit," the meaning to be given to the words "length," "area," (defined before only for the case of straight segments or for flat polynomial surfaces) is specified for the case of others lines or surfaces.

I will proceed now examining the *second* of the three meanings mentioned by Proclus as being assigned to the difference between axioms and postulates. It can be characterized by saying that all the propositions (not demonstrated) that, because they state the properties common to any kind of quantities, are valid and relevant even outside the field of Geometry, are *axioms*. Instead the other undemonstrated propositions where some purely geometrical fact is considered, or some property that has meaning only for figures' and entities' equality, or the relationship between "whole" and "part," are classified among the axioms, while instead the proposition "all the right angles are equal" is included among the postulates, even though, as is observed by Proclus himself, such a proposition, not containing any assertion of existence or constructability, should be classified among the axioms, in the case of us following the criterion we have discussed before. Even this second meaning, as with the first one, needs only to be clarified to manifest itself as connected to an important distinction to which the recent research on the principles of geometry tends to give importance. It is known, in fact, how such research tends to make the most abstract parts of mathematics assume the aspect of a series of deductions aiming to determine which are the properties possessed by a given system of relations and operations, defined only by assigning them a certain number of fundamental properties. The results obtained this way can be applied to any special system of relations and operations, provided that the group of properties that has been taken as assumption at the basis of the reasoning is verified.

The propositions, now, where it is affirmed that a given special system of relations and operations actually satisfies the conditions provided by the general theory and required for its application, constitute a further group of premises that have to be assumed by the special theory in question and that are to be well distinguished from those that are at basis of the general theory.

By indicating the latter with the name of *axioms*, and reserving the name "postulates" for the special premises of any single theory, we would end up attributing to these two technical terms a sense not much different from the one that they would assume according to this second interpretation of the three given by Proclus.

All that is left now is to consider the third, where Proclus refers to the authority of Aristotle, according to which the axioms are those, among the fundamental propositions, that are valid *"in themselves"* (καθ' ἑαυτά), i.e. by virtue of the meaning itself of the terms present in them, while the postulates are those others which, even though evident and undeniable, nevertheless are not a "necessary" consequence (ἐξ ἀνάγκης) of the definitions adopted for the terms present in them, therefore they could be denied by someone who accepts such definitions, without the possibility of convincing them that they are in contradiction.

Against this third way of conceiving the distinction between axioms and postulates, we should first of all object that, given that it contains the truth of axioms as a consequence of the meaning in itself of the terms that they contain, the axioms would no longer be part of the fundamental propositions of Geometry, and they would descend to the rank of simple theorems, demonstrable by substituting the terms that they contain with their respective definitions.

However, if we examine a little more in depth in which sense we can assert that, for example, the axiom "Two quantities equal to a third are equal to each other" is true by *definition*, we are induced to conclude that the only possible sense is the following: that the property of the relationship of equality, stated in the aforementioned proposition, belongs to those propositions that contribute to our concept of "equality," or in other words, that such a property is included by us among those that must be possessed by the relationships that we distinguish from the others by the name of equality.

In this way we characterize "axioms" in only a slightly differently way than the second way which we examined previously, and which consists of considering them as propositions with the role of contributing to "defining" a system of relationships and operations, by means of the enunciation of certain properties which it should satisfy.

The "definitions" with which we are dealing, in short, are nothing but those that are ordinarily designed with the name of "*definitions by means of postulates*" (or better "*by means of axioms*"): that is, those that do *not* declare that the meaning of the sign for a relationship or operation that we are defining is equivalent to that expressed by a group of signs with an already known meaning, but rather by asserting that some expression with a given shape, *in each of which appears the sign of the relationship or of the operation to be defined*, are deducible from one another. This happens, for example, when we define equality as a relationship that the two renowned characteristic properties (transitivity, symmetry) possess.[4]

These are the kinds of definitions that we need to resort to any time we have to determine the meaning of signs of relationships and operations that we assumed as "primitive" (that is incapable of being analyzed or determined by a definition in the strict sense of the term), and only by referring to them can we justly assert that the treatises in pure mathematics, given that they tend to develop deductively the properties of a system of relationships and of operations defined in such a way, do not have any need of postulates or admission, besides the general principles of logic that are at the basis of any kind of deductive reasoning.

References

Friedlein, Gottfried, ed. 1873. *Procli Diadochi in primum Euclidis Elementorum librum commentarii*. Teubner. Repr. Hildesheim: Olms 1992.

Morrow, Glenn R. 1970. *A commentary on the first book of Euclid's Elements*. Princeton, N.J.: Princeton University Press, 1992.

Vailati, Giovanni. 1904. Intorno al significato della differenza tra gli assiomi ed i postulati nella geometria greca. In *Verhandlungen des III Interna-*

---

[4]With definitions of this kind, the meaning of the *names of class* which design such entities, between which it is possible to establish relationships or operations possessing the considered properties, is also indirectly defined; as for example when we define the name of a quantity as the name of a class of such entities between which a relationship can be established with the renowned properties of the signs $>$ and $<$, that is, transitive and asymmetric. In this way we have "implicit" definitions, among which an important particular case is represented by the so-called definitions "*by abstraction*" (Peano), such as, for example, the definition of "ratio" (λόγος) in Book V by Euclid.

tionalen Mathematiker Kongresses in Heidelberg 8-13 aug. 1903. Leipzig: Teubner, 1905. Repr. in Vailati (1911), pages 547-552.

Vailati, Giovanni. 1911. *Scritti di G. Vailati, 1863-1909*. Leipzig-Firenze: Barth.

10

The Art of Asking Questions†

Whoever has read this precious little manual of pedagogic psychology, *Talks to teachers*[1] by James, cannot have forgotten a charming anecdote that he relates to demonstrate how hard it is to have an idea of the meaning attributed by a child to the abstract words that his teacher asks him to repeat. James tells of an acquaintance of his who, trying to explain to a little girl the meaning of the grammatical term "passive voice," said: "Suppose that you kill me: you who do the killing are in the active voice, and I, who am killed, am in the passive voice." "But how can you speak if you are killed?" said the child. "Oh, well, you may suppose that I am not quite dead!" The next day the child was asked, in class, to explain the passive voice, and said "It's the kind of voice you speak with when you ain't quite dead."

This little experience certainly should not have encouraged the teacher to persist in using the method that he had believed to be the most suitable to introduce the little girl to the mysteries of grammar.

Nevertheless, he would have been wrong in abandoning it to go back to the most commonly followed method, consisting in the enunciation and request for repetition of a more or less satisfactory definition of the term at issue. In this way he would have easily succeeded in enabling the girl to give to whoever might ask her the meaning of "passive voice," an answer no worse than a professional philologist could give.

However, the child would not have been any closer to understanding,

---

† "Sull'arte di interrogare." First published in *Rivista di Psicologia*, 1(2), March-April 1905, repr. in Vailati (1911), pages 572-576 (Vailati, 1905).

[1] W. James, *Talks to teachers on Psychology and to students on some of life's Ideals*. Longmans, Green and Co., London, 1901, p. 152; translated into Italian by G. C. Ferrari *Gli ideali della vita*, Turin, Bocca, 1901. [See James 1899, p. 152.]

Logic and Pragmatism. Selected Essays by Giovanni Vailati.
C. Arrighi, P. Cantù, M. De Zan, and P. Suppes.
Copyright © 2009, CSLI Publications.

even in a vague way, the meaning of the word. She would have just learned to conceal, to mask her ignorance, an ignorance that, moreover, would have certainly manifested itself later on, when faced with an invitation to apply her presumed knowledge to a real case.

The following observation is common place in didactics, that is, if the meaning of a word is too obscure to be explained to a child by means of examples and instances, it will be even less likely to be understood by way of a definition, which inevitably would contain even more abstract and difficult to understand words than the one we are trying to define.

Even conceding that even this norm has exceptions, and that "more abstract" does not always mean "more difficult to understand," one thing can certainly be asserted: the worst way to evaluate the level of knowledge that an individual, especially a child, has of something is to ask the individual what that something is. The frequent use of questions of this kind, in the various stages of teaching, and their role in our schools in examination procedures and proficiency evaluations, are in my opinion among the most characteristic symptoms of the backward condition of our didactic technique compared to the present state of the psychology of intellectual processes. Nowhere else do we notice, in fact, such a strident contrast between the didactic procedures usually followed and the fundamental tendency of modern psychology to consider general concepts as mere instruments (*Denkmittel*), with no other purpose than that of allowing us to order, classify, and shape the raw material of particular experiences to determined tasks. In conformity with such a view, not being able to *apply* a concept, not being able to *distinguish* facts contained within it from other opposing ones, is the same as not grasping the concept at all and not having yet acquired it, regardless of the ability we may have to repeat some words which purportedly define or explain it. An entire school, and by no means the least important, of contemporary psychology extends this consideration beyond the acquisition of concepts to that of any knowledge or abstract doctrine, and claims that not just the usefulness but the *meaning* itself that can be attributed to a hypothesis, or a theory, is nothing but the *factual ("pragmatic") knowledge* that we are able to derive from it, compared to that which would be derived from its negation or from the acceptance of some other different hypothesis or theory.

By means of a very suggestive image, Mach compares the position of a scientist in front of a familiar theory to that of a musician in front of a sheet of music. For the musician the sheet of music would be useless except that it tells him to execute specific movements to produce the sounds it represents, and in the same way the scientist, for example the physicist, cannot consider himself to have mastered any given theory if he is not able to clearly picture which experiences or experimental verifications he should perform in order to test its validity or, in other words, which events *should* happen if the theory were true.

And if this is true for a scientist, then so much truer it must be for someone who is taking his first steps in the domain of theoretical abstractions—for the child whose spontaneous reasoning processes have not yet undergone any organizational discipline, for the even more mature student who is approaching a new subject of study without any preparation that would have provided him with concrete material on which to practice his discriminating and generalizing activity.

As a teacher of mathematics at middle school I have occasion to notice daily, in its most characteristic forms, the infantile minds' natural resistance to new general ideas when the definitions of such are presented but not preceded or accompanied by a sufficient amount of practical examples.

For example, after having defined a parallelogram as a quadrilateral with parallel opposing sides, if I ask a student to draw a parallelogram, it is rare to find a case where the student does not draw a rectangle. Similarly, if I ask a student, who has already defined a triangle as a part of the plane delimited by three straight lines, to draw a triangle, I can expect, with little chance of mistake, that he will draw an equilateral triangle, and in this case, if I ask him to draw *another* triangle, I can be certain that he will think he is completely satisfying my request by drawing another... equilateral triangle—just as the boy in the anecdote who, after mentioning a rhino as an example of a pachyderm, is required to mention another example, and so replies: "Another rhino."

It is very normal for this to happen. In order for a definition, as it should, to be able to draw the attention of the person learning it to the traits that it has in common with objects that bear the name that we are defining, it is necessary for these traits to be present in the person's mind in a sufficient number and variety. In this way the person can distinguish these traits from all the other traits in the objects of that class that are more familiar to this person, or that are more easily recalled by previously established verbal associations.

To avoid this inconvenience it is not necessary that the person who understands the definition have actual experience of the various kinds of cases included in the definition. Instead, it is actually the definition itself that usually induces the mind through imagination to complete its experience, to elaborate the experiential data in order to introduce the highest number of individual divergences compatible with the conditions stated in the definition. But this is, in any case, an effort, and an effort that is so much more painful and difficult since it is less supported by impressions or experiences already recorded in memory.

To help the student in this effort, to show the most suggestive and appropriate concrete examples to his senses or his imagination, to direct his attention to the traits that make the examples similar, to teach him to recognize the presence of these traits even in cases that can seem different at first sight, etc., is all certainly more difficult and laborious than simply teaching him to repeat some stereotypical sentences or to increase the number of verbal *clichés* in his mind. But the belief that it is possible to communicate cognitions or to transfer ideas in a different way is an expectation that may seem as absurd and ridiculous as that of the farmer who, wishing to send his son a pair of shoes, hangs them from the telegraph cables. In the previously mentioned work James writes about a boy who was asked the following question: "Suppose you should dig a hole in the ground, hundreds of feet deep. How would you find conditions at the bottom, warmer or colder that at the top?" Given that the boy did not answer, in order to help him, the teacher repeated the question in a different way: "What *temperature conditions* are in the interior of the globe?" And the boy then answered triumphantly: "The interior of the globe is in a condition of 'igneous fusion'."[2]

Who knows what a condition of "igneous fusion" in the center of the globe represented for him if he was not able to tell if it would be colder or warmer there than in the school!

The first formulation under which the question was asked represents, in my opinion rather characteristically, the type of question teachers should move towards as much as possible, either with the purpose of stimulating the student to reflect, or with the purpose of testing the condition of his knowledge.

The best questions, for both purposes, are the ones that refer to the *prediction* of a specific fact, those where, after describing a given situation and a series of specific operations to the student, we ask what he would *expect* to find or to obtain if he were to perform them, or how he would *act* if he wanted to achieve a specific result given the circumstances.

The convenience of using these kinds of questions (the convenience, that is, of asking questions in a conditional, or we could say "*pragmatic*," form) is not limited to elementary school education or to the first stages of intellectual development.

To someone who already has sufficient knowledge of physics it could seem the same to ask "What is the specific weight of mercury?" as to ask instead "How many liters of water would we need to pour into a

---

[2] [See James 1899, p. 150.]

container in order for it to weigh as much as if it contained a liter of mercury?" Nevertheless it is not the same thing for someone who is on his way to acquiring and familiarizing himself with the experiences that the expression "specific weight" has the purpose of representing. The difference between the two kinds of questions is even clearer when we move from the more basic parts of physics to those where, as in the case of thermodynamics and electrotechnics, we deal with concepts that symbolize and summarize operations and reactions which are a lot more complex than balancing dishes on a scale.

Neglecting, in this case, to put the concepts in immediate and direct relation to concrete procedures of measurement, comparison and verification, from which those concepts derive their *meaning*, not only makes the theoretical studies almost useless, but is also detrimental to the advantages of experimental training. A student is prepared, instead, to receive maximum benefit when the theoretical discipline, to which he has been exposed, has helped create in him the disposition to consider any abstract enunciation as a more or less artificial way of stating the consequences and the results that whoever operates in a certain way under certain circumstances, *has to expect*.

Getting a student used to conceiving *"knowledge"* as the propensity to answer questions of this kind promptly and precisely, making him aware that the standard to which he is able to satisfy this requirement constitutes the essential criterion for his proficiency. This is the best way, I should say the only way, to fight his tendency, as natural as it is detrimental, to mistake the mnemonic effort of learning verbal formulas with the effort that leads to the effective acquisition of new concepts and knowledge.

Florence, February 12, 1905.

References

James, William. 1899. *Talks to teachers on Psychology and to students on some of life's Ideals*. London: Longmans, Green and Co, 1901.

Vailati, Giovanni. 1905. Sull'arte di interrogare. *Rivista di Psicologia* 1(2). Repr. in Vailati (1911), pages 572-576.

Vailati, Giovanni. 1911. *Scritti di G. Vailati, 1863-1909*. Leipzig-Firenze: Barth.

11

The Distinction Between Knowledge and Will[†]

for the soothsayer ought to know only the signs
of things that are about to come to pass,
but to whom the suffering or not suffering
of these things will be for the best,
can no more be decided by the soothsayer
than by one who is no soothsayer.
Plato, *Laches*, 195–6[1]

The study of the influence of desires and practical necessities on opinions and beliefs is not only interesting for those who want to use feelings to modify opinions, their own or someone else's, but also for those who want to protect themselves or others from the influence that feelings may exercise on beliefs.

An interesting question to consider regards the fact that sentimental differences and differences in taste and interests have a tendency to appear as differences of opinion.

Franz Brentano[2] owns the merit of having insisted, more than any

---

[†] "La distinzione tra conoscere e volere." First published in *Leonardo*, year III, June-August 1905, repr. in Vailati (1911), pages 626-629 (Vailati, 1905).

[1] [Translation in English from Jowett 1892, p. 105.]

[2] *Psychologie vom empirischen Standpunkte.* Leipzig, 1874 [Brentano 1874].

Logic and Pragmatism. Selected Essays by Giovanni Vailati.
C. Arrighi, P. Cantù, M. De Zan, and P. Suppes.
Copyright © 2009, CSLI Publications.

other psychologist, on the absolute difference and heterogeneity between the act of accepting or rejecting a given opinion or belief, and the act of declaring our way of evaluating certain goals and their different levels of desirability or importance.

The difference between one case and the other can be briefly characterized by saying that in the first case our assertions imply, directly or indirectly, a prediction about what is going to happen or what would happen if certain circumstances were verified, but in the second case we only express our desire that such circumstances be verified, and our disposition to act in such a way as to produce them or prevent them.

While for the first kind there exists what the logicians call the principle of non contradiction given that if two people have different opinions and they both make predictions about the same fact, one that it will happen, the other that it will not, they cannot both be right, in the second case the same is not true, in fact we cannot even talk about someone being right or wrong, unless in a metaphorical way, just as when we say that it is wrong to desire a certain thing, meaning only that we would no longer desire it if we knew its qualities or effects better.

Typical examples of the tendency of assertions of the second kind to assume the appearance of those of the first kind are provided by those sentences where the following words appear: "function," "duty," "mission," etc., just as when we say that it is a function of the state to do this or that, or that it is a person's duty to act in such and such a way, etc. The fact that they appear in the grammatical *indicative* form, instead of the *imperative* one, is one of the reasons that favor the tendency to mistake them for assertions implying something more than a desire or an aspiration, either our own or someone else's.

This case is similar to that found in sentences where we use the present tense to indicate our expectation of a future event, saying that, for example, we *are* mortal, in order to say that we *will die*, or that an object *is* fragile in order to say that we predict that it *would break* if hit, etc.

This analogy is also very useful for pointing out another characteristic which distinguishes assertions in the strict sense of the word from what could be called manifestations of will or desire. In fact while the former indicate ways or means that could be used to realize a fact that does not yet exist, the latter can only describe a state of consciousness or a fact that we recognize as *present*. The former do not refer to what we want, but rather to what we *could do if we wanted to*, so such assertions concern not just ourselves, but also whoever has completely opposite desires to our own, because they would indicate from which actions he should abstain in order to avoid producing what he does not want.

What have been pompously called the "responses" of science tend to get evermore closer to the condition of "neutrality" of the first kind of assertions. This is just one effect among many, deriving from the division of labor in the intellectual field, and from the growing convenience of separating theoretical research from the application and utilization of the results it produces.

The idea that scientists, as scientists and because they are scientists, have some special authority in deciding the value of the goals which their science tries to reach, represents only a surviving opinion that was useful in other times, when the distinction between the task of the scientist and that of the statesman, the educator, the moralist, the priest, the poet, etc. was not made like it is in the present day. This does not mean that the social condition of scientists is destined to descend to the point of being regarded as "mercenaries," at the service of any cause which offers them sufficiently remunerative conditions; but it means only that they should get used to regarding their science as an instrument that they must keep effective and increasingly powerful, leaving behind any pretence of being the only judges on its proper use.

There is another form of the tendency to see differences in opinion or belief where there exist, instead, only differences in taste and aspirations.

Those psychologists who went farthest in the analysis of the concept of "cause" were induced to conclude that only its (or one of its) constant antecedents can be considered the cause of a certain fact; another fact, that is, that the first one invariably follows. Without contesting the importance and legitimacy of this analysis "so far as it goes,"[3] it seems to me to be in need of completion, introducing the consideration of another element that contributes, no less than the preceding ones, to the meaning of the word "cause" in ordinary language.

The impression that talking about the "constant antecedent" of a fact does not express everything that we want to say when talking about "its cause," finds its justification in this: that in the majority of cases, what is called a cause of a fact represents only a small part of the entire group of circumstances whose comprehensive verification constantly precedes the verification of the fact itself.

Such a part is chosen by us, and considered separate from the others, not because it contributes more than the others in *producing* the effect, but because we are interested in keeping it in mind as the more variable

---

[3] [In English in the original.]

or modifiable, or as that part on which we hope to be able to have more influence: as the one, in short, about whose need and indispensability we have more reason to want to be informed. So, for example, no one would think that the cause of the death of a man who fell in the water was the fact that he was alive, even though life is undoubtedly a constant and invariable antecedent of any kind of death, including the one in question. By saying instead that the cause was that of not being able to swim or the depth of the water or how slippery the bottom was or the absence of people who could have seen the danger in time to bring help, etc., we mention all of these in turn, among the antecedents which suggest regret, or indicate responsibility or point out how the effect *could have* been prevented.

And this is also clearly expressed by the original meaning of the words designating the cause: the Greek name for cause is the same as fault, and the Latin word "causa" seems to be linked to the verb "caveo," and therefore also to the concept of means or remedy *against* the effect.

References

Brentano, Franz. 1874. *Psychologie vom empirischen Standpunkte*, vol. 1. Leipzig: Dunker & Humboldt.

Jowett, B. 1892. *The dialogues of Plato: Charmides. Lysis. Laches. Protagoras. Euthydemus. Cratylus. Phaedrus. Ion. Symposium*. Clarendon press, 3rd edn.

Vailati, Giovanni. 1905. La distinzione tra conoscere e volere. *Leonardo* 3. Repr. in Vailati (1911), pages 626-629.

Vailati, Giovanni. 1911. *Scritti di G. Vailati, 1863-1909*. Leipzig-Firenze: Barth.

12

Pragmatism and Mathematical Logic[†]

It is certainly not one of the least of the merits of the *Leonardo* that it has established lines of communication and encouraged the exchange of ideas between exponents of philosophical studies belonging to the most diverse and distant intellectual fields—between logicians and estheticians, between moralists and economists, mathematicians and mystics, biologists and poets.

Pending the possibility of a comparative examination of the results obtained, or prepared, by the development and exchange of ideas in all these various directions, it will not be irrelevant to summarize here in a schematic synopsis such of these results as relate to one of the most important lines of communication which the *Leonardo* has helped to construct and keep in operation, that is, the line which joins the various domains of Pragmatism with those occupied and cultivated by the "mathematical logicians." A significant indication of the intimate connection between these two fields of philosophical research may be deduced from the fact that the sponsor of the denomination and concept of "Pragmatism" (Ch. S. Peirce) is himself likewise the initiator and promoter of an original trend in logico-mathematical studies.

It is not, however, from the labors of the school of Peirce, but rather from those of the Italian school, headed by Peano, that I purpose here

[†] "Il Pragmatismo e la Logica Matematica," first published in *Leonardo*, February 1906, pages 16–25. Repr. in Vailati 1911, pages 689–694. This is a reprint of the Engl. transl. by H. D. Austin "Pragmatism and mathematical logic," *Monist* 16:481–491, 1906 (Vailati, 1906).

to take my material for the determination of what might be called the "pragmatic characteristics" of the new logical theories.

One point of contact between logic and pragmatism is found in their common tendency to regard the value, and even the meaning, of every assertion as being intimately related to the use which can be made, or which it may be desired to make, of it for the deduction and construction of particular consequences or groups of consequences. This tendency is manifest, among the mathematical logicians, especially in their revision of the criteria employed in the choice and determination of *postulates*, that is, in the choice of those propositions which in each separate branch of deductive science are to be admitted without demonstration. Instead of conceiving of the difference between postulates and the other propositions which are demonstrated by means of them as consisting in the possession on the part of the former of some special character which renders them *per se* more acceptable, more evident, less disputable, and so on; the mathematical logicians regard postulates as propositions *on a par with all the others*. The choice of such "postulates" may differ according to the *end* in view, and must, in any case, depend upon an examination of the relations of dependence or connection which may be established between these "postulates" and the remaining propositions of a given theory, and upon a comparison with the form into which the treatment as a whole would develop under conditions of varying choices. If the relations between postulates and dependent propositions might formerly have been likened to those which subsist, in a state under autocratic *regime*, between the monarch or the privileged class and the rest of the social body, the work of the mathematical logicians has been somewhat similar to that of the inaugurators of a constitutional or democratic *régime*, under which the choice of the rulers depends, at least theoretically, upon their recognized ability to exercise temporarily determined functions, to the public welfare. Postulates have had to relinquish that species of "divine right" with which their pretended evidence seemed to invest them, and resign themselves to becoming, instead of the arbiters, the *servi servorum*—the employees simply—of the great "associations" of propositions which make up the various branches of mathematics. With this same tendency are connected also the requirements regarding the maximum reduction of their number and pregnancy, the exact determination of their applicabilities and spheres of validity, and so forth.

A second resemblance, of not less importance, between the pragmatists and the mathematical logicians appears in their common repugnance to the vague, indefinite, generic; and in their care to analyze every assertion into its simplest terms, whether referring directly to *facts*, or to *connections between facts*. It is thus that both constituencies have come, each for itself and in its own way, to recognize the unreality of a great part of the distinctions which have been handed down from Scholastic logic to the modern "theories of knowledge," and to subject others of these distinctions to critical analyses from which they have emerged in a sense transfigured, restored, enriched with new and more important significances. Thus, by introducing the conception of "possible definition" a clear recognition has been reached of the wholly relative character of the distinction between the "essential properties" of a given figure or mathematical entity and the other properties possessed by it. In like manner the distinction between affirmative propositions and negative, and that between particular propositions and general, have been absorbed in the one and more important distinction between propositions affirming the interdependence of two facts and propositions affirming the *possibility* or the "*non-absurdity*" of the coexistence of two or more facts. This involves, too, the invalidating of the distinction between categorical and hypothetical general propositions.

The recognition of the hypothetical nature of general propositions has also helped to turn attention to the "tacit restrictions," or unspecified limitations, upon which their validity depends. A good example of this is the observation of Maxwell (cited by Roiti in his *Elementi di Fisica*, 1894, p. 65 [Roiti 1887]): that even the simplest propositions as to areas, e. g., that "the area of a triangle is given by one-half the product of the base by the altitude," would cease to be true if, instead of taking as the unit of measure of areas the square with side of unit length, one were to take the triangle having such unit as base and altitude. These considerations are intimately connected with those by which the pragmatists have been led to a more precise determination of the difference expressed in ordinary speech by opposing "laws" to facts; and to put on an entirely new basis the classic controversy between determinists and freedomists. (See *Leonardo*, April, 1905, p. 57, and Poincaré, *Valeur de la science*.)[1]

A third point of contact between pragmatists and mathematical logicians consists in the interest shown on both sides for historical researches in the development of scientific theories. Both consider these essential as a means of recognizing the equivalence or identity of theories, under the various forms which they have assumed in different epochs or fields—all the time expressing substantially the same facts and serving the same ends. The logicians as well as the pragmatists have thus contributed to destroy a number of prejudices attributed to

---

[1] [See Vailati 1905, this volume, chap. 14, p. 194 and Poincaré 1905.]

supposed incompatibilities between the theories now current and the views of the great scientists or thinkers of antiquity. The fact has been brought to light that many, and those not the least important, among the discoveries of modern mathematicians, have consisted in nothing more than the introduction of new methods or notation for processes formerly employed or considered under other names by their predecessors. In the *Formulario* of Peano the importance given to historical data has steadily increased, especially under the inspiration of one of the principal collaborators, Vacca (among other things an enthusiastic investigator of the development of mathematics in the Far East);[2] and the importance attributed to articles of this kind now constitutes one of the most noteworthy among the distinctive characteristics of the method of treatment of the various branches of mathematics that the said *Formulario* presents.[3] Theories are therein expounded, not as in the ordinary treatment, under their "static" aspect—as one might express it,—their aspect of repose; but under that of movement and development—not in the conventional attitudes of stuffed animals, with glass eyes; but as organisms, which live, eat, struggle, reproduce: or at least like figures in a cinematograph, with some naturalness of progression and development. To this tendency to recognize the identity of theories, beyond or under differences of expression, symbolism, language, representative conventions and the rest, is to be attributed also the constant interest of the mathematical logicians in linguistic questions—from Grassmann, at once the author of the *Ausdehnungslehre* and of the *Wörterbuch zum Rig-Veda*, to Nagy, student of the transmission of Greek thought through the Syriac and Arabic commentaries; from Couturat, joint author with Leau of a History of the Projects of "Universal Language," to Peano, inventor and propagandist of one of the most practical among them: the *"latino non flexo."*[4]

Quite a different series of relations between pragmatists and mathematical logicians is offered by the important progress made by the latter in the theory of "definition." First of all, the traditional method which makes definitions consist in the search for *genera* and *specific differences*, i.e., in the search for classes from which the class to be defined may result through the mediation of a "logical product," has been broadened so as to include every case in which the class to be defined may be obtained *as a function* of known classes, by means of any previously admitted operation or series of operations.

---

[2] [See Vacca 1905.]
[3] [See Peano 1901.]
[4] [See Grassmann 1844, 1873, Nagy 1893, Nagy 1897, Nagy 1898, Couturat and Leau 1903, Vailati 1904, Peano 1903b, Peano 1903a, Peano 1904b, and Peano 1904a.]

In another direction the Scholastic methods of definition have been broadened by taking into consideration the cases in which that which is defined is not an isolated word but a group of words or phrases in which this word appears (*implicit definitions*). Hereby we have come to recognize more clearly than did, say, Aristotle, that definitions of isolated words are only a particular case, the simplest, in the vaster field of "implicit definitions." We see, for example, that to define a noun A signifies nothing more nor less than to indicate the sense which would be attributed to the phrase: "this thing or that is an A." Moreover it has become possible to characterize and justify the procedure, already instinctively followed by mathematicians, of employing successively diverse definitions of one and the same notation, according to the fields (whether inclusive or not) in which arises the opportunity of making use of groups of symbols in which this notation figures (definitions preceded by hypotheses limiting, and varying with, the variation of the definitions).

Particular interest, in their relations to pragmatism, is presented by what were called (Peano) "*definitions by abstraction*";[5] in which, from the fact that a given relation presents some of the characteristic properties of equality, occasion is taken to fashion a new concept: as, for example, from the fact that two straight lines parallel to a third are parallel to each other, is drawn the concept "direction"; or, from the fact that two amounts of merchandise exchanged for one and the same amount of a third commodity are mutually exchangeable, is evolved the concept "value."

A character common to the latter and to the other above-mentioned innovation, among those introduced by the mathematical logicians into the traditional theory of definition, consists in their tendency to bring to light the various orders of circumstances upon which may depend the fact that of a given word, taken by itself, a definition in the ordinary sense cannot be given; that is, a phrase cannot be enunciated which will indicate directly the characteristic or characteristics belonging to the objects to which the word in question is applied.

Not only has mathematical logic led to a recognition of the fact that to speak of the "definability" or "non-definability" of a given word or concept is to use a meaningless phrase, so long as no precise indication is given as to what *other words* or concepts may be used in the desired definition; but it has also afforded an explanation of the fact that many among the most important words of science and philosophy are found to be among those very ones of which it is unreasonable to ask

---

[5][See this volume, footnote 10 to chapter 16.]

or to seek a definition, in the Scholastic sense. Mathematical logic has thus contributed most efficaciously to the defence of the position of the pragmatists against the "agnostic" prejudice which attributes the impossibility of the resolution of such problems to a pretended incapacity of the human mind to penetrate the "essence" of things.

The so-called "definitions by postulates"—i.e., those which consist in determining the significance of a sign of operation or of relation by enunciating a certain number of norms which, by hypothesis, are to regulate its application—have, on the other hand, affinities with pragmatism in that they conduce to a clearer recognition of the arbitrary character of postulates, as well as of definitions. These appear in their true quality as propositions which possess the function of determining, in view of given ends or applications, the various fields of research; that is, as propositions whose sole justification consists in the importance and utility of the *consequences* which it may be possible to deduce therefrom.

Another characteristic of mathematical logic, in which, perhaps even more than in any of the afore-mentioned, is shown its affinity to pragmatism, is that which relates to the function which has come to be assumed by the search for and construction of "particular interpretations" or concrete examples, as criteria for determining the mutual independence, or the compatibility, of given affirmations or hypotheses. Originally considered as simply a means of ascertaining the *necessity* (indispensability) of given premises, or the impossibility of reaching determinate conclusions without their aid, this search for particular examples has come to be regarded as the *only* process capable of guaranteeing that any group of hypotheses does not contain "implicit contradictions." That is, the construction of concrete interpretations, by which all the premises or hypotheses underlying a given deductive theory may be simultaneously verified, has assumed the importance of a condition in the absence of which even the most rigorous lines of reasoning can lead only to conclusions liable to contradiction by others, which may be obtained through deductions not less rigorous *than the premises themselves.*

Furthermore, in the choice of examples *hierarchies* have come to be formed, according to their degree of concreteness and determinateness. To such of these as are the most concrete and determinate of all— i.e., to the examples which belong to the field of arithmetic—has been attributed for the above-mentioned purpose, by some, a superiority over all others; particularly over those which imply considerations of continuity, or which belong to fields in which it is found more difficult to effect an exact and complete characterization or formulation of the facts adduced.

In this need of reinforcement by particular facts which is inherent in the more abstract theories (and this need is in direct proportion to their abstractness)—not, indeed, a need of facts which shall serve to confirm or to render inductively probable the separate premises upon which they are based; but of facts which shall guarantee the possibility of the *coexistence* and *cooperation* of such premises:—in this need of pure logic to derive strength, like Antaeus, from periodic contact with the earth, one cannot fail to recognize one of the most significant indications of that mysterious alliance between "the extremes of theoretic activity" (the intuition *of the particular* and the impulse to abstraction and generalization) which it is not the least of the merits of the pragmatic theories to have noted and proclaimed.[6]

Pragmatists and mathematicians find themselves in agreement, too, in their efforts toward the maximum of *conciseness* and *rapidity* of expression—in their tendency to eliminate all superfluity and redundancy both of wording and of concept.

Both find the value of theories and doctrines not only in that which is said but also in what is *unmentioned* and whereof exposition or consideration is suppressed. See the article of Giuliano il Sofista on the Nourishment of Fasting (*Leonardo*, April, 1905).[7]

One of the principal achievements of mathematical logic consists in this very recognition of the fact that so many of what pass for *mathematical truths* owe their existence solely to imperfections of notation, which permit the enunciation of the same fact in different ways—to have afterward the pleasure of recognizing it as one and the same under its divers expressions. An example of this is to be found in the propositions of trigonometry, which reenunciate, in new garb, theorems of elementary geometry; and, furthermore, re-enunciate them in manifold forms, of which the trigonometrical identities do no more than to express the equivalence. By the introduction of other new symbols the number of "truths" of this kind might be increased indefinitely—repeating in science the miracle of the multiplication of the loaves and fishes; with the difference only that the results thus obtained would serve much more to distend than to nourish the minds to which they should be communicated. Indeed in this connection, as my friend G. Vacca observes, one might enunciate a law in form analogous to Malthus's Law, consisting in this: that when the concepts or the words which are introduced into a theory increase in arithmetical ratio, the corresponding proposi-

---

[6]See G. Papini, "Les extrêmes de l'activité théorique" (in *Comptes rendus du IIᵉ Congrès internationale de philosophie*). Genève: Kündig, 1905 [Papini 1905].

[7][See Prezzolini 1905.]

tions—whose truth or falsity the "science," to be complete, must needs decide—increase more rapidly than any geometrical progression (following an exponential law, enunciated by Clifford. See Peano, *Calcolo geometrico*, 1888).[8]

Against a similar fatty degeneration of theories pragmatism, likewise, represents an energetic reaction; insisting as it does on the *instrumental* character of theories affirming that they are not an *end in themselves*, but *media* and "organisms" whose efficacy and value is rigorously dependent upon their agility, upon the absence of encumbrances and hindrances to their movements, upon their resemblance rather to lions and tigers than to hippopotami and mastodons. The favorite dictum of Plato: "the half is preferable to the whole" is no less applicable to scientific theories than to any other branch of human activity.[9]

References

Couturat, Louis and Léopold Leau. 1903. *Histoire de la langue universelle.* Paris: Hachette.

Grassmann, Hermann. 1844. *Die Wissenschaft der extensiven Grösse oder die Ausdehnungslehre.* Leipzig: Wigand. Engl. transl. by L. C. Kannenberg, *A New Branch of Mathematics. The Ausdehnungslehre of 1844, and Other Works*, Chicago and La Salle, Illinois: Open Court, 1995.

Grassmann, Hermann. 1873. *Wörterbuch zum Rig-Veda.* Leipzig: Brockhaus.

Nagy, Albino. 1893. Notizie intorno alla retorica d'Al-Farabi. *Rendiconti della R. Accademia dei Lincei* .

Nagy, Albino. 1897. *Die philosophischen Abhandlungen des Ja'qub Ben Ishaq Al-Kindi.* Munster: Aschendorffschen.

Nagy, Albino. 1898. Una versione siriaca inedita degli Analitici d'Aristotele. *Rendiconti della R. Accademia dei Lincei* 7(12).

Papini, Giovanni. 1905. Les extrêmes de l'activité théorique. In *Comptes rendus du IIe Congrès internationale de philosophie*, pages 473–480. Genève: Kündig. Rpt., Nendeln, Liechtenstein: Kraus Reprint, 1968.

Peano, Giuseppe. 1888. *Calcolo geometrico secondo l'Ausdehnungslehre di Hermann Grassmann, preceduto dalle operazioni della logica deduttiva.* Torino: Bocca.

Peano, Giuseppe, ed. 1901. *Formulaire de Mathématiques.* Torino: Bocca-Clausen.

Peano, Giuseppe. 1903a. De latino sine-flexione: lingua auxiliare internationale. *Rivista di Matematica* 8:84–87.

Peano, Giuseppe. 1903b. Principio de permanentia: exercitio de latino recto. *Rivista di Matematica* 8:84–87.

---

[8][Peano 1888]

[9][In Greek in the text: κρεῖττον ἥμισυ παντός. This aphorism from Hesiod is quoted by Plato in *Republic* 466c and in *Laws* 690e.]

Peano, Giuseppe. 1904a. Il latino, quale lingua ausiliare internazionale. *Atti della Reale accademia delle Scienze di Torino* 39:273–283.

Peano, Giuseppe. 1904b. *Vocabulario de latino internationale, comparato cum Anglo, Franco, Germano, Hispano, Italo, Russo, Graeco et Sanscrito.* Torino: Cooperativa.

Poincaré, Henri. 1905. *La Valeur de la science.* Paris: Flammarion.

Prezzolini, Giuseppe. 1905. La nutrizione del digiuno. *Leonardo. Rivista d'idee* 3:60–63.

Roiti, Antonio. 1887. *Elementi di fisica.* Firenze: Le Monnier, 1894. 2 voll.

Vacca, Giovanni. 1905. Sulla matematica degli antichi cinesi. *Bollettino di bibliografia e storia delle scienze matematiche* .

Vailati, Giovanni. 1904. Recensione a L. Couturat e L. Leau, Histoire de la langue universelle, Hachette, Paris 1904. *Rivista Filosofica* 4. Repr. in Vailati (1911), pages 541–545.

Vailati, Giovanni. 1905. La caccia alle antitesi. *Leonardo* 3:53–57. Engl. trans. The Attack on Distinctions, *Journal of Philosophy, Psychology and Scientific Methods*, 4(25), December 5, 1907. Repr. this volume, chap. 14.

Vailati, Giovanni. 1906. Il Pragmatismo e la Logica Matematica. *Leonardo* 4(1):16–25. Repr. in Vailati (1911), pages 689–694.

Vailati, Giovanni. 1911. *Scritti di G. Vailati, 1863-1909.* Leipzig-Firenze: Barth.

13

A Study of Platonic Terminology[†]

Researches relating to the introduction and the changes in meaning of the technical terms of philosophy and logic present a striking contrast to analogous researches about the terminology of the physical sciences. Whereas, in the latter, the introduction of a new term, or of a new meaning for a term already in use, is generally due to the need of giving expression to some new idea or distinction, or of giving a name to some new object hitherto unknown; in the field of philosophy, on the contrary, the chief impulse to transformations of nomenclature arises from a totally different cause, *viz.*: from the inability of the terms referring to the more abstract ideas, which occur in philosophical researches, to retain for long the precise and well-defined meaning originally attributed to them, and from their tendency to become imbued with associations incompatible with the function assigned to them by those who introduced them.

That is, the majority of the changes in philosophical nomenclature are due to the need of substituting, for expressions that have become unfit to express a given idea clearly and with sufficient definiteness, other expressions in which the same idea or the same distinction is characterised in a form less apt to give rise to confusions or misunderstandings.

This is not the least important of the causes that combine to bring

---

[†]Translation of selected passages from "La teoria del definire e classificare in Platone e i rapporti di essa con la teoria delle idee" (*Rivista Filosofica Pavia*, January-February 1906), repr. in Vailati (1911), pages 673–679 [Vailati 1906a] and "Per un'analisi pragmatista della nomenclatura filosofica" (*Leonardo*, year IV, April-May 1906), repr. in Vailati (1911), pages 701–708 [Vailati 1906b]. Reprinted from *Mind*, New Series, Vol. 15, No. 60 (Oct. 1906), pp. 473–485 (Vailati, 1906c).

Logic and Pragmatism. Selected Essays by Giovanni Vailati.
C. Arrighi, P. Cantù, M. De Zan, and P. Suppes.
Copyright © 2009, CSLI Publications.

about the result that the contribution made by each philosopher, the advances and the improvements represented by his work, compared with that of his predecessors, are more difficult to recognise and appraise then the degree of originality of scientists properly so-called.

The historian of philosophy is far more exposed than are the historians of the sciences to the danger of mistaking for new opinions and discoveries what is only a new expression of ideas and distinctions recognised long ago, and of seeing contrasts and differences of opinion where there are only differences in the manner of representing and characterising the same facts and the same doctrines.

This danger is, however, rendered still more serious by another circumstance, which especially concerns those modifications of technical philosophical language which aim at expressing *new* ideas or *new* distinctions.

These modifications often present themselves, in the first place, not in the form of new *terms*, but in that of dew *phrases*, which, though composed of terms, each of which, in other phrases, continues to be understood in its usual sense, nevertheless assumes a different technical meaning in the phrase in question.

That the appearance of technical *phrases* of this kind should precede the introduction of technical *terms*, properly so called, is a natural consequence of the fact that the introduction of a new word, or the assignment of a new meaning to a term already in use, represents a greater divergency from ordinary usage than the attribution of a special meaning to some new combination of terms already in use, without any alteration of the meaning of these terms in any other combinations.

Among the words which lend themselves most easily to serve in this way the aims of philosophic language, appear, in the first place, as is natural, those which are called by logicians "*syncategorematic*," *i.e.* those words, which, like prepositions and articles, differ from the other parts of speech, precisely in this: *viz.*: that their meaning more strictly depends on, and is more subject to vary with, the contexts in which they appear.

It is only later, and when the meaning of the phrases thus introduced is sufficiently important to render their frequent repetition inevitable, that the need arises of some "*categorematic*" term (a noun or a verb) to express in a more concise way the idea or the distinction in question, *i.e.*, the need arises of having at one's disposal, for such an object, not only technical *phrases*, but also technical *terms*.

The cases in which such terms are not introduced by the same philosopher who introduced the use of the corresponding phrase, may induce the imprudent historian, who is more preoccupied with the changes in meaning of a given word than with the various expressions and the development of a given idea or distinction, to attribute the discovery of these last, not to the philosopher to whom it is really due, but to the one who characterises it for the first time by a special technical denomination.

No formal rule can better help us to avoid the danger of erroneous interpretations arising from either of these two causes than that which advises us to determine the meaning of every phrase or abstract proposition by means of the examination of the *consequences* which are involved in it, or the *applications* which are made of it, and to regard two phrases or propositions as equivalent, or as two ways of saying the same thing (Peirce), whenever they are employed, by any one who adopts them, as a means of arriving at the same particular conclusions.

The application of this criterion to the history of philosophy is only apparently inconsistent with the oft-quoted precept of Batteux that "we must never apply to the ancient philosophers the consequences of their premises or the premises of their conclusions."

In fact the *consequences*, referred to in our case, are not the consequences which the historian or the critic believes *can* be drawn from given affirmations of the philosophers studied by him, but the consequences which the philosophers themselves have drawn, or have shown that they believed could be drawn, from them.

An inquiry which seems to me especially adapted to serve as an example for the application of the general considerations expounded above is that which relates to the first phases of the development of that important distinction which is expressed in modern Logic by opposing the *connotation* of general terms to their *denotation*.

In those of the Platonic *Dialogues* in which there appears no technical term to indicate the characteristics common to the different objects designated by the same name, the problem of seeking such common characteristics is usually formulated in one or other of the following ways:

I. By the question: *What is* ? (τί ποτέ ἐστι), followed by the word whose signification is to be determined. E.g. *Gorgias*, 502, E; *Anterastae*, 133, B C; *Theages*, 122, C; *Alcibiades, minor*, 138, D, etc.

II. By asking: "Why (διὰ τί) or to what end (πρός ἄλλο τι τέλος ἀποβλέψαντες), (*Protag.*, 354, C-E) do you call the different objects in question by the same name?" In the same sense the preposition κατά is used, *e.g.*, (*Protag.*, 354 D C) κατὰ τόδε ἀγαθὰ αὐτὰ καλεῖτε; especially in the phrases: καθ' ὅ, καθ' ὅσον. Similar use is made also of the particles: ἦ, πῆ, ταύτη, etc., the first being often used as an equivalent of καθ' ὅσον. In the *Protagoras* πῆ is used correlatively with διότι.

III. By the phrases indicating *resemblance* or *difference*, followed by the preposition κατά or by the dative or any of the particles mentioned above.

IV. By asking what they call by the same name *in* each of the objects in a given class, or what is that which, being *in* them, makes them be what they are. *E.g.*, in the *Laches* (192), Socrates, after examining the different cases of ἀνδρεία asks: τί ὄν ἐν πᾶσι τούτοις ταὐτόν ἐστιν; adducing the example of the various kinds of velocity; τί ὅ ἐν πᾶσι ὀνομάζεις ταχυτῆτα εἶναι; and, similarly, in the *Hipparchus*, after speaking of good and evil gain: τί ταὐτόν ἐν ἀμφοτέροις ὁρῶν κέρδος καλεῖς; 230, E.

The meaning attributed to such questions is perfectly determined by the answers which are given to them, answers which consist in *defining* (ὁρίζειν) the word in question. *E.g.*, in the *Hipparchus*, 230 D, to the question: "What is there in common between good and bad food?" the answer is made: διότι ἀμφότερα ζηρά τροφή σώματός ἐστι· τοῦτο γὰρ εἶναι σιτίον ὁμολογοῖς.

The prepositions, διά, κατά are, however, often used with the sense, as seen above, of the preposition, ἐν. *E.g.*, in the *Theaetetus* and in the *Meno*: ταὐτὸν διά πάντων, ταὐτὸν κατά πάντων. Also the analogous use of the preposition ἐπί (ταὐτὸν ἐπί πᾶσι) must be kept quite distinct from the other which is seen, for instance, in the *Protagoras* and in other dialogues, comparable, in its turn, to that of the preposition *of* in the phrases: "*Of* what is such and such a word the name?" and other analogous ones expressing denotation rather than connotation. *E.g.*, in the *Charmides* (175 B) and repeatedly also in the *Sophist* (218 G τὸ δὲ ἔργον ἐφ' ᾧκαλοῦμεν).

Other equivalent expressions are those in which the prepositions, παρά, πρός appear in composition with the verbs *to be, to become, e.g.*, παραγίγνεσθαι, παρεῖναι.

The metaphor implied in these expressions is used explicitly in the *Hippias major* (290) where beautiful things are said to be such through the *presence* of something, in the same way as great things are such by the presence *of the excess* by which they surpass smaller things.

But the above-mentioned ways of indicating the possession of a common-characteristic on the part of all the objects denoted by the same name were not sufficient to enable Plato to indicate so fundamental a difference as that which subsists between such characteristics and the objects which possess them.

One of the first manifestations of the need of having special terms at his disposal for such an object appears in the use he makes of the expression αὐτὸ τό, or even simply τό, as in the phrase (*Hippias major*,

287 D): οὗ τί ἐστι καλόν, ἀλλ' ὃ τί ἐστι τὸ καλόν; But the position occupied in the *Dialogues* by the search for the character, or the sum of the characteristics common to all the objects designated by a certain name, also rendered indispensable the introduction of a technical term to denote just that which was the object of the search.

It is not easy to determine what were the reasons that impelled Plato to choose for this office the term, εἶδος. It is, however, not the only term that is used by him for that purpose. There is even a Dialogue—the *Philebus*—in which he seems to have taken care to avoid the use of it, substituting ἰδέα (ἰδέαν ἔχειν, 127, 132, 134), φύσις (φύσιν ἔχειν, 122), τύπος (τύπος ἔχειν, 82, 113), μοῖρα (μετέχειν τῆς μοῖρας, 60 B) γένος, δύναμις, etc. We even find the phrases: φύσις τοῦ εἴδους, φύσις τοῦ γενοῦς used in a sense which differs little from that expressed, conversely, in the *Republic*, by εἶδος τῆς φυσέως. On the other hand, the term εἶδος itself, besides keeping, in Plato, all the sufficiently varied meanings which it has in the ordinary language, sometimes assumes, in phrases having a technical meaning, a signification remarkably different from that indicated above. E.g., in the phrase, ἐνί εἴδει περιλαμβάνειν, it seems to stand in the place of ὄνομα or λόγος. Cf. *Sophist*: ἐνί ὀνόματι περιλαβεῖν (226 E), (ibid.). In the fourth book of the *Republic*, courage, temperance, wisdom are often indicated as εἴδη, while at the same time the expressions εἶδος τοῦ πολεμίκου, etc., are used to indicate the different classes of society.

Both senses are combined in the phrase: ταὐτά ἐστι ἐν ἑκάστῳ ἡμῶν εἴδη καὶ ἤθη ἅπερ ἐν τῆ, πόλει. The first of these is, however, the one that predominates. E.g. (*Rep.*, 434, D) after defining in what Justice consists, the conclusion is reached that: ἐὰν ἡμῖν καὶ εἰς ἕνα ἕκαστον τῶν ἀνθρώπων τὸ εἶδος τοῦτο ὁμολογῆται καὶ ἐκεῖ δικαιοσύνην εἶναι (*Rep.*, 434 D).

Among the passages in which the meaning which is to be attached to such expressions comes out most clearly defined are to be included those in which the importance of recognising the distinction that they express is asserted in opposition to some interlocutor who refuses or neglects to make it, or fails to understand its significance. One of the most notable is that (*Meno*, 74) in which Socrates is represented in the act of protesting against the disposition of his interlocutor to think that, in order to answer the question: "What is ἀρετή?" it is enough to enumerate a certain number of ἀρεταί (of the man, the woman, the child, the slave, etc.). Socrates, after congratulating himself on the fact that, instead of a single thing of which he was in search, he had a swarm before him, insists, altering his question, on determining in what they agree. Resuming the examination of one of the ἀρεταί enumerated, justice, he asks if it is ἀρετή or *an* ἀρετή (ἀρετή τίς) and, taking the example of form (σχῆμα) and its particular cases (τὸ στρόγγυλον, τὸ εὐθύ) asks: "What is it which is equally present in each one of these (τί ἐστι ταὐτὸν ἐπὶ πᾶσι 75 A) and of which the word 'form' is the name (ὃ δὴ ὀνομάζεις σχῆμα)?" A perfectly identical situation is, as is well known, reproduced in the *Theaetetus* (147) when Socrates, ironically answering Theaetetus, who had enumerated to him a series of particular sciences, thanks him for having supplied him with many and various things instead of that one thing for which he had asked him (ἓν αἰτηθείς) and, again repeating the question, makes it more exact by adding: "The question is not to state how many sciences there are nor to enumerate them (ἀριθμῆσαι) but to know what science is *in itself.*" And the distinction is further elucidated by adducing the example of one who, being asked what mud (πηλός) is, instead of answering that it is earth mixed with water, "enumerates the various kinds of it: that used by potters, workmen in a furnace, etc.; and concludes by reproving Theaetetus for taking such a long and interminable (ἀπέραντον) road when it was in his power to answer easily and briefly.

The following is a passage in which the term εἶδος is more distinctly applied to express the contrast between the meaning or connotation of a general name and the whole of the objects which the name denotes: οὐ τοῦτό σοι διεκελευόμην ἕν τι ἢ δύο με διδάξαι τῶν πολλῶν ὁσίων, ἀλλ' ἐκεῖνο αὐτὸ τὸ εἶδος ᾧπάντα τὰ ὅσια, ὅσιά ἐστιν (*Euthyphr.* 5 D). The correspondence between the sense in which, in passages like this, the word εἴδη is understood and that which the word *property* has in modern Logic, is brought out still more clearly by the frequency of the phrases which recall precisely the image of possession: εἶδος ἔχειν (*cf. Hippias maj.*, 298 B; *Symposium*, 204 G; *Meno*, 72 G ; *Rep.*, IV., etc.).

With these phrases are classed also those in which the objects are said *to share* or have part in the possession (μετιεχειν, μεταλαμβάνειν) of a certain εἶδος, or to enjoy it in common (κοινωνεῖν).

It is to be noted, however, that these last suggest also at the same time another image, already applied, as was seen before also, in the use of the preposition *in*, and of the words indicating presence, *viz.*: the image of the εἴδη as ingredients or elements taking part in the composition of single objects and in the determination of those resemblances among them which justify their being called by the same name.

No less important than this metaphor of participation (μέθεξις) is the other of imitation (μίμησις) according to which the εἴδη are described as *models* and all things, on the other hand, as copies (ὁμοιώματα) of them.

A sample of a discussion of the difficulties connected with a too literal and material interpretation of both these metaphors is afforded us in the *Parmenides*, where Socrates tries to evade them by having recourse to other comparisons, *e.g.*, that of a *sail* spread over the heads of a group of people, or of the *day*, which is the same in different places, which comparisons are ably utilised by Parmenides for the deducing of more and more absurd conclusions, as confutations of the theory.

One striking point in this discussion is that in which Socrates explicitly declares that, by speaking of the *participation* of things in the εἴδη, his fundamental meaning is to express merely a resemblance between the εἴδη and the things corresponding to them. With which declaration it is useful to compare the well-known observation of Aristotle (*Metaph.*, I, 6) in which, comparing the Platonic theory of the εἴδη with the views of the Pythagoreans, he describes the former as consisting only in the mere substitution of one word for another (Πλάτων τοὔνομα μεταβαλών).

In contrast with other material objects, visible and tangible (ὁρώμενα καὶ μεταχειριζόμενα), the εἴδη are described as accessible only to the mind (διάνοια) and the reason (λογός, λόγισμος) (*Rep.*, vi., 134 A, 135 E).

The position taken up by Plato when dealing with those who for such a reason refused to admit that the εἴδη were *something*, is represented in the clearest manner in the *Sophist*, where the *stranger*, after laying stress on the necessity of exactly defining what must be understood by *existing* (τί ποθ' οἱ λέγοντες αὐτὸ [τὸ ὄν] δηλοῦν ἡγοῦνται—τί ποτε βούλεσθε σημαίνειν ὁπόταν ὄν φθέγγεσθε, *Soph.*, 244 A) brings forward, poetically comparing their opposition to the struggle of the Titans against the Gods (γιγαντομαχία),on the one side those for whom what exists is only what can be grasped and seen, and on the other those who affirm and strive (βιαζόμενοι) to establish the existence of incorporeal things, only to be apprehended by thought. Both parties, *i.e.*, both those who refuse to describe as *existing* what they cannot touch and press with their hands (ταῖς χερσί πιέζειν) and the others whom he describes as the friends of the ideas (τῶν εἴδων φίλοι) are induced to admit that everything *exists* which has any capacity (δύναμις) for acting and suffering actions (ποιεῖν ἢ παθεῖν) in however small a degree (καὶ σμικρότατον) and *even only for once* (καὶ εἰ μόνον εἰς ἅπαξ, *Soph.*, 247. E). But Plato is not contented with concluding that the εἴδη exist (εἶναι τί) . They are for him something even more truly existing (ἀληθῶς ὄν) than material things, something superior to them in value and power (πρέσβει καὶ δυνάμει ὑπερέχοντα, *Rep.*). The argument by which he most frequently supports his assertion consists in saying that it is by the εἴδη, by their presence or by resemblance to them, that material things themselves exist and *are what they are.*

A comparison of this phrase with the others in which the capacity of beholding the εἴδη is described as a necessary condition of being able to reply to questions of the type: *What is such a thing?* and of deciding whether an object deserves or not to be called by a given name (*Euthyphr.*, 6 E., εἰς ἐκείνην ἀποβλέπων καὶ χρώμενος αὐτῇ παραδείγματι ὃ μὲν τοιοῦτον ἂν 'ῇ, φῶ ὅσιον εἶναι ὃ δ'ἂν μὴ τοιοῦτον μὴ φῶ; *cf.* also *Meno,* 72 G) suffices to convince us of the perfect correspondence of the sense attributed by Plato to the word with that which the word assumes in Aristotle, and also with that now expressed by the words *meaning* or *connotation.*

The very observations which have been made on that phrase of Porphyry (*Isag.*, c. iii.) in which the *essential* properties of a given thing are defined as those with the cessation of which it would cease to be what it is, may in fact be applied here also, inasmuch as to say that it is by the presence of a given εἴδος or by resemblance to it that a given thing is, or continues to be, what it is, is not fundamentally different from saying that it is on account of such presence or resemblance that we call it by *its own* name and that we should cease to call it so if such presence or resemblance ceased or were shown to be illusory.

It seems to me indispensable to keep in mind the consideration mentioned above in order to recognise the meaning and force of the phrases in which the εἴδη are described as not subject to change and alteration (μεταβολὴν ἡτινοῦν οὐκ ἐνδεχόμενα—ἀλλοίωσιν οὐδεμίαν ἐνδεχόμενα, *Phaedo,* 78); as always equal to themselves (ὡσαύτος ἀεὶ ἔχοντα κατὰ ταὐτά—ἀεὶ κατὰ ταὐτὰ ὄντα, *ibid.*); as *pure* (καθαρός, ἄμικτά) in contrast to sensations which are *confused, mixed,* or *unstable, transient* (ῥέοντες), imperfect (ἐνδεέστεροι), incapable of perfectly resembling the εἴδη corresponding to them (οὐ δυνάται τοιοῦτον εἶναι οἷον ἐκεῖνο—προθυμεῖται πάντα ταῦτα εἶναι οἷον ἐκεῖνο, *Phaedo,* 74).

One of the most suggestive examples used by Plato to illustrate the contrast mentioned above is that which consists in contrasting *the equal in itself* (τὸ ἴσον) with *equal* things (τὰ ἴσα) which are always imperfectly so and always apt to cease to be so. It is difficult to find another that could serve better than this to illustrate the assertion, expressed by Aristotle (*Metaphys.*, xii., 4) that the first motive of the introduction of the εἴδη was the need of finding a defence or a point of support against the destructive tendencies of those philosophical theories, which, by insisting on the continual mutability and *corruptibility* of material things, seemed to remove every basis for any formal doctrine and to distrust any distinction whatever between vulgar opinions (δόξαι) and scientific knowledge (ἐπιστήμη) represented at that time especially by the mathematical sciences.

On this point it may be said that the theory of Ideas fulfilled to a certain extent the same office for these latter sciences as is now fulfilled for the physical and mechanical sciences by the so-called *law of causality*, inasmuch as this law also consists precisely in anticipating and imagining as existing among phenomena regularities and uniformities greater than, and surpassing, those which superficial observation could have made to appear possible.

The characteristics of invariableness, purity, and precision which, as we have seen, were attributed by Plato to the εἴδη, do not, in fact, differ from those which are attributed by modern logicians to *natural laws* as contrasted with merely *empirical* generalisations. There are passages in which Plato speaks of the analysis of, and search for the εἴδη, in terms which might be adopted, without any change, to describe the tracing of the single causes or laws which cooperate or combine in the production of a complex effect.

When the Platonic theory is divested of the ethical and aesthetic implications which, to a certain extent, constitute an accessory characteristic of it, it manifests itself as an energetic assertion of the right of the scientist or the philosopher to form or construct a more regular, simpler, more perfect world, than the one whose existence the data furnished by the senses and the inductions based on these data, would, by themselves, lead one to admit.

That is, it manifests itself as an assertion of the heuristic efficacy of that process of inquiry, which, taking as a starting point, idealistic and simplifying concepts and hypotheses, not having any exact counterpart in what is called the *reality of things*, arrives, precisely by means of deductions from these, and by means of what have been recently called (Mach) "experiments in thought" (Gedankenexperimente) at analysing, comprehending, dominating this reality and discovering in it and under it, independently of recourse to direct experiment, regularity, laws, standards, which direct and passive observation would never have been able to reveal.

So understood the theory of ideas appears more intimately connected than would be generally admitted with the other great innovation in method attributed to Plato, *viz.*: the employment of deductive reasoning in the choice and the rejection of the various hypothetical alternatives which present themselves as possible with regard to a given subject.

Plato found an example of the efficacy of both these processes together in Astronomy, understanding that term, as the Greeks always understood it, to mean the science that aimed at explaining and *reduc-*

ing to order (συγκοσμεῖν, to use the word employed by Aristotle (*De Caelo*, ii., 13), almost in jest, against the Pythagoreans) the irregularities and anomalies of the apparent motions of the stars on the celestial sphere, making them result as consequences of certain hypotheses with regard to their real motions in space.

It is in these first applications of mathematical doctrines to the explanation and prevision of the phenomena of the physical world, that Plato found the most convincing proof and confirmation of the power that the human mind is capable of acquiring by means of the logical discipline by which it is enabled, to use the phrase of Timaeus reported by Proclus (in *Eucl.* i.), t,o recognise as connected and akin things apparently most diverse and opposite (φίλα τὰ μαξόμενα καὶ συμπαθῆ καὶ προσήγορα τὰ διεστῶτα, *Prologus*, i., 22) *i.e.*, to trace, in the chaos of the facts which present themselves to observation and experiment, the invariable laws to which these facts conform.

Of the position in which Plato maintained that the philosopher and the scientist stood in this respect, he gives us a symbolical representation in the famous image of the cave and the bound prisoners in it who were obliged to look only at the shadows projected on a wall by objects passing behind their backs.

It is to this very situation that the sentences refer, in which the study of geometry is described as having an *elevating* (ὁλκὸν ψυχῆς) and *purifying* force; as capable of rekindling that organ of the soul, which, stained and blinded by all sorts of occupations, is more precious and worthy of being cared for and protected than ten thousand eyes. (ὁλκὸν ψυχῆς ἐκκαθαίρεταί τε καὶ ἀναζωπυρεῖται, ἀπολλύμενον καὶ τυφλούμενον ὑπὸ τῶν ἄλλων ἐπιτηδευμάτων, κρεῖττον ὂν σωθῆναι μυρίων ὀμμάτων, *Rep.*, 527.)

No less intimately connected with the subject of the meaning of general terms is the use which Plato makes of the word εἴδη in the phrase: κατ' εἴδη διαιρεῖ, and other analogous phrases which appear chiefly in the *Dialogues* which are considered to be the later ones.

It is not always easy to decide when, in such phrases and analogous ones, the word εἴδη is to be understood in the usual sense of "class," like γένος, μέρος, and when, on the other hand, in the sense of character, as it seems, for instance, that it must be understood in the *Cratylus* (424 G).

Such an ambiguity is rendered still more serious by the fact that the preposition κατά may be interpreted at the same time as equivalent to the Latin *in* (e.g., in the phrase: dividere in partes) or to the Latin *secundum*, in the sense of "according to."

In the *Phaedrus*, the proceeding of one who divides (ὁρίζομενος) is represented as correlative with, and complementary to, the other which consists in uniting under one and the same concept facts or objects apparently different, and both are described as contributing equally to constitute the true art of discussing (διαλεκτική) (*Phaedr.*, 265 D).

The same distinction is also referred to in the passage in *Rep.*, vi. in which those who are capable of *dividing* κατ'εἴδη are contrasted with those who, being incapable of emancipating themselves from verbal suggestions (κατὰ τὸ ὄνομα διώκοντες), are more disposed to litigate than to argue (ἔριδι οὐ διαλέκτῳ χρώμνεοι), *Rep.*, vi., 454 A, B. Similarly, in the *Politicus*, the method of dividing *by species* (κατ' εἴδη διαιρεῖν) is described as the best calculated to render people capable of inquiry and discussion.

Such a method is there (263) described still more precisely by the citation of examples of cases which do not conform to it, among the rest that of the division of men into Greeks and Barbarians, to which Plato objects as being based on ignorance of the fact that the nations included under the single denomination (μιᾷ κλήσει) of Barbarians differ less from one another in language and race than the Greeks from each of them. Similar remarks are repeated with regard to other divisions, *e.g.*, that of animals into two classes, one including men, and the other all other animals, as if the latter became a class solely by the fact that there is at our disposal a single word ("beasts," θηρία) to denote them all. With the same right, he adds, any other animal, *e.g.*, the cranes, if they were to occupy themselves with classifications, might divide animals into two classes, one including themselves, and the other all the rest, not excluding men.

No less suggestive is the other example of defective division, which is also adduced by Plato, *viz.*: that of the man who should divide numbers into two classes, one composed of those under, *e.g.*, ten thousand, and the other including all the others. By citing in contrast to this the other division of numbers into even and uneven, or of human beings into men and women, he seems to wish to indicate, as by the phrase: *dividere* κατ' εἴδη, still more than divisions according to certain properties, he means divisions according to qualities which are *important* because of their consequences. Inability to divide κατ' εἴδη is compared in the *Phaedrus* to the inability of the bad cook who does not know how to cut meat without breaking bones.

From the point of view of terminology, that passage of the *Politicus* is important in which a difference of meaning is established between εἶδος and μέρος, by assigning to the term μέρος the office of denoting more particularly the classes which do not satisfy the requirements of the διαίρεσις κατ' εἴδη. This difference is defined still more precisely by saying that every εἶδος gives rise to a μέρος but not every μέρος to an εἶδος. And moreover allusion is made to it in the phrase: τὸ μέρος ἅμα εἶδος ἐχέτω (Politicus, 262 B), by which he prescribes that every class ought to be determined by the presence of some characteristic common to all the objects that belong to it, and to them alone. In the Politicus as well as in the Republic, the words μέρη, μορία, are used to denote the various individual qualities which contribute to constitute one complex quality, e.g. (Politic., 290 G) mention is made of διακόνου τέχνης μορία, and hence they assume a meaning which is very nearly akin to that which is attributed to them when they are used in speaking of parts of the connotation of a term.

The image of the general characteristics as constituent parts or ingredients of the objects and concrete facts (πράγματα),already implied, as we have seen, in the phrases expressing participation, is brought still more clearly into relief by the comparison to which Plato often has recourse (Theaetetus, Politicus), like Galileo, and Huygens in later times, of scientific inquiry, to the efforts of one who is learning to read or to decipher a writing.

In connexion with this comparison, the εἴδη are described as the elements (στοιχεῖα) which, by their transposition (μετατιθεμέναι) and combination (συμμίγνυσθαι) give rise to those more complex groups (συλλαβαί, συμπλοκαί) which are concrete facts (Politic., 278, B, C ; Sophist, 253).

In this Plato is pretty near to conceiving the analogy between the relation of a whole to its parts and the relation that subsists, on the other hand, among the characters of a species and those corresponding to the different genera to which it belongs; an analogy expressed by Aristotle so clearly and explicitly in the fourth book of the Metaphysics, when he says that the name of parts may be given as well to the various classes into which a genus is divided as to the single characters that compose the definition of a species (ἔτι τὰ ἐν τῷ δηλοῦντι ἕκαστον καὶ ταῦτα μορία τοῦ ὅλου), and that, in the first sense, the species is a part of the genus, in the second, the genus is a part of the species: διὸ τὸ γένος τοῦ εἴδους καὶ μέρος λέγεται, ἄλλως δὲ τὸ εἶδος τοῦ γένους μέρος (Metaphys., iv., 23).

References

Vailati, Giovanni. 1906a. La teoria del definire e classificare in Platone e i rapporti di essa con la teoria delle idee. Rivista Filosofica Repr. in Vailati (1911), pages 673–679.

Vailati, Giovanni. 1906b. Per un'analisi pragmatista della nomenclatura filosofica. Leonardo 4. Repr. in Vailati (1911), pages 701–708.

Vailati, Giovanni. 1906c. A study of Platonic terminology. *Mind* 15(60):473–485.

Vailati, Giovanni. 1911. *Scritti di G. Vailati, 1863-1909*. Leipzig-Firenze: Barth.

14

The Attack on Distinctions[†]

To discover differences and contrasts between things that resemble each other and to find points of similarity between dissimilar things are two kinds of mental activity which, although they appear opposite and contrary, are often found united. To employ them by turns is no less indispensable to progress in any kind of knowledge than are the two opposite movements of a piston to the rotation of the wheel which it sets in motion.

Their relative importance, however, varies in the different fields of research, and as there are sciences, or phases of scientific development, in which the first predominates, so there are others in which the tendency prevails to distinguish or establish oppositions and contrasts among facts instead of connections or analogies.

It may be asked into which of the two classes in particular do the speculations of philosophers fall?

If the Scholastic precept "Distingue frequenter" seems to assign in these greater importance to the determination of differences, on the other hand the usual conception of philosophy as the search for the highest generalities, the universal, the absolute, etc., would seem to justify a diametrically opposite conclusion.

And of this latter conclusion it may be thought that we have further confirmation when, instead of attending to what philosophers have told us of their doings, we proceed to examine what they have actually done or are wont to do.

[†] "La caccia alle antitesi," *Leonardo*, 3:53–57, April 1905, repr. in Vailati (1911), pages. English translation reprinted from *The Journal of Philosophy, Psychology and Scientific Methods*, Vol. 4, No. 26 (Dec. 19, 1907), pp. 701–709 (Vailati, 1905).

As a matter of fact, the form under which results of philosophical inquiries appear to us is not that of the recognition or determination of fresh distinctions and differences, but, on the contrary, that of the criticism or rejection of distinctions commonly admitted.

Before drawing from this fact a conclusion favorable to the conception of philosophy as an activity predominantly unifying and aiming at the suppression of every distinction and opposition, it will, however, be opportune to examine the different modes by which philosophers have proceeded in their struggles against distinctions and differences. These various modes, as it seems to me, may be divided into the three following classes:

1. Those which consist in showing that there exists no precise line of demarcation between facts which are regarded as distinct, *i.e.*, in showing that the transition from one set to another is made by a series of intermediate gradations or shadings, in which the characters supposed to be distinctive are reconciled and the contrast between them disappears or becomes intangible.

2. Those which consist in showing that the properties in which the difference between the two classes of facts in question is supposed to consist, are possessed in equal degrees by both these classes, or by neither. As, for example, when the distinction between *egoism* and *altruism* is disputed by saying that even the so-called altruistic motives or aims are not effectual except in so far as those who are stimulated to action by them regard the result of the action as desirable and pleasing and regard its non-realization as a pain or want of satisfaction to themselves.

3. Those which consist in showing that the property, or properties, whose presence or absence is taken as a criterion of the distinction can be regarded, at the same time, as possessed and not possessed by any one of the objects in question according to the choice of the other objects with which we compare it. This is the case of the so-called *relative properties*, or *properties of relation*. So, for example, with numbers, the contrast between the words *preceding* and *succeeding* does not correspond to any distinction among them inasmuch as the fact that a number follows another does not prevent its preceding in its turn the one that follows itself.

Now, as to the processes of the first class, it is evident that the distinctions which they aim at destroying vanish only to reappear under another form, or even to return—like the demon, in the Gospel story, cast out of the man possessed—accompanied by other distinctions more powerful, and able to resist every further effort of dissolving analysis.

For instance, in answer to one who thought that the antithesis between "unity" and "plurality" could be destroyed by saying that from the *one* transition may be made to the *many* by successive additions, it might be observed that this is equivalent to a recognition that there are so many classes of *plurality*, *i.e.*, that, besides the distinction between the me and the *many*, there are others between the different *manys*, and that, therefore, by attempting to destroy the distinction in question he at once brings a hornet's nest about his ears, like the monkey in the fable who, being angry with his image reflected in a mirror, broke it in pieces and only succeeded in multiplying the figure which he had expected to annihilate.

Nor is it to be believed that more success attends attempts of the second class, those by means of which the value of a distinction is disputed by showing that some of the characteristics which were supposed to differentiate the two classes established by them are common to both.

A typical example on this point is offered us by the criticism of the distinction between the mere succession of two facts and what is expressed by saying that one of them has *produced*, or has been the *cause* of, the other. The result of such criticism has been to make it more apparent what are the distinctive characteristics whose possession confers, on the successions to which the names of "cause" and "effect" are applied, such superior importance in comparison with all the other classes of successions that experience presents to us.

"To say that a given fact is 'produced' by another," observe the critics of the idea of cause, "means nothing more than this: that the first has been succeeded by the second and that we have reason to believe something similar to the second will happen every time that anything happens similar to the first: and that something similar to the first has happened whenever anything happens similar to the second."

But surely this does not imply that all successions are of the same theoretical and practical importance. It is rather an acknowledgment that, among them, are some whose investigation contributes, in a particular way, to widen the field of our previsions and actions, and which, just on that account, deserve to be kept distinct from all others— whatever, on the other hand, may be the name that is adopted for this purpose.

The case of distinctions to which only greater prominence is given by every effort directed to the obliteration of the line of demarcation established by them is not the only one to be considered among those of the second class, mentioned above. Another case, no less important, is that of distinctions in regard to which such efforts, although they do not succeed in destroying, nevertheless succeed in *shifting*, the aforesaid line of demarcation, carrying it on to intersect one or other of the two classes which it at first separated.

Such shifting, however, is not followed by the complete disappearance of the original line of separation, but in most cases only by a diminution of its importance in comparison with the new one which is introduced.

If the latter absorbs and attracts to itself some of the offices of the first one, this may, nevertheless, still keep some others of them, and eventually acquire new ones which it did not possess at first. It not seldom happens that a distinction, by such successive transplantings and shiftings, gives rise to a series of subordinate distinctions or "segmentations."

The position which is finally assumed by the original line of demarcation corresponds ordinarily to a distinction of greater importance than those corresponding to the successive positions abandoned by it. Sometimes, however, the distinction in question, after having served to produce a series of others, more or less important, is finally reduced to cutting, so to speak, in the void, like a blade which has under it none of the material which it is intended to cut.

Of all the various changes that ordinarily accompany what we may call the *shifting of distinctions*, we have an example in the history of the distinction between *appearance* (phenomenon) and *reality* (essence, noumenon).

The very word "phenomenon," from its use as a technical term in Greek astronomy denoting the contrast between the "apparent" motions of the sun and the stars in the celestial sphere and their real motions in space, seems to have been very soon transferred by philosophers (Democritus) to denote, by analogy, the contrast between the properties of bodies which "appear" to our senses (colors, flavors, etc.) and their *real* structure, consisting of the respective positions and motions of the indivisible particles (atoms) of which they were supposed to be made up.

The word thus assumed the fresh office of distinguishing the properties which in later times were called the *secondary* properties of bodies from the so-called *primary* properties (such as form, resistance, weight, etc.). But even here a new shifting could not be long in taking place. Philosophers did not fail to ask themselves what reasons there were for conferring any privilege on these last properties on account of their being perceived "by means" of our touch or muscular contractions instead of "by means" of our eyes or our palate. To believe that a thing which we *feel extended* is *really extended*, observed they, is as unreasonable as to believe that a thing which we *see* red or green is "really" so, in itself, independently of our visual organs.

To find a new employment for the distinction, which thus became useless, two ways were open. It was possible, in conformity with the common use of the words, to employ it in the humble office of distinguishing the impressions of the man awake, with his senses in their normal condition, from those of one under hallucination. That would have led philosophers to a clearer recognition of the properties by which the former are distinguished from the latter (coherency, their being common to more than one person, their ability to be foreseen, etc.). Unfortunately, other prepossessions (especially sentimental ones) spurred on philosophical speculation in a diametrically opposite direction. From the admission that all properties, known or knowable, of bodies were alike "apparent," the conclusion was inevitably drawn that to ask whether bodies do really exist, would be to raise a question beyond the limits of the capacity of the human mind—a question to be classed among the insoluble "enigmas" of the universe. With this last evolution, the word "phenomenon" finally came to denote anything of which one might speak, knowing what he is talking about, and its contrary (noumenon, thing in itself) to denote nothing but our desire to have at our disposal a word that has no meaning.

It remains for us to consider the third of the three methods employed by philosophers in the criticisms of distinctions. It consists in claiming for a distinction concerning comparisons or relations between different objects a sense independent of the consideration of such comparisons and relations, and in regarding the fruitlessness of the attempts directed to such an aim as a proof of the unreality and invalidity of the distinction in question.

An example will explain better how this comes about. It is difficult to find, in the whole field of logic, a distinction which is so radical and important as that between affirmation and negation. And this is so, notwithstanding the fact that to ask oneself whether a given proposition is affirmative or negative, has as little sense as to ask oneself whether an object is larger or smaller without stating with what other object one wishes to compare it. There is, in fact, no affirmation that can not be regarded as the negation of some other affirmation, and if we disregard grammatical niceties, it is just as exact to say that every affirmation is a negation as to say that every negation is an affirmation. But shall we then have to say that there is no difference between affirming *anything* and denying it? The true distinction, therefore, is not between propositions of one class and propositions of another, but between *every* proposition and the *corresponding* negation, in the same way as the words "east" and "west" do not express any quality of the regions to which they are applied, but only indicate that these regions are in a given situation with regard to each other.

The illusions occasioned by the above-mentioned tendency to interpret a sentence which expresses a relation between different objects as if it must have a meaning for each of them taken separately, has some affinity with those exemplified by that class of sophisms which Scholastic logic describes as taking what is said *secundum quid* as if it were said *simpliciter*, *i.e.*, the sophisms consisting in passing from an affirmation which is only true under certain restrictions, or in relation to given circumstances, to another in which such restrictions are lost sight of.

The only difference between the one case and the other is this, that, in our case, the conclusions arrived at can not even be false, inasmuch as the sentences which enunciate them have no meaning at all, as if one were to say, for instance, that two quantities were proportional without saying to what other two, or that a straight line was perpendicular without saying to what straight line or superficies.

Among the most characteristic and instructive cases of this class must certainly be placed those furnished by the recent discussion on the axioms of mechanics, especially on the meaning of the law of inertia.

The usual way of enunciating this law is liable to the objection that to assert that a body is moving in a straight line and with uniform motion can have no meaning, unless we determine:

1. To what body, supposed to be fixed, the successive positions of the body declared to move in a straight line are to be referred. A straight line drawn on a sheet of paper, while it is moving, does not imply a rectilinear motion of the point with which it is drawn; and, *vice versa*, given any motion of a point, the possibility is never excluded of so moving a sheet of paper in relation to it as to obtain a straight line upon the paper.

2. What is the measure that we adopt for *time!measure of*; in other words, by what standard are two successive intervals of time to be judged as equal or unequal. For instance, according as we choose for that purpose the apparent motion of the sun or that of the fixed stars, the same motion will appear uniform or not uniform; and no appeal can be made here, as in the case of two persons whose clocks do not agree, to any common criterion, since it is just on the choice of the criterion that the dispute turns, *i.e.*, the choice of the "standard" motion by which all others shall be measured. To say that the motion adopted as "standard" is uniform, without saying *with regard to what other motion* (just as, in the case of points of reference, to say that a body is stationary without saying in regard *to what other bodies*), is as unreasonable as to say that

a man is a "contemporary" without saying of what other person.

Attempts have not been lacking to draw—from the admission of the dependence of the law of inertia on the choice of points of reference and of a fixed measure of time—the conclusion that such a law is only the result of a convention and does not correspond to any real fact, as if the very *possibility* of choosing points of reference and measures of time, in regard to which the law of inertia subsists, were not itself a fact: a fact of which we only take advantage in order to construct our science of mechanics, in the same way as we take advantage of the weight of lead to make a plumb-line, or of the instability of certain chemical compounds to make lucifer matches. If the world in which we live did not furnish us with this *fact*, no choice of conventions could combine to create it, or even to conceal its absence. The only difference between it and the more ordinary facts of our experience consists in its complexity, which is due to its implying the consideration, not only of the motion of a body with regard to another body, but also the comparison of one motion with another motion.

Distinctions based on properties that can at the same time be said to be possessed or not possessed by a given object, according to the other objects with which it is compared, are so far from being less important than others that they even form the principal object of scientific research, and tend ordinarily to acquire more prominence and importance in a science in proportion to the growth of that science in precision and power.

To prove this, we need only observe the prominent place that distinctions of this kind occupy in the sciences to which mathematical methods can be applied. To the example from mechanics, mentioned above, many others might be added no less instructive, from the distinction implied by the idea of "mass" to the more complex distinctions which come into play in other branches of physics and presuppose the choice of even more artificial points of reference and of many units of measure. The special feature of such distinctions is that the words which express them can only be defined indirectly, *i.e.*, by stating the meaning of a whole sentence in which they appear, as is the case, for instance, with the word "ratio" (λόγος) as used by Euclid, which he only defines by explaining the meaning of the assertion that the two quantities "have the same ratio to each other" as two others.

After having thus passed in review the various methods employed by philosophers for the criticism of distinctions, and having stated how each of them leads to a result diametrically opposite to the one at which it aimed, *i.e.*, leads to the increase rather than the decrease in the number and importance of the distinctions concerned, it will perhaps not be useless to consider some of the consequences which would result from the more deliberate and systematic applications of such methods to some of the most frequently discussed questions of contemporary philosophy. Let us take, as an example, the controversy between determinists and their opponents.

Taking as a point of departure what has been said before about the idea of *cause*, and keeping in mind a principle that both contending parties agree in admitting, viz., that, properly speaking, there are no facts that *repeat* themselves (in spite of appearances due to our disposition to notice only differences interesting to us), but only facts which have more or less resemblance to one another, the conclusion is inevitable that when we say the *same* causes are always followed by the *same* effects, what we mean is, in substance, this: that *effects* which *resemble* one another constantly succeed causes which *resemble* one another.

What is called the "principle of causality," in so far as it asserts nothing but the existence of certain resemblances among facts whose antecedents resemble one another, is, therefore, no more incompatible with a certain degree of indeterminateness in the "effects" of given "causes" than, for example, the laws of biological heredity are incompatible with the occurrence of *spontaneous* individual divergences and variations among the descendants of the same progenitors.

To say that the effect of a given cause is determined, can only mean that *some* of its characteristics are determined, in other words, that a class, more or less extensive, is determined, to which it must belong. Therefore, the only difference there can be between determinists and their opponents consists in regarding as possible a greater or less divergence and dissimilarity in the effects of causes having given degrees of similarity, *i.e.*, in a different estimate of the greater or less probability, or frequency, of such divergences in the various fields of scientific research, from physics and mechanics to psychology and the social sciences.

Determinism and indeterminism thus come to appear as the two extreme terms of a series of possible intermediate alternatives in which the alleged opposite characters of the two theories figure, mixed and combined in the most varied proportions.

To the above example of the application of the first of the methods, already mentioned, I will add another of the application of the second and the third. The criticism to which the idea of *quantity* has been recently subjected in the more abstract regions of mathematics has led, among other things, to a clearer recognition of the nature of the distinction between what are called "differences of degree" or "quantity" and other differences, which, in contradistinction to them, we call "differences of quality."

The conclusions arrived at on the subject may be briefly summed up as follows: Differences in *quantity* are only a *special case* of differences in *quality*. They are distinguished from the latter above all by the fact that the qualities, on which they are grounded, allow a fixed arrangement of the objects possessing them, that is, they can serve as criteria to distinguish, between any two of them, which precedes or follows the other in a certain fixed series of which they all form parts. Thus, for example, the resistance which different threads make to breaking gives rise to quantitative differences among them, inasmuch as of any two of them it can always be determined which will be broken more easily than the other. On the other hand, their differences, for example, of color (unless these concern only different gradations of the same color), can not be described as *quantitative differences*, because they are incapable of being employed as criteria for an arrangement in which a certain place belongs to each of the threads.

But if the aforesaid condition is indispensable in order that given differences may be described as *quantitative* differences, it is nevertheless insufficient to define completely the notion of quantity. For this we require the presence of further conditions, more directly connected with that special method of comparison which is denoted by the name of *mensuration*.

In other words, it is required that on the objects possessing the qualities in question some operation may be performed whose analogy to that of the arithmetical sum is sufficient to allow a precise meaning to be given to the phrase that one of them possesses the said quality in a degree double, triple, etc., that in which another possesses it.

Here also we have another example of the fact, already observed, that the methods employed by philosophers for the criticism of distinctions often result in the discovery of some new way of determining and justifying the distinctions which they aimed at destroying.

References

Vailati, Giovanni. 1905. La caccia alle antitesi. *Leonardo* 3:53–57. Repr. in Vailati (1911), pages 82–89. Engl. trans. "The Attack on Distinctions," *Journal of Philosophy, Psychology and Scientific Methods*, 4(26):701-709, December 19, 1907.

Vailati, Giovanni. 1911. *Scritti di G. Vailati, 1863-1909*. Leipzig-Firenze: Barth.

15

On Material Representations of Deductive Processes[†]

The difficulty of describing, representing, classifying, mental attitudes without having recourse to metaphors of a "physical" character has long since claimed the attention of philosophers. They have not failed to draw from it, according to their special preferences, the most opposed and disparate conclusions.

Thus, for example, while Locke ("Essay," III, 1.5 [(1690, p. 289-90)]) sees in it a proof and a verification of his thesis "that all our notions originate in sense impressions," Leibniz, on the other hand ("Nouveaux Essays," III., I.5 Leibniz 1764, pp. 289–91), seeks to draw from it conclusions favorable to the doctrine of the "primordiality" of space intuitions (intuitions of direction, distance, motion, etc.).

The advantages and inconveniences inherent in the use of these metaphors offer, however, a field of research which may be described as almost unexplored. The recent publication of a volume calling attention to the importance of this subject has afforded me an opportunity to express some observations on it.[1]

To one who proposes to make a systematic examination of the employment of physical metaphors as a means of representing mental facts two roads are open. As in hydrodynamics, when we wish to observe the

---

[†] "I Tropi della Logica," first published in *Leonardo*, February 1905, pages 3–7. Repr. in Vailati 1911, pp. 564–571. Reprinted from *The Journal of Philosophy, Psychology and Scientific Methods*, Vol. 5, No. 12 (Jun. 4, 1908), pp. 309–316 (Vailati, 1905).

[1] Lady Victoria Welby, *What is meaning?*, London, Macmillan, 1903 [Welby 1903].

Logic and Pragmatism. Selected Essays by Giovanni Vailati.
C. Arrighi, P. Cantù, M. De Zan, and P. Suppes.
Copyright © 2009, CSLI Publications.

motion of a liquid in a tube, we may consider a definite section of the tube, determining the velocity and direction of the various portions of liquid which pass successively through it, or we may, conversely, follow a given portion of the liquid, determining the various velocities and directions which it assumes in crossing the successive sections; thus here we may start from the consideration of a definite image, observing what are the various mental operations which it may be chosen to illustrate, or we may, conversely, start from a definite mental operation, and pass in review the different images by which it can be represented.

For any one having, besides a purely theoretical interest in analyzing the mechanism of mental processes, the comparatively practical intent of drawing, from such an analysis, some indications of the means of regulating the play of mental activities, researches of this second kind are found to be more important than those of the first. It is to one of them—that is, to the analysis of the various physical representations of the deductive process—that I propose here to direct the attention of the reader.

The various types of images adopted to express the fact that a given affirmation may be *deduced* from another can be roughly classified under the following headings :

I. Those in which recourse is had to the conception of "upholding" or "supporting," as, for instance, when it is said that given conclusions are "based" upon, or "founded" upon, given premises, or that they "depend" upon (or are "attached" to) them. It is thus that we speak of the "foundations" of geometry, the "basis" of morals, etc.

II. The metaphors of "ascending" or "descending," as when we speak of consequences which "descend" from or may be "traced up" to certain principles, or when we compare the "course" or running of an argument to that of a river, and speak of propositions which "derive" from, "flow" from, "spring" from, "emanate" from, the premises from which they are "drawn." In this same group we may collect also the metaphors of a biological character, in which consequences are regarded as "generated" from premises, and the premises as "roots," "germs," etc., of the corresponding conclusions.

III. The metaphors referring to the relation of "containing" or "including." These may be subdivided into two groups, according as the conclusion is regarded as "contained" in the premises, or the latter as "contained" in the conclusion. In the first case the premises are conceived as "implying" (*implicare*), in the second as "explaining" (*explicare*), the conclusion which is deduced from them. The deduction is thus often looked upon as an "analysis" or a "reduction," that is, as an operation analogous to the work of a chemist who decomposes a body into its elements.

A characteristic of the first two groups of metaphors, that is, of those by which deduction is referred to as a "supporting" or "a drawing" one assertion by or from another, consists in their lending themselves to the embodiment of one of the most radical objections that can be raised against deduction as a means of proof and ascertainment of truth. It is the objection frequently referred to by Leibniz as "difficultas Paschaliana de resolutione continuata,"[2] although Pascal was certainly not the first to raise it. (It has never ceased to be enunciated, under the most different forms, ever since the conception of deduction as a special kind of reasoning first occurred to the mind of the Greek sophists and rhetors.) It consists in observing that all processes in which an attempt is made to prove some assertion by deducing it from another must be based, in the ultimate analysis, upon assertions which, in their turn, can not be deduced from any other, upon assertions, that is, which can not be proved without recourse being had to some other process (induction, intuition, etc.) whose validity deduction can not guarantee; and that, therefore, the certainty which belongs to the conclusions of deductive reasoning can not in any way be held superior to that which we are disposed to attribute to assertions not to be justified by deduction. Deduction, therefore, far from being regarded as the type of mental process conducive to "sure" conclusions, should be looked upon only as a means of causing a greater number of assertions to participate in the certainty, which, quite independently of deductive reasoning, *some* of our beliefs *must* already possess. According to that conception of deductive reasoning, a man who only deduces could not be regarded as a *producer*, but simply as a *distributor* of "certainties"—a retail dealer in a commodity which his activity in no way contributes to bring about.

It is here worth noticing that whatever opinion we may entertain as to the existence or otherwise of premises which have no need of proof, it does not prejudice the question of the greater or less value of deduction, even if considered only as a means of ascertainment of our knowledge. Notwithstanding contrary suggestions, arising from images representing premises as "pillars" or "pegs" by which conclusions are "upheld," the advantages we derive, in regard to the certainty of our opinions, by recognizing that one proposition is deducible from another does not consist exclusively in the participation so acquired by the former in the greater certainty which the latter enjoys. The opposite case, in which the truth or certainty of conclusions, deducible from given premises, is apt to increase and consolidate the certainty of the premises them-

---

[2][See Couturat 1903, p. 220.]

selves, is no less frequent nor less important to be kept in view. The two advantages are very rarely found separated, in so far as there is hardly any branch of knowledge in which the premises are so indubitably secure that they can not receive further plausibility from their leading to conclusions immediately verifiable, while there is no assertion (except, perhaps, those relating to the so-called direct testimonials of our consciousness, in so far as they exclude all element of prevision) whose degree of credibility may not be, in some measure, increased by its agreeing with the consequences of some previously accepted belief.

The relation between premises and conclusion of a piece of deductive reasoning would not, therefore, be correctly described by saying that the latter is "supported" by the former, unless the common image of one object "supported by another" be substituted by the more general and more scientifically precise one of bodies which are "attracting each other," and which, when in contact, do support each other by reciprocal pressure. Of a pebble resting on a rock it is equally correct to say that the whole earth does support it as to say that the whole earth is supported by it.

Analogous observations may be applied to the image which represents conclusions as attached to the premises by means of a "thread" (or "chain") of reasoning. With this image also, in fact, the diffusion and communication of certainty are ordinarily conceived as acting *in one single direction*, *i.e.*, from the premises to the conclusions: no notice is taken of the fact that deduction may also act in the opposite direction, in the same way as the rope with which Alpine climbers fasten themselves in a dangerous ascent does. This rope is, in fact, a guarantee of safety to the last as well as to the first, or to any other among those who are bound by it.

Deductive processes in which the certainty of the assertions, which are taken as starting-point, is greater than the certainty of the conclusions to which they lead, are usually termed "demonstrations"; while those in which the contrary occurs, that is, those where given facts are attached to disputable premises, are usually described as "explanations." But the latter as much as the former are "deductive" processes, and in both cases there is the same need of all the apparatus and all the aids by which the operation of deduction may be made easier and more reliable.

To have taken knowledge of this—to have recognized that, even when the premises of a piece of deductive reasoning are less certain than the consequences drawn for them, it continues to be, nevertheless, important to proceed with rigor, with coherence, and with precision—is perhaps to be considered as one of the chief characteristics of the attitude of modern scientific thought as opposed to the one typically represented by Greek speculation. One is tempted to attribute to that circumstance the fact that the latter, while it showed the greatest constructive audacity in those fields in which, as in geometry, the firmness of the starting points (*axioms*) reached its highest standard, on the other hand, in fields, such as physics and mechanics, where this was not the case, it hardly succeeded in raising itself (except in astronomy) above a rough empiricism, as if it had been almost incapable of discerning any connection between facts besides those which offered themselves spontaneously to a passive observer not availing himself of any coordinating or selective preconception.

A corresponding tendency to depress and diminish the importance of deduction as compared with other processes of reasoning or of research is also countenanced by the metaphors of the third group above defined, *i.e.*, by the metaphors representing deduction as a process of "extracting" from premises that which is already "contained" in them.

To say that the conclusions of a piece of deductive reasoning are to be found, even "implicitly," "contained" in the premises, differs, indeed, very little from saying that they not only assert *nothing more*, but even assert *something less*, than what is already asserted in the premises themselves.

We know the manner in which the first great theorist of deduction, Aristotle, tried to carry this objection. He had recourse to another comparison, based upon his favorite contrast between form and matter. That is, he compared the work of one who deduces to that of the sculptor, who, by taking from a mass some of its parts, obtains something of greater value than the mass itself. If, however, instead of a statue he had spoken of an instrument or a weapon—say, of a key or of a dagger—also constructed by removing, from a given place in the raw material, certain parts whose presence would be an obstacle to the end which the instrument or the weapon was to serve, the comparison would have been also adapted to illustrate the power of deduction as an organ for the application of knowledge to the end of acquiring more of it.

In a certain sense the contrast between the process of deduction and that, purely or chiefly passive, of observation, contemplation, registration of the data of experience or of intuition, might even be compared to that between the operations of conscription, intended to secure the service of that part of a population which is fit to bear arms, and the operations of taking the census, directed only to the recognition and description of the state of population in a given country and time.

But, as we have already suggested, there is another direction, exactly opposite to the preceding, in which images referring to the relation of "containing" are capable of being employed as representing the relation subsisting between premises and conclusion in a piece of deductive reasoning. Premises, from which a given conclusion is deduced, may be regarded, not as "including" or "implying," the conclusion itself, but, on the contrary, as the more "simple" elements *of* which it is "composed" or *into* which it may be "resolved." It is the favorite image of Plato, when in the "Theaetetus" (200–208) he compares the fundamental premises of science to the letters of the alphabet (στοιχεία) from the combinations of which result syllables, words, phrases. And it was natural, as the very title of the works of Euclid shows, that this imagery should find special favor among geometricians, since no other is more fitted for refuting the objection of which we have spoken. In the light, indeed, of this comparison such an objection appears little less absurd than an attempt to dispute the genius or originality of a poet or of a musician by observing that all the words or notes used by him are registered in our dictionary, or in our gamut.

To this remarkable advantage which the images of deduction that we have called "chemical" offer in comparison with the other methods of representation before examined, there is, however, a drawback, consisting in their tendency to give rise to a false (too absolute) view of the contrast between simple and complex truths, and to present as the supreme ideal of scientific research the determination of propositions absolutely primordial, non-decomposable, atomic, capable of generating all others by their various aggregations.

This idea is found under its most determined form by Leibniz, in the comparison he establishes of truths with numerals, each of which, if it is not a prime number itself, is always apt to be decomposed, and in manner only, into a product of prime factors.

By such a metaphor as that, we are inevitably induced to lose sight of the fact that the question, whether a given proposition can be demonstrated or not, can only have a meaning if we determine what are the other propositions whose employment is to be permitted in the demonstration required.

When we speak of deduction as an *"analysis"* we must not forget that the properties of such an analysis are very unlike those of chemical analysis. In the latter, indeed, it could never happen, for example, that, among the "elements" out of which a given body is composed, some be found of which the body in question could also be considered as one of the "elements."

There is, in this last respect, a complete analogy between the process of deduction and that of definition. The latter also is, indeed, frequently represented as a process of decomposition or analysis of "ideas," or "notions" (or of the meanings of words), into more simple or more general notions or ideas. Both the relation of a complex notion to the more "elementary" notions it implies, and the converse relation of the group of individuals, coming under a given complex notion, to the other groups coming under the more "simple" notions by which the complex one is defined, are found in Aristotle[3] represented by the images of "*containing*" and of "*being contained*." Metaphors of the second group above defined, that is, those by which the passing from the premises to the conclusion is qualified as a "descent," and the seeking for the premises of a conclusion as an "ascent," or a "remounting," or "going up," have this in common with those of the type before examined, that they are applicable to the case of deduction as well as to that of definition. Defining also is, indeed, often described as a "tracing up" from particular intuitions to the more general conceptions "*under*" which they are comprised. So in the so-called "tree of Porphyry" the successive ramifications from the trunk represent notions ever more definitely determined, and which are obtained by the gradual introduction of successive specifications and qualifications, in the more general and comprehensive of all classes, *i.e.*, in the class constituted by all "existing things."

An inconvenience, not to be overlooked, which arises from this twofold employment of the metaphors of the last two groups considered— that is, from their being employed at the same time to express the relation between premises and conclusion and that between a notion and the more general notions implied by it—consists in this, that both tend to give plausibility to the conception of deduction as "a passing from the general to the particular," and to make us look upon the greater generality of premises, as compared with conclusions, as an essential characteristic of deductive reasoning. It is difficult to find a different explanation for this mode of conceiving deduction having found favor, in spite of the frequency with which demonstrative processes of quite opposite character (in which, that is, conclusions comprise some of the premises as particular cases) present themselves in the most deductive of sciences,—mathematics.

So far as regards the images which represent deduction as an "*ascent*" to principles, the aforesaid inconvenience is, however, broadly compensated for by the correspondence which they establish between the condition of one who places himself at the point of view of the premises of a deductive process and that of one who, observing a

---

[3] "the genus is called a part also of the species, and ... the species is regarded a part of the genus" *Met.* IV.25 [MacMahon 1896, p. 150].

panorama from a height, is in a position to perceive at a glance, between the various parts and regions which are before him, relations which would escape the notice of or be discovered with difficulty by one who was stationed lower down.

An analogous conception is also expressed by the phrases which characterize the process of demonstration or of explanation as a process of "throwing light," inasmuch as the presence of light has the effect of "economizing experiences" by rendering at once possible the recognition of the respective positions of objects: positions which in its absence could only be determined by subjecting oneself to the shocks and collisions inevitably ensuing from attempts to take direct cognizance of their situation.

Compared with this last metaphor, however, the one first considered, that of "ascent," presents the additional advantage of suggesting, besides the conception of seeing, that of command or power, as when we speak of a "commanding view" or of a height which "dominates" a given region.

References

Couturat, Louis. 1903. *Opuscules et fragments inédits de Leibniz: extraits des manuscrits de la Bibliothèque royale de Hanovre.* Paris: Alcan. Repr. Hildesheim-Zürich-New York: G. Olms, 1988.

Leibniz, Gottfried Wilhelm. 1764. *Nouveaux essais sur l'entendement humain.* Engl. transl. by Alfred G. Langley, *New Essay concerning human understanding,* Social Science, 2003.

Locke, John. 1690. *An essay concerning human understanding.* London: Tegg and Co.-Cheapside, 1849.

MacMahon, J. H., ed. 1896. *The Metaphysics of Aristotle.* London: G. Bell and sons.

Vailati, Giovanni. 1905. I tropi della logica. *Leonardo* 3:3–7. Repr. in Vailati (1911), pages 564-571. Engl. transl. "On material representations of deductive processes," *Journal of Philosophy, Psychology and Scientific Methods,* 5(12):309–316, 12 June 1908.

Vailati, Giovanni. 1911. *Scritti di G. Vailati, 1863-1909.* Leipzig-Firenze: Barth.

Welby, Victoria. 1903. *What is meaning?.* London: Macmillan.

16

The Grammar of Algebra[†]

When talking about algebra to some philologists and particularly when talking about it as a special language, I must beg them to be willing to attribute a slightly more generic meaning to the word "language" than the one they are used to attributing to it; to be willing, that is, to temporarily abstract away from a character in common to the languages that they study—all of which have "words" as elements—thus allowing me to apply the same name to other systems of signs which, although directed at senses other than hearing, nevertheless perform the same functions of the languages in the strict sense of the term.

Together, and preceding, the writing systems of the phonetic kind—based on a more or less satisfactory analysis and representation of the sounds or groups of recurring sounds in a spoken language—other writing systems of the "ideographic" kind have also been used since ancient times, in which the things about which information was exchanged were represented directly, without any reference to the groups of sounds that formed the name of such things in the spoken language.

To indicate the existence of certain relationships between the objects represented in this way, i.e. the relationships expressed in spoken languages by sentences or propositions, since the beginning the writings of the second kind had to use certain expedients (alterations in the shape or the order of the signs, etc.) that had an analogous pur-

---

[†] "La grammatica dell'algebra." First published in *Rivista di Psicologia Applicata*, n. 4, July–August 1908 (Vailati, 1908). For this translation we have used the version printed in Vailati (1911), where the original article was integrated with some passages added by Vailati when he used the article for a communication presented at *Congresso della Società Italiana per il Progresso delle Scienze* (Florence, October 1908), with the title "I caratteri grammaticali e sintattici del linguaggio algebrico."

Logic and Pragmatism. Selected Essays by Giovanni Vailati.
C. Arrighi, P. Cantù, M. De Zan, and P. Suppes.
Copyright © 2009, CSLI Publications.

pose to the purpose of inflections, prepositions, conjunctions, or signs of predication, interrogation, etc. in the systems of the first kind.

The examination of such expedients is particularly interesting for those systems of ideographic notations, like for example those used in algebra or music, that when used at the same time with ordinary writing, are exposed in a way to its competition, a competition to which they would have succumbed if not for some special characteristic that makes them preferable for the particular purpose to which they are applied.

In the case in which we are interested now, that of algebra, it is not enough to say that the reason for such preference lies in its predisposition to express with more brevity and precision the propositions regarding numbers and quantities. What is important is to determine how algebraic language attains the mentioned properties; that is, how much this is connected to the use of ideographic signs instead of words, and how much it is due instead to the fact that algebra uses means that are different from those of spoken languages to give meaning to the different combinations of signs used.

The use of digits in arithmetic presents us with a characteristic example of the difference between the two cases. The main advantage does not consist in the digits being shorter than the written names of the corresponding numbers, but rather in the ability that is attributed to digits to assume different meanings depending on the position they occupy in a number that has several digits.

It is my intention here to prove that the advantages presented by the algebraic language, not just as a means of expression but also as an instrument of research and demonstration, must be attributed to the kind of reasons mentioned above. These advantages are so relevant as to have induced one of the greatest algebraist of the eighteen century, Euler, to modestly ask himself the same question that Schiller asked a conceited poet in these famous verses:

If thou succeed with a verse
in a language worked out and consummate,
Shaping thy thought and thy rhyme,
think'st thou a poet thou art.[1]

In dealing with arithmetical questions, the comparison between the advantages that come with the use of digits and those which come with

---

[1] ["Weil ein Vers dir gelingt/ in einer gebildeten Sprache, // Die für dich dichtet und denkt,/ glaubst du schon Dichter zu sein." From Schiller's distich "Dilettant," appeared in the *Musen-Almanach für das Jahr 1797*, n. 88 of *Tabulae Votivae*. English translation by Paul Carus from Carus 1915, p. 59].

the use of the signs of algebra is also useful in highlighting another important distinction for our topic: that is the distinction that we have to make between systems of notations which, precisely like digits in arithmetic or musical notes, only have the function of describing, and breaking down certain groups of sensations or complex actions into their elements and the other systems which instead—just as in the case of algebra and of notations in chemistry—appear to be able to be used for the enunciation of true and proper propositions, and for the deduction of their consequences.

In cases of the first kind we cannot even say we are dealing with a particular "language," but rather with particular "nomenclatures." In fact in this case the signs and their combinations have no other purpose than that of building "names" indicating compound objects (for example, in the case of music, a chord or a melody) by means of the names (the notes) of the elements that compose them. Instead, in cases of the second kind, for example in algebra, the names which are composed in this way become part of new combinations with new signs, corresponding to those that grammarians call verbs, generating formulas, or propositions where something is stated which can be true or false, or where something is asked which is related to the objects in question.

This important class of signs is represented, in algebra, by the sign for equality ($=$) and by the two signs for inequality ($>$, $<$).

Between the simple "reading" of an algebraic formula and its "translation" into the words and sentences of ordinary language, there is a difference which anyone who has a sufficient familiarity with algebra is perfectly aware of—even when someone is not able to define it and characterize it in a precise way.

It is this difference that we have in mind when we talk about algebra as a special "language," and it is this difference that allows us to regard algebra as something more than a simple graphical artifice, or shorthand, introduced to represent the propositions about numbers and their properties in a way that is more concise and convenient than would be possible with ordinary writing.

The recognition of such a difference is equivalent to implicitly conceding that the particular effectiveness of algebra, as a means of expression and an instrument of research and demonstration, must be attributed not so much to the fact that symbols or ideographic signs are used instead of words, but rather to features of a "syntactic" nature, inherent in the way it uses them.

The question of examining closely the peculiarities of the algebraic language, or researching which features among them correspond to features that can be found, to a greater or lesser degree, in languages in the strict sense of the term, and other related questions, seem to me to deserve our interest, not only for those who want to analyze the logical procedures used in mathematical sciences, but also for those interested in a comparative study of languages and their different forms and structures.

Among the distinctions applied to the grammatical and syntactical studies of languages, the first kind encountered is that which is related to the classification and purpose of the different parts of speech.

"Language starts where interjections end" is a sentence often repeated by linguists,[2]—by which they try to determine what constitutes a specific feature of a real "language," in opposition to other less perfect forms of instinctive expression of feelings, such as those found in the inferior stages of animal life development.

If we ask ourselves, in turn, how the interjections actually differ from what the grammarians call the other parts of speech, we realize immediately that those are the only words that, even when uttered on their own, are sufficient in and of themselves to express some feeling, or some opinion, of the person who utters them, while the other kinds of words, such as nouns, adjectives, verbs, etc., cannot usually serve this purpose if not grouped together forming a sentence or a proposition.

When we utter, for example, the sound *brr*, or the sound *sst*, we do not need to add other words to make our interlocutor understand that we feel cold, or that we desire silence.

Instead if we utter for example, the name of an object without any other word (or gesture) to indicate what we mean about it—to declare, that is, whether we mean to say that we see it, that we desire it, or that we fear it, or that we are waiting for it to appear, etc.—we are not expressing any opinion or disposition, but we signal, at most, that we are thinking about that object, without saying anything about what we are thinking about it.

As a consequence interjections can be regarded as having more "meaning" than the other words in our language, and in a way, as the only ones that have some meaning per se, while the others are only able to acquire meaning when they are elected to be part of a sentence that has meaning.

The above mentioned assertion then, is the same as saying that "real

---

[2]I find it quoted, among the others, by G. Zoppi in his volume *Filosofia della Grammatica* [Philosophy of Grammar] (Verona, 1880) [Zoppi 1884], that I found full of interesting observations about the topic we are here discussing. [The quote is originally from Max Müller 1891, vol. 1, p. 507, as Vailati mentions in "The most recent definition of Mathematics," ch. 8 in this volume.]

language" starts first with the introduction of those words which, per se, have no meaning, and that a language is more perfect the more relevant words of this kind are in it, as opposed to the other kind of words, which even if uttered in isolation express some opinion, or feeling, of the speaker.

We have confirmation of this in the fact that the words that have less meaning than the others—that is those to which it is necessary to add a larger number of words to get a sentence that means something — are precisely those that appear later, both in the historical development of languages and in the individual process of learning them.

Among such words we should first of all include prepositions, because they have the purpose of indicating the different kinds of relations that can exist between the objects under discussion. In fact for this very reason, prepositions do not indicate absolutely anything if they are not accompanied by words denoting the objects with which they are asserted to have the corresponding relationship.

So, when we utter, for example, the words: *"beside," "above," "after,"* etc. without indicating the things about which we mean to assert that one is *"beside"* another, *"above"* another, etc., we do not communicate to the listener any specific information about the things we are talking about.

Similar considerations can be made about the comparison between different kinds of verbs and, in particular, the distinction commonly expressed by opposing "transitive" to "intransitive" verbs—that is, contrasting those verbs which require their enunciation to be followed by the indication of some "object" to which they refer, for example, *"I desire," "I reject," "I conceal," "I indicate,"* etc., with those verbs which instead do not need any further determination or specification, like for example, *"I sleep," "I grow," "I laugh," "I die,"* etc.[3]

Nevertheless we must observe that such a distinction— established by grammarians merely on the basis of the formal criterion consisting of whether or not the verb requires what they call a "direct complement"— does not coincide exactly with the distinction that, for our purpose, would be appropriate to highlight.

Certainly nobody would think to blame the grammarians for distinguishing those cases where the indication of the object, to which

---

[3]About the mechanism that gradually leads verbs originally intransitive to assume the character of *transitive*, we can quote the typical example of the verb *"cavalcare"* ["to ride," from the word *"cavallo,"* that is, "horse"]. While in the beginning the verb meant, in itself, "ride a horse," because it was later applied to the case of other *"cavalcature"* ["rides"] it ended up requiring the indication of those, becoming in this way transitive, as in *"cavalcare un mulo"* ["riding a mule"], etc.

the action expressed by a verb refers, happens by simply adding the name of such an object—like when we say for example: "I desire *this thing*"—from those cases where instead, the insertion of a preposition is necessary between the verb and the noun—like when we say for example: "I aspire *to this thing*."

However, the mere frequency of verbs that, although having the same meaning, belong in one language in the first category and in another language in the second category, is already proof enough of how the nature of the established distinction is, so to speak, accidental.

The question of whether it is possible to substitute such a distinction with another based on a more stable criterion—grouping together in a single class, for example, "transitive" verbs with all those others whose meanings require, even if by means of a preposition, the indication of an object to which the action that they express is referred— acquires much more interest because it is also possible to establish a similar distinction for nouns and adjectives. Even among these, in fact, there are some whose application to a given person or object requires that there is another name of a person or object following them in order to mean something. For example, it would have no meaning to say that someone is a *"contemporary"* or a *"compatriot"* without adding of whom; or to say of an object, or of a fact, that it is *"bigger"* or *"following"* without adding with respect to which other object or which other fact.

Between nouns, or adjectives, of this kind and the nouns that necessarily follow them, our language usually interposes a preposition. However, there are other languages where all that is needed is to put such words next to each other in a specific order. But for our argument, it is not necessary to distinguish one case from the other.

This, so to speak, "transitive" character of certain nouns like those mentioned before, is ordinarily indicated by qualifying them as "relative" nouns.

We have a clear example of the connection between "relative" nouns and transitive verbs in the very frequent possibility of translating sentences where a given object or person is applied to a noun expressing a relationship into other equivalent sentences where a transitive verb appears instead. For example, there is no difference in the meaning of the sentences: "this person *is the enemy* of this other person," or "this object *is higher* than this other," and these other sentences: "this person *hates* this other person," or "this object *surpasses* this other," etc.

The American mathematician and philosopher Charles Peirce, who more than any other dealt with the analysis and classification of the various types of "relations," has been induced by his research to establish a distinction between transitive verbs (or nouns or adjectives), depending on whether they require the addition of just one noun or more than one in order to acquire a determinate meaning; that is, in order to be able to assert something about the objects and the people to which they are applied.

For example, there are verbs "twice transitive" (or bivalent,[4] as they could be called with an appropriate image taken from chemistry), i.e. they require the addition of two nouns, like the following verbs: "*to teach*" (something to someone), "*to give*" (something to someone), and the corresponding nouns: "*teacher*" (of something to someone), "*donor*" (of something to someone), etc.

Some examples of "trivalent" verbs, that are able to be or must be "saturated" by adding three nouns, would be: "*to sell*," or "*to buy*" ("I sell an object A to a person B for a price C," "I buy an object A from a person B for a price C").

In the case of these "plurivalent" or multiply transitive verbs, we can clearly see the purpose of prepositions, which function almost as connective organs, and which apply the respective "complements" to each verb in an orderly fashion.

The bigger the "valence" number, the bigger, of course, the need for special signs or particles dedicated to avoiding ambiguities by assigning different complements to the same verb. To serve this purpose in ordinary language there are prepositions (or inflections) corresponding to the different "cases" of the nouns.

It could seem that the use of any preposition is always superfluous, as long as the verb, despite having more than one valence, is such that, as in the cases mentioned above, the different nouns required to complete its meaning belong to categories so clearly defined as to make it impossible for equivocation or confusion between them—when, for example, as in the case of the verb "to give," one complement must indicate a person and the other an object. In fact there is a tendency to abolish the prepositions in all those cases where there is a particular

---

[4]Perhaps it would be more appropriate to call them "trivalent," because the subject also represents a valence. Then the simply transitive verbs would be "bivalent," the intransitive verbs "univalent," and the impersonal constructions such as "*piove*," "*nevica*" ["it rains," "it snows," which have no subject in Italian] etc. would be "zero-valent" (or with no valence). The impersonal in Latin, such as "*pudet me*," "*piget me*," "*mihi videtur*," etc. would be "bivalent," the same as the transitive verbs. As an example of verbs with a valence of four we could mention the verb "exchange" in its commercial sense ("this person exchanges with that person, this thing with this other," or more simply "these two people exchange with each other these two things").

interest in saving words, for example in telegrams, in addresses, in the classified announcements on the fourth page of the newspapers. If we telegraph, for example, "send parcel secretary" there is no doubt that the parcel is the thing that is sent and the secretary is the person to whom we are sending, and not the other way round.

However, when instead, the different complements of a verb all belong to the same class—for example when they are all persons' names, like in the sentences: "I speak ill about Tom to Dick," "I speak ill to Dick about Tom"—to omit the prepositions would take away any way for the listener to distinguish the different relationships between the nouns and the verb, therefore exposing ourselves to being misunderstood.

Keeping in mind the considerations made so far, if we intend to determine which are the special grammatical and syntactical features by which algebraic language is distinguished from ordinary language, one first remarkable fact is the absence in algebraic language of any kind of "intransitive" verbs.

To clearly recognize the signs which in algebra correspond to the verbs, first of all we need to see under which form we can find the "propositions" in algebraic language.

Since by proposition we mean—according to the traditional definition— a sentence where something is affirmed or denied (a sentence, that is, where some opinion or persuasion is expressed, true or false as it may be), we should not classify among the propositions the simple "algebraic expression" or formulas, that is, where only numbers or letters appear, in whatever way combined with signs of operations or functions without the presence of any sign of equality or inequality.

Therefore the signs of equality (or inequality)—which, put between two algebraic expressions, indicate that the value of the former is, or we want it to become, equal to (or greater than) the value of the latter— serve the same purpose in algebra that verbs serve in common language, since it is through these signs, and only through these, that it is possible, using only algebraic sign, to affirm or to deny something about the objects or quantities in question.

Not only do these signs have the same task as "verbs," but they also—like the verbs "*to equal*," "*to surpass*," etc., that correspond to them in ordinary language—have the task of "transitive" verbs.

In fact, to indicate in algebraic language that a given expression "is equal" or "is greater" without saying *than such* is the same as not saying anything at all, exactly like it would be in ordinary language, to say that a given object "*accompanies*" or "*precedes*" another, without mentioning which other object is accompanied or preceded.

It may seem, at first glance, that the signs of equality and inequality in algebraic formulas should have the task of transitive verbs, rather than that of a simple "copula," and therefore that they should correspond more correctly to the words "*is*" or "*is not*" in ordinary language.

To see clearly in which sense and up to which point this could be the case, some preliminary observations are necessary on those algebraic signs that correspond to the nouns previously defined as "relative."

Among these we should first of all consider that the signs for operations such as $+, \times, -$ etc., like those relative nouns that have been qualified before as "bivalent," require the indication of two objects, or quantities (it is not relevant if they are represented by determinate numbers, or by letters representing any number whatsoever, or by whole "algebraic expressions"), on which the operation is intended to be executed.

Expressions like $a + b$, $a \times b$, $a - b$, being equal to, "the sum *of a with b*,"the product *of a and b*," "the difference *between a and b*," etc., are no different in their syntactic structure from the expressions built in ordinary language by means of "bivalent" relative nouns, such as: "the impact *of* a body *with* another," "the contempt *of* a person *for* another," "the distance *between* one point *and* another," etc.[5]

However, in algebra the signs corresponding to "simply relative," or "univalent" nouns in ordinary language, are no less important than operation signs. For example, the sign of "square root," the sign of "logarithm," and, in general, all those signs representing functions with only one variable, for example those indicating trigonometric functions.[6]

If we keep in mind the observations made before about those propositions where a relative noun appears as a predicate, and about their ability to be translated into others where a transitive verb appears instead, we can easily recognize the analogy between the procedure used in ordinary language to make this translation and the process used in algebra to build, instead, by means of the equality sign and of all the function signs or operation signs, all the other transitive verbs that are needed.

---

[5] [In Italian these examples had been chosen to show a parallelism in the use of prepositions, but this could not be replicated completely in English.]

[6] For those non mathematicians among readers to whom the word "function" could seem obscure and mysterious, I would like to inform that in algebra the word "function" refers to whatever sign or locution, that, if followed by the indication of a number (interposing, when needed, an appropriate preposition), generates a sentence indicating another determinate number. For example the words "*double*," "*half*," etc. are "function" signs because the sentences: "*the double of a number*," "*the half of a number*" indicate some *other* numbers, changing as the number in question changes.

Such procedure consists of having the equal sign followed by the sign of a function or operation, and to one side, or to both sides, appear some numbers, or letters, that almost have the purpose of pronouns, because they take the place that will be occupied by several "complements."

In the formulas built this way, as for example $a = sin\ b$, $a = b + c$, the verb is represented, not by the equality sign alone, but by such a sign together with the following function or operation. To be convinced of this it will suffice to compare such expressions with those of similar structure in ordinary language, such as: "a is a *producer* of b," "a is *son* of b and c," sentences that are immediately translatable into these others: "a produces b," "a has *been generated* by b and c," where the transitive verb appears explicitly in an active or passive form.

From what has been said about the operation signs it is clear that, with their aid, the signs for equality and inequality become suited to act not just as "bivalent" verbs, but also as verbs with any "valence" number.

If we say, for example, that a number a is greater than the sum of another two numbers b and c, we are asserting a relationship between the three numbers in question, reducing it to an assertion of a relationship between one of them, and another: $(b + c)$.

As with any other number, $(b + c)$ can assume the character of a relative noun by being followed by a new operation sign. For this reason, we will be able to express, by means of the ("bivalent") signs of equality and inequality, relationships between, not just three, but four numbers, and so on.

An important role in the construction of formulas using this procedure is that of the "parentheses," which become indispensable in avoiding the ambiguities that would inevitably arise regarding the order in which the different operations indicated are intended to be executed.

However, the similarity existing between the use of the equal sign in algebra, and that of the verb "*to be*" in ordinary language is counterbalanced by notable differences.

The only purpose of the verb "to be," for example in the propositions of the kind "the a are b" (any time, that is, that it is not used as an intransitive verb, equivalent to "to exist," "persist," etc.), is that of indicating that the persons, or the objects, to which the name a is applicable, are part of (or coincide with) those to which another given name b is applicable. On the other hand instead, the equal sign is used in algebra to express many other relationships besides this, which have only a few traits in common with this one.

We have a characteristic example in the most ancient use in Greek geometry of the corresponding adjective ἴσος, used by Euclid, as we know, to designate not only the identity or what is also now called the equality of two figures (in other words, the fact that they can be brought to coincide), but simply their ability to be taken apart in pieces that are able to be superimposed.

The relationship that Euclid asserts exists between, for example, two parallelograms with equal bases and height, when he qualifies them as "equal," does not have anything in common, as we can see, with the one that would be expressed by saying that one parallelogram *is* the other or that both *are one and the same* parallelogram.

In the same way, going from an ancient example to a modern one, when we put an equality sign between two vectors, or when we say that one is identical to the other (aside from the case where this is merely a simple definition), what is asserted is simply the existence of a certain relationship of position between the two pairs of points by which the vectors are respectively determined.

Saying that the signs in algebra that correspond to verbs are all "transitive" does not exhaust the enumeration of their characteristic properties.

They belong to a particular class of transitive verbs, distinguished from the others by a very remarkable property.

To clarify properly of what this property consists it will suffice to compare two transitive locutions, one of which has the property and the other does not.

For example, let us take two locutions obtained by using the verb "to be" followed respectively by the words "fellow-citizen" and "creditor." In the first case, when we have the following two propositions: A is a fellow-citizen of B and B is a fellow-citizen of C, we can immediately deduce the third one: A is a fellow-citizen of C. In the second case, instead, from two similar propositions: A is a creditor of B and B is a creditor of C, we cannot deduce whether or not A is a creditor of C.

Since we do not have a technical term available in grammar to designate the property possessed by the former of the two transitive locutions and not by the latter, I will temporarily indicate such a property with the name "syllogistic transitivity."

We can justify such a denomination noting that the validity of those syllogisms called by logicians of the "first figure" (that is syllogisms of the kind: A is B, B is C, therefore A is C) depends simply on the fact that the aforementioned property also belongs, among other verbs, to the verb "to be" and to its various synonyms.

In syllogisms of the kind indicated above, if we substitute any other verb besides the verb to be that possesses the same property, we obtain other kinds of reasoning which are just as valid, and for which all the rules which are valid for the syllogisms in the strict sense of the word do not cease to exist.

In any case, whatever the name used to distinguish those transitive verbs possessing the special property under discussion, the fact remains that, while there is a more or less large enough number of them in any language, the algebraic language has this special feature: all the signs in algebra that act as verbs possess this property.

The axiom that: "two quantities equal to a third one are equal to one another," and the similar axiom for the case of inequality, can in this regard be considered the fundamental specific rules of the grammar of algebra concerning the use of verbs.

Mathematicians are ever more induced to perceive the axioms of algebra in this respect, because of the extension of algebra's dominion and the consequent tendency to assign to such axioms, not the task of indicating the actual properties of certain relationships between quantities and numbers, but rather the task of indicating the properties that must be possessed by, and which are sufficient to be possessed by, any relationship, making it possible to extend the advantages of an algebraic treatment to it and to the subjects to which it refers.

Connected to this idea is the freedom which mathematicians ever more widely allow themselves, to use the same equal sign to indicate a number of other relationships beside that of coincidence between the numeric value of two expressions: a freedom that seems to justify the definition recently given to mathematics (by Poincaré), as the art of giving the same name to different things.[7]

The misunderstandings that could stem from using the same equal sign to express relationships which are very different from each other can be avoided in algebra by establishing the specific relationship that we intend to express for each different category of quantities or geometrical entities being considered. This is one of the main reasons for the importance assumed in the algebraic language by the so called "conditional" definitions, or definitions "preceded by hypothesis."

This name is used to indicate the definitions used to attribute a meaning to a given relationship or function sign, only in a "*conditional*" or "*limited*" way, i.e. only when it appears among individuals belonging to particular classes, or satisfying particular conditions, like when we say, for example: *If A and B are points*, we will indicate with *AB* the segment of which they are the extremities; *if a and b are straight lines*, we will indicate with *ab* their meeting point, etc.

---

[7] [Cf. *Science et Méthode*, I,2 (The future of mathematics): "I think I have already said somewhere that mathematics is the art of giving the same name to different things". English translation by F. Maitland in Poincaré 1908, p. 34].

The use of conditional definitions is sufficient to avoid the danger mentioned above in all those cases where the different relationships that we want to represent with the same equal sign exist between quantities or geometric entities belonging to different categories or satisfying different conditions. On the other hand it appears instead to be completely insufficient in those cases where the different relationships that should be indicated by a single sign exist among individuals of the same kind, or individuals represented by signs which are not distinguishable from one another.

So, for example, to consider a case already mentioned above, if we want to use the equal sign to indicate the relationship between two figures ordinarily called "equivalence" (i.e. the equality of their areas), we cannot use the same sign to express any other relationship between figures, like for example "equality" in the strict sense of the term (i.e. ability to be superimposed), or similitude etc.

Using the same sign to indicate completely different relationships in cases like this can generate inconveniences that could be avoided in algebra resorting to (as we do sometimes) introducing new signs which, next to those of equality and inequality, assume the purpose which in ordinary language, is assumed by the different kinds of transitive verbs.[8]

The more frequently followed procedure, however is another one. Before proceeding in characterizing it, we should mention the corresponding processes taken from ordinary language.

Ordinary language uses some means to express the result of comparisons made *from different points of view*, namely by subsequently paying attention to different qualities of the objects of a given kind, and among these means there is the assertion of equality or of inequality followed by the "abstract" name of the qualities *with respect to which* the objects in question are asserted to be equal or unequal. We say, for example, "these two people are equal *in* height," "this building is equal to this other one *in* height,"[9] "these two climates are equal *for* healthfulness," etc.

Even in this case the use of the preposition is, so to speak, accidental: in Greek, for example, it would suffice to add the name of the quality

---

[8]The suitability of resorting to this expedient, in the case of relationships between geometrical entities considered in the vector calculus, has been discussed recently, (at the *Congresso internazionale dei matematici*, held in Rome last April [1908]) regarding the presentation given on this topic by the professors Burali-Forti (from the Military Academy in Turin) and MarcoLongo (from the University of Messina) [Burali-Forti and Marcolongo 1909, Vol. 3, pp. 191–97].

[9][These two first examples are different in Italian, being two people equal "*di statura*" and two buildings being equal "*in* altezza."]

218 / Logic and Pragmatism. Selected Essays by Giovanni Vailati

in question, in the accusative case; in Latin the ablative is used.

However, there is also another form that can be assumed by propositions of this kind, and it is the one seen in the sentences: "the height of that person *is equal to that of* this other person," "the height of that building *is equal to that of* this other one," "the healthfulness of that climate *is equal to that of* this other one," etc.

These expressions, where instead of the subject and the predicate we have the names, not of the objects under discussion, but of their qualities, and of the characters with respect to which they are compared, correspond precisely to the expressions appearing in algebraic language when, to express for example that two angles *a*, *b* have the same sine, we write: $sin\ a = sin\ b$, or when, to indicate that the triangles ABC, DEF have the same area, we write: area $ABC =$ area DEF.

The two examples mentioned—the one about sine and the one about area— can be used to highlight a difference that it is important to point out.

While the meaning of the assertion that an angle has a certain sine can be perfectly defined even without considering any other angle besides the one under consideration, in the case of area the meaning of the sentence "this figure has this certain area" cannot be determined if not referring, directly or indirectly, to those operations of comparison between the area of a figure and that of another (and this other can also be, for example, the one chosen as a unit of measurement of the areas) that are required to recognize if two figures have, or do not have, the same area.

In other words, in the case of the sine of an angle we can *first* declare or define what it is, *and after* we can go on recognizing if the sine of an angle is equal to, or greater or lesser than the sine of another angle; but in the case of area, on the other hand, these two processes are inseparable, and one cannot even be conceived independently from the other.

The way in which we usually distinguish cases of one kind from those of the other is by saying that, while in cases like those of sine we define "explicitly" a new function sign, in cases like those of area the meaning of the new name introduced is determined only "implicitly" or, we can also say, by means of a *"definition by abstraction."*

The most ancient example of a definition by abstraction found in the history of the mathematical language is the definition of the word "ratio" (λόγος) which is at the basis of the treatment of proportions, in the fifth book of Euclid's Elements.

This definition, which according to tradition goes back to Eudoxus, consists in fact only in determining exactly—under a form applicable also to the case of incommensurable quantities—the sense of the sentence "those two quantities have the same ratio as these other two," or "the ratio between those two quantities *is equal to (or greater than, or lesser than)* the one between these other two quantities."

By means of this procedure, a relationship between four quantities—i.e. the relationship expressed by saying that they form a proportion—can be expressed as an equality between two terms, in each of which appears one same name, or sign, of function (between two variables); instead a definition of the word "ratio" is not given, and it is not necessary to give any other definition besides attributing a certain meaning to the sentences about equality or inequality between the ratios of two quantities.[10]

It is not appropriate to dwell on the numerous examples of the aforementioned kind of definitions that can be found in the different branches of mathematics and the various sciences where those branches find application.

It is appropriate instead to wonder which are the conditions on which the applicability of the procedure described above depends; to wonder, that is, in which circumstances the "definition by abstraction" is possible, and in which cases it is allowed, or convenient, to introduce new signs of functions by means of them.

This is the same as wondering which are the properties that must be possessed by a relationship (or a correlation) between objects of a given class in order for its existence, between two objects a and b of a certain class, to be able to be expressed by means of equalities of the kind: $fa = fb$, where we do not have any other definition of the sign f than that resulting from the meaning that is attributed to the aforementioned formula.

An indispensable condition to apply to this procedure is, first of all, this: that the relationship in question must have in common with the relationship of "equality" the property that, in this last case, is

---

[10]The name "definition by abstraction" was introduced, for the first time, by G. Peano. The recognition of the importance of the procedure that led to them, goes back to H. Grassmann (*Ausdehnungslehre*, 1844) [See Grassmann 1844]. A remarkable contribution to their analysis has recently been provided by A. Padoa (*Atti del secondo Congresso della Società Italiana di Filosofia*, Parma, September, 1907).[Burali-Forti was the first, in the Peano school, to consider definitions by abstraction, already in the first edition of his handbook of mathematical logic (Burali Forti, 1894, IV, 7, p. 140). Padoa had mentioned (and criticized) definitions by abstractions in a talk given in 1901 at a Conference of School Teachers in Livorno (Padoa, 1902). He later discussed the topic both in Padoa 1905-06 and in the article on abstraction mentioned by Vailati: Padoa 1908. Peano, who had used definitions by abstraction in his own works, published a paper on the topic in 1915, where he mentions Burali-Forti's book (Peano, 1915, p. 108).]

expressed by the axiom: if a is equal to b, and b is equal to c, then a is equal to c.

In fact, if this condition is not verified—that is, if the relationship in question were such that, from its existence between the two objects a and b, and between the other two b and c, it would not directly follow that it exists between a and c—using an expression of the kind: $fa = fb$, to indicate that it is verified between two objects a and b, will lead to the absurd consequence (or, in any case, a consequence incompatible with the fundamental property of the equality sign) that, from the equalities: $fa = fb$, and $fb = fc$ we could not deduce the other one: $fa = fc$.

For a similar reason, the relationship in question should also possess another property: it should be such that, from its existence between two objects a and b, we can also always conclude that it also exists the other way around, between b and a. Otherwise we would have to concede that from the formula $fa =$f b, we could not proceed to the other one $fb = fa$, contrary to another of the characteristic properties of equality.

This condition is satisfied, for example, by the relationships of perpendicularity and parallelism, while it is not satisfied, for example, by the relationship of divisibility, because from being a number divisible by another it certainly does not follow that the second number is divisible by the first.

The relationships that, although satisfying the first of the two conditions mentioned above, the one we have called "syllogistic transitivity," do not satisfy the second, for this very reason can be represented by any of the two signs of inequality, because in one as in the other, the former and not the latter of the two conditions mentioned above is verified.

The two aforementioned conditions, besides being necessary, are also sufficient for the application of a "definition by abstraction," and for the introduction, in this way, of a new name and a new function sign.

The only objection that can be posed is that the function sign that is introduced in this way is defined only by how it appears in expressions with a given structure—that is expressions of the kind $fa = fb$—and therefore it remains without any meaning in all the cases where we want to use it on its own, or combined in different ways with other signs of the same or different kind.

To this objection we can answer by observing that, just as we attributed a meaning to expressions of the kind $fa = fb$, in the same way nothing stops us from establishing also the meaning of other expressions where, on one side or on both sides of an equality sign, there appear not only isolated terms, such as fa or fb, but specific groups of them (like for example $fa + fb$), created by inserting certain operations signs.

In order for this to be possible, it is necessary, of course, that the relationship in question satisfies a certain number of other conditions, in addition to those that, as we have seen, are required so that the fact that it exists between two objects a and b can be expressed by a formula of the kind: $fa = fb$.

What these conditions will be, is the result of the examination of the properties that characterize the different operations whose signs appear in the formulas to be defined.

The most frequent case is the one of relationships by means of which we can attribute meaning, besides formulas of the kind $fa = fb$, also to those of the kind: $fa = fb + fc$, and as a consequence also to those of the kind: $fa = f - fc$, and also those of the kind: $fa = kfb$, where k represents a number.

An example of relationships belonging to this category, in the technical language of Physics, is the relationship expressed by saying that two certain bodies have the same "mass," or two masses have a given ratio to each other.[11]

Another example is provided by a completely different kind of relationships, namely those referring to the "exchange value" of commodities. In fact, while the economists can, and should, determine and define the exact meaning of sentences such as the following: "the value of such a commodity is equal to the value of this other," "the value of such a commodity is equal to the sum of the values of these other two," etc., they do not have any need (nor possibility, unless falling into tautologies) to define the word "value" on its own.

And such impossibility does not generate, not here nor in the other similar cases, any inconvenience or ambiguity; precisely as no inconvenience derives, in ordinary language, from the fact that we are not able to define the meaning, on their own, of the words "*stregua*," "*sollucchero*," "*josa*," "*zonzo*," "*acchito*," "*chetichella*," "*vanvera*," etc., it being enough to know the meaning of all those sentences where these words appear, that is the sentences "giudicare a una data stregua," "andare in sollucchero," "averne a josa," "andare a zonzo," "di primo acchito," etc.[12]

---

[11] I can refer the reader, who would need more clarifications, to an article that I have recently published on this matter, in *Nuovo Cimento* (Vol. XIV, 1907): "Sul miglior modo di definire la massa in una trattazione elementare della meccanica." [On the best way to define mass in an elementary treatment of Mechanics. See Vailati 1907.]

[12] [These are examples that could not be translated as they are, and for this reason

The frequent use, in the various branches of mathematics, of locutions or function signs, whose meaning is determined only by means of "definitions by abstraction," confirms what has been asserted before, when we established that one of the characteristic traits of algebraic language, compared to ordinary language, is the higher importance assumed in it by the signs which, not having any meaning that can be defined when considered on their own, are able to be defined only in an *implicit* way, that is only by indicating the meaning of whole expressions, or formulas, where the signs to be defined appear together with other signs.

To recognize as completely legitimate the use of signs or words of this kind, and as completely unreasonable the need of an "explicit" definition for them, is not without importance, theoretical or practical, even outside the area of mathematical research.

It will suffice to look at the first pages of the usual handbooks, or the elementary manuals of any branch of teaching—from grammar to constitutional law, from electronics to music—to be convinced of the great damage done to the clarity and the intelligibility (and at the same time also to the precision and rigor) of the exposition by the tendency of writers to consider the use of definitions in the strict sense of the word as the only way to determine the meaning of technical terms.

It is no doubt true that in given situations an ordinary process of definition is useful and also necessary—i.e. the one according to which, taking into consideration the notion to be defined, in isolation and independently from the sentences where it will be used to say something, the task is to break it down into its elements, making it look, in a way, like the intersection of other more general notions.

However, even without considering the fact that following such a procedure we arrive, sooner or later, at notions that cannot be reduced to others of a more general nature, even so, I say, those who teach the elements of any science should never forget to ask themselves, any time they introduce a new sign and they explain its meaning, whether the former or the latter, of the two different aforementioned ways of determining it is more convenient—i.e. between giving a definition in the strict sense of the term, or describing the meaning of the sentences where the term to be defined appears. Nor should they forget to ask themselves whether, for example, those concepts (more general than

we left the original in Italian. The meaning of some of these words is mostly forgotten ("*stregua*") or was never well-defined ("*chetichella*") but they are commonly used and understood in specific sentences and contexts. Similar examples in English could be words like "kith" (as in "kith and kin"), "lieu" ("in lieu of"), or "heebie-jeebies" ("to give the heebie-jeebies").]

the ones to be defined) to which we have to refer when we proceed in the first of the two ways, are really clearer and easier to understand, by the students or the readers, than the concept itself that is defined, and whether this concept cannot be more easily learned by means of direct observation of the facts and the relationships that it will be used to express.

The never ending discussions about time, space, substance, infinity, etc. that occupy a large part of some philosophical dissertations provide numerous and characteristic examples of the various kinds of "fictitious questions" that can be generated in the attempt to give, or receive, definitions in the strict sense of the term for those words or notions which can only be defined by relying on procedures similar to those represented, in algebra, by the "definitions by abstraction."

We have spoken so far about the means that algebra can use to express isolated propositions. But when we have a conversation, or we look for something, or we demonstrate, we need to be able to connect the propositions together; we need, that is, a means to express the relationships of dependence or independence that exist, or that we want to establish, between them.

For this purpose, in ordinary language we need those particles that the grammarians call by the name "conjunctions."

The purpose of these with respect to propositions can be compared to the purpose of prepositions with respect to nouns.

Just as a preposition between two nouns generates a locution able to function as a new noun, in the same way a conjunction between two assertions generates a new assertion, whose truth or falsity can be independent from the truth or falsity of each of them.

For a science of the deductive type, as algebra is, the most important conjunctions are those needed to indicate that, between two assertions, one is the consequence of the other.

Instead of the numerous particles, or periphrases, used for this purpose in ordinary language ("then," "therefore," "since," "whence," "for which," "if," "when," "in case that," "from which it derives," "from which it follows," "from which it results," etc.) we would need only one sign in algebra.

Other absolutely indispensable conjunctions in any algebraic dissertation that are not just a mere collection of formulae, are the following:

1. one to indicate that an uttered proposition is not true (that is, a sign corresponding to "not" in ordinary language);

2. another two corresponding respectively to "and" and "or" in ordinary language, to indicate that two propositions are simultane-

ously true, or that just one can be true.

For having introduced four special signs to indicate the aforementioned relationships between propositions, and having recognized the curious analogies that exist between the properties of such signs and those of the other signs already used in algebra, credit goes to Leibniz and the founders of what is called "mathematical logic."

One of the results obtained in the most recent phase of development of this new branch of algebra, is that of being able to express complete mathematical theories by means of the algebraic and ideographic symbols only, without the need to use ordinary language, even as an auxiliary.

The first attempt of a mathematical encyclopedia containing not only propositions and theorems, but also their demonstrations, without any use of ordinary language, is due to professor G. Peano from the University of Turin.

This is not the place to insist on the advantages of the system of notations that he initiated for the treatment of more complex and delicate questions about the foundations of arithmetic and geometry, and on the principles of the infinitesimal calculus.

The importance of the most recent progresses in mathematical logic, from the point of view of the theory of knowledge and of the analysis of the deductive procedures, has recently been brought up by the American philosopher J. Royce from Harvard University, during the inauguration speech he gave at the International Congress of Philosophy in Heidelberg (September 1908.)[13]

My purpose, in mentioning them, is simply to present another reason to the philologists, besides those previously introduced, for not excluding from the field of their studies the research on the development and features of algebra, and in general the various ideographic notations systems used in modern science, for example in geometry, in chemistry, in kinematics, not to mention the representational procedures used in geography, and the diagrams used in statistics.

I do not think it is very relevant in this case to make the objection that we deal with systems of "artificial" signs, chosen and created deliberately in view of the purposes they must serve, and whose development is not subject to the laws or uniformities of the kind that can be recognized and formulated with comparative study of the natural "languages."

It seems difficult to me, that the glottologists themselves can attribute any precise and scientific meaning to this distinction between

---

[13] [See Royce 2005, Vol. 2, pp. 681-710].

"natural" languages and "artificial" languages, given that they concede that in the formation and development of any language, even if "natural" and not educated, a non negligible part has always to be attributed to voluntary and individual factors, that determine the successive adaptation to its function as instrument of the expression and communication of certain feelings or ideas.

It would be strange, on the other hand, that while the objection to artificiality is not considered valid to exclude the study of "slang" used in the lowest classes of society from the field of glottology and semasiology, the same objection may have value in the case of what can be considered, in the worst case, ideographic "slang," used by the scholars of the most advanced of the sciences.

I will mention, finally, a consideration, of a completely practical and topical nature, that made me think it was appropriate to call the attention of philologists on the, so to speak, linguistic features of algebra.

It is becoming more and more common, in discussions about the curriculum in our high schools, to complain about the damages to the study of ancient or modern languages deriving from the use of methods which are too "grammatical" or "philological," that is deriving from the fact that so much time is spent, in the first stages of teaching, on the enumeration of grammatical rules, compared to the little time and the scarce attention paid to exercises of interpretation and conversation.

In comparison to this—which is commonly reputed to be a problem particular to the study of languages—we can see not just similar but I would say identical problems, to that part of scientific teaching which has the purpose of providing the students with the ability to use algebraic notations.

To promote a clear understanding of this kind of solidarity between these two branches of teaching, which are considered heterogeneous and without any relationship between them because of the traditional distinction between literary and scientific subjects, means to make it possible, among the scholars of the two disciplines, for there to be an exchange of ideas that will be equally fruitful for both parties.

References

Burali Forti, Cesare. 1894. *Logica matematica*. Milano: Hoepli.

Burali-Forti, Cesare and Roberto Marcolongo. 1909. Per l'unificazione delle notazioni vettoriali. In G. Castelnuovo, ed., *Atti del IV congresso internazionale dei matematici, Roma 6-11 Aprile 1908*. Roma: Tipografia dell'Accademia dei Lincei. Repr. Nendeln (Liechtenstein): Kraus, 1967.

Carus, Paul, ed. 1915. *Goethe and Schiller's Xenions*. Chicago-London: The Open Court Publishing Co., 2nd edn.

Grassmann, Hermann. 1844. *Die Wissenschaft der extensiven Grösse oder die Ausdehnungslehre.* Leipzig: Wigand. Engl. transl. by L. C. Kannenberg, *A New Branch of Mathematics. The Ausdehnungslehre of 1844, and Other Works,* Chicago and La Salle, Illinois: Open Court, 1995.

Müller, Max F. 1891. *The science of language: founded on lectures delivered at the Royal Institution in 1861 and 1863.* London: Longmans, Green.

Padoa, Alessandro. 1902. Logica matematica e matematica elementare. In *Atti del II Congresso dei Professori di Matematica delle Scuole secondarie, promosso dall'Associazione Mathesis. Livorno 1901*, pages 186–200. Livorno: Giusti.

Padoa, Alessandro. 1905-06. Che cosa è una relazione? *Atti della Accademia Reale delle Scienze di Torino* 41:818–826.

Padoa, Alessandro. 1908. Dell'astrazione matematica. concetto ed applicazioni. In *Questioni filosofiche a cura della Società Filosofica Italiana, Relazioni al II Congresso della Società Filosofica Italiana (Parma 1907)*, pages 91–104. Bologna: Chiantore Formiggini.

Peano, Giuseppe. 1915. Le definizioni per astrazione. *Bollettino della Mathesis. Società italiana di Matematica* pages 106–120. Repr. in Peano, G. 1957-59. *Opere scelte.* Roma: Cremonese, vol. 2, pages 402–416.

Poincaré, Henri. 1908. *Science et Méthode.* Paris: Flammarion. Engl. transl. by F. Maitland *Science and Method*, London: Thomas Nelson & Sons, 1914.

Royce, Josiah. 2005. The nature of truth in the light of recent discussion. Talk given at the International Congress of Philosophy in Heidelberg (September 1908). In *The Basic Writings of Josiah Royce.* New York: Fordham University Press.

Vailati, Giovanni. 1907. Sul miglior modo di definire la massa in una trattazione elementare della meccanica. *Nuovo Cimento* XIV. Repr. in Vailati (1911), pages 799–804.

Vailati, Giovanni. 1908. La grammatica dell'algebra. *Rivista di Psicologia Applicata* 4. Repr. in Vailati (1911), pages 871–889.

Vailati, Giovanni. 1911. *Scritti di G. Vailati, 1863-1909.* Leipzig-Firenze: Barth.

Zoppi, Gio Batta. 1884. *La filosofia della grammatica: studi e memorie di un maestro di scuola.* Torino: Unione tipografica editrice. Second edition revised, Verona: Tedeschi, 1891.

17

Language as an Obstacle to the Elimination of Illusory Contrasts[†]

For the sole reason that we live in a given society or at a given time, we find ourselves involved, independently of any explicit acceptance on our part or any form of "social contract," in a network of duties, responsibilities and mutual commitments, for which we are usually not able to give any specific justification. In the same way, for the sole reason that we speak a given language, we find ourselves induced, or forced, to accept a number of classifications and distinctions that none of us has contributed in creating, and of which we would be embarrassed if asked to indicate the reason or the "fundamentals."

A large number of these distinctions and classifications have their origins in circumstances, or needs, completely different from those which would guide us nowadays, if, abstracting as much as possible away from any influence of the usual forms of expression, we would want to establish an orderly inventory of our knowledge and experiences almost from the beginning.

The position of anyone who finds himself aspiring, even in the slightest, to feel and think in an original way, and to express what he thinks and feels, could be compared to that of the artist in front of a block of marble, which he knows to be filled inside with numerous, deep veins, with no relation to the shape that he wants to give to it, but which are actually suited to producing unexpected effects from his chisel, not always compatible with the effects that he would like to obtain.

[†] "Il linguaggio come ostacolo alla eliminazione di contrasti illusori." First published in *Rinnovamento*, issue 5-6, year II, 1908 (Vailati, 1908).

Logic and Pragmatism. Selected Essays by Giovanni Vailati.
C. Arrighi, P. Cantù, M. De Zan, and P. Suppes.
Copyright © 2009, CSLI Publications.

The history of any branch of scientific research presents characteristic examples of the obstacles to the formulation of even the simplest analogies and similarities between classes of facts, which derive from the tendency to passively, almost unconsciously, accept the traditional distinctions that are crystallized in the language. Such examples are found especially in those periods when the most decisive progress has been made, where the struggle between new concepts and theories and the doctrines handed down by tradition has been more lively. Let us think, for example, about the role, in Galileo's writings, of the controversy against the distinction of movements as "natural" and "violent", and against that of phenomena as "terrestrial" and "celestial."

Moreover, as it is well known, the concept of an irreducible distinction between "heavy" and "light" objects—the former with a tendency to go "down" and the latter with a tendency to go "up"—has been one of the major obstacles to the discovery and recognition of the analogies existing between the behavior of bodies under the effect of atmospheric pressure and the behavior of bodies submerged or floating in a liquid.

The same can also be observed for the distinction expressed by ordinary language when contrasting "warm" bodies with "cold" ones, as opposed to the other distinction of bodies that are "good conductors" and "bad conductors" of heat.

If we move from the field of physical research to that of mankind and its spiritual activities, the fundamental importance of the mentioned incompatibility between the distinctions, or classifications imposed by ordinary language, and those that gradually come to be recognized by individual researchers as better suited to the facts, or more conforming to the requirements of research or practical applications, is even more evident.

The first manifestation, in Greece, of a speculative impulse directed towards the independent examination and determination of the fundamental criteria of beliefs and behavior can almost be seen as coinciding with the first awakening, in Socrates and his disciples, of a clear awareness of the necessity of submitting the distinctions and the identifications implicitly accepted by ordinary language to criticism, which is an awareness of the right of every single thinker to make his adhesion to such distinctions dependent from the results of a preliminary investigation of their degree of coherence, and about the arguments that can be used to justify them. Reading the best and more elaborate of Plato's dialogues (for example the Theaetetus) we frequently have the impression of being almost defrauded of a conclusion or a definitive answer to the questions arisen, while the entire exposition seems to be exclusively dedicated to exciting the desire to obtain one, and to persuade the reader of the insufficiency of those taken under consideration in sequence.

Such an impression is due precisely to the fact that the main intent of the author is not to guide the reader towards definitive solutions to the problems addressed, but rather to give him the means of searching for such solutions on his own and "unprejudicedly,"[1] that is after being freed of all the ties generated by an excessive respect for the formulas sanctioned by ordinary language, and after having solved the difficulties due to the imprecision of the terms used in those formulas.

Among the most important attempts to systematically determine the different meanings which in ordinary language are attributed to the most important terms, and among those most frequently used in philosophical discussions, we should count the fourth book of the "Metaphysics" by Aristotle, where in fact an enumeration and determination of the different senses of such terms, stressing the connections and the differences existing between them, is attempted.

Certainly one of the more curious episodes in the history of western culture, medieval and modern, is the fact that that same exposition, intended by Aristotle to serve as a cure and preventive remedy against the effects of certain ambiguities or imperfections typical of the Greek language, ended up in turn, as a consequence of the predominance of the Aristotelian influence on the development of the medieval Latin thinking, the source of new confusion and new ambiguities which added onto those uncontemplated by Aristotle and entirely different, which were already present in using the Latin language when dealing with philosophical questions. It is enough to mention, for example, those generated by the absence of the article in Latin. In this regard the English philosopher T. Reid justly compares the scholars to sick people who have pharmaceutical products at hand to cure illnesses which are completely different from their own, but who believe they can nevertheless use them, in doing so adding other no less serious illnesses to their own, derived from the imprudent application of unsuitable remedies.

This is one reason to be added to many others, because philosophical thought, the product of a given society or a given stage of culture, can keep only part of its ability to influence other civilizations or other stages of culture.

That part, especially of philosophy, which has as its object the analysis and the criticism of the concepts and the fundamental criteria of knowledge and action, requires rethinking, so to speak, in every succes-

---

[1] [The word playfully used by Vailati is "spregiudicatamente" and means both "unprejudicedly" and "unscrupulously."]

sive generation; otherwise it risks losing any effectiveness and becoming detrimental rather than advantageous to those who are passively subject to its influence.

The processes leading to the elimination of the distinctions which are recognized little by little as superfluous or unjustified are no less necessary for the healthy development of the scientific and philosophical thought than the normal and uninterrupted activity of the secretion organs are for the life of a body.

The resistance that verbal associations give to a rapid occurrence of such processes of elimination is manifested in the most different ways.

For example, we often find ourselves forced to formulate the questions we are asking with sentences which in themselves, and independently from our intention, induce whoever wants to give an answer to implicitly accept other questions which are pre-judged, by the very shape of the question, as resolved.

To designate questions of this kind the Scholastic philosophers had a special technical term available, "exponibilia," a term which they applied to all those questions to which they had the right to refuse to answer with a yes or no during the disputes, for the reason that either answering one way or the other would be the same as admitting an essential point of the question.

Among the examples of such propositions quoted more often there were those where someone is asked when he has started or when he is going to end something. For example, if it is asked "whether we intend to start acting honestly soon," or "is it a long time since we happened to lie," we cannot answer either affirmatively or negatively without conceding, in each of the two cases, to be or to have been dishonest or liars.

Another class of "exponible" propositions, which is far more important than the previous one with regard to our subject, is constituted by those that could be called the "unsubstantial dilemmas," that is, by those questions where, by presenting the choice between two different assertions as an alternative, we are implicitly asserting, or receiving the admission, that accepting one as true implies asserting the falsity of the other.

Questions of this kind acquire plausibility because the two assertions we have to choose between are presented as though they were a contradiction of one another, so that the dilemma appears to be reduced to the question of whether one is true or false.

Every question that can be answered with a yes or no can naturally be expressed in the form of a dilemma; but on the contrary it is not true that any dilemma can correspond to a *single* question. In order for this to be true, it is necessary that the person to who the dilemma is submitted already admits that the two propositions, of which he is asked which one is true, cannot both be true, or both false. Otherwise, to request from the questioned a choice between the two propositions is equal to requesting his answer to two questions that could be completely different and independent at the same time and with a single act of assertion or negation.

Therefore this case is included in that category of sophisms which Aristotle takes into consideration (in one of the last chapters of the "Sophistical Refutations") with the name of fallacies of *"many questions."*

They are very frequently encountered in any branch of philosophical research, from the theory of knowledge, to ethics and philosophy of law.

For example, if we ask whether punishment is applied to criminals because they broke the law or because it prevents future crimes, we would be wrong if we give an answer in a way that is an acceptance of one or the other of the two assertions which seem to be in opposition. The fact that criminals are punished because they broke the law is not incompatible, rather it is actually an indispensable condition for their punishment to be effective as a means of discouraging them or others from breaking the law again. It is exactly in order for the punishment to have maximum effectiveness for this purpose that it is necessary to give it to those, and only those, who voluntarily broke the law.

Another example we can frequently find in every field of philosophical research is provided when, facing a fact produced by a set of circumstances and conditions, we ask which, among those, is the cause—which is like saying that if one of the given circumstances cooperates with the others in producing the fact, then is excluded that the others must or could cooperate as well.

Even in this case, just as in the previous one, the illusion consists of seeing an alternative, while instead the question is rather that of deciding up to which point any of the assertions, apparently in contradiction, are true, and on which circumstances their degree of truth depends.

And it is not rare to see dilemmas where one assertion is contrasted with another, but such assertion includes the other like a particular case. For example, "to believe" is opposed to "to know," even though what we "know" constitutes a part of what we "believe," notwithstanding all the reasons that justify the classification of our pieces of "knowledge" as separated from *the rest* of our "beliefs."

In the same way someone who acts by "instinct" or by "feeling" can be opposed to someone who is moved by "reasons," which is like saying that what we call "reasons" could be something different—in so far as they "move" us to action—from a special set of instincts, desires and feelings; for example, the desire of not sacrificing the present to the future, the fear of having regrets later, the need of feeling in charge of ourselves and our actions, a feeling of responsibility to uphold, of a duty, of a mission to be completed, etc.

It is rather strange that, while the majority of people interested in methodology questions concede that, with the exception of reasons of convenience or the obligation of being coherent, anyone has the right to ascribe the sense they want to the terms they intend to use—provided that they declare it expressly by means of a definition—instead only a few observe that the most important part of this right is not that which consists of the freedom of having given concepts or given classes of facts to correspond to certain sound or signs rather than others, but rather that consisting of the freedom of accepting or not accepting the classifications or the concepts which, however designated, do not seem appropriate or suited for the purposes that we have in mind in every determined circumstance.

This independence from the classifications and the grouping that we find already sanctioned in common language is far more important and valuable than the faculty of substituting certain words for certain others to designate given classes of facts, or given concepts, once they are established, or accepted.

The two languages may not even have one word in common and this notwithstanding they could be no different in their tendency to hide certain relations of similarity or of difference between facts, and to make some of them appear more important than they actually are.

References

Vailati, Giovanni. 1908. Il linguaggio come ostacolo alla eliminazione di contrasti illusori. *Rinnovamento* 2(5-6). Repr. in Vailati (1911), pages 895-99.

Vailati, Giovanni. 1911. *Scritti di G. Vailati, 1863-1909*. Leipzig-Firenze: Barth.

18

The Origins and Fundamental Idea of Pragmatism[†]

WITH MARIO CALDERONI

The term "pragmatism," according to its original creator Charles S. Peirce, appeared for the first time in 1871 in a series of debates between the members of the Metaphysical Club in Cambridge, Mass.[1] To Peirce this seemed the proper word to describe the method followed, though not formulated, by Berkeley in his investigations of the concepts of "substance," "matter," "reality," etc.

It is well known that Berkeley showed, or tried to show, that when we say, for instance, "that object exists," we do not mean, and we are not able to mean, anything but the following: if we, or beings similar to us, found ourselves in specific circumstances, we would have specific experiences or sensations. In other words, the term "reality," as well as the similar "substance," "matter," etc. refer to nothing but specific "possibilities of sensations."

Peirce thought that this procedure used by Berkeley was an example of a more general methodological process, which could be described as

---

[†] "Le origini e l'idea fondamentale del Pragmatismo." First published in *Rivista di psicologia applicata*, n. I, January-February 1909 (Vailati and Calderoni, 1909). Vailati intended for this essay to be the first chapter of a volume on pragmatism on which he and Calderoni were working before Vailati's untimely death in 1909. The second chapter would have been the essay "Pragmatism and the various ways of saying nothing," this volume, chap. 19.

[1] [See Peirce 1908, p. 109: "In 1871, in a Metaphysical Club in Cambridge, Mass., I used to preach this principle as a sort of logical gospel, representing the unformulated method followed by Berkeley, and in conversation about it I called it 'Pragmatism'."]

Logic and Pragmatism. Selected Essays by Giovanni Vailati.
C. Arrighi, P. Cantù, M. De Zan, and P. Suppes.
Copyright © 2009, CSLI Publications.

follows:

The only means to determine and clarify the meaning of an asser-tion is to indicate which particular experiences, according to such an assertion, are going to take place, or would take place under specific given circumstances.

Amongst the "specific circumstances" mentioned, our actions (move-ments, contacts, clashes, etc.) are a major component. For this reason, Peirce thought it possible to define the mentioned methodological pro-cess in the following way: the meaning of an assertion consists of the effects indicated by such an assertion as derived from, or able to be derived from, specific actions of ours.

Peirce also stated such in a much less precise form, saying that "the meaning of a concept consists of its practical consequences."

This statement, however clear its meaning when reconnected to the aforementioned train of thought, has been the cause of many misunder-standings which have contributed to the popularity of the pragmatic doctrine; a popularity that such a doctrine could hardly aspire to oth-erwise.

First of all, amongst these misunderstandings, we should mention the perception of pragmatism as a sort of "utilitarianism" applied to logic; that is, a doctrine that, in order to evaluate the truth or falsehood of beliefs, uses a criterion based on the consequences of such beliefs being more or less useful, or agreeable, etc.

It is not hard to see how little this interpretation has to do with the intentions and the scope of the original Peircean definition of "pragma-tism."

The methodological rule, as stated by Peirce, does not wish to define the distinction between true and false beliefs as something more arbi-trary, more "subjective," and more dependent on individual opinions and feelings. In fact its purpose is the exact opposite.

Such methodological rule is nothing more than an invitation to trans-late our assertions into a form that makes it possible to apply, in an easier and more direct fashion, those very criteria of true and false which are more "objective," less dependent on individual impressions and preferences. This form would be able to indicate more clearly what kind of experiments or observations can and need to be performed, by us or others, to decide whether, and to what extent, our assertions are true.

"Pragmatism" can only be conceived as having a "utilitarian" char-acter to the extent that it makes it possible to get rid of a certain number of "useless" issues—but "useless" for no other reason than that they are only apparent issues, or more precisely, that they are not issues at all.

For instance, when we have two assertions and we are not able to identify the particular experiences that should occur in order to make one of the assertions true and not the other, it is not proper to inquire which of the two is true. In a case like this, the two assertions, according to Peirce, must be considered simply as two different ways of saying the same thing.

Nevertheless, all this has not prevented some scholars from interpreting the pragmatic doctrine in a way that identifies it with that attributed to Protagoras, which is expressed in the well known aphorism "Man is the measure of all things"—that is, the doctrine according to which there is no other criteria to determine the truth of an assertion than merely the personal senses, intuition and beliefs of the person uttering the assertion.

This misinterpretation is particularly surprising if we think that the main document on which our knowledge of Protagoras' ideas is based (i.e. Plato's *Theaetetus*) contains Socrates' defense, against Protagoras, of the same thesis that Peirce has proposed under the name "pragmatism."

When Socrates asks what is "knowledge," Theaetetus replies that whatever is known by someone, is only known in so far as the person is conscious of it, or has sensory experience of it. Therefore, science is nothing but these sensory experiences or states of consciousness. To this, Socrates replies:

> Suppose now, that we ask Protagoras, or one of his disciples, a question: O, Protagoras, we will say to him, Man is, as you declare, the measure of all things—white, heavy, light: of all such things he is the judge; for he has the criterion of them in himself, and when he thinks that things are such as he experiences them to be, he thinks what is and is true to himself. Is it not so?

> And do you extend your doctrine, Protagoras (as we shall further say), to the *future* as well as to the present; and has he the criterion not only of what in his opinion is but of what will be, and do things always happen to him as he expected? For example, take the case of heat:— When an ordinary man thinks that he is going to have a fever, and that this kind of heat is coming on, and another person, who is a physician, thinks the contrary, whose opinion is likely to prove right? Or are they both right?—he will have a heat and fever in his own judgment, and not have a fever in the physician's judgment?

> [. . .] And the vinegrower, if I am not mistaken, is a better judge of the sweetness or dryness of the vintage which is not yet gathered than the harp-player? [. . .] And in musical composition—the musician will

know better than the training master what the training master himself *will hereafter think* harmonious or the reverse? And the cook will be a better judge than the guest, who is not a cook, of the pleasure to be derived from the dinner which is in preparation; for of present or past pleasure we are not as yet arguing; but can we say that every one will be to himself the best judge of the pleasure which *will seem to be* and *will be* to him in the future?—nay.[2]

These observations by Socrates are interesting not just as a confutation of Protagoras' doctrine, but also because they acknowledge the truthfulness of part of it. In fact, they not only defend the distinction between reality and appearances, but they also acknowledge that there are facts where this distinction cannot be made.

For any thought we entertain that does not have nor imply any reference to the future, that is, no prediction or expectation, the opinion of any of us cannot be refuted.

Any disagreement regarding the personal experience perceived by any of us is an ultimate fact that can be regarded as a datum, but which can never be the subject of controversy.

The question of truth or falsehood can only be posed when the perception or experience under scrutiny suggests or predicts other perceptions, the latter being not present and actual, but rather future and possible—that is, when and because the immediate perceptions and experiences are connected to *expectations* or *predictions* of any sort.

Peirce's methodological rule appears to be, in so far as what has previously been said, an indication of the importance of examining our assertions to identify a part that implies some predictions, because that is the part that can be confirmed or refuted by further experiences. The other part refers, instead, to some of our present state of mind (perceptions, taste, appreciation, etc.) and it cannot be the source of the kind of controversies that could be solved by calling upon new facts.

Pragmatists consider experience not only as a means of verifying or proving a theory, but also as a way of determining and stressing which part of the theory can be the object of useful discussion.

The issue of determining *what we mean* when we utter a certain proposition is a completely separate issue from deciding whether the *proposition is true or false*—and moreover, the former is an issue that needs to be solved before the latter can even be approached.

Pragmatism represents, in a way, a reaction to the prevailing philosophical tendency to neglect such a basic methodological norm, engaging instead in controversies which lack the clear determination of the

---

[2][Translated in English by Benjamin Jowett in Jowett 1892, p. 237. Italics added by Vailati.]

contended thesis. It is because of this that such debates go on indefinitely and appear to be unsolvable or transcendent to the abilities of the human mind.

In the presence of this kind of debate, the pragmatist's response is a refusal to participate, unless one of the two opponents explicitly indicates the facts that they believe to be the case, in order to be able to pronounce one of the two theses as true.

To entertain a certain belief instead of another means, for the pragmatist, to have a certain kind of expectation, different from the expectations he would have if he had a different belief.

This identification of "believing" with "having expectations" could seem an arbitrary limitation of the meaning of the term "believe." Having an expectation is the same as having the belief that that certain thing will happen. But on the other hand, it does not seem to be acceptable to say that every belief implies some sort of expectation.

In fact, alongside our beliefs regarding the future, we have an equally significant number of other beliefs that, apparently, only regard facts from the present or the past. Nevertheless, if we look closer at such beliefs we can see that a reference to the future is always an essential part of their meaning. A typical example of this, examined by Berkeley, is represented by judgments made on the existence of material objects. In his *Theory of Vision* [1732]—which is, after all, in every respect a theory of "prevision"—Berkeley criticizes the common opinion according to which the size, position and distance of objects are perceived in the same way as we perceive their color. Instead our visual perceptions are not able to provide this kind of information immediately, and distances, shapes, and dimensions of objects are not "seen" by us, but rather "fore-seen," or inferred from the signs provided by actual visual perceptions.

Distances, shapes, and dimensions are read and interpreted through a process similar to the process that allows us to read and interpret any other kind of "signs." We can say that we "see" these things only in a metaphorical sense, in the same way we say, for instance, that we see the intelligence or stupidity of someone when we read this person's writings. Our judgments about objects "having" certain distances, shapes, or dimensions are judgments which do not rely on actual perceptions, but rather on perceptions that we could or we will be able to experience.

Following this line of inquiry, Berkeley also extended this same conclusion to those assertions regarding, not just the position or shape of objects, but also their own "existence"—that is, when we assert that a given object "exists," what we are asserting is not the presence of some specific perception or experience, but instead it is merely our expectation that certain perceptions or experiences will occur, or would occur, given specific conditions.

This conclusion is summarized by Berkeley with the sentence "*esse est percipi*," but it could be better expressed by the sentence "*esse est posse percipi*." Far from destroying the distinction between "to be" and "to be perceived," Berkeley instead was clarifying the basis and meaning of such a distinction, showing how the *being or existence of an object is nothing but the "potential being" of certain experiences*. Plato had already acknowledged, up to a certain point, that assertions about the existence of objects can be reduced, in the end, to assertions made on the possibility of certain experiences. In his *Dialogues* there are several passages that can be considered an anticipation of Berkeley's aforementioned doctrine. It will suffice to quote that passage from *Sophist*, where it is asserted that "a suitable definition to characterize objects which exist consists in saying that they are powers or capacities" (δυνάμεις) (Soph., 347 E.).[3]

Judgments about the existence of objects and judgments made on their position or shape are not the only kind of judgments where we can see this tendency to present assertions which imply a reference to the future in the shape of judgments about present existence. In fact the same thing can be observed in all those assertions about an object possessing qualities—such as dilatability, elasticity etc.—which are related to the way the object would behave or react under specified circumstances.

For instance, the sentence "this object is fragile" would seem to be an assertion about the present state of the object, but it is only apparently so. Its grammatical form notwithstanding, the assertion refers to the future, not the present. That is, it does not express a fact occurring or which has occurred; instead, it expresses something that will occur, or would occur, if the object in question were to clash with something or be hit.

This shows that if the main verb of a preposition is in a present tense and not a future one, this cannot be considered enough evidence to establish that the preposition does not make any reference to future facts. In fact, any language has several means, beyond the mere verb tense, to indicate such a reference to the future.

In a way, we could also talk about the "future" and "conditional" of names and adjectives, in the same fashion we do for verbs. Everybody can see the difference between saying that someone is "irritable" or is

---

[3] [Vailati is probably referring to Soph, 247 E: "I hold that the definition of being is simply power." English translation by B. Jowett in Jowett 1892, p. 379.]

"irritated," or between saying that something is "movable" or "moved."

It is not always the case that the relationship between the meanings of two words is reflected in their composition. For example, the relationship between "movable" and "moved" is the same one that holds between "credulous" and "fooled," "capacious" and "containing," "heavy" (or difficult to lift) and "lifted with difficulty."

These same observations can apply, in general, to all judgments where it is stated that a certain object has or possesses a certain property, a property considered to exist even when we do not perceive or examine the facts in which it manifests itself.

Therefore, when we say that an object is of a certain color, we do not mean to say that we perceive such color, but that we would perceive it given certain circumstances (given a certain light, given that we are looking in its direction, etc.) As every good painter knows, the color "presented" by an object in a given moment can be completely different from the color that the object "has."

The previous observations made about how our assertions may be translated in terms of expectations or predictions need to be clarified and completed by adding some observations on the *different kinds of predictions* that can be involved.

An important distinction, to which I have already alluded, must be considered immediately, between the expectation that some event *will happen* for sure, and the expectation that some event *would happen*, if some other events were to happen (conditional predictions).

The relationship between conditional predictions and predictions in the strict sense of the term can be explained by saying that to have a conditional expectation is the same as being in a situation where it is enough to verify the presence of a certain fact, or to wait for the occurrence of a certain fact, in order to have the expectation, no longer conditional but a proper one, of another fact.

Explaining the distinction at issue in this way has the advantage of enlightening the relationship between this kind of distinction and the fundamental distinction of "particular" or "general" assertions, as indicated by logicians.

If we say, for example, that "some As are Bs," what is then expressed is our expectations of finding that some of the given objects have at the same time the properties indicated by A and those indicated by B.

If we say, instead, that "every A is B" what we want to say is that if we found, or expected to find, objects with A properties, we would also expect to find in these objects the properties indicated by B.

This way of describing the difference between general and particular propositions differs only in form from that adopted by Leibniz, and later by Brentano and by the logical mathematicians of Boole's school of thought. It consists in considering the general propositions as negating, and the particular propositions as asserting, the existence of two given kinds of objects.

In fact, when we state that "every A is a B" we express our belief that if we were to find some As, they would also be Bs, and this is the same as stating that there is not an A (or that we do not expect to find any A) that would not also be a B at the same time.

The strong connection between this idea of the distinction between general and particular propositions, and the idea about natural laws as recently presented by E. Mach, where natural laws are described as "limitations of expectations," is clear.

The assertions expressing not actual but only conditional predictions can be further distinguished in different classes, depending on the different nature of their conditions.

First of all we have the kind where the conditions consist of certain *deliberate* acts of ours.

The importance of this kind of conditions was in some way already recognized by Berkeley, Hume and Müller, but it has recently been highlighted by J. Pikler.[4]

Pikler reached some conclusions that are especially remarkable, in so far that they represent a complement and an extension of the conclusions reached by the three philosophers.

Pikler observes that when we assert that a given object "exists" or that it has a "certain property," we are not simply asserting the possibility of given experiences under given conditions, but we assert that these experiences can be obtained *by means of certain deliberate actions on our part.*

In other words, Pikler maintains that, when the conditions needed for the production of the given experiences are not such as to be produced or triggered by a voluntary act of ours, the belief in the connection between those experiences and the corresponding conditions is not the same as the belief in the "existence" of something, or in the possession of some existing property, even when it is not perceived. Instead, it is simply a belief in the constant succession of certain facts from others, or at most it could be a belief in the existence of a relationship of cause and effect.

On the other hand, whenever we know that the voluntary production

---

[4] *The Psychology of the Belief in Objective Existence*, London, Williams and Norgate, 1890 [See Pikler 1890, and Müller 1891].

of certain facts leads to, and could not but lead to, certain experiences, this belief tends to take the shape of a belief in the existence of something.

Proof of this can be found, in Pikler's view, in our judgments on the existence of time and space.

The question is, how do we reach the belief that, beyond the portion of space that is perceived as connected to our experience (of color, taste, touch, sound, etc.), other portions of space—the rest of space—exist at the same time? Pikler replies:

> We believe that of the extension or portion of space which is presented to us at any moment, in any of our presentations, we may through will (namely, by the motion of our eyes, our heads, our extremities, or by the propulsion of our whole bodies) obtain the presentation of another portion of space, to the right, to the left, in the front, in the rear, upwards and downwards, of the already presented portion of space, and then again of other portions of space in all the above directions from the former, and of other portions of space again, further and further on, without any limits. Hence, while there is present to us at any moment a portion of space, we believe that, had it been our will at a certain preceding period, any of these numberless other portions of space, standing in certain space-relations to the presented one, might be presented to us at the present moment; and we express this belief in this way, that numberless other portions of space exist, or that an indefinite Space exists at this moment, of which the portion of space happening to be presented forms part. [...]
>
> Our belief in the permanent objective existence of Space is therefore nothing else but our belief, expressed in other words, that certain space-presentations are permanently capable of being presented to us through our volition, just as our belief in the momentary objective existence of some of the attributes of our presentations is nothing else but the expression, in other words, of our belief that certain attribute-presentations can be presented to us momentarily through volition.[5]

Pikler also reaches the same conclusion regarding time: the belief in the "existence" of time, i.e. in its regular "passing" independent of our awareness, is nothing but the belief in the possibility of achieving, by means of our voluntary actions, specific experience of length, succession, coexistence in correspondence with any of our series of experiences, and also the possibility of achieving, starting from any of these experiences, the experience of an uninterrupted elapsing of time.

This is also, Pikler continues, the way in which we talk about the "existence" of something other than objects and their properties, i.e.

---

[5][Pikler 1890, p. 24–25.]

things like our attitudes, concepts, memories, etc.

When we say, for example, that, in a certain person, the cognition of a given fact "exists," we do not intend to say that this person is constantly thinking about this given fact; we only mean that this person would think, or could think, about the fact if his attention were induced or forced to do so.

In the same way we should interpret the sentences which assert the "existence" in us, or others, of certain memories. And when we assert that, in someone, certain qualities of character, for instance being afraid or irritable, "exist" we do not intend to say that this person is at the moment frightened or angry, but only that, to frighten or anger him, we simply need certain conditions and stimuli that would not be sufficient to make another person frightened or angry.

It follows from what has been considered so far that our belief in the connection between some experiences and some of our actions can lead to judgments about existence, and not only in those cases of facts that we think could actually be produced by an action, but also in the case that the experiences at issue, even if no longer able to be produced, have nevertheless been able to be produced in the past, or could be imagined as able to be produced in the future.

The "possibility," or attainability of these experiences, to which reference is made in the analysis performed so far on the topic of judgments of existence, is not to be thought of only in terms of an "actual" dependency on our actions. It can also be merely a "virtual" dependency, which may become real only if certain conditions happen to hold, but this could not depend on our will.

For example, when I say that this present table "exists," I am referring to experiences that, if I so desire, I can immediately obtain. When instead I say that a table exists in a room where I am not present, I refer to experiences that I may have only if I were to enter that room, even in the case in which I am not able to actually do so.

In the same fashion, the assertion that Constantinople "exists" is not an assertion that has meaning only when uttered by people who are actually, at the moment of utterance, in the condition (money available, time available, etc.) to actually go there, so that over there they could receive certain sensations—when the very possibility of those sensations is indeed what they assert when they assert the existence of that city.

From these kinds of conditions, in which we do not perhaps actually find ourselves but in which possibly, or probably, we could find ourselves from one moment to another, or even which, if we so wished, we could produce, we move gradually to others, whose realization is extremely unlikely, or even impossible.

This is the case, for example, of the physicist who makes assertions about the constituents of matter, or about the movements of particles— hypotheses whose direct verification would require tools of observation far more powerful than anything he may ever hope to have available.

An extreme example of this case is given both by our judgments about past events and our judgments about someone else's experiences. In fact, if we try to analyze these kinds of judgments in the way we have done so far, we could easily translate them in terms of "conditional expectations"—but the conditions that would appear in the translation are even, allow me to say, "more impossible" than those examined before.

When we state that something existed, or that some fact happened, in the past, such an assertion implies that, if we were to have lived at that time, we would have had, or could have had, certain experiences.

Now, it is evident that such a condition (at least for those who do not accept the hypothesis of the "eternal return"), is completely unrealizable.

And just as unrealizable are the conditions we need in the latter of the two aforementioned cases, that is the conditions we would state when we say "if I were that person, instead of myself...," etc.

However, it does not follow that the translations of these latter kinds of judgments in terms of conditional expectations do not represent an analysis of their meaning, exactly as in the case of the judgments previously mentioned.

On the contrary, such an analysis is even more important given its role in clarifying the special character of this sort of judgment. The special character is the following: judgments of this kind, unlike those of other kinds, cannot be verified or ascertained "directly."

The only kind of verification they are passable under is the sort we could call "indirect," i.e. that which consists in the verification of *other* affirmations that we can deduce from them.

In this process of deduction of directly verifiable propositions from others that are not, pragmatists are inclined to see, not only a tool to determine the truth or falsehood of these unverifiable propositions, but also a tool to determine their meaning.

Applying, even in this case, a criterion such as we have previously seen applied to directly verifiable propositions, pragmatists tend to consider two directly unverifiable propositions as "equivalent," or having the same meaning, when it is not possible to find a directly verifiable assertion that can be deduced by one of the two propositions but not from the other.

But if we apply this criterion to judgments regarding the existence of other "minds" beyond our own, we find a difficulty which we should examine here.

The conviction held by all, that other minds exist beyond our own, cannot be considered founded on any direct observation.

If someone asks us what the reasons are for why we believe, for example, that a child is suffering when he cries, we can only answer by pointing to the similarities between his behavior and some of our behavior, which we know is connected with the presence, "inside us," of some kind of pain.

In other words, the existence of "other people" minds is known to us by means of a certain number of signs, such as the behaviors of certain "things" ("animate" bodies) in some circumstances. There is no doubt that these reactions are the only proof that we have for our aforementioned belief.

The assertion that there are other "conscious" beings besides ourselves seems to be, therefore, a "hypothesis" that we use to explain some facts of our experience.

This is not the only conceivable hypothesis; there are explanations of the same facts that are completely different, and do not imply the existence of other "conscious" beings beyond ourselves. It is proof of this that there are philosophical doctrines which refer to these different hypotheses.

For example, the Cartesian theory of the automata-animals is well-known. Intended by its author as a way of making a sharper distinction between animals and humans, it could not be accepted for animals if it was not also possible, in principle, to apply it to humans.

To concede the possibility that there could be an automaton so perfect that it reacts, to any stimulus, in a way identical to the way a supposedly conscious human would react, is the same as conceding that there is no difference between the hypotesis of the presence of consciousness or that of an automaton for what concerns the predictions that we can deduce from either hypothesis.

If we were to apply the previously mentioned criterion, which pragmatists would like to use to determine whether there is a difference in meaning between two propositions, this would lead to a paradoxical conclusion, i.e. that when we assert the existence of other "conscious" beings other than ourselves, we are not saying anything different from asserting that, instead, such conscious beings do not exist—unless we intend, with the latter assertion, to deny any of those reactions or behaviors which are distinctive features of those bodies that we refuse to think of as having consciousness.

This problem is less serious than may appear once we take into consideration that pragmatists, with their analysis of meaning of propositions in terms of predictions, are not trying to give a complete description of the contents of all our beliefs—they try instead, as mentioned before, to put focus on *the only part of content whose discussion could be useful.*

As to the rest of the contents, that is the part regarding the judgments previously mentioned, not the behaviors or reactions, but rather the existence of consciousness in animated bodies, we can apply considerations similar to those pertinent to the case of relative affirmations about our own states of consciousness.

We must notice, moreover, that the alternative mentioned above is not available between the hypothesis of "consciousness" and that of "automaticity." In order to be able to provide predictions comparable in precision and extension to the ones effectively provided by the consciousness hypothesis, this latter hypothesis needs to take a determined shape or form, exposing itself to the possibility of refutations in the presence of any negative outcome of some *experimentum crucis.*

The previously stated considerations about the possibility of analyzing our assertions in terms of predictions need to be completed by adding something about the kind of assertions that seem to be referring merely to immediate observations—for instance those concerning how something "appears" to us in a given moment, or those expressing a certain present sensation or feeling, etc.

Where these kinds of assertions are concerned, we do not usually entertain the possibility of being wrong, of recognizing them as false.

This can be explained considering, first of all, that when we say something like "I'm cold," or "the color I see is red," or "I'm tired," "happy," etc. we are not just merely acknowledging some feelings, but we pair the acknowledgment with a certain number of predictions about the length, the constancy, the possible repetition, and various accompanying circumstances or consequences of those same sensations.

Even when these predictions are not clearly present in mind, as is often the case, they become evident as soon as the person is invited to validate his assertions.

So, when we say, for instance, that maybe our happiness is illusory, that our tiredness is more apparent than it really is, that we think we feel something but maybe we do not, etc., what we mean is that these states of mind will be fleeting, that the actions we would take if tested would confute them, etc.

It is in this same sense that we talk about "false pleasures," "wrong preferences," even though pleasures and our preferences are immediate and irrefutable things. What we intend when using these expressions is simply that the individual appreciation would be different, if we were aware of some overlooked consequence, or if we were reminded of some momentarily forgotten facts.

Another case in which a person's appreciations and his very beliefs may be considered as merely "apparent" is given when this person's actions do not "conform" with them, that is if the person does not seem to be inclined to make those choices or sacrifices that we would consider proof of those appreciations and beliefs. In cases like these we talk about fake compassion or fake enthusiasm; we say that a person thinks they love, but do not, showing that when we assert that someone is enthusiastic or in love, we do not intend to assert the presence, in this person, of a state of mind, but also the presence of plans of "actions" or dispositions to act in specific ways.

Finally, in order to mention all the possibilities of error that may be hidden in what look like immediate acknowledgments, we must remember that to express acknowledgments, as we do with any assertions, we need to have general terms available which presuppose a classification of the designed objects. To classify means to recognize the existence of similarities and differences, and the comparisons we need to make for this purpose are procedures that we may repeat (directly, or on the impressions left in our minds) and that, therefore, can generate confirmation or refutations of the judgments under discussion.

We can object that the set of analyses of meaning and content of our assertions and beliefs, as attempted by pragmatists, leads to bad psychology , in so far as they explain what "there is" in our minds by means of what, mostly, "there is not."

Everybody makes judgments and entertains beliefs; nobody realizes that this means making predictions. To this objection we can reply that it is one thing to claim that we are not aware, most of the time, of these predictions—but it is a completely different thing to claim that these predictions are not present in us, or are not implied in our judgments.

At this point it is proper to apply the Pikler analysis, as presented before, about the meaning of the term "existence" when applied to mental processes or attitudes.

The "internal" world, no less than the "external" one, does not consist only of what is "in act," in a given moment, but it also consists of what is "in potency." Pikler's sentence, "the 'would-be' of presentation is the 'is' of objective existence," can be applied to one as well as the other.[6]

Many of the predictions we have discussed are "in potency" in our

---

[6] [In English in the original. Pikler 1890, p. 54].

beliefs, in our judgments. As we have seen, they are latent until the thought process flows automatically with no difficulties, but they are ready to appear in moments of doubt. They are almost reserves drawn upon only in case of necessity.

It is completely in keeping with the goals of pragmatist doctrine, which are "logical" rather than psychological goals, to put the focus on such kinds of predictive elements, which are always implicit in our assertions, even when absent from our present consciousness.

The objection to this logical procedure has no more value than the objections to syllogistic logic, based on the argument that syllogism is not an exact description of our actual ways of reasoning.

We can point out, even in this case, what has been observed by Mill regarding this kind of objection, that is, we are not dealing with an analysis of the conscious processes we use in reasoning or thinking, but rather we are establishing a validity criterion for our reasoning and thinking, and we are indicating in which kind of expressions our ways of reasoning must be able to be translated when valid, and in which our beliefs must be able to be expressed, when they have some meaning.[7]

References

Berkeley, George. 1732. *An essay towards a new theory of vision*. London: J. Tonson.

Jowett, B., ed. 1892. *The dialogues of Plato: Parmenides. Theaetetus. Sophist. State man. Philebus*, vol. 4. New York: Macmillian and Co., 3rd edn.

Mill, John Stuart. 1865. *An examination of Sir William Hamilton's philosophy, and of the principal philosophical questions discussed in his writings*. London: Longman, Roberts & Green, 1872.

Müller, Max F. 1891. *The science of language: founded on lectures delivered at the Royal Institution in 1861 and 1863*. London: Longmans, Green.

Peirce, Charles Sanders. 1908. A neglected argument for the reality of God. *Hibbert Journal* 7(1):90–112.

Pikler, J. 1890. *The psychology of the belief in objective existence*. London: Williams and Norgate.

Vailati, Giovanni. 1911. *Scritti di G. Vailati, 1863-1909*. Leipzig-Firenze: Barth.

Vailati, Giovanni and Mario Calderoni. 1909. Le origini e l'idea fondamentale del Pragmatismo. *Rivista di Psicologia applicata* 5(1). Repr. in Vailati (1911), pages 920–32.

---

[7] *Examination of sir W. Hamilton's Philosophy*, London, 1872, cap. XXII, p. 513 [Mill 1865].

19

Pragmatism and the Various Ways of Saying Nothing[†]

WITH MARIO CALDERONI

Until now,[1] we have been concerned with the applicability of an analysis, in terms of predictions, of several kinds of assertions, rather than pointing out the advantages of such an application.

First of all, these advantages consist, as previously mentioned, of the possibility of having ways to express our beliefs, or those of other people, so that it is easier to specify the procedures and the kind of research we need to carry out in order to prove or refute such expressions. Secondly, among our assertions, it is easier to distinguish those that can actually be proved or refuted from the ones that are not subject to any proper proof or refutation. This is because they refer to mind-states of which each individual subject is the only irrevocable judge, and also because these assertions are only apparent, and they are, in fact, sentences with *no meaning*.

At first glance, it could seem strange, and hardly justifiable, that propositions with no meaning appear meaningful, and that we need special tools to recognize them. Apart from exceptional cases, where some individuals may have a temporary interest in appearing to be saying something while they are not, or where they have nothing to say,

---

[†] "Il Pragmatismo e i vari modi di non dir niente." First published in *Rivista di psicologia applicata*, n. 9, July–August 1909 (Vailati and Calderoni, 1909).

[1] [Vailati intended for this essay to be the second chapter of a volume on pragmatism on which he and Calderoni were working before Vailati's untimely death in 1909. The first chapter would have been the essay "The fundamental idea of pragmatism" (this volume, ch. 18) to which the expression "Until now" is referring.]

in all other cases language is used by humans as a way of expressing thoughts or feelings.

However, this does not prevent them from deluding themselves— more often than we may think—and believing that they *are* saying something, even when they are not saying anything. This may seem less strange if we think that not only the elements and words that form our speech, but also many expressions and idioms, are adopted and divulged simply as a result of tradition or imitation. In this way, expressions that originally had a meaning can still be used very often, and are still in use, even when they no longer have any meaning, for one or another of the reasons I am about to examine.

1) One of the most important cases concerns sentences or idioms that were once meaningful, but that, due to changes in meaning of some of the terms that they contain, end up becoming *"true by definition"* and in this case they no longer represent an assertion that can be confirmed or refuted through new experiences, but are merely indications or statements relative to the sense in which a certain word is used or we would like it to be used.

The history of physical sciences also provides very instructive examples. For instance, let us examine the ordinary enunciation of the "law of inertia": a body unsolicited by any force continues to move indefinitely with the same velocity and in the same direction. This proposition was full of meaning for the original scientists who formulated it, because they were aiming to refute the traditional opinion that the effect of a force "impressed" on a body would "extinguish," independently from the action of any obstacle the body might find on its path. However, the same proposition means almost nothing at all, and becomes a simple repetition that is not worth uttering, if we consider it in the context of any treatise on Mechanics where, as commonly happens these days, the word *force* has no other meaning if not being the cause of any change in the velocity or direction of a body.

Instead, the proposition merely becomes a *fragment of definition*, from which we cannot obtain any information on the circumstances that influence the changes in velocity or direction of movement of the bodies. It is only useful to remind us that in order to distinguish between the cases in which a moving body varies in velocity and direction and those cases where velocity and direction are constant, we can use, besides other expressions, the proposition that states that in the former case the body is "animated" or "solicited" by some kind of force, and in the latter the body moves without solicitation by any force.

The distinction between the two kinds of propositions we have mentioned (i.e. the ones we use to assert something about the objects under discussion, and those which indicate, instead, only the intention of the speaker of giving these words one meaning rather than another) is present in one form or another, in every logical treatise or theory of knowledge.

The different pairs of technical terms subsequently used for this purpose by several philosophers characteristically reflect their different ways of considering the importance or the purpose of one or the other of the said two kinds of propositions.

Aristotle expresses this distinction by contrasting propositions that assert the "essence" or "genus," with those in which what is asserted is an "accident" or a "peculiar property." The classification of the different kinds of "predicables" he introduced is intended to point out the importance of the distinction between the two kinds of propositions under discussion, as clearly results from what he says on this issue in his *Topics* (I, c.80).

Locke expresses the same distinction by qualifying the propositions from the former of the two mentioned kinds as "verbal" or "trifling" propositions, and the propositions from the latter as "real" propositions.

The way in which the distinction we are talking about is expressed more frequently nowadays is the one introduced by Kant, consisting of calling the first kind of propositions "analytic" judgments and the second "synthetic" judgments, which is meant to suggest that the propositions of the former kind are used to analyze or decompose our concepts into the elements of which they are constituted (or we want them to be constituted) and the propositions of the second kind are used to indicate that the objects to which we can apply a given concept present not only those characteristics that constitute the concept itself, but also other characteristics not implied in the concept.

As previously noted, the fact that sometimes propositions, synthetic to begin with, become analytic, even though their exterior form is unaltered—that is, without this transformation being indicated by any special verbal sign which allows us to recognize it independently from the examination of the context of speech—far from taking away from the importance of the distinction between the two aforementioned kinds, is, on the contrary, one of the reasons why it is important to insist on it.

Such a fact is the source of a number of equivocal and illusory argumentations, among which we must highlight, first of all, those based on the apparent character of certainty and evidence that is conferred to this kind of assertions, only because they can be interpreted, at the same time or in rapid succession, as belonging to one or the other of the aforementioned kinds. Therefore, there are propositions that, while working in their ordinary applications as true assertions, relative to facts which can either be produced or not and would induce us to declare such propositions as false, can, at the same time, also be presented as propositions whose truth cannot be contested, if not by someone who doubts the meaning attributed to some of the words in the proposition. Thus, they are exempted, whenever necessary, from any need of proof or possibility of confutation.

The most frequent form in which these types of paralogisms are seen consists of saying that such an object has such a property because it is its *"essential"* property (or inherent to its *"nature"*), because without such a property the object in question would no longer be what it is—or, in other words, what the thing should be if it could be given the name we had begun using for it.

Locke observed, regarding propositions concerning the "essence" or the "substance," that they cannot be considered absolutely certain and irrefutable, unless they are emptied first of any instructive content, while they cannot become "instructive," unless they renounce their self evidence, and often their certainty and universality.[2]

An example of this, such as that already observed, by Bernard Bolzano in an interesting passage of his *Wissenschaftslehre*, is provided by the sentence ordinarily used to state the so-called *"principle of causality,"* i.e. that "every effect must necessarily have its cause."[3] There have been many attempts to regard this principle as necessary, or self evident, saying that an effect without a cause would not be an effect. Now, it is clear that the aforementioned principle, so interpreted, is irrefutable, but neither does it tell us anything anymore, because in the face of whatever fact or event, to decide if it is an effect will be as difficult as deciding if it has a cause. If we interpret the principle, instead, as saying that every fact, or event, has a cause, then it is saying something to us, and certainly something important to know—but at the same time it ceases to be self evident and necessary, and the exceptions to such a principle cease to be impossible or absurd "a priori."

We can also attribute to similar causes the emergence and establishing of the opinion according to which geometry principles are entitled not only to a higher grade of certainty, but in some way to a certainty of a different kind and origin, compared to the pieces of knowledge that are called, almost derogatively, "empirical," or of "experimental" origin.

---

[2] Essay, B. IV, Ch. VIII, 9. [Locke 1690, p. 455]
[3] [See *Wissenschaftslehre*, II, 182.6. English translation by B. Terrell from Bolzano 1837, p. 265.]

In geometry, as in any other deductive science, we are forced to start from suppositions that cannot be found perfectly actualized on any concrete occasion, representing only ideal simplifications of the forms that experience presents to us. This is why the fundamental propositions of geometry acquire not the appearance of assertions relative to the properties owned, or allegedly owned, by the things at issue, but the appearance of conventions that we use to clarify some concepts and to limit the area of our research. As a consequence, these fundamental suppositions can assume, without any unexpected obstacles, the form of definitions, so far as we add some assertions to them (postulates), to affirm or make it possible to demonstrate that figures corresponding to such definitions "exist" or "can be constructed." When the bases of a science are posed in this fashion, whatever objections are going to be moved against whichever of the fundamental propositions assumed will appear not only as unfounded but also absurd.

For example, if someone doubts that a straight line enjoys the properties that are attributed to it by the definitions in an ordinary geometry treatise, we could answer that this is impossible, because in this case it would not be a straight line anymore—and with this sentence we are saying, basically, nothing but that it should be called, in that treatise, by another name, and this is nothing but a matter of nomenclature.

The Greek geometers that first adopted the most rigorous form of exposition were perfectly aware that in order to be able to deduce conclusions that were not merely verbal from simple definitions, it is necessary to assume, or demonstrate by means of propositions already assumed, the existence or constructability of figures or things that satisfy the conditions posed in the definitions.[4]

So, for example, the definition of "parallel straight lines" as "straight lines that, lying on the same plane, never meet each other" appears in Euclid's treatise as subordinate to the proposition, which he previously demonstrated, which says that if on a plane we draw two straight lines perpendicular to a third straight line (or creating equal corresponding angles with this third line) then the lines we draw cannot meet. If Euclid had instead adopted the other definition, which may appear more "natural," based on the property of parallel lines always maintaining

---

[4]Against the sophisms that can rise from this path seems to be directed Aristotle's observation that ([Book II] ch. 7 in *Posterior Analytics*) "the existence is not essence" (τὸ δ' εἶναι οὐχ οὐσία οὐδενί), that is, it cannot be said of anything that it exists by definition. [Engl. transl. by Edward Poste from Poste 1850, p. 105.] We can find a typical example of non-observance of such a precept in the demonstration of God's existence, as conceived by Anselm of Canterbury and adopted, with slight modifications, even by Descartes; demonstration known to scholars of the history of philosophy by the name of "ontological proof."

the same distance from each other, it would have been impossible for him to deduce from the fundamental propositions, used in the first case, the existence or constructability of parallel lines in this second sense.

Not being able to recognize this, i.e. believing that these other fundamental propositions could be made superfluous by adopting the latter definition instead of the former, was the mistake of those geometers, like Borelli for instance against whom Gerolamo Saccheri had to fight in his work *Euclides ab omni naevo vindicatus* [1733], which is so important for the history of modern ideas regarding non-Euclidean geometry.

The kind of sophism they made was qualified by Saccheri as "fallacia definitionis complexae," because it consists of believing that the definitions which attribute simultaneous possession of several properties could be used in demonstrations without verifying the compatibility of those properties beforehand.

2) If on the one hand we have the case, discussed so far, of sentences that do not assert anything because they are, or they ended up being, "true by definition," on the other there is the case of sentences that do not assert anything for a somewhat opposite reason, either because they are, or ended up being, "false by definition." It does not appear possible for propositions of this sort—i.e. propositions where the term acting as subject implies, because of its meaning, not the possession but rather the non-possession of the quality, or of some qualities expressed by the predicate—to be regarded by anyone, not even for a moment, as having meaning. But this happens more frequently than thought.

Among the main causes of this we should account for the tendency to use words or sentences, referring to some *relations*, as if they could have some meaning independent of the referents implied in their own definition.

From the fact that these sentences have, or can have, meaning *whatever the choice* of referents indicated, we can easily go on to believe that they have meaning *independent of any consideration of referent whatsoever*. So in the end we do not realize that, for example, the notion of an "*absolute*" motion of a body implies a contradiction in terms, no less so than the notion of a general increase in prices, including currency.

We should note, however, that contradictions created by changes in the meaning of the terms of an assertion can sometimes be only apparent.

Like we have terms in a given proposition that can undergo such changes in their meaning that the proposition can become a mere tautology, we could also have, by inverse procedure, a proposition that, given a certain meaning of its terms, does not assert anything because it is "true by definition," and then starts asserting something only because the term acting as subject in it assumes a new meaning, which no longer includes the characteristic expressed by the predicate. In this case the *negation* of such a proposition, which becomes possible or at least conceivable, can appear to someone, not really aware of the change that has taken place, as a contradiction in terms, while this is definitely not the case.

Amongst the most typical examples of this kind of apparent contradictions, we can mention those generated, in elementary algebra, by the successive generalizations of the concept of number.

So, for example, extending the concept of multiplication to the case of fractional numbers, we can claim without contradiction, that a product can be smaller than one of its factors. This assertion, for anyone conceiving the product of two numbers as is usually conceived in the case of integers, cannot fail to appear as a contradiction in terms. In the same way, extending the concept of addition to the case of negative numbers not only allows but forces us to reject the axiom that a sum is greater than its parts.

Similar consequences derive from further generalizations of the concept of addition, like for example the generalization that induces us to consider the sum of two segments and what is called their resultant as the same thing.

In the same way, extending the concept of equality, and the concepts of whole and part, to the case of compound aggregates consisting of an infinite number of elements, leads to the apparent paradox that part of an aggregate can be equivalent to the whole aggregate, just as when we say that, for example, the even numbers are as many as all the numbers, even though they are only part of them, and so on.

Assertions, like the ones considered above, and for the same reasons as those considered above, which present an illegitimate paradoxical appearance, can also be found in the field of philosophical research, where we should point out their influence on leading not only laymen, or followers or teachers of philosophical doctrines, but often the philosophers themselves to attribute a more radical and revolutionary importance to their theories than that which those theories should really have.

It has very often come about that the promoters of a new philosophical theory, and not only their opponents, have come to the conclusion (or, what is almost the same thing, they spoke as if they had come to the conclusion) that their analysis and their new definitions were going to uproot from its foundations the whole system of assertions uttered through terms that they had analyzed or redefined.

For example, the attempts to clarify or analyze the criteria at the basis of very important distinctions, such as reality and appearance, cause and effect, voluntary and involuntary actions, justice and profit etc., and the efforts to formulate them, to reduce them to simpler expressions, to make them applicable with more confidence in ambiguous or uncertain cases, were interpreted as attempts to undermine those distinctions which they were actually attempting to investigate, or to destroy or reveal the groundlessness of them.

It was completely useless for Berkeley to have tried to persuade his opponents of the fact that it was their theory, and not his, that was giving leeway to the skeptics' objections against the "reality of the external world." It was pointless his declaring over and over again that his purpose was only that of clarifying and determining what we intend to say when we assert that things "exist."

Nevertheless, he was still accused of wanting to suppress the common held distinction between "real" things and the illusions of our imagination, in the same way in which Hume is still accused of wanting to "destroy" the concept of cause and dissipate the distinction that such a concept allows us to express.

In a similar way also originates the tendency, common to more than one kind of contemporary Positivism, to grant that, or better to sustain that, science and philosophy cannot know anything about the "nature of things" or the "true causes" of the universe, and that their only legitimate function is *limited* to determining the laws of succession and co-existence of phenomena.

As if, amongst the problems formulated by previous philosophers with sentences including the words "cause," "nature of things," etc., we could find *at least one* problem that could not be translated into the new nomenclature, and as if the resolution of *not dealing* with anything else but questions that can be formulated in terms of succession or co-existence, would not imply for itself any refusal to deal with any problem which is truly such.

3) We can find a third source of questions and assertions with no meaning in the tendency to forget that what is called the "generalization process" is nothing other than a means to certain logical or practical goals, and that there are limits, surpassing which would entail the impossibility of reaching those goals.

The same impulse that leads mankind to desire an end that has been previously desired as a means—for example, that leads them to desire knowledge or understanding independently from the advantages and powers that derive from them,—induces them, or tends to induce them, also to consider those simple means or stratagems used in order to gain knowledge and understanding as ends in themselves, with value and esteem independently from any kind of result, *even if purely epistemic*, independently from any alleged effectiveness in the growth or consolidation of our knowledge and our predictions.

The reason why we shape general concepts is that of establishing "classes" of objects, or, in other words, of distinguishing some objects from others, about which there is, or could be, something more or less important to be asserted or denied, as opposed to what can be asserted or denied about others.

By shaping evermore general concepts, or transforming the more particular concepts into more general ones, we make them applicable to a greater number of objects; but we can only do this at the cost of diminishing the number of characteristics expressed by those concepts, that is, the characteristics that must be possessed in order for those same concepts to be applied to them, also diminishing in this way the number of assertions, important or not, that we can make about those same objects.

This process can go on so far as to reach the point where a concept is no longer useful in distinguishing anything from anything else; and because this distinction is the main advantage of using concepts, the bottom line will be to have rendered the corresponding word useless for the uses it was applied to before, and to have made necessary the introduction of new words necessary to indicate *the same distinctions* that were formerly indicated by that word.

For example, asserting that *everything is an illusion* or that *all our actions are involuntary* does not exempt us from having to introduce later distinctions between kinds of "illusions," and between kinds of "involuntary actions," those same distinctions that were formerly expressed by the terms "reality" and "appearances," "voluntary" and "involuntary."

In the same way, someone, who says that all voluntary actions are *egotistical* because the person performing them likes performing them best the way he does, is then obliged to distinguish between different kinds of "egotistical" actions, some of which come to coincide with those that others, who have not yet generalized so much, are still calling altruistic.

Those who generalize in this way often fall for the illusion of believing, for the fact that they use names such as "life," "concrete fact," "lived experience," etc., that they have left the field of abstraction, without noticing that all the aforementioned terms, including the term *concrete fact*, are among the most abstract we can imagine, in so far as the concept, for example, of concrete fact is so wide that it can embrace any fact whatsoever which happens.

As a consequence of this way of reasoning, we are led to sentences that end up saying so little that their meaning is no different from the meaning of other sentences that would deny the same thing; for example, it would be hard to indicate how asserting that everything is an illusion is different from asserting that nothing is an illusion.

Perhaps this is the cause that induced some philosophers, who were abusing of this kind of generalization, to think that in some areas of philosophy the principle of non-contradiction is no longer valid—in this they were partially right, because between the assertion or the negation of these sentences there is, more or less, the same difference that in mathematics we have between a zero with a positive sign and one with a negative sign.

4) The abovementioned case of processes of generalization is not the only one where our tendency to automatically extend our thought-processes beyond the point where those processes are justified by the goals prefixed, leads us to consider mere mutations in terminology or forms of expression as effectual results.

Another source of illusion of this same kind is to be found in the process of *explanation*, because it leads us to consider certain assertions as sufficient causes of facts that we are trying to explain, assertions that are just re-stating the same facts in a different fashion.

The most frequent example of this consists of resorting to the use of terms expressing properties, qualities, etc. (as in the famous case "*opium makes people sleep because it has a sleeping virtue*").[5]

This is also the case of all the explanations condemned by Comte under the name of "metaphysical explanations"—explanations where, in spite of the wording, the fact to be explained is simply described again in abstract terms, without linking it back to any more general law, from which it would result as a consequence; of such link would consist an explanation that is effective and not merely apparent. Philosophers have looked into the inherent dangers of this tendency. Among the best remedies are those suggested by Locke and Leibniz, when they suggest translating any assertion containing "abstract" words into an equivalent assertion where those words are substituted by the corresponding concrete things;[6] a rule of which pragmatism represents nothing but an

---

[5] [In Latin in the original ("opium facit dormire quia habet virtutem dormitivam"). The quote is taken from Molière, *The Imaginary Invalid*.]

[6] See Locke, *Essay*, B. III, ch. X, XI. [See also ch. VIII, 1, Locke 1690, p. 334.] Leibniz believes that the philosophical language could do without abstract terms: "The philosophical language can do without abstract terms (Carere potest abstractis in lingua philosophica)" (Fragments et opuscules inédits de Leibniz, publiés par L. Couturat, Paris, 1902, p. 243 [Couturat 1903]); "We will do philosophy in an extremely safe way without recurring to abstract terms (Tutissime philosophabimur abstinendo ab astractis)" (ibid. p. 400).

extension and complementation.

References

Bolzano, Bernard. 1837. *Wissenschaftslehre*. Prag: Sulzbach. Engl. transl. by B. Terrell in J. Berg (ed.) *Theory of Science: A Selection, with an Introduction*, Dordrecht: Reidel, 1973.

Couturat, Louis. 1903. *Opuscules et fragments inédits de Leibniz: extraits des manuscrits de la Bibliothèque royale de Hanovre*. Paris: Alcan. Repr. Hildesheim-Zürich-New York: G. Olms, 1988.

Locke, John. 1690. *An Essay Concerning Human Understanding*. London: Tegg, 1841, 29th edn.

Molière, Jean Baptiste Poquelin de. 1673. *Le malade imaginaire*.

Poste, E., ed. 1850. *The logic of science: a translation of the Posterior Analytics of Aristotle*. Oxford: Francis MacPherson.

Saccheri, Gerolamo. 1733. *Euclides ab omni nævo vindicatus; sive conatus Geometricus quo stabiliuntur geometriæ principia*. Milan. Engl. transl. by G. B. Halstead, Chicago-London: The Open Court, 1920.

Vailati, Giovanni. 1911. *Scritti di G. Vailati, 1863-1909*. Leipzig-Firenze: Barth.

Vailati, Giovanni and Mario Calderoni. 1909. Il Pragmatismo e i vari modi di non dir niente. *Rivista di Psicologia applicata* 5(9). Repr. in Vailati (1911), pages 933–41.

Part III

A Selected Bibliography

References

1963. [Atti del convegno di studi sul pensiero di Giovanni Vailati, Milano-Crema, 4-5 maggio 1963]. In *Rivista Critica di Storia della Filosofia*, vol. 18, pages 275–523.

Amendola, G., Norberto Bobbio, and Luigi Einaudi. 1999. *Scritti su Vailati*. Centro Studi Vailati.

Binanti, Luigino. 1979. *Giovanni Vailati. Filosofia e scienza*. L'Aquila: Japadre.

Bozzi, Paolo. 1956. Il pragmatismo italiano: Giovanni Vailati. *Rivista critica di storia della filosofia* 11(2):149–173.

Bruni, Luigino. 2002. *Vilfredo Pareto and the Birth of Modern Microeconomics*. Cheltenham-UK, Northampton-USA: Edward Elgar.

Calderoni, Mario. 1904. Le varietà del Pragmatismo. *Leonardo* 2:3.

Calderoni, Mario. 1905. Variazioni sul pragmatismo. *Leonardo* 3(2):15–21.

Calderoni, Mario. 1924. Giovanni Vailati, commemorazione letta a Crema il 20 giugno 1909. In O. Campa, ed., *Scritti*, vol. 2, pages 161–180. Firenze: La Voce.

Calderoni, Mario and Giovanni Vailati. 1915. *Il Pragmatismo*. Lanciano: Carabba.

Cantù, Paola. 2000. L'insegnamento della geometria nelle scuole medie inferiori. Una lettera inedita di Giuseppe Veronese a Giovanni Vailati. *Il Voltaire* 5:109–118.

Cantù, Paola. 2007. Il carteggio Padoa-Vailati. Un'introduzione alle lettere inviate da Chioggia. *Chioggia. Rivista di Studi e ricerche* 30:45–70.

Cappelli, Rosa. 1972. Vailati: una metodologia pragmatica al di là del pragmatismo. *Il Protagora* 84.

Casini, Paolo. 2002. *Alle origini del Novecento. Leonardo, 1903-1907*. Bologna: Il Mulino.

Chisholm, Roderick M. and Michael Corrado. 1982. The Brentano-Vailati Correspondence. *Topoi* 1:3–30.

Colella, E. Paul. 2005. Reflex action and the Pragmatism of Giovanni Papini. *The Journal of Speculative Philosophy* 19(3):187–215.

Dal Pra, Mario. 1984. *Studi sul pragmatismo italiano.* Napoli: Bibliopolis.

De Rose, Maria. 1986. *L'educazione dell'intelletto: il pragmatismo di Giovanni Vailati.* Napoli: Guida Editori.

De Zan, Mauro. 1996. Attualità di Giovanni Vailati e superamento della classe come struttura base dell'organizzazione scolastica. In D. Generali and F. Minazzi, eds., *La scuola italiana. Tra delusione e utopia*, pages 183–193. Padova: Edizioni Sapere.

De Zan, Mauro, ed. 1999. *Lezioni su Vailati.* Crema: Centro Studi Vailati.

De Zan, Mauro, ed. 2000. *I Mondi di Carta di Giovanni Vailati.* Milano: Angeli.

De Zan, Mauro. 2003. Sul carteggio tra Vito Volterra e Giovanni Vailati. *Annuario del Centro Studi Giovanni Vailati* 1:79–89.

De Zan, Mauro. 2004. I carteggi europei di Vailati. *Annuario del Centro Studi Vailati* 2:19–52.

De Zan, Mauro. 2005-06. Il Carteggio Vailati-Schiaparelli (1897-1900). *Annuario del Centro Studi Vailati* pages 107–118.

De Zan, Mauro. 2009. *La formazione di Giovanni Vailati.* Lecce: Congedo.

Demofonti, Laura. 2003. *La riforma dell'Italia del primo Novecento.* Roma: Edizioni di Storia e Letteratura.

Dewey, John. 1909. *How we think.* London: Heath.

Duporcq, Ernest, ed. 1902. *Compte rendu du deuxième Congrès international des mathematiciens tenu à Paris du 6 au 12 août 1900.* Paris: Gauthier-Villars.

Evans, Valmai Burwood. 1930. The pragmatism of Giovanni Vailati. *International Journal of Ethics* XL(3):416–424.

Ferrari, Massimo. 1989. Giovanni Vailati e la "rinascita leibniziana". *Rivista di storia della filosofia* 44:249–84.

Ferrari, Massimo. 2006. *Non solo idealismo: filosofi e filosofie in Italia tra Ottocento e Novecento.* Firenze: Le Lettere.

Frege, Gottlob. 1980. *Philosophical and Mathematical Correspondence.* Chicago: University of Chicago Press.

Garin, Eugenio. 1946. Note sul pensiero italiano del '900. *Leonardo. Rassegna bibliografica* 15:22–32; 78–86; 201–210.

Garin, Eugenio. 1955. *Cronache di filosofia italiana (1900-1943).* Bari: Laterza.

Gentili, Sandro and Gloria Manghetti, eds. 2003. *Papini, Giovanni - Prezzolini, Giuseppe, Carteggio.*, vol. 1. 1900-1907. Dagli "Uomini Liberi" alla fine del "Leonardo". Roma: Edizioni di Storia e Letteratura.

Geymonat, Ludovico. 1931. *Il problema della conoscenza nel positivismo*. Torino: Bocca.

Gullace, Giovanni. 1962. The pragmatist movement in Italy. *Journal of the History of Ideas* 23:91–105.

Haack, Susan. 2006. Introduction. In S. Haack, ed., *Pragmatism, old and new. Selected writings*, pages 15–67. New York: Prometheus Books.

Harris, H.S. 1963. Giovanni Vailati 1863-1963. Notes and reflections upon a centennial. *Dialogue* 3:328–336.

Hookway, Christopher. 2008. Pragmatism. In E. N. Zalta, ed., *The Stanford Encyclopedia of Philosophy (Summer 2008 Edition)*. URL = http://plato.stanford.edu/entries/pragmatism/.

Innis, Robert E. 2002. Paleo-pragmatism's linguistic turn. Lessons from Giovanni Vailati. In *Pragmatism and the Forms of Sense: Language, Perception, Technics*, pages 99–130. Penn State Press.

James, William. 1890. *The Principles of Psychology*. New York: Henry Holt. (Reprinted Bristol: Thoemmes Press, 1999).

James, William. 1896. The will to believe. In *The will to believe, and other essays in popular philosophy*. New York: Longmans, Green, and Co., 1897.

James, William. 1899. *Talks to teachers on psychology and to students on some of life's Ideals*. London: Longmans, Green and Co, 1901.

James, William. 1906. G. Papini and the pragmatist movement in Italy. *The Journal of Philosophy, Psychology and Scientific Methods* 3(13):337–341.

James, William. 1908. *Pragmatism*. New York: Longmans & Green.

James, William. 1969. *The letters of William James*. Boston: Athlantic Monthly Press.

Kennedy, Hubert. 2002. *Eight mathematical biographies*. San Francisco: Peremptory Publications.

Kühn, Eva. 1960. *Vita con Giovanni Amendola*. Firenze: Parenti.

Lanaro, G. 1985. Vailati e il positivismo. In E. Papa, ed., *Il positivismo e la cultura italiana*. Milano: Franco Angeli.

Lee, Vernon. 1912. *Vital lies; studies of some varieties of recent obscurantism*. London, New York: J. Lane.

Lolli, Gabriele. 1985. Le forme della logica: G. Vailati. In G. Lolli, ed., *Le ragioni fisiche e le dimostrazioni matematiche*, pages 107–132. Bologna: Il Mulino.

Maddalena, Giovanni and Giovanni Tuzet, eds. 2007. *I pragmatisti italiani. Tra alleati e nemici*. Alboversorio.

Magnani De Donadio, D. 1969. Deducciòn y experiencia en el pensamiento de Juan Vailati. *Dialogos, Revista del departemento de Filosofia, Universidad de Puerto Rico* 6(14):117–129.

Micheli, Gianni. 1980. Scienza e filosofia da Vico ad oggi. In G. Micheli, ed., *Storia d'Italia. Annali. 3. Scienza e tecnica nella cultura e nella società Dal Rinascimento ad oggi*, pages 648–49. Torino: Einaudi.

Milanesi, Vincenzo. 1979. *Un intellettuale non 'organico': Vailati e la filosofia della prassi*. Padova: Liviana.

Milanesi, Vincenzo. 1983. *Prassi e psiche: etica e scienze dell'uomo nella cultura filosofica italiana del primo Novecento*. Trento: Verifiche.

Minazzi, Fabio, ed. 2006. *Giovanni Vailati intellettuale europeo*. Milano: Edizioni Thélema.

Modenato, Francesca. 1993. Conoscere e volere. L'incontro di Vailati e Calderoni con Brentano. In L. Albertazzi and R. Poli, eds., *Brentano in Italia*, pages 47–66. Milano: Guerini.

Palmieri, Paolo. 2008. The empirical basis of equilibrium: Mach, Vailati, and the lever. *Studies in History and Philosophy of Science* 39:42–53.

Papini, Giovanni. 1902. La teoria psicologica della previsione. *Archivio per l'Antropologia e l'Etnologia* 32(2):351–375.

Papini, Giovanni. 1905. Pragmatismo messo in ordine. *Leonardo* 3(2):45–48.

Papini, Giovanni. 1907. Non bisogna essere monisti. In *Ricerche e Studi di Psichiatria, Nevrologia, Antropologia e Filosofia*. Milano: Vallardi. Repr. in *Sul pragmatismo (Saggi e Ricerche) 1903-1911*. Milano: Libreria Editrice Milanese. 1913, pages 83-102.

Papini, Giovanni and Giuseppe Prezzolini. 1906. *La coltura italiana*. Firenze: Lumachi.

Peano, Giuseppe, ed. 1901. *Formulaire de Mathématiques*. Torino: Bocca-Clausen.

Pedrazzi, Luigi. 1952. Il pragmatismo in Italia (1903-1911). *Il Mulino* 1(10-11):495–520.

Pettoello, Renato. 2005-06. Il carteggio Pikler-Vailati (1892-1908). *Annuario del Centro Studi Vailati* 3:83–106.

Ponzio, Augusto. 1986. Significs and semantics: Victoria Welby and Giovanni Vailati. In W. H. Schmitz, ed., *Essays on significs*, pages 165–78. Amsterdam-Philadelphia: Benjamins.

Ponzio, Augusto. 1988. L'eredità di Giovanni Vailati nel pensiero di Rossi-Landi. In *Rossi-Landi e la filosofia del linguaggio*, pages 183–198. Bari: Adriatica.

Pozzoni, Ivan, ed. 2009. *Cent'anni di Giovanni Vailati*. Villasanta (Milano): Limina Mentis.

Prezzolini, Giuseppe. 1905. Il mio prammatismo. *Leonardo* 3(2):48.

Quaranta, Mario, ed. 1989. *G. Vailati nella cultura del '900*. Bologna: Forni.

Quaranta, Mario, ed. 2003. *Giovanni Vailati. Gli strumenti della ragione*. Il Poligrafo.

Reggiani Montanari, M. 1985. *Il pragmatismo logico di G. Vailati è ancora attuale*. Bologna: Pontenuovo.

Renan, Ernest. 1876. *Dialogues et fragments philosophiques*. Paris: Calmann-Lévy.

Rénauld, J.F. 1960. Quelques notes sur un économiste oublié: Otto Effertz, qu'avaient loué Charles Andler et Giovanni Vailati. *Sèvriennes d'hier et d'aujourd'hui* 21:3–10.

Rénauld, J.F. 1964. Le retour à Vailati. *Revue de Synthèse* 1:65–84.

Rizza, Cinzia, ed. 2006. *Benedetto Croce – Giovanni Vailati Carteggio (1899-1905)*. Acireale-Roma: Bonanno.

Ronchetti, Lucia, ed. 1998. *L'archivio Giovanni Vailati*. No. 34 in Quaderni di Acme. Bologna: Cisalpino Istituto Editoriale Universitario. Dipartimento di Filosofia, Università degli Studi di Milano.

Rossi, Mario Manlio. 1923. Il pragmatismo italiano. *Rivista di psicologia* 19(1):8–23.

Rossi, Mario Manlio. 1925. Per Mario Calderoni. *La Voce* Firenze.

Santucci, Antonio. 1963. *Il Pragmatismo in Italia*. Bologna: Il Mulino.

Santucci, Antonio. 1988. Filosofia italiana e filosofia statunitense: il pragmatismo e il naturalismo. *Rivista di filosofia* 79(2-3):271–309.

Santucci, Antonio. 1992. *Storia del pragmatismo*. Roma: Laterza.

Santucci, Antonio. 2004. *Ricerche sul Pensiero italiano tra Ottocento e Novecento*. Bologna: Clueb.

Scarpelli, Uberto. 1992. Con il "magico" e irrazionalista Papini e il "logico" Vailati anche l'Italia ha avuto il suo pragmatismo. Un' arma contro i modi del non dir niente. *Il Sole 24 Ore* .

Schiller, F.C.S. 1905. The definitions of pragmatism. *Leonardo* 3(2):44–45.

Sciacca, Michele F. 1942. *Il secolo XX. Parte I. Dal Pragmatismo allo Spiritualismo cristiano*. Milano: Bocca.

Sciacca, Michele F., ed. 1959. *Scritti di metodologia scientifica e analisi del linguaggio*. Milano-Messina: Principato.

Silvestri, G. 1987. Metodologia come filosofia. La deduzione in G. Vailati. *Contributo* 1:3–23.

Silvestri, G. 1998. The fictions of deduction. Patterns, idealisation and concretisation: on Vailati's and Pareto's epistemology. *Metalogicon* 11(1):17–48.

Suppes, Patrick. 2009. Some philosophical reflections on de Finetti's thought. In M. C. Galavotti, ed., *Bruno de Finetti: Radical Probabilist*, pages 19–39. London: College Publications.

Thayer, Horace Standish. 1981. *Meaning and action: a critical history of pragmatism*.

Vailati, Giovanni. 1891a. Le proprietà fondamentali delle operazioni della logica deduttiva studiate dal punto di vista d'una teoria generale dello operazioni. *Rivista di Matematica* 1. Repr. in Vailati (1911), pages 2–8.

Vailati, Giovanni. 1891b. Un teorema di logica matematica. *Rivista di Matematica* 1. Repr. in Vailati (1911), page 1.

Vailati, Giovanni. 1892a. Dipendenza fra le proprietà delle Relazioni. *Rivista di Matematica* 2. Repr. in Vailati (1911), pages 14–17.

Vailati, Giovanni. 1892b. Sui principi fondamentali della geometria della retta. *Rivista di Matematica* 2. Repr. in Vailati (1911), pages 9–13.

Vailati, Giovanni. 1893. Recensione a A. Nagy, Principi di logica esposti secondo le teorie moderne. *Rivista di Matematica* 3. Repr. in Vailati (1911), pages 18–19.

Vailati, Giovanni. 1894a. Recensione a C. Burali-Forti, Logica matematica (Milano, Hoepli, 1894). *Rivista di matematica* Repr. in Vailati (1911), pages 22–25.

Vailati, Giovanni. 1894b. Recensione a Catalogue of University of Texas for 1893-94. *Rivista di Matematica* 4. Repr. in Vailati (1911), pages 20–21.

Vailati, Giovanni. 1895a. Sulle proprietà caratteristiche delle varietà a una dimensione. *Rivista di Matematica* V:183–185. Repr. in Vailati (1911), pages 30–32.

Vailati, Giovanni. 1895b. Sulle relazioni di posizione tra punti d'una linea chiusa. *Rivista di Matematica* 5. Repr. in Vailati (1911), pages 26–29.

Vailati, Giovanni. 1896a. Recensione a E. Mach, Populär-wissenschaftliche Vorlesungen. *Rivista sperimentale di Freniatria* 22(3). Repr. in Vailati (1911), pages 43–45.

Vailati, Giovanni. 1896b. Recensione a E. Mach, Populär-wissenschaftliche Vorlesungen. *Rivista di Studi Psichici* Repr. in Vailati (1911), pages 60–63.

Vailati, Giovanni. 1896c. Recensione a E. Perez, El cultivo de la Matematica y la forma deductiva de la inferencia. *Rivista di Matematica* 6. Repr. in Vailati (1911), pages 33–34.

Vailati, Giovanni. 1897a. Del concetto di Centro di Gravità nella Statica di Archimede. *Atti della Regia Accademia delle Scienze di Torino* 32. Repr. in Vailati (1911), pages 79–90.

Vailati, Giovanni. 1897b. Di una dimostrazione del Principio della Leva, attribuita ad Euclide. *Bollettino di Storia e Bibliografia Matematica* Repr. in Vailati (1911), pages 115–117.

Vailati, Giovanni. 1897c. Il pensiero di Crookes sulle Ricerche Psichiche. *Archivio di Psichiatria, Scienze Penali ed Antropologia criminale* 18(4). Repr. in Vailati (1911), pages 112-114.

Vailati, Giovanni. 1897d. Il principio dei Lavori Virtuali da Aristotele a Erone d'Alessandria. *Atti della Regia Accademia delle Scienze di Torino* 32. Repr. in Vailati (1911), pages 91–106.

Vailati, Giovanni. 1897e. *Sull'importanza delle Ricerche relative alla Storia delle Scienze. Prolusione a un corso sulla Storia della meccanica, letta il 4 dicembre 1896 nell'Università di Torino*. Torino: Roux e Frassati. Repr. in Vailati (1911), pages 64–78. Engl. transl. "On the importance of research regarding the history of science," this volume, chap. 1.

Vailati, Giovanni. 1898a. *Il Metodo Deduttivo come Strumento di Ricerca. Prolusione ad un corso libero di Storia della Meccanica, 1897-1898*. Torino: Roux-Frassati. Repr. in Vailati (1911), pages 118–148. Engl. transl. "The deductive method as an instrument of research," this volume, chap. 2.

Vailati, Giovanni. 1898b. Le méthode déductive comme instrument de recherche. *Revue de Métaphysique et de Morale* 6:667–703.

Vailati, Giovanni. 1898c. Le speculazioni di Giovanni Benedetti sul moto dei gravi. *Atti della Regia Accademia delle Scienze di Torino* 33. Repr. in Vailati (1911), pages 161–178.

Vailati, Giovanni. 1898d. Recensione a C. Guastella, Saggi sulla Teoria della Conoscenza. *Il Nuovo Risorgimento* 8(9-10). Repr. in Vailati (1911), pages 198–201.

Vailati, Giovanni. 1898e. Recensione a G. Schiaparelli, Studio comparativo tra le forme organiche naturali e le forme geometriche pure, Hoepli, Milano 1898. *Archivio di Psichiatria, Scienze Penali ed Antropologia criminale* 19(4). Repr. in Vailati (1911), pages 192–197.

Vailati, Giovanni. 1898f. Recensione a Joseph Hontheim, Der Logische Algorithmus in seinem Wesen, in seiner Anwendung und in seiner philosophichen Bedeutung. *Rivista di Matematica* 6. Repr. in Vailati (1911), pages 149–153.

Vailati, Giovanni. 1899a. *Alcune osservazioni sulle Questioni di Parole nella Storia della Scienza e della Cultura. Prolusione ad un corso libero di Storia della Meccanica, 1898-98*. Torino: Bocca. Repr. in Vailati (1911), pages 203–228. Engl. transl. "Some observations on the questions of words in the History of Science and Culture," this volume, chap. 3.

Vailati, Giovanni. 1899b. La logique mathématique et sa nouvelle phase de développement dans les écrits de M. J. Peano. *Revue de Métaphysique et de Morale* 7(1). Repr. in Vailati (1911), pages 229–242.

Vailati, Giovanni. 1899c. Recensione a C. Guastella, Saggi sulla Teoria della Conoscenza, Sandron, Palermo 1898. *Rivista di Studi Psichici* 5. Repr. in Vailati (1911), pages 278–279.

Vailati, Giovanni. 1899d. Recensione a C. Laisant. La Mathématique: philosophie, enseignement. Paris: Carré et Naud 1898. *Il Nuovo Risorgimento* 9(8). Repr. in Vailati (1911), pages 258–259.

Vailati, Giovanni. 1899e. Recensione a C. Trivero, Classificazione delle Scienze. Hoepli, Milano 1899. *Rivista italiana di Sociologia* 3(4). Repr. in Vailati (1911), pages 249–250.

Vailati, Giovanni. 1899f. Recensione a W. James, Principii di Psicologia, traduzione italiana, Società Editrice Libraria, Milano 1900. *Rivista di Studi Psichici* 5. Repr. in Vailati (1911), pages 280–281.

Vailati, Giovanni. 1899g. Recensione a W. James, The will to believe and other essays in popular philosophy, Longmans Green & Co., New York 1897. *Rivista sperimentale di Freniatria* 25(3-4). Repr. in Vailati (1911), pages 269–272.

Vailati, Giovanni. 1900a. Recensione a J.P. Durand (De Gros), Aperçus de taxinomie générale, Alcan, Paris 1900. *Rivista di Scienze Biologiche* 1-2. Repr. in Vailati (1911), pages 298–299.

Vailati, Giovanni. 1900b. Recensione a W. Lutoslavski, Seelenmacht. Abriss einer zeitgemässe Weltanschauung, Engelmann, Leipzig 1899. *Rivista di Scienze Biologiche* (6-7). Repr. in Vailati (1911), pages 302–304.

Vailati, Giovanni. 1901a. Des difficultés qui s'opposent à une classification rationelle des sciences. In *Bibliothèque du Congrès international de Philosophie. Paris 1900*, vol. 3. Logique et Histoire des Sciences. Paris: Colin. Repr. in Vailati (1911), pages 324–335. Ital. transl. in Quaranta (2003), pages 179–202. Engl. transl. "The difficulties involved in a rational classification of sciences," this volume, chap. 4.

Vailati, Giovanni. 1901b. Recensione a E. Mach. Analyse der Empfindungen und das Verhältnis des Physischen zum Psychischen. Jena: Fischer 1900. *Rivista di Biologia generale* 1-2. Repr. in Vailati (1911), pages 346–350.

Vailati, Giovanni. 1901c. Recensione a L. Couturat, La logique de Leibniz d'après des documents inédits, Alcan, Paris 1901. *Rivista di matematica* 7. Repr. in Vailati (1987), vol. 2, pages 193–204.

Vailati, Giovanni. 1901d. Recensione a L. Couturat, La logique de Leibniz d'après des documents inédits, Alcan, Paris 1901. *Bollettino di Bibliografia e Storia delle Scienze Matematiche* Repr. in Vailati (1911), pages 382–388.

Vailati, Giovanni. 1901e. Recensione a M. Begey *Del lavoro manuale educativo*. torino: Paravia 1900. *Rivista di Biologia generale* 1-2. Repr. in Vailati (1911), pages 343–345.

Vailati, Giovanni. 1901f. Sulla portata logica della classificazione dei fatti mentali proposta dal prof. Franz Brentano (Comunicazione presentata al III Congresso Internazionale di psicologia di Parigi, agosto 1900). *Rivista Filosofica* 2(1). Repr. in Vailati (1911), pages 336–340. Engl. transl. "On the logical import of the classification of mental facts proposed by Franz Brentano," this volume chap. 5.

Vailati, Giovanni. 1902a. Aggiunte alle Note Storiche del Formulario. *Rivista di Matematica* 8(3). Repr. in Vailati (1911), pages 449–453.

Vailati, Giovanni. 1902b. *Di un modo di riattaccare la teoria delle Proporzioni fra segmenti e quella dell'Equivalenza (II Congresso degli Insegnanti di Matematica delle Scuole secondarie, promosso dall'Associazione Mathesis, Livorno 17-22 agosto 1901)*. Livorno: Giusti. Repr. in Vailati (1911), pages 399–402.

Vailati, Giovanni. 1902c. Recensione a A. Naville, Nouvelle classification des sciences. Alcan, Paris 1901. *Rivista di Biologia generale* 3. Repr. in Vailati (1911), pages 429–439.

Vailati, Giovanni. 1903a. Di un'opera dimenticata del P. Gerolamo Saccheri ("Logica Demonstrativa" 1697). *Rivista Filosofica* 4. Repr. in Vailati (1911), pages 477–484.

Vailati, Giovanni. 1903b. La teoria aristotelica della definizione. *Rivista di Filosofia e scienze affini* 2(5). Repr. in Vailati (1911), pages 485–496. Engl. transl. "The Aristotelian theory of definition," this volume, chap. 7.

Vailati, Giovanni. 1903c. Sull'applicabilità dei concetti di causa e di effetto nelle scienze storiche. International Conference of Historical Sciences, Rome, April 1903. *Rivista Italiana di Sociologia* 7(3). Repr. in Vailati (1911), pages 459–464. Engl. transl. "On the applicability of the concepts of cause and effect in historical sciences," this volume, chap. 6.

Vailati, Giovanni. 1904a. Intorno al significato della differenza tra gli assiomi ed i postulati nella geometria greca. In *Verhandlungen des III Internationalen Mathematiker Kongresses in Heidelberg 8–13 aug. 1903*. Leipzig: Teubner, 1905. Repr. in Vailati (1911), pages 547–552. Engl. transl. "On the meaning of the difference between axioms and postulates in Greek geometry," this volume, chap. 9.

Vailati, Giovanni. 1904b. La dimostrazione del principio delle leva data da Archimede nel libro primo sull'equilibrio delle figure piane. In *Atti del Congresso Internazionale di Scienze Storiche, Roma, 1903*, vol. 11. Roma: Lincei. Repr. in Vailati (1911), pages 497–502.

Vailati, Giovanni. 1904c. La più recente definizione della matematica. *Leonardo* pages 7–10. Repr. in Vailati (1911), pages 528–533. Engl. transl. "The most recent definition of mathematics," this volume, chap. 8.

Vailati, Giovanni. 1904d. Recensione a L. Couturat e L. Leau, Histoire de la langue universelle, Hachette, Paris 1904. *Rivista Filosofica* 4. Repr. in Vailati (1911), pages 541–545.

Vailati, Giovanni. 1905a. I tropi della logica. *Leonardo* 3:3–7. Repr. in Vailati (1911), pages 564–571. Engl. transl. "On material representations of deductive processes," *Journal of Philosophy, Psychology and Scientific Methods*, 5(12):309–316, 12 June 1908, this volume, chap. 15.

Vailati, Giovanni. 1905b. La caccia alle antitesi. *Leonardo* 3:53–57. Engl. trans. The Attack on Distinctions, *Journal of Philosophy, Psychology and Scientific Methods*, 4(26):701–709, December 19, 1907. Repr. this volume, chap. 14.

Vailati, Giovanni. 1905c. La distinzione tra conoscere e volere. *Leonardo* 3. Repr. in Vailati (1911), pages 626–629. Engl. transl. "The Distinction Between Knowledge and Will," this volume, chap. 11.

Vailati, Giovanni. 1905d. Recensione a E. Mach. Erkenntnis und Irrtum. Skizzen zur Psychologie der Forschung. Barth: Leipzig 1905. *Leonardo* pages 193–94. Repr. in Vailati (1911), pages 667–69.

Vailati, Giovanni. 1905e. Sull'arte di interrogare. *Rivista di Psicologia* 1(2). Repr. in Vailati (1911), pages 572–576. Engl. transl. "The art of asking questions," this volume, chap. 10.

Vailati, Giovanni. 1906a. Idee pedagogiche di H.G. Wells. *Rivista di Psicologia applicata alla Pedagogia ed alla Psicopatologia* 2(3). Repr. in Vailati (1911), pages 713–717.

Vailati, Giovanni. 1906b. Il pragmatismo e la logica matematica. *Leonardo* 4(1):16–25. Repr. in Vailati (1911), pages 689–694. Engl. transl. by H. D. Austin "Pragmatism and mathematical logic," *Monist* 16:481–491, 1906. Repr. this volume, chap. 12.

Vailati, Giovanni. 1906c. La teoria del definire e classificare in Platone e i rapporti di essa con la teoria delle idee. *Rivista Filosofica* Repr. in Vailati (1911), pages 673–679.

Vailati, Giovanni. 1906d. Per un'analisi pragmatista della nomenclatura filosofica. *Leonardo* 4. Repr. in Vailati (1911), pages 701–708.

Vailati, Giovanni. 1906e. Recensione a E. Schröder, Vorlesungen über die Algebra der Logik, Teubner, Leipzig 1905. *Leonardo* 4. Repr. in Vailati (1911), page 712.

Vailati, Giovanni. 1906f. A study of Platonic terminology. *Mind* 15(60):473–485. Repr. this volume, chap. 13.

Vailati, Giovanni. 1907a. Dal monismo al pragmatismo. *Rivista di Psicologia applicata alla Pedagogia ed alla Psicopatologia* 3(4). Repr. in Vailati (1911), pages 787–790.

Vailati, Giovanni. 1907b. L'insegnamento della matematica nel primo triennio della scuola secondaria. *Bollettino di Matematica* 6(8-9). Repr. in Vailati (1911), pages 805–809.

Vailati, Giovanni. 1908a. Il linguaggio come ostacolo alla eliminazione di contrasti illusori. *Rinnovamento* 2(5-6). Repr. in Vailati (1911), pages 895–99. Engl. transl. "Language as an obstacle to the elimination of illusory contrasts," this volume, chap. 17.

Vailati, Giovanni. 1908b. La grammatica dell'algebra. *Rivista di Psicologia Applicata* 4. Repr. in Vailati (1911), pages 871–889. Engl. transl. "The grammar of algebra," this volume, chap. 16.

Vailati, Giovanni, ed. 1911a. *Il primo libro della metafisica - Aristotele ; saggio di traduzione dal greco di G.V. con notizie su Aristotele e le opere sue.*. Lanciano: Carabba. Repr. G.A. Lucchetta, ed. *Metafisica 1. La sophia degli antichi. Vailati traduce Aristotele*, Lanciano: Carabba, 2009.

Vailati, Giovanni. 1911b. *Scritti di G. Vailati, 1863-1909*. Leipzig-Firenze: Barth-Seeber.

Vailati, Giovanni. 1919. *Gli strumenti della conoscenza*. Lanciano: Carabba. Repr. 2009.

Vailati, Giovanni. 1924. Sulla teoria delle proporzioni. In F. Enriques, ed., *Questioni riguardanti le matematiche elementari*, pages 143–191. Bologna: Zanichelli.

Vailati, Giovanni. 1947. *Contributiòn a la historia de la mecànica*. Buenos Aires: Espasa-Calpe. Spanish translation by Hugo Incarnato.

Vailati, Giovanni. 1957. *Il metodo della filosofia. Saggi scelti*. Bari: Laterza. Repr. 1967.

Vailati, Giovanni. 1971. *Epistolario, 1891-1909*. Torino: Einaudi. G. Lanaro (ed.).

Vailati, Giovanni. 1987. *Scritti*. Bologna: Forni. M. Quaranta (ed.), 3 vols.

Vailati, Giovanni and G. Amato Pojero. 1993. *Epistolario: 1898-1908*. Milano: Angeli. A. Brancaforte, ed.

Vailati, Giovanni and Mario Calderoni. 1909a. Il Pragmatismo e i vari modi di non dir niente. *Rivista di Psicologia applicata* 5(9). Repr. in Vailati (1911), pages 933–41. Engl. transl. "Pragmatism and the various ways of saying nothing," this volume, chap. 19.

Vailati, Giovanni and Mario Calderoni. 1909b. Le origini e l'idea fondamentale del Pragmatismo. *Rivista di Psicologia applicata* 5(1). Repr. in Vailati (1911), pages 920–32. Engl. transl. "The origins and fundamental idea of pragmatism," this volume, chap. 18.

Verrecchia, Anacleto. 1978. *La catastrofe di Nietzsche a Torino*. Torino: Einaudi.

Villa, Giovanni. 1962. Sul pragmatismo logico di Vailati e Calderoni: la questione delle varietà del pragmatismo. *Memorie della Accademia delle Scienze di Bologna. Classe di scienze morali* (5) 10:88–213.

Volterra, Vito. 1902a. Betti, Brioschi, Casorati, trois analystes italiens et trois manières d'envisager les questions d'analyse. In *Compte rendu du deuxième Congrès International des mathématiciens, Paris 1900*, pages 43–57. Paris: Gauthier-Villars.

Volterra, Vito. 1902b. Sur les équations aux dérivées partielles. In *Compte rendu du deuxième Congrès International des mathématiciens, Paris 1900*, pages 377–378. Paris: Gauthier-Villar.

Wiener, Philip P. 1973-74. Pragmatism. In *The Dictionary of the History of Ideas: Studies of Selected Pivotal Ideas*, vol. 3, pages 551–570. New York: Charles Scribner's Sons.

Zanoni, C. P. 1979. Development of logical pragmatism in Italy. *Journal of the History of Ideas* 40(4):603–619.

Index

naturalistic conception, lxxxiii
pragmatic, 154
production of, xxviii
scientific, 180
theory of, xxiii, liii, lxxiii, 77n,
103, 165, 224, 231, 251
transmission of, xxxi
Koyré, xxix
Kuhn, xxix, lxxxvii

Lagrange, 17, 19
Lamarck, xciv
Lambert, 132n, 135
Lanaro, ix, xlin
Landry, lviii
language, xli
algebraic, lvii, 206, 207, 212,
216, 218
ideographic, lvii, 205–207, 224,
225
ordinary, xxxi, xxxiii, xxxviii,
xliii, xlvi, lv, lvii, 25, 26,
66, 67, 75, 87, 124, 142,
161, 174, 177, 207, 211–214,
217, 221–224, 228, 229
phonetic, lvii, 205
positional, lvii
technical, xiii, xxxiii, xlvi, 66,
68, 72, 80, 87, 109, 124,
125, 128, 150, 175, 177,
222, 230, 251
in astronomy, 190
in logic, 127, 128, 173
in philosophy, 173
Lasson, lviii
Lavisse, 7n
Lazarus, 35n
Leau, 166
Lee, lix
Leibniz, xiv, xxvii, 7, 14, 14n, 15,
15n, 30n, 87, 133n, 134, 147,
197, 199, 202, 224, 240, 258,
258n
Leonardo da Vinci, xxix, 58
Lessona, xxii
Lewis, 87n

linguistics, *see also* philology;
language; grammar, xxii,
xxxiv, xlvi, 36, 97
Lobatchevski, 132n
Locke, xxiii, liv, 10, 39n, 41, 68n,
197, 251, 252, 258, 258n
logic, ix, xxv, xxxvi, 103, 133,
151, 164, 173
Aristotelian, 74, 128
history of, 135
mathematical, x, xxiv–xxvi,
xxxiv, xxxvi, xliv, xlv,
xlvii, xlix, liv, lv, lviii, lix,
lxxix, lxxxivn, lxxxixn, 91,
141, 163–170, 219, 224
modern, 175
pure, 169
Scholastic, 148, 165
Lombroso, C., xxii, xxiii
Lombroso, P., 140n
Loria, xl
Lubbock, xxii, 8
Lucretius, 32n
Lutoslavski, 128n

Macfarlane, xxiv
Mach, ix, xxvi–xxviii, xxx, xli,
lxxxvi, 10, 10n, 18n, 34n, 50,
84, 154, 181, 240
MacLaurin, 18n
Malebranche, 3
Malthus's Law, 169
Mandsley, xxii
Marcolongo, lviii, 217n
Marcus Aurelius, lviii
Marx, xxxixn, 54, 84n, 110
mathematics, xxii, xxiv, xxv,
xxvii, xxviii, xxxiii, xxxiv,
xxxvi, xliv–xlvi, xlix, l, 11,
14, 29, 32, 35, 39, 49, 83, 102,
104, 138, 141, 149, 151, 208,
219, 222, 258
and deductive method, 24
definitions of
by Poincaré, 216
by Russell, 137, 139